Industrial Policy

This is Volume 44 in the series of studies commissioned as part of the research program of the Royal Commission on the Economic Union and Development Prospects for Canada.

The studies contained in this volume reflect the views of their authors and do not imply endorsement by the Chairman or Commissioners.

Industrial Policy

ANDRÉ BLAIS
Research Coordinator

Published by the University of Toronto Press in cooperation with the Royal Commission on the Economic Union and Development Prospects for Canada and the Canadian Government Publishing Centre, Supply and Services Canada

University of Toronto Press
Toronto   Buffalo   London

Grateful acknowledgment is made to the following for permission to reprint previously published and unpublished material: Basic Books, Inc.; Basil Blackwell Ltd.; Business Council on National Issues; Cambridge University Press; Cornell University Press; Jonathan Cape Ltd.; Centre for the Study of Public Policy, Glasgow; Helga Greene Literary Agency; Holt, Rinehart & Winston; Macmillan Publishing Company, Inc.; Basil Merton Ltd.; Russell Press Ltd.; Science Council of Canada; United Nations Organization; Vintage Books.

©Minister of Supply and Services Canada 1986

Printed in Canada
ISBN 0-8020-7289-5
ISSN 0829-2396
Cat. No. Z1-1983/1-41-44E

CANADIAN CATALOGUING IN PUBLICATION DATA

Main entry under title:
Industrial policy

(The Collected research studies / Royal Commission on the Economic Union and Development Prospects for Canada,
ISSN 0829-2396 ; 44)
Includes bibliographical references.
ISBN 0-8020-7289-5

1. Industry and state — Canada — Addresses, essays, lectures. 2. Industry and state — Addresses, essays, lectures. I. Blais, André. II. Royal Commission on the Economic Union and Development Prospects for Canada. III. Series: The Collected research studies (Royal Commission on the Economic Union and Development Prospects for Canada) ; 44.

HD3616.C33C35 1985   338.971   C85-099607-4

PUBLISHING COORDINATION: Ampersand Communications Services Inc.
COVER DESIGN: Will Rueter
INTERIOR DESIGN: Brant Cowie/Artplus Limited

CONTENTS

FOREWORD

When the members of the Rowell-Sirois Commission began their collective task in 1937, very little was known about the evolution of the Canadian economy. What was known, moreover, had not been extensively analyzed by the slender cadre of social scientists of the day.

When we set out upon our task nearly 50 years later, we enjoyed a substantial advantage over our predecessors; we had a wealth of information. We inherited the work of scholars at universities across Canada and we had the benefit of the work of experts from private research institutes and publicly sponsored organizations such as the Ontario Economic Council and the Economic Council of Canada. Although there were still important gaps, our problem was not a shortage of information; it was to interrelate and integrate — to synthesize — the results of much of the information we already had.

The mandate of this Commission is unusually broad. It encompasses many of the fundamental policy issues expected to confront the people of Canada and their governments for the next several decades. The nature of the mandate also identified, in advance, the subject matter for much of the research and suggested the scope of enquiry and the need for vigorous efforts to interrelate and integrate the research disciplines. The resulting research program, therefore, is particularly noteworthy in three respects: along with original research studies, it includes survey papers which synthesize work already done in specialized fields; it avoids duplication of work which, in the judgment of the Canadian research community, has already been well done; and, considered as a whole, it is the most thorough examination of the Canadian economic, political and legal systems ever undertaken by an independent agency.

The Commission's research program was carried out under the joint direction of three prominent and highly respected Canadian scholars: Dr. Ivan Bernier (*Law and Constitutional Issues*), Dr. Alan Cairns (*Politics and Institutions of Government*) and Dr. David C. Smith (*Economics*).

Dr. Ivan Bernier is Dean of the Faculty of Law at Laval University. Dr. Alan Cairns is former Head of the Department of Political Science at the University of British Columbia and, prior to joining the Commission, was William Lyon Mackenzie King Visiting Professor of Canadian Studies at Harvard University. Dr. David C. Smith, former Head of the Department of Economics at Queen's University in Kingston, is now Principal of that University. When Dr. Smith assumed his new responsibilities at Queen's in September 1984, he was succeeded by Dr. Kenneth Norrie of the University of Alberta and John Sargent of the federal Department of Finance, who together acted as Co-directors of Research for the concluding phase of the Economics research program.

I am confident that the efforts of the Research Directors, research coordinators and authors whose work appears in this and other volumes, have provided the community of Canadian scholars and policy makers with a series of publications that will continue to be of value for many years to come. And I hope that the value of the research program to Canadian scholarship will be enhanced by the fact that Commission research is being made available to interested readers in both English and French.

I extend my personal thanks, and that of my fellow Commissioners, to the Research Directors and those immediately associated with them in the Commission's research program. I also want to thank the members of the many research advisory groups whose counsel contributed so substantially to this undertaking.

DONALD S. MACDONALD

At its most general level, the Royal Commission's research program has examined how the Canadian political economy can better adapt to change. As a basis of enquiry, this question reflects our belief that the future will always take us partly by surprise. Our political, legal and economic institutions should therefore be flexible enough to accommodate surprises and yet solid enough to ensure that they help us meet our future goals. This theme of an adaptive political economy led us to explore the interdependencies between political, legal and economic systems and drew our research efforts in an interdisciplinary direction.

The sheer magnitude of the research output (more than 280 separate studies in 70+ volumes) as well as its disciplinary and ideological diversity have, however, made complete integration impossible and, we have concluded, undesirable. The research output as a whole brings varying perspectives and methodologies to the study of common problems and we therefore urge readers to look beyond their particular field of interest and to explore topics across disciplines.

The three research areas, — *Law and Constitutional Issues*, under Ivan Bernier; *Politics and Institutions of Government*, under Alan Cairns; and *Economics*, under David C. Smith (co-directed with Kenneth Norrie and John Sargent for the concluding phase of the research program) — were further divided into 19 sections headed by research coordinators.

The area *Law and Constitutional Issues* has been organized into five major sections headed by the research coordinators identified below.

- Law, Society and the Economy — *Ivan Bernier and Andrée Lajoie*
- The International Legal Environment — *John J. Quinn*
- The Canadian Economic Union — *Mark Krasnick*

- Harmonization of Laws in Canada — *Ronald C.C. Cuming*
- Institutional and Constitutional Arrangements — *Clare F. Beckton and A. Wayne MacKay*

Since law in its numerous manifestations is the most fundamental means of implementing state policy, it was necessary to investigate how and when law could be mobilized most effectively to address the problems raised by the Commission's mandate. Adopting a broad perspective, researchers examined Canada's legal system from the standpoint of how law evolves as a result of social, economic and political changes and how, in turn, law brings about changes in our social, economic and political conduct.

Within *Politics and Institutions of Government*, research has been organized into seven major sections.

- Canada and the International Political Economy — *Denis Stairs and Gilbert Winham*
- State and Society in the Modern Era — *Keith Banting*
- Constitutionalism, Citizenship and Society — *Alan Cairns and Cynthia Williams*
- The Politics of Canadian Federalism — *Richard Simeon*
- Representative Institutions — *Peter Aucoin*
- The Politics of Economic Policy — *G. Bruce Doern*
- Industrial Policy — *André Blais*

This area examines a number of developments which have led Canadians to question their ability to govern themselves wisely and effectively. Many of these developments are not unique to Canada and a number of comparative studies canvass and assess how others have coped with similar problems. Within the context of the Canadian heritage of parliamentary government, federalism, a mixed economy, and a bilingual and multicultural society, the research also explores ways of rearranging the relationships of power and influence among institutions to restore and enhance the fundamental democratic principles of representativeness, responsiveness and accountability.

Economics research was organized into seven major sections.

- Macroeconomics — *John Sargent*
- Federalism and the Economic Union — *Kenneth Norrie*
- Industrial Structure — *Donald G. McFetridge*
- International Trade — *John Whalley*
- Income Distribution and Economic Security — *François Vaillancourt*
- Labour Markets and Labour Relations — *Craig Riddell*
- Economic Ideas and Social Issues — *David Laidler*

Economics research examines the allocation of Canada's human and other resources, the ways in which institutions and policies affect this allocation, and the distribution of the gains from their use. It also considers the nature of economic development, the forces that shape our regional and industrial structure, and our economic interdependence with other countries. The thrust of the research in economics is to increase our comprehension of what determines our economic potential and how instruments of economic policy may move us closer to our future goals.

One section from each of the three research areas — The Canadian Economic Union, The Politics of Canadian Federalism, and Federalism and the Economic Union — have been blended into one unified research effort. Consequently, the volumes on Federalism and the Economic Union as well as the volume on The North are the results of an inter-disciplinary research effort.

We owe a special debt to the research coordinators. Not only did they organize, assemble and analyze the many research studies and combine their major findings in overviews, but they also made substantial contributions to the Final Report. We wish to thank them for their performance, often under heavy pressure.

Unfortunately, space does not permit us to thank all members of the Commission staff individually. However, we are particularly grateful to the Chairman, The Hon. Donald S. Macdonald; the Commission's Executive Director, J. Gerald Godsoe; and the Director of Policy, Alan Nymark, all of whom were closely involved with the Research Program and played key roles in the contribution of Research to the Final Report. We wish to express our appreciation to the Commission's Administrative Advisor, Harry Stewart, for his guidance and advice, and to the Director of Publishing, Ed Matheson, who managed the research publication process. A special thanks to Jamie Benidickson, Policy Coordinator and Special Assistant to the Chairman, who played a valuable liaison role between Research and the Chairman and Commissioners. We are also grateful to our office administrator, Donna Stebbing, and to our secretarial staff, Monique Carpentier, Barbara Cowtan, Tina DeLuca, Françoise Guilbault and Marilyn Sheldon.

Finally, a well deserved thank you to our closest assistants: Jacques J.M. Shore, *Law and Constitutional Issues*; Cynthia Williams and her successor Karen Jackson, *Politics and Institutions of Government*; and I. Lilla Connidis, *Economics*. We appreciate not only their individual contribution to each research area, but also their cooperative contribution to the research program and the Commission.

IVAN BERNIER
ALAN CAIRNS
DAVID C. SMITH

This volume consists of ten papers. The first, by André Blais, presents an overall view of the industrial policy in the advanced capitalist democracies. It proposes a definition of industrial policy, defines the main tendencies and orientations of government intervention, and analyzes the causes of these tendencies and orientations. The second, also by Blais, deals with the debate on industrial policy in Canada. As in the United States and Europe, industrial policy is a part of the political agenda in Canada, and it is therefore important to examine the terms of debate. This article identifies the main options defended as well as the arguments used to support them. It shows in particular how the dominant values of society influence the structure and evolution of debate.

The next three studies deal with three of the large issues in industrial policy. First, the question of private investment is discussed by David Marsh (chap. 3). All discussion on the possibilities and limits of state intervention must take account of the place of private investment in capitalist democracies. Lindblom, in particular, put forth the hypothesis that the business community is in a better position to influence the decisions of governments because the latter depend on private investment. Marsh examines this hypothesis in detail and points out some of its limitations.

Foreign investment creates even more serious problems. Lynn Krieger Mytelka (chap. 4) analyzes the numerous measures adopted with regard to foreign investment in the main countries in the Organization for Economic Co-operation and Development and presents case studies of Australia and France. She shows that the conditions leading to state intervention are complex and specific to a given historical conjuncture. She also underlines the lack of information available on the real impact of government policies.

Of all the political issues raised by industrial policy, however, none is more complex and delicate than that of industrial decline. What can be done about industries or regions that are in a state of decline? Marsha Chandler's significant paper (chap. 5) traces a profile of the policies adopted in six countries and identifies the main political factors that might account for the differences among them. She demonstrates that the options are not limited to laissez-faire and protectionism and that several forms of adjustment are possible.

The last five papers deal with the role of the main players in the development and implementation of industrial policy. Conrad Winn (chap. 6) first discusses the rationality of leading politicians. He stresses the multiplicity of ministerial roles and motivations and the limits of their power. Michael Atkinson, on the other hand (chap. 7), summarizes and comments on the three "images" of bureaucracy that are found in the literature. He studies the implications of each of these images for the development and implementation of industrial policy. He concludes that it is more necessary to concentrate on the problems of responsibility associated with a strong bureaucracy than to become preoccupied with the vices of an ineffective or incoherent one.

The two papers that follow deal with the respective roles of business and unions. Andrew Gollner (chap. 8) distinguishes three types of industrial policy and shows how the choice between these approaches is largely influenced by the nature of business-government relations. Steven Wolinetz (chap. 9) emphasizes the small influence unions have in countries as different as France, the Netherlands, Sweden and the United Kingdom.

The volume concludes with an analysis of the impact of federalism on Canadian industrial policy. Allan Tupper, after examining the roles of the federal and provincial governments in the area of industrial policy, examines the breadth of cooperation and conflict among the governments. He shows that while there is little coordination the policies are rarely clearly contradictory. He concludes that Canadian federalism poses certain problems of coordination but that it also has advantages, particularly in the area of "sensitivity" to regional interests.

ANDRÉ BLAIS

ACKNOWLEDGMENTS

I would particularly like to thank the many people who supported me, in various ways, in the development and realization of this project. First, the members of my advisory committee: Herman Bakvis, David Cameron, Michael Jenkin and Robert Young. They foresaw the main weaknesses of the initial project and made interesting suggestions for its improvement. Their comments on the first drafts of the texts were very useful to the various authors. In the same vein, I would like to stress the conscientious work of the anonymous evaluators. Their pertinent remarks were an important element in my discussions with the authors concerning changes to be made to the final version of their texts. My own research assistants, Claude Desranleau and Yves Vanier, were also valuable collaborators for the two texts I drafted.

For my Director of Research, Alan Cairns, I reserve a large part of my gratitude. Despite his heavy responsibilities elsewhere, he gave me support throughout the project, accepting my hesitations and dilemmas and lavishing me with good advice. His great intellectual curiosity became an important stimulus for which I am sincerely grateful. His assistants, Cynthia Williams and Karen Jackson, did all they could to facilitate the administration of the project. I appreciate both their efficient work and their willingness to coordinate everything to contribute to the quality of the work. Finally, I would like to stress the collaboration of the other research coordinators, in particular Bruce Doern, Richard Simeon, Keith Banting, François Vaillancourt and Donald McFetridge. Our formal and informal exchanges could only have improved the final product.

A.B.

1

Industrial Policy in
Advanced Capitalist Democracies

ANDRÉ BLAIS

Industrial policy, whatever it is or is not, or should or should not be, is on the political agenda in Canada as it is in the United States and Europe. It is the subject of lively debate and has created an entire clientele of businesses dependent to some degree on government assistance; an increasing number of observers are jumping into the discussion of its logic and its contradictions. It will be seen later in this paper that the concept of industrial policy is not without ambiguity. However, this is certainly not sufficient reason to avoid or ignore the debate: the term has found its way into the public arena, and the recent proliferation of studies devoted to industrial policy attest to the popularity of the issue. Industrial policy is a political issue, and it is in that light that it will be examined here.

Industrial policy, like any government policy, raises three major questions (Blais, 1980). The first relates to the content of state intervention: what governments do. The second deals with causes: why governments do the things they do. The third concerns the consequences of the policy: what government action alters. All three questions will be dealt with here. Emphasis will, however, be placed on analysis of the causes of industrial policy. We shall seek primarily to grasp the sociopolitical dynamic that leads governments to intervene, or not to intervene, in industrial development, and to intervene in one particular way rather than another.

One could not, however, examine the "why" of industrial policy without considering the other two facets. A firmly grounded knowledge of the content of state intervention, its evolution, and its spatial variations would seem to be indispensable. One section will thus be devoted to a description of major trends in industrial policy. The effects of government measures will also be considered, since these effects —

real, imagined or anticipated — may influence the initiation, maintenance or abolition of industrial policy.

The sociopolitical dynamic may be approached in many ways. Of particular interest is the policy calculation that motivates governments to adopt a particular strategy. This study will attempt to discover the logic of government intervention, the reasons for which political leaders take or refrain from taking action. As the predominant trend in the literature is to examine the *economic* "rationality" (or "irrationality") of industrial policy, the necessity for a study on its *political* rationality (or irrationality) appears obvious. Also, the strategy of political leaders does not develop in a vacuum: it takes into account, in particular, the position and influence — real, imagined or anticipated — of other agents in society. This situation arises from what games theory refers to as the interdependence of choices (Lemieux, 1979). In this way, the relationship of social forces conditions the whole of government strategy.

The universe studied consists of the advanced capitalist democracies. It is sufficiently homogeneous that useful comparisons can be drawn (Castles, 1982; Blais, 1986). Special attention will of course be given to industrial policy in Canada. The comparative approach would appear to be essential. By identifying points of similarity or dissimilarity in the industrial policies of different countries, we are able to understand the reasons behind these policies, as well as what is specific to the Canadian case. We are also interested in industrial policies adopted since the end of World War II: this is a sufficiently long period for the variations that have occurred over time to be analyzed. With such a frame of reference, however, analyzing one particular measure in depth is out of the question. The objective is rather to highlight the most noteworthy trends.

This study consists of four sections. The first defines "industrial policy." The conceptual and operational problems linked with the concept are discussed, and a definition proposed. The second section discusses the content of industrial policy: the major trends and broad policy directions of state intervention are described. The last two sections deal with the causes behind these trends and directions. First the *scope* of government intervention in time and space are considered. Industrial policy raises the question of the respective roles of the market and the state in the economy, and this paper will attempt to explain why state intervention is more pronounced in some countries and at certain times. The last section deals with the *management* of industrial policy, that is, the distribution of government assistance. As will be seen, the state clearly seeks to promote certain industries or activities at the expense of others. The question is why.

Defining Industrial Policy

Two preliminary observations may be made. First, the term "industrial policy" is relatively recent. Nearly all the works on the subject have been published since 1975. Since reflection on the issue has only just begun, so to speak, it may be expected that it will take a certain amount of time before what has been said on the subject is put into order. Second, the need for an exact definition of the term has not been strongly felt. In a number of works no definition is provided (Stoffaës, 1978; Young and Lowe, 1975; Pinder, 1982; Warnecke, 1978; de Banot, 1977; Galambert, 1982; Diebold, 1980). Where a definition is proposed, it is generally disposed of in a paragraph, with the author not taking care either to justify the definition or to indicate some of the problems it may contain. It is as if defining the term were an unimportant task, to be dashed off as quickly as possible. The following seems to reflect the general attitude fairly well: "Rather than use more space on definition, we hope the reader will recognize this ungainly animal in the examples and analysis that follow" (Pinder et al., 1979, p. 3). Moreover, no author seems to feel it worth while to set his or her own definition against those proposed by other writers on the subject.[1] Yet one of the elementary precautions in any research is to compile previous definitions and discover their relative merits or weaknesses (Selltiz et al., 1976, p. 72).

We propose as a starting point the most "official" definition of any kind to appear so far, the OECD definition: "Industrial policies are concerned with promoting industrial growth and efficiency" (OECD, 1975, p. 7). Industrial policy is thus defined in relation to its target clientele, industry, and to the objectives of growth and efficiency. The first element is more or less self-evident: it would be surprising if "industry" did not appear in the definition. Also, differentiation of policies according to target is current practice in policy analysis (Froman, 1968). The sense of the term "industry" remains to be specified, a point to which I shall return.

The second element refers to "objectives" of growth and efficiency. This implies that the government's intentions must be interpreted (Blais and Faucher, 1981). It must be recognized, however, that most definitions of industrial policy make reference to objectives, as will be seen shortly.[2] By contrast, the choice of growth and efficiency as objectives is debatable, to say the least. Industrial policy also responds to social concerns (Hager, 1982) or political concerns (Zysman, 1983), which have nothing to do with growth or efficiency.

The objective that recurs most often in the literature is that of altering industrial organization. So it is that Pinder et al. (1979, p. 3) state that "industrial policy aims directly to affect the structure of industry." According to Warnecke (1975, p. 4), industrial policy attempts to influence the structure of production, location of businesses and industrial organization. Watson (1983, p. 2) defines it as "any policy that involves a conscious attempt to alter the composition of either the outputs produced in the non-governmental sector of the economy or the inputs used to produce the output." Even in a recent OECD work on positive adjustment policies (1983b, p. 48), the section on industrial policy began:

"governments try to influence directly the structural composition of production."

There is one final feature of industrial policy that should be emphasized: its selective character. I have already strongly stressed this dimension, which would appear to be essential: "The state seeks, through industrial policy, to direct investment, promote (or protect) certain forms of production, and facilitate (or prohibit) some exchanges" (Blais and Faucher, 1981, p. 5, translation). The same stress is found in Curzon Price (1981, p. 18), who defines industrial policy as "any *selective* government or set of measures to prevent or promote structural change on a *specific* ad hoc basis" (emphasis mine). Similarly, Young and Lowe (1975, p. 27) note "the increasing emphasis on incorporating the principle of discrimination into industrial policymaking."

I therefore propose the following definition of industrial policy: *the set of selective measures adopted by the state to alter industrial organization.* I noted earlier the ambiguity inherent in the term "industry," which can refer to the whole of production, the manufacturing sector only, the whole of the primary and secondary sectors, or, finally, the primary and secondary sectors excluding agriculture. The predominant trend in the literature has been to limit the definition to the manufacturing industry. Systematically, those specific branches that have been examined belong to the manufacturing sector. The studies in Pinder's book (1982) deal with four industries: textiles, synthetic fibres, shipbuilding and aeronautics. Curzon Price (1981, chap. 4) includes an analysis of steelmaking, shipbuilding, textiles and chemicals. This sort of direction appears to be narrow, to say the least, especially since the exact differentiation between which are processing industries and which are not may sometimes be a delicate matter. I have opted for the broadest possible definition, one encompassing the primary, secondary and tertiary sectors.

No definition is ever entirely satisfactory. Any breakdown is, in the final analysis, arbitrary. I hope to show, however, that the proposed definition succeeds in reconciling the two essential qualities, however opposite, of any good definition, namely, being relatively clear and at the same time corresponding fairly closely to current usage of the term. This twofold concern led me to include government objectives in the definition, while favouring the objective that appeared most relevant.

This definition must be made operational. The government measures included in the definition, as well as those that are excluded should be indicated. This is a thorny issue, which is usually skirted, and principles of inclusion in most cases remain implicit. I have selected the following instruments from a previous work (Blais and Faucher, 1981):

• government enterprise;
• direct financial or technical assistance;
• tax allowances;

- tariff protection; and
- regulation of competition and foreign investment.

Two items, which are described in my study on aid to industry (Blais, 1986), should be added to this list: government markets and special protection against imports.

This set of instruments would seem to cover the essence of what is usually designated by the term "industrial policy." The few authors who have been explicit on the point tend to be more restrictive in their definition. Davenport et al. (1982, chap. 2) consider five instruments of intervention — tax allowances, financial assistance, technical assistance,[3] government markets, and protection against imports[4] — to which Watson (1983, p. 12) adds government enterprise. In chapter 10 of this volume Tupper limits himself to government markets, financial assistance, and government enterprise. My own definition should thus lead to a fairly complete picture of what is meant by industrial policy.

Trends in Intervention

Any analysis of industrial policy should first trace the broad outlines of state intervention. Three issues will be examined. The first concerns the form of intervention: seven instruments of industrial policy have just been pinpointed, and it is important that the relative use made of each of these instruments be assessed. The second issue concerns the source of intervention: by definition, the source is always the state, but questions may be raised as to the respective roles of different levels of government in developing industrial policy. This issue is obviously of special interest to Canada, where the theme of "province-building" has been amply developed. The third issue relates to the targets of intervention: industrial policy, like any other government policy, is never without its winners and losers, and it is important to specify which types of enterprise, industry or activity are primarily promoted by state intervention. In each case, the most significant changes that have occurred during the selected period will be highlighted, as well as national variations.

Instruments

Attempts to compare instruments of intervention for which modes of operation are quite diverse are, at the very least, audacious. The exercise is indispensable, however, in providing an overview of industrial policy. A number of studies (Economic Council of Canada, 1983; Morici and Megna, 1983; Corden and Fels, 1976) have thus attempted to quantify the implicit subsidy associated with different measures. On the basis of this research and information obtained elsewhere, Blais (1986) concludes that tariffs are still the most important measure. The average tariff in advanced capitalist democracies will be around 4 percent in

1987, when the period of adjustment in the Tokyo Round of GATT agreements has come to an end. Direct financial assistance and tax allowances represent 3 percent and 1 to 2 percent respectively of the gross domestic product (GDP).[5] Government markets, technical assistance, and special protection (quotas in particular) have a fairly low overall impact.

This study does not, however, take into consideration either government enterprise or regulation of competition and foreign investment. The case of regulation of competition is relatively straightforward. All indications are that antimonopoly legislation is not very tough. As for Canada, the study by Gorecki and Stanbury (1979) showed that the law is rather permissive, and the penalties imposed on violators hardly very strict. With regard to monitoring foreign investment, the picture is more complicated. On the one hand, all governments have adopted measures aimed at regulating foreign investment, either through authorization procedures or by reserving certain sectors for national investors (Mytelka, chap. 4 of this volume). On the other hand, intervention is very flexible in practice: "Cases of refusal turn out in practice to be either non-existent or very few in comparison to the number of authorizations given" (OECD, 1975, p. 115). Also, the share of foreign investment in total investment has grown constantly (Mytelka, chap. 4 of this volume). This suggests that regulation is not rigorously applied.

The role of government enterprise is far from negligible. It is responsible for approximately 5 percent of employment and 15 percent of investment (Saunders and Klau, 1985, pp. 81–82, Tables 20 and 21). But how can its place in industrial policy be assessed? One approach is to compare the output of private and government enterprise, and consider the divergence as an implicit subsidy to certain production factors (or to consumers of the product). To my knowledge, only Sègre (1974) and Le Pors (1977) have engaged in this sort of exercise (for France). They arrived at an estimate on the order of Fr15 billion for 1969 and Fr20 billion for 1974, or approximately 2 percent of the GDP. However, France is a country where government enterprise occupies a considerable place in the economy. In Canada, the only data we have are from Boardman (1984, Table 3) on the Canada Development Corporation. The corporation's return on average annual assets from 1973 to 1982 was 2.9 percent. The average return for seven "comparable" enterprises during the same period was 5.8 percent, or almost 3 percent higher. If this divergence is representative, the implicit subsidy would be on the order of $4.2 billion in 1981, or 1.2 percent of the GDP.[6] Government enterprise would thus be an important tool in industrial policy, as important as tax allowances but a little less so than direct financial assistance.

In a more dynamic perspective, the most substantial changes are, on the one hand, reduction of tariff protection, with the average tariff dropping from 9 percent to 4 percent from 1967 to 1987 (Blais, 1986, Table 1), and, on the other hand, an increase in subsidies, which rose from 1.8 percent to 3.1 percent of the GDP from 1965 to 1980 (ibid., Table 12). More recently, a resurgence of quotas has also been observed, although their effect is less extensive than is generally claimed. In the manufacturing sector, at any rate, these quotas apply to commodities for which tariffs are already high, and the degree of additional protection they offer is generally low. Also, the industries affected are not numerous. The equivalent tariff for all quotas in the United States in 1976 was 0.4 percent (Morici and Megna, 1983, p. 8). The amount of tax allowances has been nearly stable for the same period. The same is true for government enterprise (Blais and Faucher, 1981).

The fact that the decline in tariffs has been accompanied by an increase in non-tariff barriers has given rise to a whole school of thought, widely predominant at present, which claims that a new protectionism is emerging (Krauss, 1978; Balassa, 1978, 1979; Lazar, 1981; Mahon and Mytelka, 1983). It is important to place things in perspective. In spite of certain contrary trends, the process of trade liberalization has continued. Since 1965, tariffs have decreased by more than five percentage points, and financial assistance has increased by a little over one point. Quotas have become more numerous, but the drop in tariffs has clearly been more substantial. International trade continues to expand. For those countries that concern us, the average value of total imports and exports compared to the GDP rose from 52 percent to 58 percent between 1970 and 1975, and from 58 percent to 66 percent between 1975 and 1980 (Blais, 1986, Tables 23 and 24). It was, in fact, during the 1970s, and not the 1960s, that international trade experienced its real expansion, which was just as strong in the second half of the decade as in the first. The percentages have even continued to rise slightly since that time, reaching 67 percent in 1982, the last year for which figures are available. Talk about the new protectionism is thus somewhat short-sighted in that it fails to take into consideration what is still the predominant trend, trade liberalization.

The trend varies slightly, of course, from one country to another. Tariffs are particularly high in Austria, New Zealand and Australia, and particularly low in the Scandinavian countries, Switzerland and, more recently, the United States and Japan. Canada occupies an intermediate position, as does the European Economic Community. On the domestic level, government intervention is higher in Europe, and clearly lower in the United States, with Canada once again occupying an intermediate position (Blais, 1986, chap. 1).

The Role of Different Levels of Government

In Canada, "the growing strength of the provincial states has fascinated many observers . . . most provincial governments appear increasingly powerful, self-confident, and ambitious" (Tupper, 1982, p. 25). Moreover, "the most controversial dimension of contemporary provincial power is the provinces' growing economic importance" (ibid.). It is thus desirable to examine the respective place of the federal and provincial governments in industrial policy.

First, certain instruments are controlled solely by the federal government. This is true for protection against imports (tariffs and special measures) and for regulation of competition and foreign investment. The same is almost true of tax allowances. Seventy percent of revenues from taxes on corporate profits come back to the federal government (Statistics Canada, *Consolidated Government Finance*, Catalogue 68-202). In eight of the provinces, provincial taxes are determined (except in regard to tax rates) by the federal government, and Quebec tax laws are practically a copy of federal legislation (Thirsk, 1983, pp. 448–49). Also, the federal government provides three times more grants and loans than do the provincial governments (Blais, 1986, Table 10); it also spends three times as much for trade and industry development (Jenkin, 1983, p. 171). Only in government markets and government enterprise does the provincial government predominate. With regard to purchasing, policies of federal and provincial governments are similar (Tupper, chap. 10 of this volume), but the scope of purchasing is greater at the provincial level (Science Council of Canada, 1984, p. 21, Table 1). In 1981, the assets of provincial government enterprise, $94 billion, were almost double the assets of federal government enterprise, which were $51 billion (Statistics Canada, *Federal Government Enterprise Finance*, Catalogue 61-203, and *Provincial Government Enterprise Finance*, Catalogue 61-204). On the whole, however, federal intervention is clearly higher than provincial intervention. This does not rule out the fact that the role of provincial governments has grown over time; this is manifestly the case for subsidies and government enterprise. This development should not, however, obscure the predominant role of the federal government. This balance is amply confirmed by data from Whalley (1983) on barriers to interprovincial trade, data which indicate that the largest barriers come from the federal government. In my view, those who hold to "province-building" as a depiction of industrial policy seem, like the proponents of the new protectionism, to be shortsighted.

Tupper's position (chap. 10 of this volume) is different. Although he acknowledges the considerable powers of the federal government ("the federal government wields powerful industrial policy levers comparable to that of a unitary state") his thesis is to the effect that there is no real domination: "a concern with measuring which level of government is dominant is not useful, because such a focus overlooks federalism's combination of active governments in Ottawa and the provinces." The thesis is unconvincing, however. For one thing, the Canadian state can only with great difficulty be described as interventionist, if we take the European experience into consideration (Blais, 1986, chap. 1).[7] For another, it is difficult to understand why it would be irrelevant to compare the weight of the two levels of government in industrial policy. Further in his study Tupper quotes Cairns (1977) to the effect that neither of the two levels of government "can dominate the other."

It is important, however, to distinguish between the issues. Clearly, the influence of the federal government is greater than that of provincial governments in the area of industrial policy, as in most other areas (Young, Faucher and Blais, 1984). What Tupper emphasizes, by contrast, is that provincial governments sometimes succeed in influencing federal policy:

> provincial government critiques exert major, albeit sometimes subtle, influences on public policy. In a very direct way, incessant provincial criticisms of federal industrial policy have converted debates about industrial policy into intergovernmental wrangles about the location of economic activity.

The observation is a relevant one. "Domination" by the federal government is certainly not total domination, and the federal government cannot ignore pressure from the provincial governments. But one may well wonder whether this pressure would be any less strong if there were no provincial governments, given the nature of regionalism in Canada. It might be more appropriate, however, to wonder whether federal policies do not exert more influence over provincial policies, rather than vice versa. The example of regional development (Careless, 1977) is particularly striking here. As Binhammer et al. note (1980, p. 30), "the programs which used to be initiated and financed entirely from provincial budgets have been overtaken by special programs cost-shared with the federal government. . . ." It should also be kept in mind that it is the federal government that controls trade policy, which, as will be seen later, pervades the whole of industrial policy.

The division of powers raises the question, finally, of the degree of cooperation between governments. In this regard, Tupper (chap. 10 of this volume) arrives at the following conclusion:

> while governments seldom pursue industrial policies that are clearly contradictory, there remains a lack of policy coordination between the federal and provincial governments and between the provincial governments themselves. In most major areas of industrial policy, each government pursues its ends with scant reference to the goals of other actors.

The thesis is somewhat exaggerated, since, as we have just seen, policies of different levels of government cannot help but influence each other: every government takes account of what other governments are doing. The fact remains that coordination, in the strict sense of the term, is almost non-existent. But this may not in fact be a problem. It can just as easily be maintained that competition is preferable to coordination (Bélanger, 1982), especially since cases where they contradict each other are rare.

Finally, the Canadian experience may be compared to that of other federations. Information here is quite fragmentary. Tupper hints that the powers of regional governments are even weaker in the United States and Australia, which may explain the concerns of some observers. In fact, the central government is responsible for 97 percent of subsidies to industry in the United States and 84 percent in Australia, compared to 79 percent in Canada, in 1981 (Blais, 1986, Table 9). By contrast, the central government's share is lower in West Germany (69 percent) and Switzerland (63 percent), two federations not examined by Tupper. The Canadian position thus appears to be a fairly halfway one. Even in Australia and the United States, "governments, in defiance of constitutional guarantees, have erected various internal barriers to trade," such that "differences between federal states are those of degree, not of kind" (Tupper, 1982, p. 3).

To summarize then, in Canada as in other federations, the central government plays a preponderant role. The importance of regional governments has certainly increased during the period under study, but domination by the central government persists. One may complain about the lack of coordination of measures between different levels of government, but it remains to be demonstrated that coordination has more advantages than has competition.

Targets

We have just seen that the central government remains the principal author of industrial policy. It now remains to determine who is mainly affected by the policy. Toward whom is industrial policy directed? The question may be approached in various ways. On the sectoral level, it is important to specify which branches of industry are targetted by the state. Geographically, the question should be asked as to whether industrial policy favours poorer or richer regions. Finally, at a yet more specific level, the influence of size and ownership is of interest.

Let us begin with industrial sectors. The situation, of course, varies from one instrument to another. The clothing industry is protected by the highest tariffs, and agriculture by the strictest quotas. Agriculture, shipbuilding, aeronautics, data processing and steelmaking are favoured with respect to direct financial assistance. The mining industry is favoured by the tax system (Blais, 1986, chap. 1). Lastly, government enterprise appears primarily in the transportation and energy sectors, as well as in the steel and auto industries (Pryor, 1973; King, 1973; Blais and Faucher, 1981; Monsen and Walters, 1983). Overall, agriculture and clothing are probably the two main targets of industrial policy.

What are the major characteristics of this sectoral breakdown? Work done to date has borne primarily on tariff protection, for which data are more readily available. A number of authors have examined the whole area of protection, including non-tariff barriers, but the results are doubtful at best, given the highly incomplete range of measures considered.[8] As concerns tariffs, the industries most spared from the liberalization process are those with a large number of employees and facing stiff competition from abroad (Blais, 1986, chap. 1). Financial assistance is directed primarily to industries in which the unemployment rate is high (Denton, 1976). Government enterprise is found in the most highly concentrated sectors (Pryor, 1973, chap. 2). State intervention is thus primarily aimed at "problem" industries. This does not mean that governments are not concerned with leading-edge industries; on the contrary, a number of measures have been directly addressed toward these (George, 1983); declining industries, however, enjoy even more special status.

Industrial policy is also strongly directed toward regional development. This is particularly the case for direct financial assistance. Enterprises in the poorest areas of Canada benefit most from federal government aid programs (Blais et al., 1983); this trend is found in almost every country (Blais, 1986, chap. 1). In Canada, Quebec industry receives the most tariff protection (Pinchin, 1979), in the United States, enterprises located in rural areas (Lavergne, 1983).

At the level of enterprises, governments tend to favour large firms. These receive a high proportion of government subsidies (Blais, 1986, chap. 1), but are also the most likely to be nationalized (Blais and Faucher, 1981). Governments do not, however, appear to systematically favour the large enterprise, and a new interest in small business has been observed for a number of years (Blais, 1986, chap. 3).

Finally, there is the "national" dimension. Do governments deal differently with domestic and foreign capital? Available information on the subject is quite fragmentary and does not enable a definitive answer. All things considered, any favour that might be shown to domestic capital appears rather limited. As has been noted previously, regulation of foreign investment is not very strict. Foreign enterprise is somewhat at a disadvantage in terms of taxation, but not in respect of financial assistance. On the other hand, the nationalist orientation is more pronounced in high-technology or defence-related industries (Blais, 1986, chap. 1). Similarly, foreign firms are more likely to be nationalized (Bergsten et al., 1978). The predominant trend, however, appears to be in the direction of treating foreign capital in a relatively neutral manner.

In summary, among the industrial policy instruments used, the most important are, in order, tariffs, direct financial assistance, tax allowances, and government enterprise. A substantial reduction of tariffs has occurred, counterbalanced in part by an increase in subsidies. Government intervention tends to be most pronounced in Europe. In all countries, the central government has prime responsibility for industrial policy, although the role of regional governments has grown slightly. Finally, industrial policy attempts to support first declining industries and regions, and then technology. Large enterprise and domestic capital are slightly favoured.

The Scope of Industrial Policy: The Role of the State and the Market

In this section, the reasons behind the trends in industrial policy will be examined. Industrial policy is more vigorous in different countries and at different times; these variations will be described, looking first at variations over time, and then at variations between countries.

The Evolution of Industrial Policy

Industrial policy over the past forty years has been marked mainly by a sharp decrease in tariffs and an increase in subsidies to industry, with the changes appearing more particularly in the last twenty years. The basic direction has been toward liberalization of trade exchanges. There are two major interpretations of this movement, one political (the hegemony thesis) and the other economic (the economic conjuncture thesis).

The hegemony thesis stipulates that "the existence of a state possessing clear superiority over its nearest rivals — the United Kingdom in much of the 19th century and the United States in much of the 20th — is a necessary and sufficient condition for an open system to emerge" (McKeown, 1983, p. 73). The argument appears plausible when applied to the recent past: the United States played a dominant role in establishing GATT and in various rounds of negotiation (Lipson, 1983, p. 235). By contrast, the Kennedy Round, and especially the Tokyo Round, took place at a time when U.S. power was in relative decline (Krasner, 1976). With regard to the 19th century, McKeown (1983) concludes that England's efforts to win tariff reductions from other countries were rather weak. In addition, "British efforts simply were not successful in inducing major changes in other states' tariffs; when tariff liberalization occurred, it was in the absence of British pressure" (p. 88). In sum, even though it appears that the hegemonic power generally tends to adopt a more open trade policy, the thesis is not very enlightening as to "the motivations and capabilities of the nonhegemonic states that are most likely to rival the hegemonic power" (McKeown, 1983, p. 76), and cannot account for changes over time (Lawson, 1983; Stern, 1984).

According to McKeown (1984) and Gallarotti (1985), the liberalization process intervenes in periods of prosperity, and protectionism intervenes in periods of recession. Their data on the growth of tariffs in the United States and Germany during the 19th century seem to corroborate this hypothesis. Viewed in this light, the unprecedented growth after

World War II apparently greatly favoured the reduction of tariff protection, and the economic difficulties of the 1970s would explain why the protectionist temptation is greater now.

Why is this so? According to McKeown (1984, p. 219), protectionist pressure is stronger in periods of recession for the following reasons:

Since rates of entry into a sector tend to be positively related to that sector's rate of demand growth, we would expect entry rates to be smaller during a depression than during a period of prosperity. This implies that for a given level of protection the producer's surplus created by protective measures will be bid away by new entrants more slowly during the trough of a business cycle than during the peak. . . . Moreover, since during the trough the expected utility of exit into a more remunerative line of business is lower than at the peak, firms are more likely to resort to voice (i.e., political action) at such a time.

The study by Takacs (1981) confirms this interpretation. In the United States, representations to the government for adoption of safeguard measures increase substantially when the economic conjuncture is unfavourable. How do governments react to this sort of pressure? They are certainly not insensitive to it, since trade policy is in fact affected by the economic conjuncture. But neither do they respond automatically to such pressure. Takacs (p. 691) observes that decision making by the U.S. administration is only slightly influenced by the economic conjuncture, so that "although the pressure for protection increases in times of economic stress, the government does not necessarily respond to it."

Governments appear, therefore, to have an unfavourable bias against protectionism and to resist pressure from special-interest groups. This point cannot be overemphasized, since the predominant model in economics, when it comes to describing trade policy, is that of the pressure group (Lavergne, 1983). This model postulates that, although free trade favours growth and efficiency, it can hurt some groups. Compared with proponents of free trade these can more readily organize and exert pressure on politicians to obtain protective measures. The model is not unattractive: Bauer et al. (1972) note that, in fact, protectionist forces are more easily mobilized than are free trade groups. The postulates of the model in regard to the position of governments, by contrast, are not as valid. Governments are presented as being essentially passive and responding mechanically to protectionist demand. It could just as well be assumed that political leaders subscribe to certain principles or rules that influence their decision making to the same extent (Lavergne, 1983).

Empirical data do not confirm the pressure-group model. For one thing, even though protectionist groups are better organized, the trade liberalization process has been the predominant trend, suggesting that other, more decisive factors are at work in the other direction. For another, forecasts of tariff structures by the model have been invalidated. Lavergne (1983, p. 155), whose study is by far the most thorough and systematic one on the subject, concludes thus: "When all the analysis is done, the pressure-group variables must be said to perform very weakly. As a group . . . they play a minor role in each of the regressions or tend to yield contradictory results."

This is not surprising. The voluminous study by Bauer et al. (1972) on U.S. trade policy demonstrated that even protectionist groups are much less organized than is generally thought, and that in any case the interest of a business or an industry is often ambiguous:

> The formal acts of economic calculation acquire their concrete content only through acts of communication and social influence. . . . Neither a study of influence processes nor a simple study of economic interests without their interaction could have yielded much understanding of the behavior of our business respondents. (Bauer et al, 1972, p. 4572)

It would certainly be foolhardy to claim that pressure groups have no influence over trade policy. One might, at the very least, maintain that their influence is not decisive and that governments respond as well to other concerns.

Why, in fact, do governments have a favourable bias toward free trade and resist protectionist pressure? Three factors seem to be at work. First, to the extent that a government's popularity is affected by the performance of the economy (Winn and Marsh, chaps. 6 and 3 of this volume) and that free trade promotes growth (Harris with Cox, 1984), it is in the government's interest to resist protectionism. Support for free trade is certainly not unreserved, since governments look for relatively stable rather than maximum growth (Krasner, 1978, p. 40; Mosley, 1976); they prefer a gradual, cautious liberalization of trade. Second, to the extent that politics consists in large part of symbols (Edelman, 1964), it must be acknowledged that free trade has rallied public opinion (see chap. 2 of this volume). The Depression and the two world wars have succeeded in creating a negative image for protectionist ideas, which are readily associated with narrow nationalism. Third, the major capitalist countries form part of a military coalition, a fact that can only stimulate governments to resist protectionist temptation, a temptation that may have considerable political consequences (McKeown, 1984).

The strategy of governments seems then to have consisted in ensuring that the movement toward trade liberalization continued, while yielding to certain protectionist pressures in certain sectors and at times when the economic situation was particularly unfavourable. The strategy may not be as clear or coherent as some people would wish, but this ambiguity results from the political necessity of reconciling partly contradictory objectives, such as growth, stability and jobs, not to mention political-military considerations. Combining these objectives may even prove to be wise, as Lavergne suggests in the last sentence of his book (1983, p. 187). "If the conservative adoption of linear and non-linear cuts has been accepted as a mechanism for *easing* the general downward movement of tariffs, then it is conceivable that the overall strategy that this represents may have been close to optimum."

The period has also been marked by an increase in direct financial assistance to industry. Several factors are responsible for this development. The principal one seems to lie in the reduction of tariff protection, with which we have just dealt. In the manufacturing sector, the sector most directly affected by tariffs, the link between these two developments appears clearly. Fels (1976, p. 92) notes that

> during the 1960s, a shift occurred in West Germany's industrial assistance policy from assistance by trade barriers to domestic subsidies and tax allowances. The reason for this is obvious: trade policy was becoming subject to multinational agreement in which liberalization and significant tariff reductions were being achieved.

Similarly, the Canadian government's first assistance programs were directed toward the defence industry, following the Canada–U.S. agreement on production sharing in this sector, and toward shipyards, for which customs tariffs proved to be inoperative as a result of the British Commonwealth Shipping Agreement (Blais, Faucher and Young, 1983). It has also been observed that, all things being equal, subsidies to industry are more substantial in countries where tariff protection is weakest (Blais, 1986, Table 30).

This type of reaction says a great deal about the concerns of governments. On the one hand, they appear favourable to free trade, which promises growth and efficiency. On the other hand, they are very nervous over the fact that liberalization might benefit certain countries or industries more than others, and that because of this it carries with it great uncertainty. Financial assistance thus attempts in some degree to cushion the potential shocks associated with free trade.

A second cause of the increase in subsidies to industry is the general trend toward a drop in profits (Bosworth, 1982). If it is true that investment depends on anticipated profits and governments depend on this investment to maintain their popularity (chaps. 3 and 6 of this volume), it comes as no surprise that politicians are enormously concerned with the investment issue and seek to counterbalance the drop in business profits. Hager (1982, p. 243) presents this point of view most clearly:

> the logic of industrial policy . . . may be described as the politics of compensation . . . the state and society remove with one hand the resources (and conditions) that allow industry to prosper and give them back with the other. Both operations are carried out in the name of social objectives.

The fact that a correlation is observed between the size of subsidies to industry in a country and the tax burden of business in that country (Blais, 1986, Table 30) tends to give credence to this thesis. Subsidies to industry apparently also compensate in part for the reduction in tariffs and profits. This indicates as well that investors hold a privileged political position in the development of industrial policy (Marsh, chap. 3 of this volume).

A third explanation for the growth of subsidies lies in the increase of the unemployment rate since 1974. Since a sizable proportion of government assistance is directed toward declining industries and regions, the demand for the intervention becomes more urgent as unemployment rises. All things being equal, subsidies become larger in a country as its unemployment rate rises (Blais, 1986, Table 30). Unemployment rates rose on an average by nearly two percentage points between 1974 and 1979, and by two points again from 1980 to 1982 (OECD, 1984), a rise that could not help but contribute to the increase in subsidies to industry.

National Variations

While all governments have reduced their tariffs and increased their financial assistance to industry, the trend has been more noticeable in some countries than in others. First the question of why tariffs and subsidies to industry are higher in one country than in another will be discussed. Then two studies offering general interpretations of the role of the state in industrial growth will be examined. The first is Zysman's study (1983), which, based on a comparative analysis of the situation in France, the United Kingdom, West Germany, the United States and Japan, attempts to explain why the industrial adjustment process is managed by the state in some countries and left to private enterprise in others. The second study is contained in a special issue of the *Journal of Public Policy* (February 1983) devoted to industrial policy. That issue includes an introduction by McKay and Grant (1983) on prior conditions for adoption of an industrial strategy, and eight articles, each bearing on industrial policy in a particular country.

Tariff Protection
Nearly all studies on customs tariffs deal with the tariff structure, that is, the breakdown of tariffs by industry. To my knowledge, only Conybeare (1983) and Blais (1986) have concerned themselves with national variations. Conybeare analyzes the average manufacturing tariff in 35 countries for 1971, and tests four explanatory models. The model yielding the best results is the "rational domestic economic policy" model, which postulates that tariffs depend essentially on the country's level of economic development. This result is doubtful, however, because Conybeare's sample is quite heterogeneous. Blais (1986, chap. 2) compares the average manufacturing tariff with the size, wealth and agricultural employment of 18 advanced capitalist democracies. The three variables appear to have no significant impact. All in all, it is not really known why some countries are more protectionist than others. Only

more in-depth studies, taking historical continuity into account (Lavergne, 1983), may enable an answer to be found.

Subsidies to Industry

Blais (1986, chap. 2) is also concerned with the size of subsidies to industry in advanced capitalist democracies. Nine independent variables were examined: size, resources, size of agriculture, unemployment rate, composition of government by political party, tax burden borne by business, average manufacturing tariff, size of the government, and spending on social security. As previously noted, subsidies are negatively associated with tariffs and positively associated with the business tax burden and the unemployment rate. Subsidies are also higher in countries where agriculture holds an important place in the economy, where the social security system is less developed, and where the left is in power. I would like to emphasize the last result: left-wing governments give more subsidies to industries than do right-wing governments; the difference is even more marked than the difference in total expenditures. The greater propensity of left-wing governments to intervene is even stronger in the industrial sector. Industrial policy, therefore, is well and truly an effect of political will. These results are along the same lines as those of Chandler (1982), who showed that left-wing governments in Canada were more likely to create government enterprise, and Castles (1982), who found that the orientation of the party in power had a substantial influence on government spending.

Zysman's Thesis: The Financial System

Zysman (1983) sought to explain why adjustment in the industrial sector is more a function of the state in some countries, and left more to private enterprise in others. The explanation favoured by Zysman is related to certain features of the financial system. He finds three situations (p. 94, fig. 2.1): a) a credit-based system, where the state determines the cost of credit; b) a system based on the capital market; and c) a system also based on credit, but in which private financial institutions predominate. Zysman maintains that industrial adjustment is managed by the state in the first case, left to private enterprise in the second, and negotiated between the state and its social partners in the third. He attempts to demonstrate the validity of this proposition by examining the financial system and industrial policy of five countries: France, the United Kingdom, West Germany, the United States, and Japan.

We are faced here with two assumptions, relating to two dimensions of the financial system. First, the state plays a more active role in countries where the capital market is less developed. Second, among those countries where financing is created essentially through credit, the state intervenes more in countries where it controls credit than in countries where private institutions predominate. These two assumptions must be looked at separately, as one cannot, a priori, preclude the possibility that one is valid and the other is not.

It is not very easy to assess Zysman's argument, since it is not supported by strict, systematic data on the dependent variable (the politics of industrial change), which ought to be the very centre of the analysis (Blais, 1980). Zysman's work contains useful information on the financial systems of the five countries, but there is almost no description of industrial policy in those countries. Zysman acknowledges at the outset (1983, p. 95) that there is a measurement problem, a problem whose implications he seems to underestimate. How indeed can one appraise the thesis, when the term "the politics of industrial change" is never defined and the indicators are never discussed? We do not know exactly with which aspects of government intervention the author is concerned. References to the literature on industrial policy, which is quite extensive, are rare in Zysman's work. To cite only one example, Zysman states (p. 257) that in West Germany "the traditional determination to resist demands for subsidy from declining industries appears to be holding firm," while another study estimates that two-thirds of financial assistance to industry in that country is directed toward declining industries (Ohlin, 1978, p. 26).

Let us return more specifically to the assumptions. Zysman clearly accords greater importance to the second than to the first. The West German example is revealing in this regard. Zysman (1983, p. 257) stresses the state's nonintervention in that country, comparing it in particular to the situation in France. The West German case, however, differs from the French case in respect of the second assumption, and not in respect of the first. Thus it is apparently state control of credit that is the determining factor.

According to Zysman (p. 63), industrial credit appears to be the favoured instrument of industrial policy, and comprehensive control of credit a necessary condition for utilization of this instrument as part of industrial policy: "the universality of finance enables a single agency to exert influence across a range of issues without having to develop regulatory or administrative apparatus for each specific case." Unfortunately, he does not go to the trouble of systematically comparing industrial credit with other instruments of industrial policy. Data used by Le Pors (1977, p. 44) on state-industry transfers in France cast a great deal of doubt on Zysman's thesis: the flow of loans to industry is in fact much lower than subsidies properly speaking, such that it is hard to believe that credit is as key an instrument as Zysman claims it is (Blais, 1986, chap. 1).

Finally, the importance attributed by Zysman (1983, p. 85) to what he calls the state's "capacity" for intervention should be stressed. The term is used abundantly: "Our task is to fit finance into an interpretation of the state's capacity for managing industrial adjustment." This sort of explanation gives rise to several difficulties. First, how can one measure the capacity for intervening, and how can one distinguish the *potential* for intervening from intervention itself? Also, according to this logic, what would account for differences between countries would not be the pressures exerted on the state or the ideological concepts of politicians or bureaucrats, but rather the available instruments. Zysman tries hard to incorporate these other elements into his analysis, but he presents them as being dependent on the power of the state. Thus, in approaching the adjustment process from the politician's point of view, he states that the calculation depends on the instruments available: "A state strategy of purposive development requires a distinct set of capacities" (p. 86). It must also be determined, however, what leads governments to wish or not wish to intervene. Zysman is quite aware of the importance of this question, as he deals with political objectives, but in the final analysis he assumes these objectives to be closely dependent on the available means of intervention: "How a government establishes the purposes of its policy . . . is entertwined with its administrative capacity to act in industrial affairs" (ibid.). The converse, that is, the assumption that instruments arise out of objectives, may in fact be more plausible.

In sum, Zysman's thesis is unconvincing. Factual data on the content of industrial policy is almost nonexistent. The crucial role of credit as an instrument of intervention is more presumed than demonstrated. Therefore, one must look elsewhere for a satisfactory explanation of national variations in industrial policy.

The McKay-Grant Hypothesis

According to McKay and Grant (1983, p. 9), adoption of a coherent industrial strategy depends on two factors: first, "a broad acceptance among political elites of the need for government to play an active part in helping industry adapt to change," and, second, "the existence of good communication between political/bureaucratic and economic actors, including a broad acceptance by private investors of the need for government intervention." The authors acknowledge that industrial policy directions are always controversial, but add that consensus on the need for government intervention is indispensable.

Like Zysman's thesis, the McKay-Grant hypothesis is not really verified empirically. The authors present their analysis as being exploratory. It is regrettable, however, that they offer no discussion of the criteria whereby one may recognize the presence or absence of an industrial strategy on the one hand, and of consensus on the other. Once again, the argument is remarkably vague.

The interpretation is not unattractive, however. It correctly places emphasis on the dynamic of government-industry relations. It attributes a veto power to industrialists, in the sense that their cooperation appears to be indispensable. The statement of the problem is also more interesting than in Zysman, as the interplay of the actors is taken directly into consideration. Unfortunately, the articles on which McKay and Grant base their argument yield only a little information on the position of the industrial community, and it is almost impossible to rule on the validity of the hypothesis. Moreover, the distinction between consensus on the timeliness of an industrial policy and disagreement on possible directions for that policy appears superficial. It may be assumed that assessment by one group of the necessity for government intervention is closely linked with the assessment it makes of the management, present or anticipated, of that intervention.

Consensus remains a quite superficial explanation, unless its origin is also examined. Let us assume for the time being that the authors are right, and that consent of the parties involved is in fact a necessary condition for the development of industrial policy. This implies, as previously noted, that the industrial community plays a decisive role, which would confirm the thesis that the business community occupies a privileged position in capitalist societies. It remains then to explain why industrialists react differently to government intervention in different countries. If cultural explanations are excluded, the most plausible interpretation is that the industrialist's calculation depends on measures already in place. In countries where government intervention is already firmly established (Katzenstein, 1978), business people would judge that it is was not in their interest to oppose industrial policy. Equally, weakness in the industrial community would allow for a "coherent" industrial strategy (Gollner, chap. 8 of this volume).

Here, it would seem, we are touching on the crux of the question. What are the interests of industrialists with respect to industrial policy? The question is especially complex, as these interests vary by sector, region, and type of enterprise. The perspective may also be different depending on whether the short or the long term is considered. This is a fundamental question, however, and one can only regret that it is almost never directly dealt with in the literature. In my opinion, in spite of all the fine distinctions that should be made, it is in the interests of the industrial community overall that governments intervene as little as possible in the economy. Even industrial assistance programs cannot be considered "gifts," since they arc accompanied by conditions that reduce the firm's margin of manoeuvre. This represents a considerable political cost, if it is felt, as Vogel feels (1978), that management autonomy is at the very heart of power in business. More generally, "there exists a large common interest of business, less often articulated but still generally understood, in curbing excessive expenditure . . ." (Young, 1983, p. 353).

If such is the case, a vigorous industrial policy can emerge only in countries where the state is able to impose its directions on an industrial community too weak to oppose it. In steelmaking in France, for example, "after extended negotiations and much against its will, the industry, in the form of its trade association, agreed to the plan because it was in desperate need of substantial government financial assistance"

(Zysman, 1977, p. 71). The consensus would thus be more apparent than real, the result of industrialists resigning themselves to the situation. It should be recalled in this respect that subsidies to industry are linked to the composition of the government. Left and right have different positions on this issue, as on others, and if there is consensus it can be explained only by the power relationships that exist in society.

In sum, the McKay-Grant hypothesis seems to be quite unsatisfactory. It is of interest because it draws attention to a key actor, industrialists, but we learn so little as to the nature and origin of the so-called consensus that the author's interpretation raises doubts, to say the least.

Conclusion

We must conclude that, while national variations in industrial policy have been subject to several interpretations, these interpretations have, on the whole, been rather unconvincing. This analysis of studies on the subject has, however, brought out three points. First, industrial policy is part of a broader debate on the role of the state; as a result, politicians approach the issue partly from the angle of the place the government and the market ought, in their view, to occupy in the economy. Second, government-industry relations are crucial in developing industrial policy, and politicians always bear in mind, in planning strategy, the industrialists' possible reactions, their mobilizing power, and the means at their disposal to invest elsewhere. Third, economic performance influences the scope of industrial policy. Subsidies to industry are more substantial in countries where the unemployment rate is higher.

The Management of Industrial Policy: Winners and Losers

When government intervenes in industrial development, it is clearly for the purpose of promoting certain activities or industries at the expense of others; thus it is important to examine who benefits most, and who benefits least, from government intervention, and to explain why this is so. We saw in the second section of this study that industrial policy is primarily directed toward declining industries and regions, and secondly toward leading-edge, high-technology industry. We also noted that large enterprises and domestic enterprises were slightly favoured. These are the five principal issues raised by industrial policy in relation to distribution of government assistance.

Industrial Decline

It is paradoxical to say the least that industrial policy addresses itself primarily to industries and businesses in difficulty. The paradox arises from the fact that the discussion of industrial policy revolves around the themes of growth, productivity and efficiency. In the United States, those who propose a true industrial policy (Reich, 1982; Thurow, 1980; Magaziner and Reich, 1982) insist on the necessity of giving more encouragement to industries of the future, while sceptics hint that this is still only a pious wish, given the natural bent of the political apparatus: "an industrial policy that seeks to direct resources to winners might find itself funneling massive funds to politically adept losers" (Badaracco and Yoffie, 1983, p. 102).

The argument most often advanced to describe this state of affairs goes back to the process of mobilizing interests: "only those who are losers in the marketplace are likely to be interested in developing the political clout to promote an industrial policy" (Krauss, 1978, p. 73). The argument has a certain plausibility. Aggarwal in particular has documented fully the pressure exerted by the American Cotton Manufacturers Institute to initiate agreements on voluntary restraints in the textile industry during the 1950s. The explanation is incomplete, however. A high proportion of textile workers, for example, are women and immigrants (OECD, 1983a; Matthews, 1980), generally not highly organized. Similarly, the favoured treatment enjoyed by agriculture could not possibly be explained by the strong organization of farm associations. As Cable emphasizes (1983, p. 228), "there is no mechanical process by which politicians weigh votes and bureaucrats defer to economic power and good organization. There is also an important ideological component: lobbies need to capture a sense of what is both 'fair' and in the national interest." Politicians are not passive, and hence it is important to understand how they perceive industrial decline.

Why, in fact, are politicians so concerned with declining industries, and exactly what objectives are they pursuing? On this point nearly all studies are in agreement: the major concern is clearly jobs. Denton (1976, p. 161) states that "without doubt the one problem above all of these in provoking the growth of financial aid to industry has been unemployment." Denton et al. (1975) observe as well, in the United Kingdom, a close correlation between the size of subsidies and the unemployment rate in a given industry. In the same vein, Kreile (1983, p. 215) concludes that in Italy "the dominant patterns of industrial policy has been short-term crisis management, ad hoc interventions that were aimed at safeguarding employment and ensuring the financial survival of floundering companies." In the United States, tariffs decrease least in industries facing heightened competition from foreign producers and having a large number of employees (Lavergne, 1983); it is also in industries with many employees and where employment is declining that retaliatory measures are most frequent (Herander and Schwartz, 1984; Finger, Hall and Nelson, 1982).

Why is the safeguarding of jobs so important? The simplest answer is that politicians' concerns reflect the value system of the society in which they live. Work is held to be a source of well-being more important than the financial situation (Campbell et al, 1976, p. 85). Job security is more highly valued than the level of remuneration: 84 percent of Canadians prefer stable employment to higher wages (*Decima Quarterly Report*, Winter 1982, question 545; Bellemare and Poulin-Simon, 1983, p. 68; Campbell et al., 1976, p. 299). Finally, while it is true that growth of income may contribute to a feeling of well-being, the negative impact of unemployment is much more pronounced, especially as this impact is in large part independent of the resulting loss of income, involving as it does one's self-esteem (Campbell et al., 1976, p. 318; Campbell, 1981, pp. 120–22; Bellemare and Poulin-Simon, 1983, p. 68). This leads as "liberal" an economist as Baldwin (1979, p. 238) to conclude: "Our social values and income levels are such that we should be able to reduce output in noncompetitive industries slowly enough to enable most of those currently employed in such industries to remain if they wish." Grant (1982, p. 16) notes that in the British textile industry "most of the managers . . . identify closely with their companies [and] . . . prefer to continue to make low profits rather than sell out."

Of the political necessity for aid to declining industries there can be no doubt. The problem is set out clearly by Brenner and Courville (1985):

> there are risks, associated with domestic and international turmoil, that a government, by definition, is supposed to reduce. Industrial policies are one of the means by which such disturbances can be mitigated. In order to diminish these risks, people may be willing to pay, directly or indirectly, the costs of insurance by subsidizing some provinces, regions or industries.

Such aid also serves the purpose of facilitating the trade liberalization process. As McKeown emphasizes (1984, p. 231), in the 19th century "the lack of alternative policy instruments and heavy political burdens thus carried by the tariff imply that the stakes in tariff setting were high and that actors deprived in this issue area could not readily be compensated by payoffs in other areas."

The question of intervention strategy in the face of industrial decline still arises. Chandler, in her study (chap. 5 in this volume), refers to Magaziner and Reich (1982), who distinguish among three strategies: a) laissez faire; b) protection, which consists of preserving the status quo and hence impeding industrial adjustment; and c) a policy to facilitate the adjustment process. A fourth possible strategy, which Chandler mentions in passing, is the management of decline, which cushions the adverse effects of the decline by stretching it out over a longer period of time (Blais, 1986).

It is then a matter of determining which of these strategies predominates, and whether variations among countries are significant. The question is quite complex. Data on employment in specific industries are rarely available on a comparative basis. Information on government programs is fragmentary, and almost nothing is known about their real impact (Grant, 1983). Generalizations on the subject cannot help but be risky.

One way to attack the problem is to examine the concrete result, that is, changes in employment in the declining industries. In textiles and clothing, probably the cases most often cited, job losses since 1963 have been progressing at an average annual rate of 3 percent (Blais, 1986, Table 32). This data suggests that governments seek essentially to manage industrial decline, that is, to slow down the rate of job loss. As OECD notes (1983a, p. 120), "Government policies for the textiles and clothing industries have primarily affected the rate at which change has occurred, rather than the direction or broad thrust of change." The strategy is quite understandable. On the one hand, unemployment has considerable impact on the popularity of governments. On the other, it is particularly in the government's interest to prevent unemployment in a given industry from exceeding a certain tolerance threshold:

> Within the context of the "satisficing" theory we may interpret these changes as responses to the straying of a target variable into a "forbidden" region: when unemployment begins to take on "unsatisfactory" values, red lights, as it were, begin to flash and the authorities deploy their instruments in instinctive Pavlovian fashion until the offending target variable has moved back into the satisfactory region. (Mosley, 1976, p. 65)

It is a matter, in sum, of ensuring that the decline occurs gently, and is spread out over a longer period of time, so as to be less painful.

Chandler, for her part (chap. 5 of this volume), is more interested in the differences among countries. In so doing, she has probably tended to exaggerate the differences and minimize the similarities. In the case of France, for example, she notes that "protection through quotas, tariffs and preferential public procurement continue to be employed. . . ." One could be even more explicit: within the manufacturing sector, the tariff structure is remarkably similar from one country to another. In practically every country, clothing is the most protected industry. Agreements on voluntary restraints are perhaps more numerous in the United States, but they are to be found in Europe as well, particularly in textiles and automobiles (Blais, 1986, chap. 1). The constants appear to me to be even more significant than the national variations.

Still, these variations are not negligible. Chandler's thesis is the following:

> In France, West Germany and Japan, the more successful states to deal with decline, there is much evidence that state-led or encouraged restructuring has been accompanied by assistance to hard-hit regions and redundant workers. If anything distinguishes Britain, Canada and the United States from the other three countries here, it is the way in which they respond to

the social costs of economic change: Britain, Canada and the United States tend to shield workers and regions *from* change rather than support them *through* change.

It is important to emphasize that the picture applies only to the manufacturing sector, with which the studies cited by Chandler are concerned. In agriculture, the situation is altogether different. Quotas imposed by Japan and the EEC are clearly stricter than those set by the U.S. government (Cline et al., 1978; Blais, 1986, chap. 1). This is a facet of Japanese industrial policy that is too easily forgotten:

> Agriculture has been the most heavily protected of industries . . . in agriculture the political system, far from exhibiting special capacities for adapting economic activity to favor the high-growth sectors, has been unable even to provide incentives for a shift of resources from rice growing to those farm sectors . . . in which productivity gains promise to be greatest. (Trezise, 1976, p. 773–74).

Within the manufacturing sector, the description is probably fairly accurate on the whole, although again distinctions must be drawn. In Japan, for example, the government is still "reluctant to abandon existing industries" (ibid., p. 800). In West Germany, it is true that the central government avoids "rescue" operations, but "politically this abstinence was made easier by the Regional (*Land*) governments frequently stepping in . . . to rescue failing firms" (Shepherd, 1983, p. 37). But it is the French case especially that creates a problem. Here, the assessment of the situation made by the French themselves is clearly less positive than that of foreign observers. Even among the latter, the picture they paint is not always rosy: "only limited efforts to rationalize production were undertaken by the largest cotton textile companies, as they took over smaller firms" (Mytelka, 1982, p. 148). But the judgment of French analysts is even harsher. Stoffaës, for example (1978, pp. 708–709), describes a study on the structural adjustment occurring in the jute industry:

> Three types of reaction were observed in the face of competition from developing countries . . .
> • The United States opened its market and gave free play to competition which led to rapid elimination of national production.
> • France brought protective measures and quotas into play.
> • Great Britain adopted an intermediate process, of free entry into its market, but with an equalization tax intended to be gradually reduced. . . . [Translation]

The picture is similar in the case of steelmaking (Padioleau, 1981).

In order to describe these variations among countries, Chandler looks at five independent variables: the presence or absence of consensus, the party in power, the bureaucratic organization, the banking system, and the structure of private sector representation. The interpretation is essentially political. Chandler acknowledges that there are also determining economic factors, but stresses the necessity of analyzing the political dynamic. In principle, I can only agree. However, she seems to overlook the considerable political impact of unemployment. For my part, I feel that a policy directed at the outset toward industrial adjustment is possible only if the unemployment rate is not too high. A high unemployment rate has social and political implications such that a certain dose of protectionism is required. The West German case is quite interesting in this respect. If my analysis is accurate, it is only because unemployment is low in that country and the social security system more highly developed that protectionist pressure is not more strongly exerted.[9]

For a number of years now, agreements on voluntary restraints have represented an important instrument for managing industrial decline, and it is important to ask why. The principal factor in the explanation has already been described. Increases in the unemployment rate have intensified protectionist pressure, and quotas are the protective measure par excellence. The logic of quotas is relatively straightforward: they are an ideal instrument for stabilizing industry.

> a quota stabilises the circumstances of domestic producers for any downward shift of the foreign-supply curve. . . . Thus in a situation in which there is considerable uncertainty as to the future position of the foreign-supply curve — even in its position in the immediate future — there is a case for a protectionist government to choose a quota system rather than a tariff. (Hindley, 1980, p. 32)

Consequently, "with quotas, the employment effect is certain" (Pearson and Salembier, 1983, p. 27). As the majority of the population is "risk-averse" (Johnston, 1985), quotas are an attractive solution to alleviate the difficulties an industry is experiencing. Seen from this point of view, the voluntary restraint agreement, because it is limited to one or a few countries, is less effective than unilateral quotas. It does, however, have the additional advantage of clearly identifying a few countries practising it and accusing them of being the source of the industrial problem. Restraints are essentially directed toward countries where wages are much lower than those in the importing country; they reflect the "moral" judgment of the population and its political leaders, namely that the foreign competition is "unfair" (Cable, 1983). It comes then as no surprise that voluntary restraint agreements are highly accepted by the population. A clear majority of Canadians and Americans approve, to varying degrees, of restrictions on imports of Japanese cars (*Decima Quarterly Report*, Fall 1982, question 515; *Public Opinion*, vol. 8, April–May 1985, p. 30). Similarly, a survey of business leaders conducted by the Conference Board of Canada (Adamek, 1984) revealed that voluntary restraints were the only measure they wished to see utilized more often.

However, if the "specialists" are consulted, the point of view is quite different. They are nearly unanimous in opposing this type of intervention, whether they are proponents or opponents of a vigorous industrial policy. This is because quotas are seen as having considerable adverse effects. Tyson and Zysman (1983, p. 53) summarize these effects quite well:

> OMAs [orderly market adjustments] tend to have three main consequences. The first is well understood: the restriction of imports from one country encourages new producers to spring up quickly in other places. The second is even more serious: if one limits the volume of imports, it is in the interest of foreign producers to move into higher value goods to achieve the largest possible value of total sales. Finally, foreign producers may alter the composition of the goods they produce to escape the quantitative limits on certain imports.

Moreover, quotas are a very costly measure. Jenkins (1980) estimated that quotas in clothing cost Canadian consumers nearly $200 million in 1979, an amount equivalent to a subsidy of $33,000 for each job saved. U.S. restrictions on Japanese automobiles apparently raised the price of imported cars by over $1,000, and the price of domestic cars by around $400 (Maskus, 1984; Crandall, 1984). The cost per job saved in 1983 would be in the order of $160,000 (Crandall, 1984).

The economic cost of quotas is thus enormous. It is possible that the cost has low visibility and is underestimated by the population. However, it is hard to see how governments could give up use of this instrument, since safeguarding jobs is a prime objective of industrial policy:

> safeguard clauses are accepted by most observers of international commercial diplomacy — even the most liberal — as an essential pre-condition of obtaining liberalizing trade agreements. Behind this acceptance lies the idea that an unduly rapid contraction of a domestic industry due to imports is politically embarrassing and socially costly. . . . It is believed that governments will not commit themselves to liberalization unless they are assured that they can avoid such costs should they arise. (Hindley, 1980, pp. 315–16)

Another indicator of the political necessity of voluntary restraint agreements is the fact they are largely tolerated even though they contravene the fundamental GATT principle that any safeguard measure should be multilateral and not make distinctions between countries (Merciai, 1981; Lipson, 1983). This complicity is easily explained:

> the complicity which exists between governments when one of them is forced to take unpopular trade measures because it has a domestic problem on its hands. All governments know what it is to be subject to such pressures, and they are usually prepared to be indulgent with each other because

they do not know when they will be forced to ask for sympathy and understanding themselves. (Curzon and Curzon, 1976, p. 222)

It is also important to emphasize the temporary character of voluntary restraints. Critics maintain that they have a tendency to stretch out unduly, or even indefinitely (Aggarwal, 1983). This is undoubtedly the case in textiles. In other sectors, however, even if restraints are often extended, they are destined to end fairly quickly, more quickly at any rate than programs of direct financial assistance (Faucher et al., 1985; Blais, Faucher and Young, 1983). Restraints are thus a relatively flexible instrument of intervention.

In sum, management of industrial decline is the most important, and also the most delicate, issue in industrial policy. In practice, governments give priority to this question, hence reflecting the general concern among citizens for stability and jobs. The predominant strategy consists of preventing the decline in employment from taking place too abruptly. One instrument particularly used for this purpose is the voluntary restraint agreement. Such agreements include substantial benefits, but are very costly. It would appear that politicians make only moderate use of them. When unemployment is high, when foreign competition seems "unfair," and penetration by imports becomes too strong, restraint agreements are a weapon that can be resorted to, but only temporarily and for a limited number of commodities.

Regional Development

Industrial policy is also strongly directed toward regional development. The traditional formula is the subsidy to investment, where the rate is typically 25 percent, intended for investments in designated regions, which usually include a third of the population (Yuill, Allen and Hull, 1980). In recent years there has been a tendency to add subsidies for hiring (McKersie and Sengenberger, 1983, p. 99). It was during the 1960s that aid for regional development truly grew. Yuill, Allen and Hull (1980, p. 219) describe the period this way:

In sum, the second phase of policy — what could be termed the heyday of regional policy — saw the introduction of increasingly valuable incentives and of a wider range of incentive types. It was, moreover, a period of great innovation and experimentation, reflected not only in the constant chopping and changing found in many countries, but also in attempts to target policy in a very specific manner through highly discriminatory schemes. . . .

The predominant trend in the 1970s appears to have been the status quo, as the major programs were hardly modified (ibid., p. 221).

Moreover, aid to declining industries often has a strong regional component as well. Miles (1976), for example, notes that in Britain the footwear industry is much less supported by the state than is the textile industry. Yet the two industries face similar problems. The footwear industry, however, is characterized by being much more scattered throughout the country than is the textile industry. Similarly, the favoured treatment enjoyed by shipbuilding in nearly every country is explained in large part by its geographical concentration. As de Closets notes (1982, p. 243), in France "if shipbuilding had been broken up into thousands of small and medium-sized enterprises located all over the country, it would no doubt have collapsed and not have received the assistance of public funds" [translation]. Lavergne's data (1983) indicate that, in the United States, industry located in rural areas and whose survival is even more essential to the area in which it is established has seen its tariffs reduced less rapidly than has industry located in urban areas. It is often on a regional basis that political mobilization in favour of an industry emerges. In steelmaking in the United States, "in addition to industry and labor activity, the pressure came from a newly created Steel Communities Coalition composed of public officials representing two dozen communities in traditional steel working areas" (Walters, 1982, p. 112).

Why is this so? An initial observation appears necessary, and that is the great legitimacy of regional development as a target of government intervention. In Europe, 79 percent of the population agree to contribute through taxes to the development of disadvantaged regions (Urich, 1983, Appendix 7). Similarly, 83 percent of Canadians feel that the federal government should concentrate its efforts on disadvantaged regions (*Decima Quarterly Report*, 1981–83, question 375). Thus there is a desire that the government have a regional policy.

If such a desire exists, it is because people's attachment to their immediate surroundings is very strong. In Europe, more people identify with their community than with their country (Urich, 1983, Appendix 9). In the United States, most people, especially in rural areas, do not want to move away from the community in which they live (Campbell et al., 1976, pp. 260–61). Consequently, "despite the shortcomings that can be found in almost every situation, most of us are at least moderately satisfied with our communities, our neighbourhoods, and our dwelling units, and we change our location only with reluctance and under pressure of circumstances" (Campbell, 1981, p. 159). In Canada, attachment to one's region is a widespread feeling, and attachment to one's province is practically as great as to the country (Johnston, 1985).

To talk about regional development presupposes that there is a regional "problem." The problem is defined essentially in terms of jobs (Ashcroft, 1980, p. 19). It lies in the fact that one of the solutions suggested to resolve the serious problem of regional unemployment, namely the migration of workers to parts of the country where the job outlook is more attractive, is unacceptable because of the strength of attachment to the community. The only option remaining is to encourage firms to migrate to where the workers are.

What is the real impact of incentives to investment? This question is the cause of much debate. It is a matter of determining the extent to which incentives in fact influence decision making by a firm; if the firm would have invested without the incentives, there is really no additional benefit. In Canada, studies based on interviews suggest that the rate of additional benefit is between 30 and 80 percent (Economic Council of Canada, 1977). In addition, creation of the Department of Regional Economic Expansion coincided with a shrinking by one percent of the gap between the unemployment rate in the Atlantic provinces and the rate for all of Canada (ibid., p. 168). Of course, it is not certain that DREE policies were entirely responsible for this situation (Usher, 1983), but the data tend at any rate to confirm the hypothesis of a not inconsiderable impact. This led the Economic Council to conclude (ibid., p. 172):

> The RDIA part of DREE expenditures does seem to work, in the sense that enough firms are encouraged to relocate by the grants to cause national output to be higher than otherwise, as a result of making use of labour that would otherwise be unemployed.

This conclusion, it seems, should apply to all countries. Ashcroft's summary (1980, p. 102) of econometric studies of the impact of regional incentives in six European countries is the following:

> A summary of some of the key results suggested that regional policies had induced 13.6 percent of assisted investments in the GA areas of Germany, 16.0 percent of total investment in the Northern Region of the Netherlands and 20.0 percent of total investment in the three main DA regions of the United Kingdom. For employment, it appeared that regional policies had raised employment by 1.26, 1.23 and 1.19 jobs per annum per thousand of the population in respectively the GA areas of Germany, the Designated Areas of Ireland and the four main DA regions of the United Kingdom. In Denmark and Belgium, no quantitative studies of the effects of policy were available. However, for Denmark, one study could be interpreted as indicating that 0.79 jobs per annum per thousand of the population had been created by regional policy in that land. In Belgium, there was evidence that suggested a redistribution of investment in favour of the assisted areas.

Ashcroft concludes that "the effect appears to be substantial" (p. 53). In the same vein, an OECD study (1983c) estimates that, in general, incentives to investments influence investment decisions very little, but that their impact on the place of investment, within a given large economic region, is greater. The OECD study seems to indicate as well that this impact has been growing in recent years.

The fact that regional incentives are aimed at investment rather than employment is often presented as an inconsistency. Woodward's argument (1974, p. 173) is a traditional one in this regard:

> the capital bias of DREE's maximum-incentive formula, of the constraint affecting most industries and of the majority of offers is inconsistent with the department's primary objective — employment. The inconsistency occurs

because a capital bias implies that the designated regions' extra employment attributable to the grant program is less, and investment more, than would have occurred if the incentives had been neutral or labour biased.

The strategy of government may not, however, be as illogical as it seems at first glance. Although governments are primarily concerned with jobs, they must rely on private enterprise to create those jobs. But company executives think in terms of investment, not in terms of jobs, and governments must take this logic into account in seeking to influence their decisions. This would explain the fact that incentive bonuses for job creation seem to be less effective than incentives to investment. They are less attractive to employers, who take less advantage of them than they might (OECD, 1982b), and the budget cost per job tends to be high (McKersie and Sengenberger, 1983). Also, "there is no satisfactory evidence that policy has induced firms to substitute the factor subsidized for a non-subsidized factor" (Ashcroft, 1980, p. 104).

Why then do governments resort to subsidies rather than to other forms of aid, such as tax allowances? It is because they are anxious to demonstrate that they are acting in favour of regional development, and are keenly concerned with the visibility of their interventions. Subsidies to specific firms are of great interest in this regard (McAllister, 1982, p. 52; Lewis, 1984, p. 144). A minister or MP may announce that the government is giving a subsidy toward the establishment of a firm in a given locality. The political dividends of such a measure are probably overestimated. Some studies indicate, in fact, that the electoral impact of very selective interventions is rather marginal. Agricultural policy, for example, is often decried for its vote-getting character. Systematic analysis of the effect of agricultural policy on election results in Quebec, however, leads to the conclusion that the effect is weak, and that the government's popularity is more dependent on the overall situation of agriculture and its short-term fluctuations (Blais, 1978). Similarly, a study of the distribution of facilities in London and New York indicates that this distribution influences voting at the next election very little (Glassberg, 1973). This does not mean this aspect of the question can be disregarded. It is in the politicians' interest that their interventions in regional policy be publicized. But it is the visibility of the result, that is, a change in the unemployment rate in a given area, that counts the most (Blais, 1986, chap. 4).

Technology

While the state is concerned first with "losers," it still does not overlook "winners." Nearly all governments have set up incentive programs for industrial innovation (OECD, 1978b). In data processing, governments tend to make their purchases from domestic producers only (Blais, 1986, chap. 1). Research and development enjoy special tax treatment: R&D

expenditures may generally be depreciated over a short period of time, sometimes in the same year in which they are made; to this are added special deductions and tax credits on the level of or increase in expenditures compared to a given previous period (McFetridge and Warda, 1983).

The interest in technology may appear quite well founded, given that technological capacity is considered today as one of the main engines of economic growth (Economic Council of Canada, 1983). The role played by the creation and dissemination of technology, and the place of the state in the process, give rise to no less lively a debate. Assistance to research and development is usually justified by maintaining that the collective rate of return on applied research is higher than the private rate (ibid., p. 40). Thus there is apparently an "externality" that would legitimize government intervention to promote this type of activity. In an international perspective, by contrast, where technology may be disseminated at low cost, it could just as well be argued that a given country, especially a small country, has a greater interest in benefiting from technological innovation designed elsewhere (McFetridge and Warda, 1983, p. 91).

There is another argument in support of a vigorous government policy in technological innovation: the Schumpeterian thesis concerning barriers to entry, and, more particularly, the opinion that technological competition has an irreversible character and favours those who innovate, success necessarily begetting more success (Harris, 1985). Data in this regard are often contradictory, however. Thus it is that Kamien and Schwarts (1982, p. 75), while acknowledging that some studies seem to confirm the hypothesis according to which success leads to success, add: "there is also some evidence that 'success begets failure'. Either initial success leads to complacency or the successful firm is not as hungry as the newcomer, or the behaviour that led to the first success is maintained until it becomes obsolete in a changing environment."

Governments have not waited for the debate to be resolved before intervening. The underlying logic seems to have been the following: in the 1960s, at a time when states agreed to play the international competition game and when, as a consequence, each state began to compare its production structure to that of others, a profound feeling of insecurity emerged in many countries. The United States quickly appeared as both a reference point and a threat. The symbolic impact of the American challenge, especially during the 1960s and even today, cannot be overemphasized. The presence of an economic giant at the forefront of technological development leaves hardly any choice for the governments of other countries: they must do something in order not to be swallowed up by the U.S. power. Zysman (1977, p. 143) is very clear on this point. In France, "simple insecurity was at the bottom of the technology gap debate." Warnecke (1978, p. 9) also points out this emulation effect: "the industries [governments] wish to emulate at home are frequently those they believe enhance other nations' political and economic power." At a time when international competition is becoming keener, and technology seems to be called upon to play an increasingly important role, governments wish to ensure, at the very least, that the country's industry does not find itself suddenly outclassed by foreign producers.

On the economic level, one may at least doubt the relevance of such a strategy. The advantages associated with high-tech industries in the early 1960s have quickly vanished: "the differential between the high returns in technologically advanced industries and the earnings of others disappeared between 1965 and 1970" (Bergsten et al., 1978, p. 266). While all governments "have to some extent made attempts to discover which industries are likely to become winners" (George, 1983, p. 41), the exercise is no less delicate, inasmuch as elements of "success" change with time. Similarly, countries that have invested most in research and development have not experienced higher growth rates: "statistically, in fact, there is a weak negative association, i.e. the countries who have devoted an above-average share of the output to research and development have, if anything, experienced below-average rates of growth" (Norris and Vaizey, 1973, p. 123). Whatever the case may be, only with difficulty can governments resist the temptation to intervene in technological innovation, because of the high degree of uncertainty that prevails. Technological expansion being what it is, governments are concerned with the eventuality that a particular innovation may endanger an entire domestic production sector, especially in a context of trade liberalization.

Governments are also motivated by the prestige associated with high technology:

> computers have come to symbolize the essential power of the second industrial revolution; and the efforts . . . to preserve a national computer industry in the face of immense technological and economic odds are not so much a fight against the apparent rationality of industrial specialization as an attempt to retain some form of real power by preserving the symbol of power. (Norris and Vaizey, 1973, p. 195)

In addition, since the concern with prestige is greater in large countries likely to compare themselves to the United States, it should not be surprising that "the drive for an independent computer industry is closely linked with a country's size" (ibid., p. 202).

Such preoccupations are not confined to the elites. Eighty percent of Canadians wish the federal government to invest large amounts of money in the development of new technology (*Decima Quarterly Report*, 1981–83, question 373). Research and development are highly regarded in modern society, as is indicated by the high social status of researchers

(Hodge, Siegel and Rossi, 1966; Treiman, 1977). Research and innovation are seen as worthwhile objectives in themselves. Collectively, a society needs to see itself as having a degree of excellence. The pride aroused by the exploits of a nation's athletes at the Olympics demonstrates this. A government, then, may only with difficulty allow itself not to have a policy on technology.

The desire to see the government intervene vigorously in the field of technology is generally expressed by organizations made up of scientists and technologists. In Canada, the Science Council has become the chief proponent of this option. This should not be surprising, since "the main beneficiaries of research and development aimed at producing significant technical advances are likely to be scientists in the jobs thereby created" (Daly and Globerman, 1976, p. 6). While it appears plausible that researchers may not be impartial actors, their real influence is still doubtful, especially in comparison with that of the industrial community. As we have just seen, the desire to see the government act is far from being limited to this group alone.

Intervention by the state in technology has two major components: on the one hand, general incentives to research and development, especially through taxation, and, on the other, special measures directed toward specific projects. All indications are that the first strategy is increasingly favoured by the state (Blais, 1986, chap. 4). However, the emphasis placed on research and development is debatable, to say the least (Mansfield, 1985). R&D is an activity that lends itself easily to quantification, and it is statistics on amounts allocated to R&D that are most often cited in discussing technology. In Canada, the low level of total expenditure on R&D and the meagre contribution of multinationals to this activity are at the forefront of the debate now taking place on industrial policy (chap. 2 of this volume). If it is in the interests of governments to appear to be keenly interested in seeing technology develop, they must make or encourage sufficient expenditures in this sector. It is not surprising that the Canadian tax system is generous in this regard (McFetridge and Warda, 1983), since Canada's performance is very poor (Bernstein, 1985, Table 1-1). Pressure being exerted to have the government correct this "anomaly" is very strong as a result.

Governments would be ill advised to resist this pressure, since there is every reason to believe that incentives are beneficial. Studies on the impact of tax incentives indicate they in fact contribute to an increase in research and development, although the cost (tax loss) is fairly high (Mansfield, 1985; McFetridge, 1977). In addition, research and development seem to drive up the number of patents, the most common indicator of innovation (McFetridge, 1977).

Governments have especially observed that it is in their interest to adopt the least selective approach possible, as the technology sector is probably where industrial policy has experienced its most resounding failures. Wescott (1983, p. 112) reports that "the return from research and development tends to be lower in those fields where much of it is supported by the U.S. government." Zysman's study (1977) on data processing in France shows how government intervention has had the effect of weakening the trade position of firms that depended on public assistance. Ilgen's analysis (1983, p. 680) on the chemical industry concludes that "an industry that relies on innovation as its engine of growth needs a setting where individuals and firms have maximum freedom to pursue their innovative instincts." If, in practice, commercial failures like the Concorde are the rule rather than the exception, one can only agree with Trebilcock (1986) when he states that general incentive measures represent the best economic policy toward industrial R&D attainable in our political system, and with Mansfield (1985), for whom the available indices suggest "that governments seem to be most successful in stimulating civilian technology when they emphasize relatively broad policies rather than attempting to make detailed decisions concerning which specific designs and types of commercial products should be developed and at what pace."

This seems to be the conclusion gradually being reached by most governments. Of course, assistance for given branches of industry or specific projects will not be abolished overnight. But the infatuation with national champions is much less evident. There seems to be a learning process taking place, with governments refocussing their efforts in order to correct past mistakes, especially the more glaring ones. In a field where the risks are so high, it is not at all in their interest to be closely associated with any project whatsoever, since they have much more to lose from a miserable failure than they have to gain from a noticeable success.

Business Size

On the whole, government intervention does not systematically benefit either large or small enterprise. There are, however, exceptions to the rule. Thus more direct financial assistance goes to large enterprise (Blais, 1986, chap. 1). This situation, however, is in large part the indirect consequence of measures that are not based on the size of the firm. For example, national security concerns lead governments to favour the defence industry, a highly concentrated industry; thus, large firms find themselves at an advantage, even though this is not the prime objective of government intervention. At the other end, agriculture is the most highly subsidized industrial sector, and the sector in which family businesses still predominate. In this industry, governments have manifestly not encouraged concentration (Leanos, 1984).

The shutdown of a large firm, or the risk of shutdown, is of greater concern to governments than the shutdown of a small firm, as the impact on regional unemployment is much more substantial. Governments worry about the decline of small establishments only if they are concentrated in a given area. Large firms are thus more likely to be "saved" than are small firms. As Hager emphasizes (1982), while it is true that more assistance is given to large firms, those favoured are "the worst performers among them" (p. 244). This preference is not the result of indulgence on the part of political leaders toward big capital. It is dictated by the concern with preventing disequilibrium in the regional economy as the result of a large firm's demise. By contrast, it is the large firm that is most often nationalized (Blais and Faucher, 1981), usually against its wishes.

Governments in fact have no interest in creating the impression of unduly favouring big business. It is politically unfeasible for them to defend big capital openly:

> the decision-makers are extremely anxious to avoid any suggestion that they favour large firms over small ones: they are, of course, painfully aware that rival politicians and the mass media are always ready to pounce upon even the slightest hint of an instance of favoritism. (Braam, 1981, p. 264)

Even the Conservative party in Britain "has to appeal to a broad electoral base and too close an identification with big business might run counter to the populist suspicion of 'bigness' among many of the voters likely to support the Conservatives" (Grant, 1980, p. 151).

As in the tale of David and Goliath, virtue is on the side of the little guy, and wrong on the side of the big guy. Small business does not miss its chance to exploit this belief fully. It likes to be seen as the true representative of genuine capitalism, often given a rough ride by the unfair activities of high finance and large industrialists. In the United States, the data in this regard are clear:

> Big corporations were given highly favourable rating by 10–16 per cent, while the percentages having such positive feelings about small business companies ranged from 35 to 41 per cent. About one third of the respondents . . . gave big business either not too favourable or unfavourable ratings, compared to the one twentieth who evaluated small companies in a negative light. (Lipset and Schneider, 1983, pp. 81–82)

Obviously, this has not prevented governments from slightly favouring large business, showing there are limits to ideology. But neither can the gap between talk and action be too large. The very fact that in certain respects large business is at an advantage has forced governments to set up programs specifically for small business. Financing assistance for small businesses represents a particularly interesting case. All available data indicate that the economic rationality of such aid is doubtful:

> small businesses are not treated in a substantially different fashion than are larger firms. Small businesses, in fact, receive more favourable treatment by

the banks in terms of the amount of financing obtained, the loan conditions imposed on the business and the time taken by the banks to reach a decision. (Hatch et al., 1982, p. 8)

The political calculation seems to be the following: on the one hand, the government must show it is interested in the fate of small business; on the other hand, credit is a relatively inexpensive form of aid. In 1979 in Canada, the treasury cost of loans from the Federal Business Development Bank was only $20 million, and the cost of guarantees under the Small Businesses Loans Act only $1.5 million (Economic Council of Canada, 1982, p. 140, Table A-2, and p. 142, Table A-4). Also, the underlying mistrust of banks (Facsym Research Limited, 1981) justifies the government's intervention in this area of activity. According to this analysis, the guarantee is apparently less costly and more advantageous than the loan. For a given budget, guarantees enable the government to come to the aid of a greater number of firms.

The search for neutrality with respect to the size of enterprise has not always been so fashionable. During the 1960s, several European governments seemed to have a fondness for big business: "there has been a . . . tendency to use large national enterprises in an effort to solve specific problems as if they were agencies of the state" (Vernon, 1974, p. 3). Thus, governments encouraged mergers (Blais and Faucher, 1981). This attitude was based on the idea that trade liberalization, by broadening markets, would increase economies of scale, and thereby put large business in a better position to benefit from the new situation. As it is essentially large firms that export (Galbraith, 1984, Table 1), the analysis appears plausible. In practice, however, mergers did not produce the expected effects (Blair, 1972, pp. 185–95), and the strategy was gradually abandoned.

There seem to be two lessons to be drawn from this episode. First, it is difficult for governments to predict what the industrial organization of the future will be and to adopt the measures most likely to favour that organization (George, 1983). In this case in particular, all indications are that governments have underestimated both the enormous transition difficulties posed by mergers and the weight of centrifugal forces creating diseconomies of scale (Blair, 1972, Part 2). Second, the fact that the strategy was abandoned demonstrates that governments are capable of correcting at least some of the mistakes they make along the way.

The hopes placed in large business have quickly faded: "the 'merger mania' of the late 1960s has now been replaced by a fashionable belief that small firms are the key to economic revival" (Grant, 1982, p. 32). The OECD (1983b) notes a trend since the mid-1970s toward giving special consideration to measures in favour of small firms. Some now proclaim that it is dynamic small firms that create jobs. In Canada, establishments with fewer than 50 employees were responsible for nearly 90 percent of net job creation in the manufacturing sector from 1971 to 1981 (Blais, 1986, Table 33). In the United States, establishments with fewer than 20 employees created two-thirds of new jobs from 1969 to 1976, and those with fewer than 100 employees about 80 percent (Birch, 1981).

It is important, however, to place things in perspective. On the one hand, small establishments are more likely than large ones to close their doors (Blais, 1986, Table 33), so that jobs in these establishments are less stable. On the other hand, the picture is somewhat different when we examine the data concerning firms rather than establishments. In the United States, at any rate, "a significant portion of the growing small establishments are branches or subsidiaries of large firms" (Armington and Odle, 1982, p. 14). From 1978 to 1982, establishments with fewer than 100 employees created 78 percent of jobs, but the majority of those jobs came from firms having several establishments; the share of firms having fewer than 100 employees was only 34 percent. In sum, small establishments had the advantage of creating more jobs, and the disadvantage of offering less stable jobs. Small firms had the same disadvantage, but without the same advantage. While governments have no interest in openly favouring large business, neither is it in their interest to go in the opposite direction.

Foreign Capital

The treatment of foreign capital is one of the major issues in industrial policy. Only one dimension of this issue, namely, regulation of foreign investment, will be examined here. Mytelka's study (chap. 4 of this volume) indicates that:

- in nearly half the OECD countries, foreign investment is normally subject to formal authorization; by contrast, regulation is rarely in an act bearing specifically on foreign investment, and only in Canada and Australia have screening agencies been set up;
- in four countries — the United States, the United Kingdom, Italy and West Germany (OECD, 1982a, also mentions the Netherlands and Switzerland) — there is no formal authorization procedure, although other policies may sometimes have the same effect; and
- in several countries, authorization is required only in special circumstances (acquisitions, investment over a certain amount, etc.).

It is obviously important to assess the real scope of these regulations. On this point the existing studies are not very enlightening. We learn little about the concrete application of policies. Governments, for their part, stress the liberal character of the measures adopted (OECD, 1975, p. 128). We are led to believe that this corresponds to the facts, and that regulation is on the whole flexible. The predominant policy would thus appear to be "open-door," with governments reserving the right to intervene if necessary. Also, according to Mytelka's study, a number of sectors, in particular public services, transportation and communications, and financial institutions, are more or less closed to foreign investment. Regulation in these areas is more often implicit than explicit, since the most frequent obstacle is the formation of public monopolies.

As in the case of the development of technology, insecurity seems to be at the root of government intervention. Even though governments have a favourable bias toward investors, whatever their nationality, they see multinationals as a threat to which they feel very vulnerable (Black et al., 1982; Graham, 1982). The anxiety is primarily because of the power of the multinationals, a power that derives from their high mobility (Marsh, chap. 3 of this volume). Also the question arises as to whether multinationals show more favour to the economic development of their country of origin or to that of the host country. In this regard, centralization of research and development in the country of origin (Rugman, 1981; Economic Council of Canada, 1983) is a constant concern of governments. Although foreign investment seems to benefit the country of origin and the host country equally (Bergsten et al., 1978), it is a source of tension.

Consequently, multinational firms inspire a great deal of mistrust. Multinationals are one of the institutions Canadians trust the least. Only unions are seen in a more negative way. Public opinion of multinationals is even less favourable than of the federal government and the public service (Johnston, 1986). Multinationals have the double drawback of being both large and foreign (on mistrust of large institutions, see Lipset and Schneider, 1983; and Blais, 1986, chap. 3). The attitude of the elites is more moderate, the predominant trend being "a moderately favourable overall appraisal" (Fayerweather, 1982, p. 4), but "always simmering behind the surface are basic nationalistic views" (ibid., p. 18).

This wariness of multinationals makes regulation of foreign investment reasonably attractive. In fact, 60 percent of Canadians say they are favourable, in principle, to screening of foreign investment (*Decima Quarterly Report*, 1980–83, question 208). The same attitude is found among executives (Sales, 1983, Table 9, p. 34). But, as Johnston emphasizes (1985), support for screening is quite timid. More than half the people in favour were so only on condition that screening not reduce employment (*Decima Quarterly Report*, 1980–83, question 209). Since job creation is seen as the principal advantage of foreign investment (Murray and LeDuc, 1982, Table 10.2, p. 233), and since the majority of Canadians feel a reduction in this investment would cause a decrease in employment (Johnston, 1985), it can only be concluded that "support for nationalist measures seems shallow" (ibid., chap. 5).

Thus it can be easily understood that the predominant strategy is one of cautious openness. Governments depend on foreign investment for job creation, but also see it as a threat calling for vigilance. They are similar to "a fairly constant proportion of the Canadian public . . . waiting and watching, not seeing foreign investment as an immediate problem to be dealt with but rather as one that might become more serious over time" (Murray and LeDuc, 1982, p. 226).

Another strategy consists of setting up an agency whose purpose is to orient foreign investment in the national interest. Only in Canada and Australia, the two countries where foreign firms seem to be most in evidence (Mytelka, chap. 4 of this volume, Tables 4-3 and 4-4), has this strategy been adopted. It is an ambitious wager. The government aims to negotiate investment conditions, cause business to do more research and development in the country, make more use of national suppliers, export in larger quantity, grant world production rights, and so on. The risk, of course, is that of driving out foreign firms who do not wish to have such conditions imposed on them. There is yet another possibility, which is that firms "yield" to conditions that they would have accepted anyway (Usher, 1983). The strategy assumes that governments have a certain margin of manoeuvre available to them, either because the firms targeted are not completely mobile, or because the decision to invest is made on the basis of other criteria, the market in particular, which clearly favour a given country already.

To my knowledge, no econometric research has been done to measure the impact of government regulation. The only data available are too specific or fragmentary. Case studies indicate that certain multinationals sometimes make sizable concessions, while others are intransigent and wish to preserve their management autonomy at any cost (Doz and Prahalad, 1980). It is nearly impossible to establish the relative frequency of the two kinds of reaction.

In Canada, two studies question the benefits government intervention may bring about in this area. The survey by Bonin and Perron (1984, pp. 16–17) on world production rights in Quebec concluded:

> The role of governments in obtaining rights is deemed negligible. . . . The hypothesis to the effect that obtaining world or regional rights will translate into an increase in the margin of autonomy enjoyed by the Canadian branch plant was not confirmed by our research. [Translation]

Similarly, Crookell's study (1985) on major appliances reveals that interventions by the Foreign Investment Review Agency sometimes yielded results opposite to those intended. This is what seems to have happened following the Canadian government's refusal to authorize the takeover of Camco by Canadian General Electric:

> The objective in blocking the CGE takeover of GSW has not been achieved. Ironically, CGE may be pleased. . . . Under its original proposal, rejected by FIRA, CGE would have paid GSW $21.6 million and would then have had

to find additional funds for modernizing Camco. Under the new, apparently acceptable, format, CGE receives a dividend from Camco of $780,000 plus $7.2 million from the proceeds of sale of 900,000 shares, and acquires majority voting control. . . . CGE may well prefer this new arrangement to the costly takeover rejected by FIRA.

The impact of regulation on the flows of investment is not much easier to assess. According to Safarian (1983, p. 82), "countries which experiment with what are considered to be significantly restrictive policies do tend to lose with such flows, and vice versa." On the other hand, Mytelka's analysis (chap. 4 of this volume) "reveals absolutely no correlation between regulation and reduction in new foreign investment in either Australia or France." Without econometric studies, it is quite difficult to draw a conclusion one way or the other. A survey by the Conference Board of Canada (McDowall, 1984; Beckman, 1984) seems to indicate that regulation may have had negative effects among ten percent of potential investors. This concurs with an OECD study (1983c), which concludes that obstacles to investment have an impact, but a moderate one.

If governments thus run the risk, however small, of losing investments, they are unwilling to put systematic regulation in place. The Canadian case is interesting in this regard. The fact that half of Canadian manufacturing production comes from foreign firms can only encourage political leaders to want to exercise some control over foreign investment. The concern is much less intense, however, when high unemployment makes job creation the most important issue; it is in periods of prosperity that nationalism is healthiest (Murray and LeDuc, 1982). Recession apparently has the effect of accentuating protectionism against foreign production, but weakening protectionism against foreign investment.

Conclusion

Industrial policy during the past forty years has been characterized essentially by the trade liberalization movement, counterbalanced by a whole series of measures intended to slow the decline of industries, firms or regions in difficulty. This strategy may be regarded as the one most appropriate, since it reconciles the public's desire to see a happy marriage between progress and stability. While the market economy is likely to ensure growth, it also brings with it disequilibria (Offe and Ronge, 1975), disequilibria that the state seeks, with some degree of success, to alleviate (Montmarquette, 1981; Alt and Chrystal, 1983; McCallum and Blais, 1985). A society that feels it is progressing, even if not to the maximum extent, avoiding major upheavals, is likely to be relatively satisfied. The political system thereby achieves the output desired by the majority of its citizens.

On the whole, then, our assessment of industrial policy is positive. Questions may be raised, of course, as to the relevance of many government measures; I shall return to this point later in this section. All things considered, however, governments handle matters not too badly.

The good performance of governments would seem to be explained primarily by the constraints to which they are subject. To the extent that politicians are particularly preoccupied with getting reelected, and to the extent that reelection depends in large part on the performance of the economy, they have every interest in seeing that their interventions promote stable growth of the economy. For this reason, analysis that suggests a strong opposition between economic rationality and political rationality (Trebilcock, 1986) seems misleading. As long as economic rationality encompasses an objective such as stability, as long as it is admitted that employment is more highly valued than income, as long as it is accepted that compromises must be made between growth, stability and full employment,[10] the two rationalities will be more convergent than divergent. This interlocking of economic and political logic has tended to become more pronounced because of the growing importance given to the economy by the media (Mosley, 1984). Consequently, the electoral calculation made by governments leads them to a concern with the economic efficiency (in the broad sense of the term) of their policies.

We have also observed that politicians have had a favourable bias toward free trade, and have resisted protectionist pressure up to a point. If this is so, it is doubtless because free trade is seen as being in line with the national interest. As Bauer et al. note (1972, pp. 397–98), "an image of the general interest which was diffused through myriad channels of mass media and citizen discussion promised in the end to triumph over rear-guard actions by even the cleverest of pressure groups." The national interest is obviously a fuzzy concept, concealing social conflicts that are at the very heart of the political dynamic. The rule whereby the state is a guarantor of the national interest is no less a principle to which politicians all adhere, and which influences their behaviour to a certain extent (Krasner, 1978). To the degree that politicians keep in mind what history will say about them,[11] they must create the impression of being motivated by noble ideals. The need to follow this rule is especially strong inasmuch as politicians are called upon to maintain relations with representatives of other countries, thereby making them even more aware of the advantages of international trade;[12] it is through this formal and informal communication that the legitimacy of an "international system" is established (Krasner, 1983).

Even though the overall direction of industrial policy seems to be nearly optimal, it does not necessarily follow that all existing measures are satisfactory. According to the analysis of government intervention presented here, governments are more justified in managing industrial decline than in promoting innovation. Of course, citizens wish to see government intervene to support technological development, and governments cannot completely stand aside from this sector. Governments have also learned to adopt less selective measures which generally prove to be more effective, economically and politically speaking. But it is probably in this field that there is virtue in leaving the market free to act (Ilgen, 1983). As Rothwell and Zegveld emphasize (1984, p. 436), "because of the very nature of the innovation process — its variability and its technological, financial and marketing uncertainties — there are inherent limitations to what public policies can achieve."

In addition, it is not certain that the mechanisms to which governments resort to manage industrial decline are the most appropriate ones. For a number of years, voluntary restraint agreements have attracted the most attention, and criticism. However, these agreements appear to represent an essential safety valve in the trade liberalization process, directly oriented toward safeguarding jobs and having a great symbolic effectiveness to the extent that they enable citizens to point a finger at those countries responsible for their domestic industrial problems. This is obviously an expensive safety valve, but it has not been abused until now. Of course these agreements could always be made more flexible, but it is hard to see how they could be abolished completely.

The most fashionable proposals at the moment consist of replacing protectionist measures with compensation measures for workers. These proposals seem to have two major shortcomings. First, they assume that the workers involved are ready to accept a risk of higher unemployment in exchange for monetary compensation. While the formula may be acceptable when the unemployment rate is low, it could, however, have the effect of arousing a great deal of resistance in a context of high unemployment to the extent that workers are risk-averse and value employment over income. Of course, programs to encourage mobility or early retirement are desirable, but could not possibly constitute the core of an adjustment policy. From this point of view, it might be more effective to attack the unemployment problem directly, through corporate institutions, for example (Schmidt, 1982; 1984), or by abolishing taxes on manpower (Rousseau and Taurand, 1984), rather than adopting the adjustment measures made politically necessary by unemployment.

Second, proposals to compensate workers seem aimed at the wrong target. The political dynamic surrounding industrial decline finds its support essentially in the regions. Only when a firm or industry in difficulty might seriously aggravate local unemployment does the problem become political. In this situation, the entire locality, and not just the workers in an industry, should be compensated. Adjustment policies should therefore be resolutely regional. The analysis in this paper has indicated that to a great degree they already are. It is my view that it would be in the interests of governments to accentuate this direction even more, and to be explicit in making the regional dimension the pivotal element of their industrial policy. The creation of agencies such as the Canadian Industrial Renewal Board (CIRB) appears to be particularly interesting in this regard. Attachment to the community being what it is, we must acknowledge that resistance to geographic mobility is quite high, and may even intensify and become more problematic with the proliferation of households with two wage earners (Gordus, 1984).

Throughout, this study has stressed the stabilizing role that has fallen to the state in capitalist societies. If the state intervenes, it is because the stability so highly valued by its citizens cannot be ensured by market mechanisms. It is important to emphasize, however, that stability, by bringing with it comfort — a desirable adjunct — involves paying a price for that comfort. As Scitovsky notes (1976), "too much seeking for comfort will reduce or eliminate pleasure in any and every activity" (p. 77). Too great a stability can lead in the long term to a dull life, and its drawbacks may be underestimated by citizens (ibid., p. 73).

In addition, various orders of stability may come into conflict with each other. In particular, a choice must be made between employment and assured income. If it is true that wage levels may influence employment (Malinvaud, 1982) and that employment is more highly valued than income, wage rigidity constitutes a problem requiring some consideration. This is the message accurately conveyed by de Closets (1982, pp. 326–27):

> Let us assume theoretically that any distribution that makes certain segments of society, because of their vested interests, a three-way winner (in terms of standard of living, guaranteed income, and job security) is a source of injustice. If we admit that our wealth is linked to the market economy, no one can lay claim to that wealth without accepting certain constraints of the system in return. We must necessarily admit a penalty on one or other of these major attributes. . . . Social justice would have everything to gain from income insecurity gradually replacing job insecurity among salaried workers. [Translation]

Raising stability to the status of an absolute good is thus out of the question. Change, with its attendant uncertainty, is just as indispensable. But, if it is true that the family — the nuclear family primarily, but the extended family as well — is still the outstanding source of satisfaction for a large majority of citizens (Bénéton, 1983, chap. 12; Campbell et al., 1976), one can understand the crucial importance of social roots. This is another reason for according even greater interest to regional policy.

Notes

This study is a translation of the original French-language text, which was completed in February 1985. I wish to express my thanks to Stéphane Dion and Robert Young for their comments on a preliminary version of this study.

1. Watson (1983) describes six definitions before offering his own, but does not discuss their advantages or disadvantages.
2. Davenport et al. (1982, p. 1) first define industrial policy in terms of impact: "An industrial policy is any program that directly affects the economic activity of an industry, company or plant," and then refers to the goal being pursued: "Industrial policies are designed to change economic structures, behaviour, and/or performance."
3. They refer mainly to non-financial (in kind) transfers, but concentrate essentially on technical assistance.
4. They refer to regulation, but stress protection against imports (tariffs and quotas).
5. Rates of subsidy and protection may be compared, since "a subsidy to production of the final product has the same effect on production as a customs duty at the same rate" (Corden, 1977, p. 37, translation).
6. Assets of government enterprise in 1981 amounted to $144 billion (Statistics Canada, 1981, *Federal Government Enterprise Finance*, Catalogue 61-203, and *Provincial Government Enterprise Finance*, Catalogue 61-204).
7. Tupper notes the problem, but this does not prevent him from referring to "interventionist" governments throughout the text.
8. Baldwin's data (1970), most often used in the U.S. case, does not include either direct financial assistance or tax allowances.
9. It is important to emphasize that, in this perspective, the key factor is not overall economic performance (rate of growth of GDP), but rather performance compared to the most relevant criterion in industrial decline, politically speaking: employment. It is too easily forgotten that different indicators of economic performance are not correlated among themselves (Schmidt, 1983). For instance, the unemployment rate in France during the 1970s was just as high as in the United Kingdom; that is why, in my view, the two countries are equally protectionist.
10. Correlations between a country's performance with respect to growth, inflation and employment are practically nil (Schmidt, 1982; 1983).
11. For example, one day in January 1984, Brian Mulroney confided to his senior policy adviser that he wanted history to remember him: "Brian just doesn't want to be Prime Minister," his friend Lucien Bouchard once observed, "He wants to live in history" (MacDonald, 1984, p. 299).
12. On the impact of travel on the attitudes of U.S. businessmen, see Bauer et al. (1972).

Bibliography

Adamek, Josef. 1984. *Business Leader's Views on Protectionism in Western Europe.* Ottawa: Conference Board of Canada.

Aggarwal, Vinod K., with Stephan Haggard. 1983. "The Politics of Protection in the U.S. Textile and Apparel Industries." In *American Industry in International Competition,* edited by John Zysman and Laura Tyson. Ithaca, N.Y.: Cornell University Press.

Alt, James E., and K. Alec Chrystal. 1983. *Political Economics.* Brighton: Harvester Press.

Armington, Catherine, and Marjorie Odle. 1982. "Small Business — How Many Jobs?" *Brookings Review* (Winter): 14–18.

Ashcroft, Brian. 1980. *The Evaluation of Regional Policy in Europe: A Survey and Critique.* Glasgow: Centre for the Study of Public Policy.

Badaracco, Joseph L. Jr., and David B. Yoffie. 1983. "Industrial Policy: It Can't Happen Here." *Harvard Business Review* (November–December): 96–106.

Balassa, Bela. 1978. "The 'New Protectionism' and the International Economy." *Journal of World Trade* 12: 409–436.

———. 1979. "The New Protectionism: Evaluation and Proposals for Reform." In *Challenges to a Liberal International Economic Order*, edited by R.C. Amacher et al. Washington, D.C.: American Enterprise Institute.

Baldwin, Robert E. 1970. *Nontariff Distortions of International Trade*. Washington, D.C.: Brookings Institution.

———. 1979. "Protectionist Pressures in the United States." In *Challenges to a Liberal International Economic Order*, edited by R.C. Amacher et al. Washington, D.C.: American Enterprise Institute.

Bauer, Raymond S., Ithiel de Sola Pool, and Lewis Anthony Dexter. 1972. *American Business and Public Policy: The Politics of Foreign Trade*. Chicago: Aldine.

Beckman, Christopher C. 1984. *The Foreign Investment Review Agency: Images and Realities*. Ottawa: The Conference Board of Canada.

Bélanger, Gérard. 1982. "Dans un système fédéral le gouvernement central doit-il essayer d'imposer l'harmonisation fiscale?" *Actualité économique* 58 (December): 493–512.

Bellemare, Diane, and Lise Poulin-Simon. 1983. *Le plein emploi pourquoi?* Montreal: Presses de l'Université du Québec.

Bénéton, Philippe. 1983. *Le fléau du bien: Essai sur les politiques sociales occidentales*. Paris: Robert Laffont.

Bergsten, C. Fred, Thomas Horst, and Théodore H. Moran. 1978. *American Multinationals and American Interests*. Washington, D.C.: Brookings Institution.

Bernstein, Jeffrey J. 1985. "Research and Development, Patents, and Grant and Tax Policies in Canada." In *Technological Change in Canadian Industry*, volume 3 of the research studies prepared for the Royal Commission on the Economic Union and Development Prospects for Canada. Toronto: University of Toronto Press.

Binhammer, H.H., L.C. McDonough, and G. Lepore. 1980. *Government Grants to Private Sector Firms*. Ottawa: Economic Council of Canada.

Birch, David L. 1981. "Who Creates Jobs?" *The Public Interest* 65 (Fall):3–14.

Black, Robert, Stephen Blank, and Elizabeth C. Hanson. 1982. *Multinationals in Contention: Responses at Governmental and International Levels*. New York: Conference Board.

Blair, John. 1972. *Economic Concentration*. New York: Harcourt Brace Jovanovitch.

Blais, André. 1978. "Politique agricole et résultats électoraux en milieu agricole au Québec." *Revue canadienne de science politique* 11 (June): 333–83.

———. 1980. "Orientation de la recherche." In *Introduction à l'analyse des politiques*, edited by Réjean Landry. Quebec: Presses de l'Université Laval.

———. 1986. *The Political Sociology of Industrial Policy*. Volume 45 of the research studies prepared for the Royal Commission on the Economic Union and Development Prospects for Canada. Toronto: University of Toronto Press.

Blais, André, and Philippe Faucher. 1981. "La politique industrielle dans les économies capitalistes avancées." *Canadian Journal of Political Science* 14 (March): 3–35.

Blais, André, Philippe Faucher, and Robert Young. 1983. *L'aide financière directe du gouvernement fédéral à l'industrie canadienne, 1960–80*. Research Paper. Montreal: Université de Montréal, Department of Political Science.

Blanc, Jacques, and Chantal Brulé. 1983. *Les nationalisations françaises en 1982*. Paris: La Documentation Française.

Boardman, Anthony. 1984. "An Evaluation of Canada Development Corporation." Mimeographed.

Bonin, Bernard, and Bruno Perron. 1984. "Les entreprises implantées au Québec et les mandats mondiaux de production." Montreal: Centre d'études en administration internationale.

Bosworth, Barry. 1982. "Capital Formation and Economic Policy." *Brookings Papers on Economic Activity* 2: 273–317.

Braam, Geert P.A. 1981. *Influence of Business Firms on the Government: An Investigation of the Distribution of Influence in Society*. The Hague: Moncton Publishers.

Brenner, Reuven, and Léon Courville. 1985. "Industrial Strategy: Inferring What It Really Is." In *Economics of Industrial Policy and Strategy*, volume 5 of the research studies prepared for the Royal Commission on the Economic Union and Development Prospects for Canada. Toronto: University of Toronto Press.

Cable, Vincent. 1983. *Protectionism and Industrial Decline*. London: Hodden and Stoughton.

Cairns, Alan. 1977. "The Governments and Societies of Canadian Federalism." *Canadian Journal of Political Science* 1 (December): 695–727.

Campbell, Angus. 1981. *The Sense of Well-Being in America: Recent Patterns and Trends*. New York: McGraw-Hill.

Campbell, Angus, Philipe Converse, and Willard L. Rodgers. 1976. *The Quality of American Life: Perceptions, Evaluations and Satisfaction*. New York: Russel Sage Foundation.

Careless, Anthony. 1977. *Initiative and Response: The Adaptation of Canadian Federalism to Regional Economic Development*. Montreal: McGill-Queen's University Press.

Castles, Francis G. 1982. "Introduction: Politics and Public Policy." In *The Impact of Parties: Politics and Policies in Democratic Capitalist States*, edited by Francis G. Castles. Beverly Hills: Sage.

Chandler, Marsha. 1982. "State Enterprise and Partisanship in Provincial Politics." *Canadian Journal of Political Science* 15 (December): 711–40.

Cline, William R., et al. 1978. *Trade Negotiations in the Tokyo Round: A Quantitative Assessment*. Washington, D.C.: Brookings Institution.

Conybeare, John A.C. 1983. "Tariff Protection in Developed and Developing Countries: A Cross-Sectional and Longitudinal Analysis." *International Organization* 37 (Summer): 441–67.

Corden, Warner, M. 1977. *La théorie de la protection*. Paris: Economica.

Corden, W.M., and Gerhard Fels, eds. 1976. *Public Assistance to Industry*. Boulder, Col.: Westview Press.

Crandall, Robert W. 1984. "Import Quotas and the Automobile Industry: The Costs of Protectionism." *Brookings Review* (Summer): 8–17.

Crookell, Harold. 1985. "The Impact of Government Intervention on the Major Appliance Industry in Canada." In *Canadian Industrial Policy in Action*, volume 4 of the research studies prepared for the Royal Commission on the Economic Union and Development Prospects for Canada. Toronto: University of Toronto Press.

Curzon, Gérard, and Victoria Curzon. 1976. "The Management of Trade Relations in the GATT." In *International Economic Relations of the Western World, 1959–1971*, vol. 1, edited by Andrew Shonfield. London: Oxford University Press.

Curzon Price, Victoria. 1981. *Industrial Policies in the European Community*. London: Trade Policy Research Centre.

Daly, D.J., and S. Globerman. 1976. *Tariff and Science Policies: Application of a Model of Nationalism*. Toronto: University of Toronto Press.

Davenport, P., C. Green, W.J. Milne, R. Saunders, and W. Watson. 1982. *Industrial Policy in Ontario and Quebec*. Toronto: Ontario Economic Council.

de Bandt, Jacques. 1977. *Politiques industrielles et objectifs d'industrialisation: essai sur le degré de cohérence des politiques industrielles*. Paris: Cujas.

de Closets, François. 1982. *Toujours Plus*. Paris: Grasset.

Denton, Geoffrey. 1976. "Financial Assistance to British Industry." In *Public Assistance to Industry*, edited by W.M. Corden and Gerhard Fels. Boulder, Col.: Westview Press.

Denton, Geoffrey, Seamus O'Cleiracain, and Sally Ash. 1975. *Trade Effects of Public Subsidies to Private Entreprise*. London: Trade Policy Research Centre.

Diebold, William. 1980. *Industrial Policy as an International Issue*. New York: McGraw-Hill.

Doz, Yves L., and C.K. Prahalad. 1980. "How MNCs Cope with Host Government Intervention." *Harvard Business Review* (March–April): 149–58.

Economic Council of Canada. 1977. *Living Together: A Study of Regional Disparities*. Ottawa: Minister of Supply and Services Canada.

———. 1982. *Intervention and Efficiency: A Study of Government Credit and Credit Guarantees to the Private Sector*. Ottawa: Minister of Supply and Services Canada.

———. 1983. *The Bottom Line: Technology, Trade and Income Growth*. Ottawa: Minister of Supply and Services Canada.

Edelman, Murray. 1964. *The Symbolic Uses of Politics*. Urbana: University of Illinois Press.

Facsym Research Limited. 1981. *Small Business Financing and Non-Bank Financial Institutions*. Ottawa: Ministry of Industry and Commerce.

Faucher, Philippe, André Blais, Robert Young, and Manuel de la Fuente. 1985. "Politique commerciale et politique industrielle du Canada." In *La nouvelle division internationale du travail et le Canada*, edited by Duncan Cameron and François Houle. Ottawa: Presses de l'Université d'Ottawa.

Fayerweather, John. 1982. "Elite Attitudes toward Multinational Firms." In *Host National Attitudes toward Multinational Corporations*, edited by John Fayerweather. New York: Praeger.

Fels, Gerhard. 1976. "Overall Assistance to German Industry." In *Public Assistance to Industry*, edited by W.M. Corden and Gerhard Fels. Boulder: Westview Press.

Finger, J.M., H. Keith Hall, and Douglas R. Nelson. 1982. "The Political Economy of Administered Protection." *American Economic Review* 72: 441–66.

Froman, Lewis A. Jr. 1968. "The Categorization of Policy Contents." In *Political Science and Public Policy*, edited by Austin Ranney. Chicago: Markham.

Galambert, Patrice. 1982. *Les sept paradoxes de notre politique industrielle*. Paris: Cerf.

Gallarotti, Guilo M. 1985. "Towards a Business Cycle Model of Tariffs." *International Organization* 39 (Winter): 155–89.

Galbraith, J. William. 1984. "When Small Is Big." *The Canadian Business Review* (Summer): 36–40.

George, Roy. 1983. *Targeting High Growth Industry*. Montreal: Institute for Research on Public Policy.

Gervais, M., et al. 1969. "Éléments de comparaisons." In *Terres, paysans et politique: structures agraires, systèmes politiques et politiques agricoles*, vol. 1, edited by Henri Mendras, and Yves Tavernier. Paris: S.E.D.E.I.S.

Glassberg, Andrew. 1973. "The Linkage between Urban Policy Outputs and Voting Behaviour: New York and London." *British Journal of Political Science* 3 (July): 341–61.

Gordus, Jeanne Prial. 1984. "The Human Resource Implications of Plant Shutdowns." *Annals of the American Academy of Political and Social Sciences* 475 (September): 66–80.

Gorecki, P.K., and W.T. Stanbury. 1979. "Canada's Combines Investigation Act: The Record of Public Law Enforcement, 1889–1976." In *Canadian Competition Policy*, edited by J.R.S. Prichard, W.T. Stanbury, and T.A. Wilson. Toronto: Butterworth.

Graham, Norman A. 1982. "Developed Countries and Multinational Corporations: Threat, Perception and Policy Response in France and the United Kingdom." In *Host National Attitudes toward Multinational Corporations*, edited by John Fayerweather. New York: Praeger.

Grant, R.M. 1983. "Appraising Selective Financial Assistance to Industry: A Review of Institutions and Methodologies in the United Kingdom, Sweden and West Germany." *Journal of Public Policy* 3 (October): 369–97.

Grant, Wyn. 1980. "Business Interest and the British Conservative Party." *Government and Opposition* 15 (Spring): 143–61.

———. 1982. *The Political Economy of Industrial Policy*. London: Butterworth.

Hager, Wolfgang. 1982. "Industrial Policy, Trade Policy and European Social Democracy." In *National Industrial Strategies and the World Economy*, edited by John Pinder. London: Croom Helm.

Harris, Richard. 1985. *Trade, Industrial Policy and International Competition*. Volume 13 of the research studies prepared for the Royal Commission on the Economic Union and Development Prospects for Canada. Toronto: University of Toronto Press.

Harris, Richard G., with David Cox. 1984. *Trade, Industrial Policy and Canadian Manufacturing*. Toronto: Ontario Economic Council.

Herander, Mark G., and J. Brand Schwartz. 1984. "An Empirical Test of the Impact of the Threat of U.S. Trade Policy: The Case of Antidumping Duties." *Southern Economic Journal* 51 (July): 59–79.

Hindley, Brian. 1980. "Voluntary Export Restraints and the GATT's Main Escape Clause." *The World Economy* 3 (November): 313–41.

Hodge, Robert W., Paul M. Siegel, and Peter H. Rossi. 1966. "Occupational Prestige in the United States: 1925–63." In *Class, Status and Power: Social Stratification in Comparative Perspective*, edited by Reinhard Bendix and Seymour Martin Lipset. New York: Free Press.

Ilgen, Thomas L. 1983. "Better Living through Chemistry: The Chemical Industry in the World Economy." *International Organization* 37: (August): 47–81.

Jenkin, Michael. 1983. *Le défi de la coopération: la politique industrielle dans la fédération canadienne*. Ottawa: Science Council of Canada.

Jenkins, Glenn P. 1980. *Costs and Consequences of the New Protectionism: The Case of Canada's Clothing Sector*. Ottawa: North-South Institute.

Jequier, Nicolas. 1974. "Computers." In *Big Business and the State: Changing Relations in Western Europe*, edited by Raymond Vernon. Cambridge, Mass.: Harvard University Press.

Johnston, Richard. 1985. *Public Opinion and Public Policy in Canada: Questions of Confidence*. Volume 35 of the research studies prepared for the Royal Commission on the Economic Union and Development Prospects for Canada. Toronto: University of Toronto Press.

Kamien, M.I., and N.L. Schwartz. 1982. *Market Structure and Innovation*. Cambridge: Cambridge University Press.

Katzenstein, Peter. 1978. "Conclusion." In *Between Power and Plenty*, edited by Peter Katzenstein. Madison: University of Wisconsin Press.

King, Anthony. 1973. "Ideas, Institutions and the Policies of Governments, A Comparative Analysis." *British Journal of Political Science* 3 (July): 291–313.

Krasner, Stephen D. 1976. "State Power and the Structure of International Trade." *World Politics* 28 (April): 317–47.

———. 1978. *Defending the National Interest: Raw Material Investments and U.S. Foreign Policy*. Princeton, N.J.: Princeton University Press.

Krasner, Stephen D., ed. 1983. *International Regimes*. Ithaca, N.Y.: Cornell University Press.

Krauss, Melvyn B. 1978. *The New Protectionism: The Welfare State and International Trade*. New York: New York University Press.

Kreile, Michael. 1983. "Public Enterprise and the Pursuit of Strategic Management: Italy." In *Industrial Crisis: A Comparative Study of the State and Industry*, edited by Kenneth Dyson and Stephen Wilks. Oxford: Martin Robertson.

Lavergne, Réal P. 1983. *The Political Economy of U.S. Tariffs: An Empirical Analysis*. Toronto: Academic Press.

Lawson, Fred. 1983. "Hegemony and the Structure of International Trade Reassessed: A View from Arabia." *International Organization* 37 (Spring): 317–39.

Lazar, Fred. 1981. *The New Protectionism*. Toronto: James Lorimer.

Leanos, Théodore P. 1984. "Concentration and Centralization of Capital in Agriculture." *Studies in Political Economy* 13 (Spring): 99–117.

Lemieux, Vincent. 1979. *Les cheminements de l'influence: systèmes, stratégies et structures du politique*. Quebec: Presses de l'Université Laval.

Le Pors, Anicet. 1977. *Les béquilles du capital: transferts État-industrie, critère de nationalisation*. Paris: Seuil.

Lewis, James R. 1984. "Regional Policy and Planning: Convergence and Contradiction." In *The State in Capitalist Europe*, edited by Stephen Bornstein et al. London: Allen and Unwin.

Lipset, Seymour M., and William Schneider. 1983. *The Confidence Gap: Business, Labor, and Government in the Public Mind*. New York: Free Press.

Lipson, Charles. 1983. "The Transformation of Trade: The Sources and Effects of Regime Change." In *International Regimes*, edited by Stephen D. Krasner. Ithaca, N.Y.: Cornell University Press.

MacDonald, L. Ian. 1984. *Mulroney: de Baie Comeau à Sussex Drive*. Montreal: Editions de l'Homme.

Magaziner, Ira C., and Robert Reich. 1982. *Minding America's Business*. New York: Harcourt Brace Jovanovich.

Mahon, Rianne, and Lynn Krieger Mytelka. 1983. "Industry, the State and the New Protectionism: Textiles in Canada and France." *International Organization* 37 (Fall): 552–81.

Malinvaud, E. 1982. "Wages and Unemployment." *Economic Journal* 92 (March): 1–13.

Mansfield, Edwin. 1985. "Technological Change and the International Diffusion of Technology: A Survey." In *Technological Change in Canadian Industry*, volume 3 of the research studies prepared for the Royal Commission on the Economic Union and Development Prospects for Canada. Toronto: University of Toronto Press.

Maskus, Keith E. 1984. "Rising Protectionism and U.S. International Trade Policy." *Economic Review* (July–August): 3–18.

Matthews, R.A. 1980. *Canadian Industry and the Challenge of Low-Cost Imports*. Study prepared for the Economic Council of Canada. Ottawa: Minister of Supply and Services Canada.

McAllister, Ian. 1982. *Regional Development and the European Community: A Canadian Perspective*. Montreal: Institute for Research on Public Policy.

McCallum, John, and André Blais. 1985. "Government, Special Interest Groups and Economic Growth." In *Responses to Economic Change*, volume 27 of the research studies prepared for the Royal Commission on the Economic Union and Development Prospects for Canada. Toronto: University of Toronto Press.

McDowall, Duncan. 1984. *A Fit Place for Investment? Foreign Investors' Perceptions of Canada in a Changing World*. Ottawa: Conference Board of Canada.

McFetridge, Donald G. 1977. *Government Support of Scientific Research and Development: An Economic Analysis*. Toronto: University of Toronto Press.

McFetridge, Donald G., and Jack P. Warda. 1983. *Canadian R&D Incentives: Their Adequacy and Impact*. Toronto: Canadian Tax Foundation.

McKay, David, and Wyn Grant. 1983. "Industrial Policies in OECD Countries: An Overview." *Journal of Public Policy* 3 (February): 1–12.

McKeown, Timothy J. 1983. "Hegemonic Stability and 19th Century Tariff Levels in Europe." *International Organization* 37 (Winter): 73–91.

———. 1984. "Firms and Tariff Regime Change: Explaining the Demand for Protection." *World Politics* 36: 215–33.

McKersie, Robert B., and Werner Sengenberger. 1983. *Les suppressions d'emplois dans l'industrie; réponses possibles des politiques de main-d'oeuvre*. Paris: OECD.

Merciai, Patrizio. 1981. "Safeguard Measures in GATT." *Journal of World Trade Law* 15 (January–February): 41–65.

Miles, Caroline. 1976. "Protection of British Textile Industry." In *Public Assistance to Industry*, edited by W.M. Cordens and G. Fels. London: Trade Policy Research Centre.

Monsen, R. Joseph, and Kenneth D. Walters. 1983. *Nationalized Companies: A Threat to American Business*. New York: McGraw-Hill.

Montmarquette, Claude. 1981. "Politique budgétaire de stabilisation et taille relative des gouvernements." *Finances publiques* 36: 244–67.

Morici, Peter, and Laura L. Megna. 1983. *U.S. Economic Policies Affecting Industrial Trade: A Quantitative Assessment*. Washington: National Planning Association.

Mosley P. 1976. "Towards a 'Satisficing' Theory of Economic Policy." *Economic Journal* 86 (March): 59–73.

———. 1984. "Popularity Functions and the Role of the Media: A Pilot Study of the Popular Press." *British Journal of Political Science* (January): 117–33.

Murray, J. Alex, and Lawrence LeDuc. 1982. "Changing Attitudes toward Foreign Investment in Canada." In *Host National Attitudes toward Multinational Corporations*, edited by John Fayerweather. New York: Praeger.

Mytelka, Lynn Krieger. 1982. "The French Textile Industry: Crisis and Adjustment." In *The Emerging International Economic Order: Dynamics Processes, Constraints and Opportunities*, edited by Harold Jacobson and Dusan Sidjanski. Beverly Hills, Cal.: Sage.

Norris, Keith, and John Vaizey. 1973. *The Economics of Research and Technology*. London: Allen and Unwin.

Offe, Claus, and Volker Ronge. 1975. "Theses on the Theory of the State." *New German Critique* 6: 137–48.

Ohlin, Gorau. 1978. "Subsidies and Other Industrial Aids." In *International Trade and Industrial Policies: Government Interventions and an Open World Economy*, edited by Steven J. Warnecke. New York: Holmes.

Organisation for Economic Co-operation and Development. 1975. *Objectifs et instruments des politiques industrielles: une étude comparative*. Paris: OECD.

———. 1978a. *Selected Industrial Policy Instruments: Objectives and Scope*. Paris: OECD.

———. 1978b. *Policies for the Stimulation of Industrial Innovation: Analytical Report*. Paris: OECD.

———. 1982a. *Controls and Impediments Affecting Inward Direct Investment in OECD Member Countries*. Paris: OECD.

———. 1982b. *Les primes d'incitation à la création des emplois*. Paris: OECD.

———. 1983a. *Textile and Clothing Industry: Structural Problems and Policies in OECD Countries*. Paris: OECD.

———. 1983b. *Positive Adjustment Policies: Managing Structural Change*. Paris: OECD.

———. 1983c. *Investment Incentives and Disincentives and the International Investment Process*. Paris: OECD.

———. 1984. *Historical Statistics, 1960–82*. Paris: OECD.

Padioleau, Jean G. 1981. *Quand la France s'enferre*. Paris: Presses universitaires de France.

Pearson, Charles, and Gerry Salembier. 1983. *Trade, Employment and Adjustment*. Montreal: Institute for Research on Public Policy.

Pinchin, Hugh M. 1979. *The Regional Impact of the Canadian Tariff*. Study prepared for the Economic Council of Canada. Ottawa: Minister of Supply and Services Canada.

Pinder, John, ed. 1982. *National Industrial Strategies and the World Economy*. London: Croom Helm.

Pinder, John, Takashi Hosomi and William Diebold. 1979. *Industrial Policy and the International Economy*. New York: Trilateral Commission.

Pryor, Frederick. 1973. *Property and Industrial Organization in Communist and Capitalist Nations*. Bloomington: Indiana University Press.

Reich, Robert. 1982. "Making Industrial Policy." *Foreign Affairs* (Spring): 852–82.

Rothwell, Roy, and Walter Zegveld. 1984. "Designing and Implementing Innovation Policy." *Policy Studies Review* 3 (May): 436–45.

Rousseau, H.P., and F. Taurand. 1984. "Financement de la sécurité du revenu et taxes sur la masse salariale." *Analyse de politiques* 10 (December): 459–68.

Rugman, A.M. 1981. "Research and Development by Multinational and Domestic Firms in Canada." *Analyse de Politique* 7: 604–616.

Safarian, A.E. 1983. *Governments and Multinationals: Policies in the Developed Countries*. Washington: British North American Committee.

Sales, Arnaud. 1983. "Interventions de l'État et positions idéologiques des dirigeants des bureaucraties publiques et privées." *Sociologie et Sociétés* 15 (April): 13–42.

Saunders, Peter and Friedrich Klau. 1985. *Le role du secteur public: causes et conséquences de l'élargissement du secteur public*. Paris: OECD.

Schmidt, Manfred G. 1982. "The Role of Parties in Shaping Macroeconomic Policy." In *The Impact of Parties: Politics and Policies in Democratic Capitalist States*, edited by Francis G. Castles. Beverly Hills, Cal.: Sage.

_____. 1983. "The Welfare State and the Economy in Periods of Economic Crisis: A Comparative Study of Twenty-three Nations." *European Journal of Political Research* 11 (March): 1–27.

_____. 1984. "The Politics of Unemployment: Rates of Unemployment and Labour Market Policy." *West European Politics* 7 (July): 5–25.

Science Council of Canada. 1984. *Canadian Industrial Development: Some Policy Directions*. Ottawa: The Council.

Scitovsky, Tibor. 1976. *The Joyless Economy: An Enquiry into Human Satisfaction and Consumer Dissatisfaction*. New York: Oxford University Press.

Sègre, Henri. 1974. "La politique monopolistique du secteur public industriel (1967–74)." *Economie et politique* 245 (December): 73–93.

Selltiz, C., L.S. Wrightsman, and S.W. Cook. 1976. *Research Methods in Social Relations*. New York: Holt, Rinehart & Winston.

Shepherd, Geoffrey. 1983. "Textiles: New Ways of Surviving in an Old Industry." In *Europe's Industries: Public and Private Strategies for Change*, edited by Geoffrey Shepherd, François Duchêne, and Christopher Saunders. Ithaca, N.Y.: Cornell University Press.

Stern, Arthur A. 1984. "The Hegemonon's Dilemma: Great Britain, the United States, and International Economic Order." *International Organizations* 38 (Spring): 355–87.

Stoffaës, Christian. 1978. *La grande menace industrielle*. Paris: Chalmann-Lévy.

Takacs, Wendy E. 1981. "Pressures for Protectionism: An Empirical Analysis." *Economic Inquiry* 19: 687–93.

Thirsk, Wayne R. 1983. "Fiscal Harmonization in the United States, Australia, West Germany, Switzerland, and the EEC." In *Federalism and the Canadian Economic Union*, edited by M.J. Trebilcock et al. Toronto: University of Toronto Press.

Thurow, Lester C. 1980. *The Zero-Sum Society*. New York: Basic Books.

Trebilcock, Michael J. 1986. *The Political Economy of Economic Adjustment: The Case of Declining Sectors*. Volume 8 of the research studies prepared for the Royal Commission on the Economic Union and Development Prospects for Canada. Toronto: University of Toronto Press.

Treiman, Donald J. 1977. *Occupational Prestige in Comparative Perspective*. New York: Academic Press.

Trezise, Philip H. 1976. "Politics, Government, and Economic Growth in Japan." In *Asia's New Giant: How the Japanese Economy Works*, edited by Hugh Patrick and Henry Rosousky. Washington: Brookings Institution.

Tupper, Allan. 1982. *Public Money in the Private Sector*. Kingston: Queen's University, Institute of Intergovernmental Relations.

Tyson, Laura, and John Zysman. 1983. "American Industry in International Competition." In *American Industry in International Competition*, edited by John Zysman and Laura Tyson. Ithaca, N.Y.: Cornell University Press.

Urich, René. 1983. *Pour une nouvelle politique de développement régional en Europe*. Paris: Economica.

Usher, Dan. 1983. *The Benefits and Cost of Firm Specific Investment Grants: A Study of Five Federal Programs*. Kingston: Queen's University, Institute for Economic Research.

Vernon, Raymond. 1974. "Entreprise and Government in Europe." In *Big Business and the State: Changing Relations in Western Europe*, edited by Raymond Vernon. Cambridge: Harvard University Press.

Vogel, David. 1978. "Why Businessmen Distrust Their State: The Political Consciousness of American Corporate Executives." *British Journal of Political Science* 1 (January): 45–78.

Walters, Robert S. 1982. "The U.S. Steel Industry: National Policies and International Trade." In *The Emerging International Economic Order: Dynamics Processes, Constraints and Opportunities*, edited by Harold K. Jacobson and Dusan Sidjanski. Beverly Hills: Sage.

Warnecke, Steven J. 1975. "Introduction." In *Industrial Policies in Western Europe*, edited by Steven J. Warnecke, and Ezran Suleiman. New York: Praeger.

———. 1978. "Government Intervention and an Open Global Trading System." In *International Trade and Industrial Policies: Government Intervention and an Open World Economy*, edited by Steven J. Warnecke. New York: Holmes and Meier.

Watson, William G. 1983. *A Primer on the Economics of Industrial Policy*. Toronto: Ontario Economic Council.

Wescott, Robert F. 1983. "U.S. Approaches to Industrial Policy." In *Industrial Policies for Growth and Competitiveness: An Economic Perspective*, edited by F. Gerard Adams and Lawrence R. Klein. Lexington: D.C. Heath.

Whalley, John. 1983. "Induced Distortion of Interprovincial Activity: An Overview of the Issues." In *Federalism and the Canadian Economic Union*, edited by M.J. Trebilcock et al. Toronto: University of Toronto Press.

Woodward, R.S. 1974. "The Capital Bias of DREE Incentives." *Canadian Journal of Economics* 7 (May): 161–74.

Young, Robert A. 1983. "Business and Budgeting: Recent Proposals for Reforming the Revenue Budgetary Process." *Canadian Public Policy* 9 (Summer): 347–61.

Young, Robert, Philippe Faucher, and André Blais. 1984. "The Concept of Province Building: A Critique." *Canadian Journal of Political Science* 17 (December): 783–819.

Young, Stephen, and A.V. Lowe. 1975. *Intervention in the Mixed Economy: The Evolution of British Industrial Policy, 1964–72*. London: Croom Helm.

Yuill, Douglas, Kevin Allen, and Chris Hull, eds. 1980. *Regional Policy in the European Community: The Role of Regional Incentives*. London: Croom Helm.

Zysman, John. 1977. *Political Strategies for Industrial Order: State, Market and Industry in France*. Berkeley: University of California Press.

———. 1983. *Governments, Markets and Growth: Financial Systems and the Politics of Industrial Change*. Ithaca, N.Y.: Cornell University Press.

2

The Debate on Canadian Industrial Policy

ANDRÉ BLAIS

The object of this study is to examine the Canadian industrial policy debate, and to analyze the principal ideas as to what this policy should — or should not — be. This analysis will deal with the subject from two points of view. First, the political agenda will be defined: while there are an infinite number of possible industrial policies, in reality the debate is limited to a few "serious" options, which thus constitute the agenda of what is foreseeable for the near future (Cobb and Elder, 1972; Kingdon, 1984). Second, the paper examines the arguments of those involved in the debate, and the main reasons given to support or oppose one proposal or another. This will permit us to delineate the structure of the debate.

From the outset the extent and the limitations of this procedure should be made clear. Since the essence of politics is the management of conflict, with politicians spending most of their time talking and juggling with ideas (Nimmo, 1978; Bell, 1975), politics quite naturally takes on the form of debate. Public discussion should therefore receive special attention from political science. However, from the point of view of a researcher analyzing government policy, as is the case in this volume, things appear somewhat different. Emphasis is placed on what the government is doing or achieving, rather than on what those in charge say they are doing; concrete actions, not the spoken or written word, serve here as the point of departure for analysis (Blais, 1980).

In this context, therefore, the discussion is of interest only if the ideas expressed influence government policy. I do not intend to prove this statement empirically; it can be considered a hypothesis. However, the sense in which it is a plausible hypothesis should be indicated. The entire issue of the role of ideology is involved here — a huge and complex question, to which there is no clear answer. While it is impossible, given the present state of knowledge, to weigh the effect of ideas compared to that of other factors, there is nonetheless good reason to believe that their effect is not nil. Thus it is that the comparative study by King (1973) on the orientation of government policy in the United States, Canada, Britain, France and West Germany emphasizes the special circumstances of the U.S. case, and explains it, essentially, "in terms of Americans' beliefs and assumptions, especially their beliefs and assumptions about governments" (p. 418). In the field of social policy, Lockart (1984, p. 344) is of the view that "what political elites think the state should do is the most important single guide to incremental change."

Above all, political debate reveals the dominant values of a society. One emerges the winner or the loser depending on whether what one advocates is legitimate or not; this legitimacy is based on what is perceived as being the public interest or the common good. Prevailing values define what constitutes this common good. Participants in the debate are aware of this, and the content of their claims, as well as the way in which they are presented, is influenced by it:

> Citizens understand that sometimes they will have to subordinate particular and immediate interests to the common good, but they also understand that those particular interests which harmonize well with it are to receive high priority. They have an interest in showing that such a harmony exists and in adjusting their claims to foster that harmony (Connolly, 1981, p. 114).

This study consists mainly of an analysis of the strategy employed by the participants in the Canadian industrial policy debate. All have available a certain number of arguments to support their proposals, arguments they choose from among the most convincing and from among those which, at least implicitly, seem to them to include the values to which they have an interest in allying themselves. These values define whether a given option is in a position of strength or of weakness. Analyzing the strategy of advocacy should therefore enable us to identify certain components of the dominant ideology, which fashions the political agenda both directly and indirectly. For this reason survey data have been used extensively as a source of information concerning the dominant values in Canadian society.

However, it is not only ideas and dominant values that underlie the political debate. The facts themselves contribute to ideological positions: "new facts may make us change our minds about what it makes sense for us to say about the facts" (Ryan, 1970, p. 167). In a society that values education and knowledge, a claim cannot be considered legitimate unless it is based on a serious analysis of the facts. Thus it is also important to examine the type of data to which the participants in the debate refer.

Because we are interested in the structure of the debate, special attention will be given to the words of those who seem to best articulate the principal options available. Generally, these are organizations whose function it is to recommend certain directions for government policy or individuals, usually university professors, who, because of their knowledge in a given area, tend to become the apostles of a particular strategy of action. Although these organizations or individuals are not, strictly speaking, political organizations or politicians, they have undoubted political influence. They contribute to a definition of the terms of the debate. Thus "social policies have been most directly influenced by middlemen at the interfaces of various groups" (Heclo, 1974, p. 308). It should not be surprising, given the subject and their status, that most of these are economists. Heclo notes that even "social policy has developed in the interstices allowed to it by 'sound economic thinking'" (ibid., p. 310). The role of economists may have declined recently, but it "is not yet so low that politicians can afford to have them lined up in outspoken opposition to proposed policies" (Watson, 1983, p. 97).

The industrial policy debate in Canada does not take place behind closed doors, however. It is fed in part by what is taking place in other countries, particularly the United States. The industrial policies adopted by other governments are a point of reference for Canadians. Throughout this analysis, I shall therefore attempt to place the Canadian debate within an international context. This cannot be achieved in as systematic a manner as I should have liked, however, because of the paucity of data available. Nevertheless, it should be possible to bring out certain characteristics specific to the Canadian case.

The approach is an anthropological one. Since we are seeking to understand how the debate is structured, there would be no point in imposing a model or typology on the material studied. Rather, the objective is to reduce the underlying structure from a detailed study of the debate itself. Clearly, this is a hazardous undertaking. Indeed, analysts may be subconsciously influenced by a model, which leads them to analyze the data in their possession in one way rather than another. Similarly, there is no rigorous measure of the importance or the position of the various proposals in play; so that analysts might, for reasons of personal inclination, be led to favour or to neglect certain avenues. These are the limitations of the method, and they are very real. However, I believe that this method is the most appropriate, given the objectives of the study.

Until recently, the debate concerning Canadian industrial policy was dominated by the proposals of two organizations: the Economic Council of Canada and the Science Council of Canada. When putting forward "the main industrial strategies currently being proposed for Canada," Norrie (1979) observed that "ironically, it is two research agencies sponsored by the federal government that have become the main proponents of each of these opposing views. These are the Economic Council of Canada and the Science Council of Canada" (1979, pp. 66 and 67). Similarly, in their study of "competing approaches to industrial policy," Morici, Smith and Lea (1982, chap. 7) mention first the "free trade/ domestic non-interventionist" model and refer to the Economic Council; next, when they consider the interventionist model, they quote the Science Council. They also refer to a third approach, which would combine free trade and fairly vigorous government intervention. The authors imply that "many influential policy advisers appear to embrace important elements of this view, and the policies of the current government as well as the previous Trudeau government reflect this approach in numerous ways" (p. 81). But this position is not presented in a coherent fashion, and does not emerge in official discussion, which is what is of interest here. Thus, one may conclude that there are really only two schools of thought confronting one another.

This simple opposition is in the process of transformation. First, the economist Richard Harris (1985) made an attempt to reconcile the theses of the Economic Council and the Science Council in pronouncing in favour of both free trade and a vigorous technological policy. Next, many economists, while favourable to the idea of free trade, insist on compensation mechanisms for workers who risk losing their jobs in a period of transition. In many respects, this position is a direct extension of that of the Economic Council which, in *Looking Outward: A New Trade Strategy for Canada* (1975) had earlier envisaged adjustment measures. But thinking on this question has developed a great deal since and merits particular attention. Finally, there is the argument that the best industrial policy is one that involves minimal government intervention and the fewest selective measures. Watson (1983) has defended this position.

The other issue in the debate has been the regional question. The clearest position is that taken by the economist Courchene (1970; 1978), who claims that mobility is the best remedy for regional disparities. The debate has revolved around the merits and the implications of this thesis, with the most virulent criticism coming from the sociologist Matthews (1981), who appeals to the dependency model.

Free Trade

In 1975, the Economic Council proposed, in *Looking Outward*, a policy based on liberalization of trade. It was particularly interested in creating a free trade zone with the United States. This approach was raised again in the report of the Standing Senate Committee on Foreign Affairs

(Canada, 1982), which recommended negotiation of a bilateral free trade agreement with the United States.

The great advantage of free trade, according to its proponents, would be an increased market for Canadian industry. This would have the effect of improving productivity, through greater specialization, lengthening production runs, or, more indirectly, increased competition (Markusen, 1985). The Economic Council (1975, p. 90) forecast that "the increase in productivity which free trade would bring would reach at least 5% of GNP, perhaps more."

The opponents of free trade either cast doubt on this advantage, or emphasized the cost of its implementation in comparison to other aspects of the question. The second strategy was more common. Wilkinson (1982), it is true, questioned the extent of gains related to free trade. He noted, for instance, that it is, at the very least, risky to think that the difference in productivity between Canada and the United States would disappear completely, since even in Canada considerable regional disparities persist. But it was clear that the free traders had the advantage, particularly since the most recent work (Harris with Cox, 1984) based on the most advanced models has confirmed and even increased initial estimates. In that study, Harris estimated the potential gains from multilateral free trade at 8.6 percent of GNP; others speak freely of as much as 10 percent (Markusen, 1985). Yet Harris's estimates were made using tariffs in effect prior to the Tokyo Round of the General Agreement on Tariffs and Trade (GATT), which will be reduced by a third by 1987.

The principal objections to free trade are, however, of a different kind. First, there is the short-term adjustment cost. Here, the free traders are on the defensive. The Wonnacotts (1982, p. 418) admit that "Canadian producers would have dislocation costs in the short run." Harris (1985) estimates that 6 to 7 percent of the labour force would have to change industries. The Economic Council (1975) forecast increased unemployment, particularly in Quebec and Ontario. Generally, the counterargument is that the experience of the European Economic Community (EEC) and of the European Free Trade Association (EFTA) indicates that these costs are not large, and that they could be absorbed through the use of appropriate corrective measures.

A second objection, that U.S. industry is better placed than its Canadian counterpart to take advantage of freer trade, has been put forward mainly by Lazar (1981). For example, the comparative advantage of the United States in research and development would be accentuated if tariffs were abolished (Lazar, 1981, p. 55). Further, "Canadian firms will have to invest heavily in advertising and other marketing costs in order to overcome lack of product familiarity in the United States market" (ibid, p. 61). Free traders reply that, on the contrary, a small country has more to gain "since its market increases more as a result of free trade" (Wonnacott and Wonnacott, 1982, p. 422), but they realize fully that this runs counter to common sense; everyone knows that in "real life," it is the "big guy" who wins, and the "little guy" who loses. The report of the Standing Senate Committee on Foreign Affairs (Canada, 1982, p. 34) cites the case of free trade between Australia and New Zealand: "During the first seven years of the agreement, trade between the two countries increased by 78%, and Australia's trade surplus declined from 4 to 1 to 2 to 1. This means that the agreement seems to have been advantageous to the weaker of the two partners." Trade relations between the two countries did indeed evolve in a manner favourable to the smaller of the two; at present, Australia's trade surplus is only 1.4 to 1 (Europa Publications, 1983). Furthermore, the growth rate of real per capita gross domestic product for New Zealand equalled that of Australia by the end of the 1960s. The case of New Zealand is not the most convincing, however, since the growth rate of GDP since 1973 is lower there than in all other countries in the Organisation for Economic Co-operation and Development (OECD, 1983, Table 3.2). Besides, the free trade experiment as experienced by the EEC and EFTA does not appear to have benefited the smallest countries (Blais, 1986). The main point to keep in mind, however, is that the free traders have great difficulty in persuading others that economic association between a small country like Canada and a giant like the United States would benefit the former more.

The third, and probably most important, objection concerns the risks of eroding Canada's political sovereignty. This fear is based on the neofunctionalist theory of integration (Haas, 1968), according to which there is a continuum from the free trade zone to customs union, common market, economic union, and, finally, political union. The difficulties inherent in each stage could lead the partners to go on to a higher form of integration. This is the "spillover" effect.

Free traders are aware that this is a weighty objection. In 1975, the Economic Council of Canada (p. 114) noted that "The deepest of all Canadian concerns is . . . the fear that a Canada–U.S. free trade arrangement would ultimately lead to political absorption by the United States." This is why free traders emphasize that only a free trade zone is being proposed, not a customs union or common market (Canada, 1982, p. 31). The spillover theory is deemed unfounded (Lyon, 1975), and it is even added that "transnational trade schemes may actually enhance the self-awareness of participants" (Economic Council of Canada, 1975, p. 115). A recent study (Soldatos, 1986) indicates, however, that some spillover has occurred within the EFTA and in the Australia–New Zealand free trade zone. In this latter case, what is particularly interesting from the Canadian point of view is that the partners went from a partial free trade zone in 1965 to total free trade in 1983. The new agreement deals not only with tariffs, but also with quotas, export subsidies, and public markets (Thakur and Gold, 1982; 1983).

In this area as well, the free traders are on the defensive. Although the spillover theory has not been proved, the risks it evokes are substantial. It must be recognized that the political will to create a Canadian nation was in good part a reaction to the very visible presence of the United States, and that the "Canadian identity" is defined principally in comparison with the U.S. model (Nossal, 1985). The American "soul" threatens to subjugate the Canadian "soul": "The danger is far more subtle and far more deeply to be dreaded. It lies in gradual assimilation, in peaceful penetration, in a spiritual bondage — the subjection of the Canadian nation's mind and soul to the mind and soul of the United States" (MacMechan, 1920, p. 347).

For the same reasons some representatives of the Canadian left are opposed to continentalism, which is deemed to undermine the very foundations of the Canadian state:

> Thus the uneven impact of continental integration on the different provinces of Canada is exposing the Canadian union to unmanageable strains. At the same time as it strengthens some of the provincial governments, and encourages them to pursue their divergent interests independently, the process of continental integration seems to make the Canadian federal government increasingly superfluous. (Stevenson, 1980, p. 26)

The force of the free trade thesis therefore resides in the economic benefits it promises. Its weakness derives from the short-term adjustments it implies, the political risks which, although they remain hypothetical, cannot be denied, and, finally, the perception that an association with the U.S. giant could benefit the latter more.

The debate concerning Canadian trade policy is polarized by the following two, diametrically opposed, schools of thought: those in favour of North American integration, and those opposed. It is difficult to adopt middle or more subtle positions. For example, it would be completely logical for a Canadian nationalist to favour free trade with the United States, if this could lead to a decrease in U.S. investment in Canada and in Canadian investment in the United States, and thus reduce the U.S. stranglehold on the Canadian economy, but such a position is held by virtually no one. On the contrary, "Paradoxically, nationalists, whose principal target hitherto has been American investment in Canada, raise the spectre of its southward flight if tariffs are removed" (Pentland, 1985, p. 33). People are pro- or anti-American across the board. There seems to be no place for any type of strategic calculation.

The dominant characteristic of the debate, however, may be the absence of an opposite position. While the free trade hypothesis does not meet with unanimous favour, those opposed to it are not advocating increased protectionism. Rather, they say that getting rid of tariffs "does not seem to provide a suitable antidote" (Science Council of Canada, 1979, p. 36) or that "changes in commercial policy should come after there is better understanding of and general agreement on the causes of Canada's problems and on policies for reconstruction" (Britton and Gilmour, 1978, p. 61). Lazar (1981) is of the view that the Canadian government should reinforce retaliatory measures in the face of so-called "disloyal" practices by foreign competitors, but this could not be considered a resolutely protectionist attitude. The Science Council (1984) reiterates the same ideas. In sum, either free trade is favoured, or a policy based on other concerns is defended. As Bauer et al. (1972) have noted, free trade has been winning the ideological battle since the end of World War II. The protectionists are on the defensive, their position viewed as narrowly isolationist:

> It has become relatively rare for a protectionist spokesman to argue for protection in principle. When they speak for protection of a particular industry, it seems that they often tacitly accept the arguments of their opponents and contend that their own industry is an exception. (ibid., p. 147)

Who, indeed, would dare to come out against freedom and trade in a society in which an open mind is considered one of the most revealing signs of an enlightened personality?

Obviously, this does not mean that no protectionist position can be defended in Canada. The report of the Task Force on the Canadian Motor Vehicle and Parts Industry (Canada, 1983), which recommends a "trade policy requiring all vehicle manufacturers who sell vehicles in the Canadian market to make binding commitments similar to those currently in effect for vehicle manufacturers who are members of the Canada–U.S. Automotive Agreement" (p. 131), is a striking example of this. However, the fact that U.S. manufacturers are subject to constraints (under the Automotive Pact) from which manufacturers in other countries are exempt can be cited as placing them in a discriminatory and "unjust" position.

The pre-eminence of the free trade doctrine is clear in opinion polls when questions are restricted to generalities. More than 80 percent of Canadians are of the opinion that Canadian industry should become more competitive in foreign markets, rather than being protected from international competition (*Decima Quarterly Report*, 1981–83, question 430). When the question is posed in general terms and symbolism is allowed free play, the free trade philosophy is clearly the winner. The more concrete the questions, however, the more qualified the replies. The majority of Canadians in all regions favour quotas for Japanese cars (*Decima Quarterly Report*, 1982–83, question 515).

When questions are directed more specifically to free trade with the United States, the replies are more ambiguous. On the one hand, slightly more than 50 percent of Canadians feel that elimination of tariffs between the two countries would be to Canada's advantage (*The Gallup*

Report, June 16, 1983, p. 2). On the other hand, only 40 percent favour an agreement to eliminate tariffs and all barriers to trade (*Decima Quarterly Report*, 1982–83, question 500). Thus, there seems to be support mixed with caution for an agreement on limited freer trade between the two countries.

In comparison to what is happening elsewhere, the vigour of the free trade option in Canada is striking. Unfavourable economic conditions at the beginning of the 1980s resulted in more protectionist talk, if not practice, in the United States and Europe. I have shown elsewhere (Blais, 1986) that trade policy is strongly influenced by economic conditions but that, by contrast, there has been no real return to protectionism. In Britain, for instance, "the debate about protection . . . is now at the centre of the discussion" (Grant, 1982, p. 128). In Canada, it is more the option of a free trade zone with the United States that has regained impetus. The phenomenon is not new: "reciprocity discussions between Canada and the United States historically have intensified when times were bad" (Granatstein, 1985, p. 70). This probably reflects Canada's peculiar situation: it is the only "small" developed country that does not participate in any form of economic union whatsoever.

Technological Sovereignty

While market size is the Economic Council's priority, the capacity for technological innovation is the cornerstone of the industrial strategy proposed by the Science Council. Canadian capacity for innovation is considered inadequate. This situation has occurred mainly because of the prevalence of foreign firms that are content to serve the Canadian market, while research and marketing are managed by the parent firm. In order to fill this gap, the Science Council (1978, chap. 4) became the apostle of a technology policy aimed at: a) increasing the demand for Canadian technology; b) changing Canadian potential for development of new techniques; c) expanding capacity for assimilation of new techniques; and d) developing among Canadian firms the means to acquire foreign technical expertise under conditions favourable to Canada's industry.

Thus the Science Council places emphasis on the technological aspect of industrial expansion. This approach is resolutely nationalist, since the objective to be attained is technological "sovereignty," and involves strong government intervention. *Forging the Links: A Technology Policy for Canada* (Science Council of Canada, 1979) makes reference to public markets, joint ventures, "sponsorship of selected companies," consortia, sectorally oriented technical centres, and regulation of some of the multinationals' activities. In a more recent work, *Canadian Industrial Development: Some Policy Directions* (Science Council of Canada, 1984), the Council returned more explicitly to some of these ideas, placing greater emphasis on assistance to encourage the growth of small but dynamic high-technology firms. It also recommended creation of metropolitan technology centres.

Generally, the starting point for the Science Council's analysis, the crucial role of technological innovation in industrial development, is not disputed. For example, the Economic Council (1983, p. 20) agrees that technological progress is a vital element in total factor productivity. However, innovation cannot be considered a panacea:

> the strategy of encouraging innovations and promoting entrepreneurship creates both benefits and costs. Entrepreneurship implies innovation which reduces the costs of production and thus eliminates competitors; in the process it creates temporary unemployment. Thus, successful entrepreneurship disturbs the status quo. This disturbance imposes a cost on society by decreasing its social stability. (Brenner and Courville, 1985)

Governments may thus have an interest, under certain circumstances, in slowing the process of innovation. This type of dialectic does not emerge in public pronouncements, however. "Enlightened" people look to the future, not the past; they do not fear change, and come down on the side of innovation and technology. The dominant tone is resolutely modernist.

The polls show astonishing results on this question. Opinions about technological change vary greatly. For example, 70 percent of Canadians feel that automation will lead to job reductions, but the majority believe that better-quality goods will be produced at lesser cost. People are almost equally divided as to the overall effect on the economy (Johnston, 1985). Two-thirds of all Canadians even think that society is too oriented toward mechanization and technology (*Decima Quarterly Report*, 1980–82, question 67).

We should therefore be justified in expecting that the support for a technological policy would be slim. However, 80 percent of Canadians hope that the federal government will invest a substantial amount of money in the development of new technology (*Decima Quarterly Report*, 1981–83, question 373). This is a fine paradox, which suggests that many are scarcely aware of the innovation/stability dialectic. The paradox may reflect the influence of the better educated. While tradition is just as valued as change by the population as a whole, those who are better educated tend to opt in greater numbers for newness (Stoetzel, 1983, pp. 29 and 30). The traditionalists are less articulate and less bold in stating their values in public. As a result, organizations like the Science Council and the Economic Council, which preach the virtues of innovation, have the upper hand.

Innovation occurs through the creation and spread of new techniques. The Science Council clearly places emphasis on the first. Naturally, it also advocates measures to reinforce capacities for absorbing new techniques, but the primary aspects of the technological policy proposed in

Forging the Links (Science Council of Canada, 1979) concern the direct production of a Canadian technology. This is understandable since, according to Gilmour (1978, p. 28), one of the principal defenders of this approach, the transfer of technology generally operates to the benefit of innovators:

> technology purchasing has a tendency to create dependence of the pur-
> chaser (nation) on the seller. It leads to increasing trade deficits because
> technology transfer substitutes itself into the importation of goods and
> inhibits the development of technological capability in the purchasing
> nation.

More recently, the Science Council (1984, p. 29) stated that production capacity is a prerequisite for the assimilation of new technologies: "some basic level of industrial R&D competence is needed to be able to locate and quickly transfer the technology developed elsewhere."

The Science Council's opponents maintain that the transfer process is at least as important as the discovery itself. Globerman (1978, p. 37) cites a number of studies that suggest that adaptation and improvement of an innovation lead to productivity gains that are just as great as those generated by the innovation itself. The Economic Council (1983, chap. 5), in countering the Science Council's attack on the foreign stranglehold over Canadian industry, goes even further and states that the transfer of innovations occurs more rapidly within the multinationals. Bird (1982, p. 30) also points out that "R&D expenditure performed within a country does not have a decisive effect on its growth rate" (see also Watson, 1984).

From this point of view, as well, an entirely logical counterproposition would be that it is in Canada's interest not to concern itself with technological production, but rather with seeking to profit to the maximum possible extent from the fallout from foreign technological innovations:

> In a world where technology can be developed in one location and used
> without compensation in many others, one may appeal to the taxpayer of a
> small country to provide a high level of support for R and D on altruistic
> grounds. An appeal based on self-interest would be much more difficult to
> sustain. (McFetridge and Warda, 1983, p. 91)

The very fact that this argument is made only indirectly shows that there is awareness of the fact that the ideological offensive belongs to the Science Council, and that a frontal attack is unlikely to be productive. This suggests that, within the dominant system of values (the values of change, to which innovation and technology are linked, being truly dominant only among the educated elite, who, however, dominate the public debate), research and innovation occupy an important place. They are not perceived exclusively, as is the case in the classical economic model,[1] as instruments of growth. It is revealing that, generally speaking, the social status of researchers is very high (Hodge, Siegel and Rossi, 1966; Treiman, 1977). Collectively, Canadian society needs to be recognized as having achieved excellence in at least some fields of advanced technology.[2]

The Science Council's position is weaker, however, when it deals with the means of government intervention. As has been noted, the Council proposes massive intervention, involving joint government and industry participation in technological development projects. The Science Council (1979, p. 21) recognizes that it is in a difficult position here:

> There would seem to be an ideological aversion on the part of federal officials to become involved in any policy which requires government cooperation with industry. As a result of official commitments to laissez-faire, government has failed to solve the serious problems now facing Canadian industry. In contrast, many foreign governments (particularly in Europe and the Far East) are not the least reluctant to intervene directly and comprehensively in their economies to achieve international trading advantages for their domestic industries.

The Science Council acknowledges that its recommendations are contrary to the dominant ideology, but adds that it is time to question thinking that prevents implementation of the appropriate measures, since other governments, which are not paralyzed by this ideology, have obtained satisfactory results. In sum, the argument is that the measures proposed by the Science Council exist in several European countries and in Japan, and that the economic performance of these countries is superior to that of Canada. The Council has in fact published a study describing the many facets of government intervention in the microelectronics industry in Europe (de Vos, 1983).

The argument is presented in almost identical fashion in Canada and the United States:

> The advocates of an industrial policy for the United States implicitly or explicitly base their conclusions on the following propositions.
> • Despite the performance of the U.S. economy in the postwar period and its potential from 1970 to the early 1980s, it has not been performing well; in particular, output has declined.
> • The economies of a number of other high-income countries have performed better over this period.
> • These countries followed some form of industrial policy which contributed to their better performance, possibly to the detriment of U.S. economic welfare.
> • If the United States were to follow some form of industrial policy in imitation or response to these policies, its economic performance would improve.
> Therefore, these advocates concluded, the United States should follow some form of industrial policy. (Lecraw, 1985b)

Opponents of the Science Council's stance begin by casting doubt on the extent of measures adopted abroad. In Japan's case, for example, they will say that the true role of the Ministry for International Trade and Industry (MITI) is ambiguous and has probably been exaggerated (Lecraw, 1985b; see also Gilder, 1983). However, they pass quickly over this point and put more emphasis on the effect of the measures that have been adopted. Lecraw's conclusion (1985b, p. 27) is worth quoting:

> This brief review of industrial policy in Japan, France and Germany does not give much support to the conclusion that industry-specific policies in other countries have been particularly successful or have made significant contributions to their economic welfare. In some cases, industrial policies have improved the competitive position of a firm, an industry or a sector in national and international markets but, in general, the cost of those policies would seem to have been high in terms of reduced national economic welfare. Although there may be a theoretical possibility for industrial policies to improve national welfare, in practice these benefits seem at best to have been difficult to attain.

It is the subtlety of this assessment which is most striking. Lecraw does not go so far as to say that government intervention has had harmful effects; he contents himself with saying that he is far from certain that it has had the beneficial effects assumed by the Science Council. Thus he remains on the defensive.

But the most forceful objection is probably that the strategy proposed by the Science Council obliges one to choose "winners," a delicate operation to say the least. According to Watson (1983, p. 50), "in general incentives — via tax credits or non-discretionary subsidies — would be preferable to attempts to choose the likely winners and losers." On the one hand, the machinery of government is sluggish:

> for reasons that have to do with the public's natural desire for financial probity and its fear of political patronage, governments are usually required to run themselves according to rules that are cumbersome. Thus their discretionary judgements often take a long time to make. (Ibid., p. 102)

On the other hand, there is nothing to indicate that the government makes better decisions; indeed, these decisions are likely worse:

> Governments do not have information about the future that is better (or worse) than that available to most banks or investment consultants, though since private agents are likely to suffer greater penalties when they get things wrong, they can be expected to work harder to get them right. (Ibid., p. 103)

Furthermore, it is more difficult for the government to step away from an industry if its investment proves unprofitable (Bird, 1982, p. 23).

The attack has real weight. Gordon (1978, p. 52) recognizes that "uneconomic private interests instead of social cost analysis may continue to exercise an undue influence in plant location decisions" and that "historical experience reveals that government involvement in industry has been unsuccessful more often than not" (p. 55). The position seems to be that it is possible to benefit from past experience and to correct one's aim; the advocates of a vigorous technological policy are on the defensive here, however. Some claim, despite the persuasiveness of most of the arguments in favour of an industrial policy (Badaracco and Yoffie, 1983, p. 97), that the political process is such that "an industrial policy that seeks to direct resources to winners might find itself funnelling massive funds to politically adept losers" (ibid, p. 102).

The Science Council focusses on a certain number of themes in order to rally opinion on this question. First, "enlightened" persons are in favour of change and technology and modern values, and are oriented toward the future rather than the past. A self-respecting country could not possibly leave an activity as prestigious as that of technological creation to other countries, limiting its efforts to the diffusion of this technology. In saying this, the Council proposes an ideal to be achieved, and points its finger at the enemy, the perpetrator of all our woes, the multinational firm, one of the institutions that inspires the least confidence in Canadians (Johnston, 1985). As a result, the technological sovereignty option appears, at least in principle, very attractive. It is when the concrete means of carrying out the option must be specified that difficulties arise. The Science Council runs up against the dominant idea that the government is generally inefficient,[3] and that there is thus no question of entrusting it with a task as complex as that of determining exactly what is the future of technology.[4]

Some Recent Proposals

Until recently, the debate concerning Canada's industrial policy was carried on essentially in terms of the opposition between the Economic Council and the Science Council. It has not progressed much, though points of disagreement have been accentuated over time. A debate over the political agenda cannot be maintained indefinitely, however. In order to retain the interest of politicians and bureaucrats, the language must be renewed and new options, or new combinations of options, proposed. Over the past few years we have been seeing the emergence of such new ideas. At least they are different from the traditional positions. Since most of the new proposals have not been discussed systematically, the debate surrounding them cannot be analyzed. Rather, the various suggestions and the manner in which they are presented will be examined.

Three of these new options seem extremely important. The first, developed by the economist Richard Harris, consists of combining free trade with a vigorous technological policy. The second, advanced by a large number of economists, concentrates on compensation measures for workers displaced by industrial change. The third, put forward principally by the economist William Watson, is a plea against government intervention in industrial development, particularly selective intervention.

Free Trade and Technological Policy

Saunders (1982) was the first to suggest a compromise between the continentalist and nationalist proposals. After outlining the limitations of the analyses of both schools of thought, he suggested an industrial strategy that would include freer trade accompanied by transition measures aimed principally toward the multinationals. On the one hand, he states, "the multinationals must be required to guarantee that their value-added in Canada will at least match pre-free trade levels in constant dollars" (p. 476). On the other hand, "it is appropriate to continue to scrutinize proposals for new foreign direct investment so as to secure world product mandates for Canadian subsidiaries" (ibid.).

While Saunders' idea has had no direct follow-up and has not affected the evolution of the debate, the attempt to reconcile the opposite points of view was astute. It was subsequently taken up by Harris with more success. Saunders, who limited himself to suggesting that "further work is needed to assess the costs and benefits of increased incentives for high technology activity" (1982, p. 476), probably made an error in not taking aim at the most appealing dimension of the nationalist option: its technological dimension. Rather, he emphasized control over foreign investment. Though the multinationals may not be viewed with favour by the general public, investment controls are not popular (Johnston, 1985).

The real work of reconciliation was led by Harris (1985). In a text that could be described as iconoclastic, he speaks highly of the virtues of free trade accompanied by a vigorous technological policy designed to increase substantially the research and development activities carried out in Canada, and directed in particular toward the small and medium-sized firms in high-technology industries for whom market penetration is costly. Harris's analysis is based on several hypotheses. First, he assumes that high-tech firms (which he describes as "Schumpeterian") can acquire "quasi-rents" in the form of higher profits and salaries. Secondly, a small country like Canada[5] has greater interest in subsidizing indigenous Schumpeterian firms which, because they are small, are more affected by barriers to entry. Finally, assistance should be provided in specific and selective ways: since a minimum threshold must be achieved and available funds are limited, giving a bit of money to several firms would be quite simply ineffective.

An entire tome would be required to discuss the theoretical and empirical bases for Harris's thesis. The principal limitations of his argument have been well exposed by McFetridge (1985). The empirical foundations of his analysis are scarcely more solid. For example, to illustrate the barriers to entry in technological innovation, Harris uses the argument that "success breeds success." But Kamien and Schwartz (1982, p. 75), to whom Harris in fact refers, while recognizing that some studies confirm this hypothesis, add that "there is also some evidence that 'success begets failure,'" which is as much as to say that the proposal is dubious.

The fact remains, nonetheless, that Harris's ideas are appealing. They have the merit of putting an end to the sterile debate between the Economic Council and the Science Council by proposing a strategy that integrates the most valid points of each. The most controversial aspect of the proposal concerns the selective nature of the assistance proposed. Harris is aware of this, and complains that too much importance is being given to this aspect of the question. Nevertheless, this selectiveness flows naturally from the analysis as a whole, and the extent to which this question brings people up short is indeed striking. It is because the image of a government choosing certain businesses it considers "truly" dynamic goes against the grain of the dominant ideology that the market best sorts out the efficient and inefficient.

Assistance to Workers

While the Science Council of Canada and Richard Harris are concerned mainly with the industry of the future, economists, for their part, are increasingly preoccupied with the industry of the past, which is in decline and prey to all sorts of difficulties. The textiles industry is a typical example. Here is an industry that is artificially maintained through high tariffs and agreements on voluntary restrictions. Would it not be more efficient to withdraw completely from this industry, and invest funds and energies in Canadian industries that already enjoy some comparative advantage? The objection to such a strategy — and, therefore, the justification of continued protection — is well known. Short-term adjustment costs would be enormous: many workers, particularly older ones, would be unable to find work, and there would be a considerable worsening of unemployment in some regions. Although the true extent of these costs may be arguable, the dominant position is that they would not be negligible: "the high levels of overall unemployment in recent years have made it increasingly unlikely that displaced workers will find new jobs quickly, especially if their skills are specific to their former employment" (Saunders, 1984, p. 3).

What should be done? Thinking on this subject has been strongly influenced by Jenkins' study (1980) on the cost of protectionism in the clothing industry. Jenkins estimates that the cost of tariffs and quantitative restrictions in this industry amounted to almost $17,000 per protected job in 1979, whereas the average annual wage in the industry was $10,000. Similar results have been reported in the United States. For example, the cost of tariffs and quantitative restrictions in the shoe industry was estimated in 1977 at $78,000 per protected job, while the average annual wage in the industry was a little over $8,000 (Maskus, 1984, Table 2). Would it not be more logical in such cases to eliminate protection entirely and compensate the employees generously? In the extreme, the government could withdraw protection completely and pay the entire wage of all the workers in these industries, and society would still gain.

The line of argument is clear. Politics are such that the most efficient choices are not made:

> Although a change in the pattern of economic activity may promote effi-
> ciency, it may do so by generating large losses for some narrowly defined
> groups within that society while generating small gains for everyone else. In
> these circumstances, we can expect to see lobbying efforts that successfully
> block or, at least, greatly delay, economic restructuring. (Saunders, 1982,
> p. 17)

As a result, "this protection and the inefficiency it generates is likely to persist unless the workers whose jobs are endangered are given gener-ous adjustment assistance" (ibid, p. 18). Naturally, care is taken to note the risks of such a policy; these are linked essentially to "moral hazard" (McFetridge, 1985), but it is added that "the case for a generous compen-sation program remains strong" (Saunders, 1982, p. 20). However, as Watson (1983, p. 95) admits straight out, "attempts to block change are inevitable; since economists are not likely to defeat such attempts outright, they should be prepared to try to deflect them in more useful directions."

Why, however, should compensation be directed toward the workers rather than the firms involved? Trebilcock (1985) gives an economic rationale — market imperfections in the training field (lack of invest-ment by firms in the general training of their employees) — and a social rationale — workers are generally less mobile than businesses, and it is more difficult to diversify human capital investment than any other type of investment. The argument is not generally well supported, but this does not lessen its appeal. Everyone "knows" that the bosses are rich and the workers are poor,[6] and that if someone is to be helped, it should be the worker. Worker assistance thus has more legitimacy than assistance to firms (Blais, 1986).

The new strategy, which is touted as more pragmatic and more refined, therefore assumes that, to achieve free trade, the support (or non-opposition) of workers in declining industries must be bought by offering generous compensation. This position is held virtually unan-imously, and is to be found in Glenday and Jenkins (1981), Glenday, Jenkins and Evans (1982), Saunders (1984), Watson (1983) and Trebilcock (1985). Opinions vary principally concerning the method of compensa-tion. What is implicit, however, is the assumption that the workers involved would themselves be eager to trade the risk of loss of employment (whether temporary or permanent) for generous compensation. After all, this type of bargaining is familiar to economists "who obviously believe in deal-making" (Watson, 1984, p. 104). But the workers' own opinion has scarcely been considered. The type of trade-off proposed may not be as appealing as it might appear at first glance if account is taken of the fact that, in general, Canadians attach much greater importance to job security than to wages (Johnston, 1985). Neither does the strategy take into account the regional aspect of Canada's industrial problems. Not only the workers but also residents in an area or region as a whole can be affected by a plant closing (Blais, 1986). Might it not be necessary to indemnify an entire region?

As early as 1971, Matthews was insisting on the necessity of adaptation measures in order to facilitate the process of moving to freer trade. However, this message has only recently received more emphasis. The free traders have understood that they must form a broader coalition if they wish their strategy to prevail. Thus was born the idea of generous compensation for workers in declining industries, an idea that incorporates the bias in favour of the "poor" worker. The formula assumes, among other things, that such workers are not clinging tooth and nail to their jobs, and that they are ready to trade them in exchange for some financial consideration. This type of calculation is customary for economists, but it is by no means certain that workers see things in the same light.

Virtues of the Market

It is Watson (1983, pp. 97–98) who attacks government intervention in industrial development most coherently. He takes care to emphasize that he is not opposed to all government intervention:

> there are many other areas of economic activity in which governments obviously have a crucial role to play and in which they can hope to be at least moderately successful. They can clearly do much good by assuring the public safety and by encouraging and enforcing the act of contract. They should probably also be active in taking resources from those who have much and giving them to those who have demonstrably little. . . . Thus to be against an active industrial policy is not necessarily to be anti-government.

Watson is favourable to compensation for workers, and wishes to dissociate himself from the "small-minded ideologues" of the extreme right who question any government intervention. Rather, each type of intervention should be examined on its own merits. This constitutes recognition that, despite what may have been said about fiscal revolt, government action is seen as legitimate (Johnston, 1985; Blais and McRoberts, 1983).

Watson's argument (1983, p. 25) is relatively simple. First, "there are at least prima facie grounds for supposing that market processes are better than alternative forms of organization at delivering an efficient allocation of resources." Here, he is in a strong position: the market is usually a guarantee of efficiency. Naturally, he admits that the market has its imperfections, which take the form of public goods and externalities, but this is not a sufficient condition:

> the existence of external benefits and costs clearly creates a potential role for government. . . . Nevertheless, the possibility of government failure cannot be dismissed. An optimal allocation requires not merely that more (or less) of those goods that create external benefits (or costs) be produced, but that production be expanded (or contracted) until the social benefit from the extra unit of output just equals its social cost. (p. 40)

The word is out. The market may be imperfect, but do not forget that "governments — perhaps occasionally, perhaps often — may operate in inefficient ways" (ibid., p. 25). On the one hand, politicians and bureaucrats have objectives to pursue which may lower the priority of the concern for efficiency. On the other hand, the government, like any apparatus of authority, has "strong thumbs, but no fingers" (ibid., p. 29). Developing an industrial strategy is more complex than distributing pensions, and the bureaucratic machinery does not have the flexibility required to do so.[7] In addition, "the public agent does not go out of business if he or she is inept" (ibid., p. 30), and incentives for efficiency are thus less great. Besides, another difficulty "with firm specific assistance is that without strict administrative control it creates abundant opportunities for corruption" (Watson, 1984, p. 208). As a result, "there is every reason to expect that government failure is as serious as market failure" (Watson, 1983, p. 30). Industrial policy is thus a misleading solution.

Watson's recommendations follow logically from these observations. First, the government should intervene as little as possible: "public policy should restrict itself to patching up obvious market failures, *when this is possible*" (ibid., p. 98, emphasis in the text). Secondly, when intervention seems justified, the measures should be as simple and as general as possible, since the administration does not have the competence or the organizational flexibility required to take decisions on details.

Watson's position is appealing both because of its contribution to the debate and because of the quality of his argument. He has succeeded in explaining in relatively simple terms what the basis is for most economists' reticence toward a vigorous industrial policy. The argument has force with regard to selective measures, since it goes back to the idea held by the general public regarding the bureaucracy: that it is an inefficient body.[8]

The Regional Question

The regional question shows up in almost every debate in Canada, and industrial policy is no exception. Regional considerations are explicitly invoked by the Economic Council and the Science Council. In *Looking Outward*, the Economic Council looks at the regional impacts of freer trade. In 1983, the Science Council published *The Challenge of Co-operation* (Jenkins, 1983), which, in the words of the Chairman, "analyses the difficult problems raised by the existence of distinct regional economies" (p. 11).

The clearest proposals put forward on this subject is that of the economist Courchene, who believes that the principal remedy for regional disparities is the marketplace, and particularly capital and labour force mobility:

> For example, suppose that real wages are higher in region A than they are in region B. . . . Under these circumstances, people will tend to move out of region B toward region A to take advantage of higher wages in region A. Investment capital, on the other hand, will tend to flow in the opposite direction to finance industry in region B and therefore to take advantage of the lower wages — i.e. lower cost labour supply. The net result will be a tendency for wages and the return on investment to be "equalized" between the two regions. (1978, p. 148)

Naturally, this position is debated. Polese (1981) in particular suggests that the selective nature of migration (in relation to age, education, etc.), as well as its multiplier effect, can, on the contrary, have the effect of increasing regional inequalities. The empirical data prove Courchene only partially correct: mobility indeed seems to contribute to a reduction in inequalities, but it is only one of the factors involved (Mansell and Copithorne, 1985). The conclusion of the Economic Council of Canada (1977, p. 179) probably expresses the dominant position: "Examination of empirical data suggests that migration might help a little to reduce regional disparities . . . but it could hardly become a panacea."

Indeed, the mobility option is advanced cautiously. As Matthews (1981) points out, Courchene himself rarely speaks explicitly of migration, preferring the concept of "natural adaptation." He recognizes that it is unlikely that regional transfers, which he attacks, will be abolished (Courchene, 1978, p. 157). The legitimacy of government intervention in regional development is widely accepted by public opinion. In Canada 83 percent are of the opinion that the federal government should concentrate its efforts in the disadvantaged regions (*Decima Quarterly Report*, 1981–83, question 375). Despite all the virtues attributed by economists to mobility, it is perceived more as a problem than a solution. The vast majority of people, particularly in rural areas, do not want to change their environment (Campbell et al., 1976, pp. 260–61). Even in urban centres, local roots are often deep (Andrew, Blais and Desrosiers, 1976). Therefore a policy explicitly and primarily based on worker mobility can be defended only with difficulty on the public platform. As noted by Bonin (1981, p. 498), "the federal government, of whatever party, would find difficulty in being without a program aimed at reducing regional economic disparities" [translation]. This does not mean that encouraging mobility is without symbolic appeal. On the contrary, in a society that values "openness," and even more strongly in "enlightened" circles, "mobility" is better than "immobility." Viewed in this light, programs to facilitate worker mobility are quite acceptable. Attachment to one's environment being what it is, however, a solution aimed at massive labour force migration is of little interest.

The most virulent criticism of Courchene's model is that of Matthews (1981), who instead proposes a "sociological" model based on the theory of dependence. The flaws in the latter, sociological, analysis have been exposed by Woodfine (1983). One of the most interesting aspects of the debate is that of the employment-income dynamic. Economists stress that regional disparities show up mainly in employment rather than income (Mansell and Copithorne, 1985). Hence the notion that it would perhaps be better to decrease workers' incomes by, for example, abolishing legislation on minimum wages and by attacking unemployment (Courchene, 1978). Matthews (1981, pp. 273–74) refuses to contemplate this possibility. However, there could be good sociological reasons for placing emphasis on safegarding employment rather than maintaining income. While it is true that "people may so value their way of life that migration is simply a last resort" (Matthews, 1981, p. 276), a lower wage could be an acceptable compromise. It is as if there were only two options: either support those who advocate reducing regional disparities across the board and demand more money and more jobs for workers, or let "unproductive" market trends prevail.

It is interesting to note that the mobility argument is really made only in the Canadian geographic context. When relations between Canada and other countries are involved, the debate centres on the free circulation of goods. The free circulation of persons, under a more open immigration policy, could have as great, or greater, impact, but this is a solution no one proposes, because it is clearly both socially and politically unacceptable. Canadians are strongly opposed to the idea that any individual who wishes to settle in their country should be able to do so by his or her own choice (Johnston, 1985) and find the vision of a tide of immigrants of all races and origins invading Canada "at will" scarcely appealing. The call for mobility must not, therefore, extend beyond Canada's borders. Even within them, the call is timid.

Conclusion

According to Edelman (1964), the dominant characteristic of political action is its symbolic dimension. Edelman showed especially how political elites seek to influence the expectations of the population, and thus to ensure its support. These manoeuvres are revealing signs of the necessity for those who govern in a democratic society to identify themselves as the legitimate representatives of its citizens. This legitimacy is, in part, conferred upon them by the method by which they are designated, that is, by elections, but it also depends on their policies. Thus the agenda resembles a competition of ideas in which the symbols that are successfully imposed as those associated with the public interest are the winning symbols: "new candidates for legitimacy symbols will be successful in direct relationship to their perceived harmonious relation to major value patterns of the society" (Merelman, 1966, p. 555).

The debate concerning Canada's industrial policy illustrates this assertion nicely. In this paper it has frequently been possible to state that certain options were proposed only indirectly or timidly because they were in opposition to the dominant ideas or values of the society. The fact that these ideas and values are not free of contradictions, however, leaves some margin of manoeuvre to those who wish to change them.

The dominant image in the field of industrial policy appears to arise from the theme of openness. The Canadian economy must be "open" to the international economy, must adapt to industrial changes; innovation and adaptation to the new international context must be encouraged. People will speak of opting for the "virtuous circle" of taking the offensive rather than the "vicious circle" of being on the defensive (Stoffaës, 1978). In the same vein, Chandler argues in this volume (chap. 5) that countries in industrial decline are those which have tended to protect workers and regions from change, rather than supporting them during change. An industrial strategy that focusses primarily on stability is thus ruled out from the start. On the other hand, the need for stability cannot be completely ignored. It is a constraint that must be taken into account when one wishes to implement a policy facilitating long-term change. Traditional values, which the majority of the population still accept, find few defenders in the debate with which we are concerned, as it is dominated by the educated, modern elite. No one dares to propose a more protectionist policy, or to advocate less research and development.

The debate concerning industrial policy also raises the question of the roles of private enterprise and the state. The ideology of free enterprise is clearly the dominant one in North America, and is particularly prevalent in the United States. Lipset and Schneider (1983, p. 282) note that "the concept of free enterprise has a powerful appeal and is typically endorsed by over 90 percent of the population." Free enterprise is perceived as conducive to a high standard of living, individual freedom, and technological development. Private enterprise is also deemed clearly more efficient than public administration. In the same vein, Chong et al. (1983, p. 407) note that "the vast majority of Americans consistently uphold such key capitalist notions as private property, the profit system, economic competition, and the general fairness of the private enterprise system." While the Canadian political culture is certainly less monolithic, the ideology of free enterprise is still dominant. Almost 60 percent of Canadians think that private industry serves the economic interests of the average citizen better than does the government (*Decima Quarterly Report*, 1982–83, question 469). On more specific matters, opposition to government mismanagement is less pronounced, but this only confirms the prejudice in favour of the values represented by free enterprise.

Thirdly, emphasis in this debate is placed more on the mobility of goods than of persons. The Economic Council of Canada has made itself the prime proponent of a free trade zone with the United States. Only at a lower level do some of the more audacious, such as Courchene, risk vaunting the virtues of mobility. For most Canadians, mobility is not considered a good but an evil which is occasionally necessary, and this type of scenario is highly unlikely to arouse enthusiasm.

Finally, we have been able to observe the considerable importance of the widely held image of "big guys" and "little guys." In popular mythology, the big guy is necessarily the "bad guy" and the little guy the "good guy." Moreover, it is necessarily the big guy who will devour the little guy. Thus it is difficult to persuade people that a free trade zone between the United States and Canada will benefit the latter. The idea of assisting workers rather than businesses appears completely legitimate, because it tends in the direction of what is considered morally good and fair. In a democratic society, the big guys are unhappy:

> The "big guys" don't dare to complain in the open; they defend themselves indirectly because they know their cause is unpopular and, at bottom, they often doubt its legitimacy. (de Closets, 1982, p. 101, translation)

Notes

This study is a translation of the original French-language text, which was completed in February 1985. I wish to thank Herman Bakvis, Alan Cairns, Stéphane Dion, Robert Young and two anonymous referees for their comments on a draft version of this text.

1. McFetridge (1977, p. 87) states this assumption explicitly: "This study has confined itself to policy recommendations which can be directed directly from a simple, albeit abstract, theory of the role of the state in economic life. This theory assumes that the principal criterion by which one evaluates proposed government actions is their effect on real per capita income." Watson (1983, p. 45) also writes that "what is profitable — not what is fashionable — should be done."

2. The possibility cannot be denied, however, that this "need" could be reassessed if the real cost of the measures put in place were clearly identified.

3. Eighty per cent of Canadians feel that the government wastes a great deal of money (Kornberg et al., 1982, p. 68, Table 3.3). See also Johnston (1985) on anti-government sentiments.

4. For this reason one may well be sceptical about the Economic Council of Canada recommendation (1983) that subsidy programs be established based on a cost-benefit analysis of each project. At the very least, it may be observed that such a measure would create jobs for economists, who are the only ones qualified to carry out the type of analysis proposed, in the same way that the strategy proposed by the Science Council favours scientists and engineers (Daly and Globerman, 1976).

5. The idea that Canada is a small country seems to go without saying among economists even though, compared to other OECD countries, it is medium-sized. But clearly it is small if the United States is the norm.

6. For a formal demolition of this attractive myth, see de Closets (1982, p. 58): "To seek inequalities among the French is not at all original . . . the 'big guys' are denounced, the 'little guys' receive pity; no one speaks of the 'middle guys'; everything is judged by a monetary yardstick. Such talk is always well received. Naturally, it elicits the righteous indignation that gives everyone the feeling of working for justice, of stealing, without any risk whatsoever, to help the poor. . . . The system that generates these inequalities cannot be reduced to the capitalist-worker dialectic. This is a shame, because this scenario, which parallels that of the 'big guys' and the 'little guys,' suits everyone." [Translation]

7. For a more detailed view of the debate surrounding this question, see the study by Atkinson in this volume (chap. 7).

8. Johnston (1985, chap. 2, p. 12) notes that everyone, or almost everyone, agrees when a proposal is made to reduce the size of the public service.

Bibliography

Andrew, Caroline, André Blais, and Rachel Desrosiers. 1976. *Les élites politiques, les bas-salariés, et la politique du logement à Hull.* Ottawa: University of Ottawa Press.

Badaracco, Joseph L. Jr, and David B. Yoffie. 1983. "Industrial Policy: It Can't Happen Here." *Harvard Business Review* (November–December): 96–106.

Bauer, Raymond A., Ithiel de Sola Pool, and Lewis Anthony Dexter. 1972. *American Business and Public Policy: The Politics of Foreign Trade.* New York: Aldine.

Bell, David V. 1975. *Power, Influence and Authority.* New York: Oxford University Press.

Bird, Richard M. 1982. *Industrial Policy in Ontario: A Preliminary View.* Toronto: Institute for Policy Analysis.

Blais, André. 1980. "Orientation de la recherche." In *Introduction à l'analyse des politiques,* edited by Réjean Landry. Quebec: Les presses de l'Université Laval.

_____. 1986. *The Political Sociology of Industrial Policy,* volume 45 of the research studies prepared for the Royal Commission on the Economic Union and Development Prospects for Canada. Toronto: University of Toronto Press.

Blais, André, and Kenneth McRoberts. 1983. "Dynamique et contraintes des finances publiques au Québec." *Politique* 3 (Winter): 27–63.

Bonin, Bernard. 1981. "Introduction." *Canadian Public Policy* 8 (Autumn): 498–500.

Brenner, Reuven, and Léon Courville. 1985. "Industrial Strategy: Inferring What It Really Is." In *Economics of Industrial Policy and Strategy,* volume 5 of the research studies prepared for the Royal Commission on the Economic Union and Development Prospects for Canada. Toronto: University of Toronto Press.

Britton, John H., and James M. Gilmour. 1978. *The Weakest Link: A Technological Perspective on Canadian Industrial Under-development.* Ottawa: Science Council of Canada.

Campbell, Angus, Philip E. Converse, and Willard L. Rodgers. 1976. *The Quality of American Life: Perceptions, Evaluations and Satisfactions.* New York: Russel Sage Foundation.

Canada. 1982. Standing Senate Committee on Foreign Affairs. *Canada–United States Relations*. Vol. 3, *Canada's Trade Relations with the United States*. Ottawa: Minister of Supply and Services Canada.

———. 1983. Department of Regional Industrial Expansion. *A Strategy for the Automobile Industry in Canada*. Report of the Task Force on the Canadian Motor Vehicle and Parts Industry. Ottawa: The Department.

Cobb, Roger W., and Charles D. Elder. 1972. *Participation in American Politics: The Dynamics of Agenda-Building*. Boston: Allyn and Bacon.

Chong, Dennis, Herbert McClosky, and John Zaller. 1983. "Patterns of Support for Democratic and Capitalist Values in the United States." *British Journal of Political Science* 13 (October): 401–440.

Connolly, William E. 1981. *Appearance and Reality in Politics*. Cambridge: Cambridge University Press.

Courchene, Thomas J. 1970. "Interprovincial Migration and Economic Adjustment." *Canadian Journal of Economics* 9 (November): 550–76.

———. 1978. "Avenues of Regional Adjustment: The Transfer System and Regional Disparities." In *Canadian Confederation at the Crossroads*, edited by M. Walker. Vancouver: Fraser Institute.

Daly, D.J., and S. Globerman. 1976. *Tariffs and Science Policies: Applications of a Model of Nationalism*. Toronto: University of Toronto Press.

de Closets, François. 1982. *Toujours Plus*. Paris: Grasset.

de Vos, Dirk. 1983. *Governments and Microelectronics*. Ottawa: Science Council of Canada.

Economic Council of Canada. 1975. *Looking Outward: A New Trade Strategy for Canada*. Ottawa: Information Canada.

———. 1977. *Living Together: A Study of Regional Disparities*. Ottawa: Minister of Supply and Services Canada.

———. 1983. *The Bottom Line: Technology, Trade and Income Growth*. Ottawa: Minister of Supply and Services Canada.

Edelman, Murray. 1964. *The Symbolic Uses of Politics*. Urbana: University of Illinois Press.

Europa Publications Limited. 1983. *The Far East and Australasia, 1963–1984*. London: Europa Publications.

Gilder, George. 1983. "A Supply Side Economics of the Left." *Public Interest* 7 (Summer): 29–44.

Gilmour, James L. 1978. "Industrialization and Technological Backwardness: The Canadian Dilemma." *Canadian Public Policy* 4 (Winter): 20–33.

Glenday, G., and G.P. Jenkins. 1981. *Labour Adjustment: An Overview of Problems and Policies*. Ottawa: Task Force on Labour Market Developments.

Glenday, G., G.P. Jenkins, and J.C. Evans. 1982. *Worker Adjustment Policies: An Alternative to Protectionism*. Ottawa: North-South Institute.

Globerman, Steven. 1978. "Canadian Science Policy and Technological Sovereignty." *Canadian Public Policy* 4 (Winter): 34–45.

Gordon, Myron J. 1978. "A World Scale National Corporation Industrial Strategy." *Canadian Public Policy* 4 (Winter): 46–56.

Granatstein, J.L. 1985. "Free Trade between Canada and the United States: The Issue That Will Not Go Away." In *The Politics of Canada's Economic Relationship with the United States*, volume 29 of the research studies prepared for the Royal Commission on the Economic Union and Development Prospects for Canada. Toronto: University of Toronto Press.

Grant, Wyn. 1982. *The Political Economy of Industrial Policy*. London: Butterworth.

Haas, Ernest B. 1968. *The Uniting of Europe: Political, Social and Economic Force, 1950–1957*. Stanford: Stanford University Press.

Harris, Richard. 1985. *Trade, Industrial Policy and International Competition*. Volume 13 of the research studies prepared for the Royal Commission on the Economic Union and Development Prospects for Canada. Toronto: University of Toronto Press.

Harris, Richard G., with David Cox. 1984. *Trade, Industrial Policy and Canadian Manufacturing*. Toronto: Ontario Economic Council.

Heclo, Hugh. 1974. *Modern Social Politics in Britain and Sweden*. New Haven, Conn.: Yale University Press.

Hodge, Robert W., Paul M. Siegel, and Peter H. Rossi. 1966. "Occupational Prestige in the United States: 1925–1963." In *Class, Status and Power: Social Stratification in Comparative Perspective*, edited by Reinhard Bendix and Seymour Martin Lipset. New York: Free Press.

Jenkin, Michael. 1983. *The Challenge of Co-operation: Industrial Policy in the Canadian Federation*. Ottawa: Science Council of Canada.

Jenkins, Glenn P. 1980. *Costs and Consequences of the New Protectionism: The Case of Canada's Clothing Sector*. Ottawa: North-South Institute.

Johnston, Richard. 1985. *Public Opinion and Public Policy in Canada: Questions of Confidence*. Volume 35 of the studies prepared for the Royal Commission on the Economic Union and Development Prospects for Canada. Toronto: University of Toronto Press.

Kamien, M.I., and N.L. Schwartz. 1982. *Market Structure and Innovation*. Cambridge: Cambridge University Press.

King, Anthony. 1973. "Ideas, Institutions and the Policies of Governments: A Comparative Analysis," Part III. *British Journal of Political Science* 3 (October): 409–423.

Kingdon, John W. 1984. *Agendas, Alternatives and Public Policies*. Boston: Little, Brown.

Kornberg, Allan et al. 1982. *Representative Democracy in the Canadian Provinces*. Scarborough: Prentice-Hall.

Lazar, Fred. 1981. *The New Protectionism: Non-Tariff Barriers and Their Effects on Canada*. Toronto: James Lorimer.

Lecraw, Donald J. 1985a. "Corporate Operation and Strategy in a Changing World Environment." In *Technological Change in Canadian Industry*, volume 3 of the research studies prepared for the Royal Commission on the Economic Union and Development Prospects for Canada. Toronto: University of Toronto Press.

_____. 1985b. "Industrial Policy in the United States: A Survey." In *Economics of Industrial Policy and Strategy*, volume 5 of the research studies prepared for the Royal Commission on the Economic Union and Development Prospects for Canada. Toronto: University of Toronto Press.

Lipset, Seymour Martin, and William Schneider. 1983. *The Confidence Gap: Business, Labor and Government in the Public Mind*. New York: Free Press.

Lockart, Charles. 1984. "Explaining Social Policy Differences among Advanced Industrial Societies." *Comparative Politics* 16 (April): 335–51.

Lyon, Peyton. 1975. *Canadian–U.S. Free Trade and Canada's Independence*. Study prepared for the Economic Council of Canada. Ottawa: Minister of Supply and Services Canada.

MacMechan, Archibald. 1920. "Canada as a Vassal State." *Canadian Historical Review* 1 (4): 347–53.

Mansell, Robert L., and Lawrence Copithorne. 1985. "Canadian Regional Economic Disparities: A Survey." In *Disparities and Interregional Adjustment*, volume 64 of the research studies prepared for the Royal Commission on the Economic Union and Development Prospects for Canada. Toronto: University of Toronto Press.

Markusen, James R. 1985. "Canadian Gains from Trade in the Presence of Scale Economies and Imperfect Competition." In *Canada–United States Free Trade*, volume 11 of the research studies prepared for the Royal Commission on the Economic Union and Development Prospects for Canada. Toronto: University of Toronto Press.

Maskus, Keith E. 1984. "Rising Protectionism and U.S. International Trade Policy." *Economic Review* (July–August): 3–18.

Matthews, R.A. 1971. *Industrial Viability in a Free Trade Economy: A Program of Adjustment Policies for Canada.* Toronto: University of Toronto Press.

———. 1981. "Two Alternative Explanations of the Problem of Regional Dependency in Canada." *Canadian Public Policy* 7 (Spring): 268–83.

McFetridge, D.G. 1977. *Government Support of Scientific Research and Development: An Economic Analysis.* Toronto: University of Toronto Press.

———. 1985. "The Economics of Industrial Structure: An Overview." In *Canadian Industry in Transition,* volume 2 of the research studies prepared for the Royal Commission on the Economic Union and Development Prospects for Canada. Toronto: University of Toronto Press.

McFetridge, Donald G., and Jacek P. Warda. 1983. *Canadian R&D Incentives: Their Adequacy and Impact.* Toronto: Canadian Fiscal Studies Association.

Merelman, Richard M. 1966. "Learning and Legitimacy." *American Political Science Review* 50 (September): 548–62.

Morici, Peter, Arthur Smith, and Sperry Lea. 1982. *Canadian Industrial Policy.* Washington, D.C.: National Planning Association.

Nimmo, Dan. 1978. *Political Communication and Public Opinion in America.* Santa Monica: Goodyear.

Norrie, Kenneth H. 1979. "Regional Economic Conflicts in Canada." In *The Politics of an Industrial Strategy: A Seminar.* Ottawa: Science Council of Canada.

Nossal, Kim R. 1985. "Economic Nationalism and Continental Integration: Assumptions, Arguments and Advocacies." In *The Politics of Canada's Economic Relationship with the United States,* volume 29 of the research studies prepared for the Royal Commission on the Economic Union and Development Prospects for Canada. Toronto: University of Toronto Press.

Organisation for Economic Co-operation and Development. 1983. *Stimuli and Obstacles to Investment and the International Investment Process.* Paris: OECD.

Pentland, Charles. 1985. "North American Integration and the Canadian Political System." In *The Politics of Canada's Economic Relationship with the United States,* volume 29 of the research studies prepared for the Royal Commission on the Economic Union and Development Prospects for Canada. Toronto: University of Toronto Press.

Polèse, Mario. 1981. "Regional Disparity, Migration and Economic Adjustments: A Reappraisal." *Canadian Public Policy* 7 (Autumn): 519–25.

Ryan, Alan. 1970. *The Philosophy of the Social Sciences.* London: Macmillan.

Saunders, Ronald S. 1982. "Continentalism and Economic Nationalism in the Manufacturing Sector: Seeking Middle Ground." *Canadian Public Policy* 8 (October): 463–80.

———. 1984. *Aid to Workers in Declining Industries.* Toronto: Ontario Economic Council.

Science Council of Canada. 1979. *Forging the Links: A Technology Policy for Canada.* Ottawa: The Council.

———. 1984. *Canadian Industrial Development: Some Policy Directions.* Ottawa: The Council.

Sears, David O., and Jack Citrin. 1982. *Tax Revolt: Something for Nothing in California.* Cambridge, Mass.: Harvard University Press.

Soldatos, P. 1986. "Free-Trade Continentalism in Canada–U.S. Relations." In *The International Legal Environment,* volume 52 of the research studies prepared for the Royal Commission on the Economic Union and Development Prospects for Canada. Toronto: University of Toronto Press.

Stevenson, Garth. 1980. "Canadian Regionalism in Continental Perspective." *Canadian Studies Review* 15 (Summer): 16–28.

Stoetzel, Jean. 1983. *Les valeurs du temps présent: une enquête.* Paris: Presses universitaires de France.

Stoffaës, Christian. 1978. *La grande menace industrielle.* Paris: Calman-Lévy.

Thakur, Ramesh, and Hyam Gold. 1982. "New Zealand and Australia: Free Trade Agreement Mark II." *The World Today* 38 (October): 402–410.

—————. 1983. "The Politics of a New Economic Relationship: Negotiating Free Trade between Australia and New Zealand." *Australian Outlook* 37 (August): 82–88.

Trebilcock, Michael J. 1985. *The Political Economy of Economic Adjustment: The Case of Declining Sectors*. Volume 8 of the research studies prepared for the Royal Commission on the Economic Union and Development Prospects for Canada. Toronto: University of Toronto Press.

Treiman, Donald J. 1977. *Occupational Prestige in Comparative Perspective*. New York: Academic Press.

Watson, William G. 1983. *A Primer on the Economics of Industrial Policy*. Toronto: Ontario Economic Council.

—————. 1984. "It's Still Not Time for an Industrial Strategy." *Canadian Public Policy* 10 (June): 201–210.

Wilkinson, B.W. 1982. "Canada–U.S. Free Trade and Some Options." *Canadian Public Policy* 8 (October): 428–40.

Wonnacott, P., and R.J. Wonnacott. 1982. "Free Trade between the United States and Canada: Fifteen Years Later." *Canadian Public Policy* 8 (October): 412–28.

Woodfine, William J. 1983. "Regional Disparities — Once Again." *Canadian Public Policy* 9 (December): 499–505.

3

The Politics of Private Investment

DAVID MARSH

Despite the fact that many politicians assert that the market is an effective, indeed the most effective, way of allocating resources, there is little doubt that in all developed capitalist societies the state is deeply, and it appears increasingly, involved in economic management. At the same time the legislative and administrative decisions of the state clearly influence the activities of business. In a market economy, capital is inevitably a crucial economic and political resource. This study is concerned with both elements of this reciprocal relationship.

The major proposition that the study examines is one put forward by structuralists, namely that because governments are dependent on private investment, the business community has a privileged position in influencing public policy. In the first section I shall examine briefly a theoretical justification of the basic proposition, leading into a series of hypotheses about the structural position of business, or capital, which can be examined empirically. The second section will attempt to test the hypotheses against available data on the political economies of the United States and western Europe. The proposition also suggests that the privileged position which capital enjoys is reflected in policy decisions taken by government, particularly in those areas that most concern capital, such as industrial policy, industrial relations policy or prices and incomes policy, and a third section will deal with this contention. As space is limited, and any case study of public policy has to be fairly detailed to be of any use, the main empirical material for this discussion is drawn from the country with which I am most familiar, Britain. However, I shall be concerned to relate the case study of Britain to a broader context. The final section of the study will then reexamine the structuralist proposition in the light of the material presented. My contention in this conclusion will be that the proposition has major limitations and that a much more sophisticated formulation of the relationship between capital and the state in modern capitalist society is necessary.

The Structuralist Position

The structuralist position within Marxism emphasizes the external constraints that prevent the state elite from developing and implementing policies contrary to the interests of capital. To a Marxist like Jessop[1] these constraints are based upon what might be called "the institutionalized right of capital withdrawal." In this view the state will be obliged to act in the interests of capital because of the threat of an investment strike by one or more sections of capital. On most occasions this threat will be implicit but nevertheless potent as the state elite is well aware of the crucial position of capital and of its flexibility. However on occasion the threat will be explicit as capital engages in organized efforts to provoke economic destabilization to influence government. The emphasis here is upon the necessary constraints imposed by the basic relations within the economic system rather than, as in the instrumentalist position, upon the activity of interest groups or political parties that forward the interests of capital.

This essentially structuralist explanation of the power of capital is not however confined to Marxism. Indeed perhaps its most influential advocate is Charles Lindblom, who would certainly not regard himself as a Marxist. In fact until the publication of his much vaunted book *Politics and Markets*,[2] Lindblom could be regarded as a leading member of the American political science pluralist establishment. His work is worthy of brief consideration here both because it offers perhaps the most convincing theoretical exposition of the proposition with which I am concerned, and because from it I can generate a series of hypotheses, derived from that proposition, which I shall test in the next section.

According to Lindblom, every political system needs a mechanism for taking decisions about jobs, prices, production and grants. Such decisions are inevitably public in two senses: they affect the standard of living and economic security of everyone, and the performance of the economy crucially influences the Government's reelection prospects. In a private enterprise system most of these decisions are made not by ministers and civil servants but by businessmen. In other words, businessmen control key decisions on all aspects of production and distribution. Moreover, capital is a flexible resource; its owners and controllers can choose whether, or where, to invest. In consequence a major, perhaps *the* major, function of government is to encourage businessmen to invest and produce, thus increasing GNP and improving everyone's standard of living.

The point is that in a market system businessmen cannot be compelled to invest in a particular way; rather, they must be offered incentives — usually subsidized services, grants, or government contracts. All this means is that, to Lindblom, businessmen are different from other interests in society:

> In the eyes of government officials, therefore, businessmen do not appear simply as the representatives of a special interest, as representatives of interest groups do. They appear as functionaires performing functions that government officials regard as indispensable. When a government official asks himself whether business needs a tax reduction, he knows he is asking a question about the welfare of the whole society and not simply about a favour to a segment of the population, which is what is typically at stake when he asks himself whether he should respond to an interest group.[3]

So businessmen act almost as public officials and in some sense their interests can be regarded as the interests of all. If business is efficient and productive it increases everyone's standard of living and economic security. To this extent what is good for General Motors *is* good for America. In effect, the structural position of business in the economy gives it a veto over government policy decisions.

To Lindblom then, the key power of capital is structural. In fact this structural constraint has two aspects. It rests partly upon capital's potential to cause economic disruption, for example through an "investment strike." This threat is implicit, rather than explicit, in that it exists regardless of whether the threat is actually expressed by business interest groups or businessmen. Indeed, the key element of the threat is perhaps the anticipatory reaction of government. Government anticipates the interest and reaction of capital without the need for interest group representations. As Lindblom puts it:

> Mutual adjustment is often impersonal and distant. It operates through unspoken deference of administrations, legislatures, and courts to the needs of business. And it relates on a multitude of common tacit understandings shared by the two groups of leaders, business and governmental, with respect to the conditions under which enterprises can or cannot profitably operate.[4]

At the same time however, Lindblom emphasizes that capital also exercises ideological control through its manipulation of the views, or in Lindblom's terms "volitions," of the population. Here the idea is that a group may exercise ideological hegemony, with the dominant ideology of society serving its real interests. The crucial point here is that if that dominant ideology legitimizes a particular group's interests as the "national interest" then that group's interests are likely to be served regardless of any representations it makes to government. This process might be best regarded as ideological control. In fact Lindblom views business as capable of, and in many cases actually exercising, such control:

Consider the possibility that businessmen achieve an indoctrination of citizens so that citizens' volitions serve not their own interests but the interests of businessmen. Citizens then become allies of businessmen. The privileged position of business comes to be widely accepted. In electoral politics, no great struggle needs to be fought.[5]

One of the major achievements of his book, however, is that it indicates how that structural constraint is clearly reflected in the decisions of government. Too many authors, particularly Marxists, talk generally of structural power without considering its translation into decision making. In contrast Lindblom clearly delineates the relationship:

Government exercises broad authority over business activities. But the exercise of its authority is curbed and shaped by the concern of government officials for possible adverse effects on business, since adverse effects can cause unemployment and other consequences that government officials are unwilling to accept.

In other areas of public policy, the authority of government is again curbed and shaped by concern for possible adverse effects on business.

Hence even the unspoken possibility of adversity for business operates as an all-pervasive constraint on government authority.

Mindful of government concern for business performance, businessmen, especially corporate executives, actively voice and negotiate demands on government, with the implicit threat of poor performance if their demands are not met.

For all these reasons, business officials are privileged not only with respect to the care with which government satisfies business needs in general but also in privileged roles as participants in policy deliberations in government.[6]

To Lindblom, then, business occupies a privileged position which no other group enjoys. Indeed other groups like unions, farmers or doctors can enjoy only limited, and often temporary, privilege. Despite this, however, capital's position is not sinister:

To understand the peculiar character of politics in market-oriented systems requires, however, no conspiracy theory of politics, no theory of common social origins uniting government and business officials, no crude allegation of power elite established by clandestine forces. Business simply needs inducements, hence a privileged position in government and politics, if it is to do its job.[7]

There is hope because, while government cannot command business, it can negotiate with it. Politics in such a system is all about trade-offs between business and government. Governments offer incentives and thus increase profitability in return for economic progress and business cooperation. "The key strategy is, in effect, to pay business to waive some of their privileges."[8] Lindblom's view of the structural position of capital, and indeed that of much of the Marxist material, suggests a number of empirically testable hypotheses:

- Private investment is crucial to contemporary capitalist economies.
- Governments' reelection chances are largely determined by economic performance.
- Capital is increasingly international and flexible.
- Capital uses its privileged position to pressurize government through the threat of investment strikes, and other such tactics.
- Governments respond to this pressure by providing increased incentives to business.
- Government incentives play an important role in the investment decisions of firms.

These hypotheses will be examined in turn.

The Significance of Private Investment

If private investment is not crucial in the economy, and the first of our hypotheses states that it is, then obviously any argument about the structural position of capital will be weakened. There is little doubt that western governments believe that private investment is important or that they have intervened increasingly to attempt to stimulate that investment. Table 3-1, which indicates the relative level of state and private investment in six European countries, shows that the private sector is the most important source of investment in all cases. In contrast, direct investment by states in 1979 was less than 18 percent of total investment in each country. At the same time, investment grants and subsidies account for a significant proportion of private investment in all the countries although it is considerably higher in Britain and Italy than elsewhere. Nevertheless, perhaps the most interesting row in the table is the last one; in no country does private enterprise provide more than two-thirds of the investment if government grants and subsidies to private enterprise are deducted. Indeed in Britain the figure drops well below 50 percent. Clearly, then, while private investment is the most important single element of investment everywhere, the state plays a larger role in some countries than in others, and in Britain in particular the state and the public sector are a more important source of investment than is the private sector.

Table 3-2, which deals with the level of investment in relation to gross domestic product (GDP) in the world's major economies, reveals another significant point. It is clear from these data that investment is particularly low in Britain and the United States and particularly high in Japan. More interestingly, if we compare Tables 3-1 and 3-2, the level of investment in relation to GDP in a country appears to bear no obvious relationship to the extent of the subsidies and grants to stimulate such investment. As I have already said, investment grants and subsidies account for a considerably greater proportion of investment in Britain

TABLE 3-1 The State versus the Private Sector as an Investor, Entrepreneur and Provider of Subsidies in Western Europe, 1979 (1975 figures in brackets)

	Belgium	West Germany	France	Italy	Holland	United Kingdom
Percent of gross fixed capital formation (GFCF) by state	17.4 (16.6)	15.4 (17.7)	13.1 (15.5)	16.3 (17.8)	14.8 (10.0)	14.6 (24.4)
Percent of GFCF by private enterprise	68.1 (47.5)	72.5 (65.0)	66.7 (66.6)	68.2 (59.6)	76.5 (73.0)	57.9 (48.2)
Percent of GFCF by public enterprise	12.9 (30.2)	10.7 (15.2)	15.0 (13.6)	13.3 (20.2)	8.2 (6.4)	16.3 (19.3)
Investment grants expressed as a percentage of GFCF by private enterprises	6.6 (3.6)	7.9 (6.5)	2.4 (3.1)	6.0 (6.6)	8.3 (6.0)	7.5 (8.6)
Investment grants & subsidies expressed as a percentage of GFCF by private enterprises	8.7 (21.5)	14.7 (13.5)	13.9 (13.7)	23.9 (21.4)	16.2 (12.3)	23.3 (33.7)
Percent of GFCF by private enterprise less grants and subsidies	62.2	61.8	57.4	51.9	64.1	44.4

Source: Eurostat National Accounts ESA Detailed Tables by Sector, 1970–80 and 1970–81.

TABLE 3-2 Gross Fixed Capital Formation as a Percentage of Gross
Domestic Product, 1962–82

	1962	1965	1970	1975	1980	1981	1982
United States	17.6	18.8	17.6	17.0	18.5	18.0	16.6
Japan	32.9	29.9	35.5	32.4	32.0	31.0	29.6
West Germany	25.7	26.1	25.5	20.4	22.8	21.9	20.5
France	21.4	23.3	23.4	23.3	21.7	21.1	20.5
United Kingdom	16.8	18.2	18.5	19.5	17.4	15.7	15.4
Italy	23.7	19.3	21.4	20.6	19.8	20.2	19.0
OECD Europe	22.2	22.7	23.0	21.9	21.1	20.4	19.5
European Economic							
Community	21.9	22.3	22.9	21.1	20.9	19.8	18.9
Total OECD							
less United States	23.3	23.8	25.3	24.1	23.5	23.3	22.2

Source: OECD Economic Outlook 34 (December 1983): 154.

and Italy than in West Germany and France; yet the level of investment is marginally higher in West Germany and France than in Italy and significantly higher than in Britain. I shall return to this point at length later when I look at material on the investment decisions of firms.

Economic Performance and Government Popularity

Government clearly offers incentives to encourage firms to invest on the assumption that such investment stimulates growth and leads to economic prosperity and, in the government's terms, reelection. But is government popularity largely determined by economic factors? Until recently the general consensus seemed to be that the answer to this question was a qualified yes. It was qualified for a number of reasons. First, researchers found that economic factors have different effects on voters with different partisanship, that is, that the bias and intensity of voters' partisanship shapes their perception and interpretation of economic data.[9] In addition, other research indicated that electors held different political parties responsible for different economic factors. Parties of the right are more likely to lose votes if inflation increases than if unemployment increases, while the reverse is true for left-wing parties.[10] At the same time the literature also makes it clear that economic factors have different effects on different social groups, and this in turn affects the voters' perception of economic conditions, and of parties' responsibility for them.[11]

More recently, more attention has been paid to the impact of political factors such as wars and scandals[12] and political events[13] on government popularity. Of the studies that consider the importance of political variables, Mackuen's is possibly the most interesting.[14] It compared the relative effects of changing economic conditions and dramatic political events on the popularity of American presidents between 1963 and 1980 and concluded that they were about equal:

> Clearly citizen evaluations are as heavily affected by the President's action in the symbolic political arena as they are by fluctuations in economic conditions. A President cannot, and need not, rely on economic success to maintain his political support.[15]

In Britain evidence on the 1979–83 Conservative Government is even more revealing. The popularity of the Conservative Government and Mrs. Thatcher declined substantially after the end of 1980. Indeed, the percentage of the electorate believing Mrs. Thatcher was doing a good job reached an all-time low for any British prime minister in August 1981.[16] Her recovery, and that of her party, in the opinion polls owed something to the internal troubles of the Labour party and the weakness of the major Opposition leader Mr. Foot, but most, if not almost all, to the military action against Argentina in the Falklands. Certainly economic factors played a minor role in her successful surge to reelection in June 1983.

Economic performance is clearly a key factor affecting government popularity, and governments are therefore crucially concerned to promote economic prosperity by, among other things, offering incentives to private enterprise to invest. However, there is an increasing amount of evidence which suggests that political factors also play a key role in government popularity, and that governments can overcome economic adversity to win elections.

The Flexibility of Capital

Capital's ability to constrain government will depend a great deal upon its flexibility. If it intends to exercise its power directly then it has to convince government that it has the capacity to move capital and to withdraw or relocate production, and that it will do so unless government cooperates. The view of capital implicit in such an argument, however, seems oversimplified. There is certainly no doubt that capital is now internationally mobile, but its degree of mobility varies, particularly as between sectors. Here I shall examine first the extent of the flexibility of capital and then the limitations upon it.

The mobility of capital is a major feature of modern economies; it has increased substantially in the last twenty years for a number of reasons. Initially there was a major expansion of world trading by the United States and her allies after 1945, backed by U.S. military strength and linked with a revolution in transportation and communications. At the same time, and in an accelerating manner, technological advances made it quite possible to locate different stages of the production process in different places. What is more, the increase in international industrial concentration led to the centralization of decision making in a few hands and gave the few decision makers considerable flexibility as to where, and in what, they invest. All these developments have been reinforced by the growing instability in the world economic order since the dissolution of the Bretton Woods agreement in 1971 and the growth of the Eurocurrency market.[17]

Of course capital can relocate production within one country, and Bluestone and Harrison chart the extent of production mobility within the United States, where this phenomenon is most developed.[18] The most dramatic and consistent movement has been from the old industrial areas extending from Maine to Michigan, the "frost belt," to the more recently industrialized southern and southwestern states, the "sun belt." Indeed Bluestone and Harrison report data that show that:

> No matter where the home offices or their own factories, corporations, insurance companies or banks may be located, the nations' capitalists are investing most of their money outside of the old industrial "frost belt". Over the [period from 1960 to 1976], for example, the Southern manufacturing capital stock grew almost twice as fast as that of the Northeast, and 65% faster than in the North Central region. The states that experienced the fastest growth of manufacturing capital lie in a band stretching from Kentucky and Tennessee south and west to Texas. The slowest growing states are those whose manufacturing plants have long made up the heartland of organized labour: Wisconsin, Michigan, Illinois, Indiana, Ohio, New York, New Jersey and Pennsylvania. The correlation between these geographical patterns of capital investment and employment shifts . . . is unmistakable.[19]

It is also worth noting that this mobility has had such a strong effect on patterns of employment that individual states have offered a wide variety of grants and incentives in order to attract capital. I shall assess the consequences of such incentives later.

While intraregional shifts are of interest, this study is most concerned with the mobility of capital between countries. Here the figures are consistently large. In the next paper in this volume, Lynn Mytelka indicates the vast scale of direct foreign investment by the major industrialized countries. However, here I shall concentrate on evidence of decisions by companies on the location and relocation of production, since it is such decisions that might be used by companies to pressure government into offering incentives or making policy concessions. For this reason I shall look in some detail at the work of Frobel et al. on West Germany[20] and Gaffikin and Nickson on Britain.[21]

Frobel et al. in effect produced three related case studies. In the first section of their work they examined the most important structural changes which have occurred in the West German textile and garment industries, investigating 214 textile and 185 garment companies in depth.

In the second section they presented data on 602 West German manufacturing companies that had at least one subsidiary abroad. The aim here was to analyze the worldwide redistribution of production sites for all West German manufacturing industry. The third section of the book was based on data from 103 countries in Asia, Africa and Latin America where, by the mid-1970s, there were literally thousands of factories producing almost exclusively for the developed countries. The authors attempted to discover whether the growth of such factories helps the development of the countries in which they are located.[22] However in doing so they also threw further light on the reasons why transnational corporations (TNCs) invest in such countries. This aspect of their work will be examined in a later section.

The overwhelming conclusion reached by Frobel et al. is that the mobility of capital has dramatically increased. The picture is similar whether only data from the garment and textile industry are considered, or data from the entire manufacturing sector are included. Indeed, the authors estimated that the number of foreign workers directly employed by West German manufacturing companies amounted to 20 percent of the total domestic manufacturing labour force.[23] As they concluded:

> [this case study illustrates] the changed conditions in the world [political economy] which are forcing industrial undertakings, regardless of size and industrial branch, to reorganize their production. In an increasing number of cases, this reorganization involves the relocation of production abroad. To conclude: the new international division of labour is manifested in the changing world distribution of, in this case, Federal German production facilities. The high level of structural unemployment in Federal Germany is an inevitable result of the transfer of industrial employment elsewhere in the world.[24]

One of the main limitations of the work of Frobel et al. is that it only deals with the period up to 1974. In contrast Gaffikin and Nickson, while their work is not nearly as thorough, look at the relocation of production from Britain in the period between 1978 and 1982. They are primarily concerned with the movement of capital, and thus jobs, out of one area of Britain, the West Midlands. However, they report data on a study of the 50 largest British manufacturing companies, most of which are multinational corporations (MNCs). In 1978–79 these companies had a combined overseas production of over $20 billion — which represented 36 percent of their global output. Indeed 9 of these companies produced over half of their global output overseas and, by 1981–82, overseas production had increased to 44 percent of their global output. At the same time, overseas production was three times as important to these companies as exports in 1978–79, and by 1981–82 it had risen by 24 percent while exports from the United Kingdom grew by only 10 percent. By 1982 only 4 of these top 50 companies had exports greater than their overseas production.[25] This is startling evidence of the mobility of capital but it is reinforced by a more detailed consideration of the activities of the 10 largest manufacturing companies in the West Midlands. Gaffikin and Nickson conclude:

> Between 1978 and 1982 the combined global output of these 10 companies rose by 4.3% p.a. from £10,722mn to £13,868mn. . . . The combined value of production by these companies in Britain, comprising output for the domestic market as well as for export, rose by only 1.7% from £7,529mn to £8,218mn, while the value of overseas production by these companies rose by 12.1% p.a. from £3,193mn to £5,650mn over the same period. As a result the share of overseas production in the combined global output of these companies rose from 30% to 41% between 1978 and 1982.[26]

This movement of production was reflected in a rapid increase in unemployment.

> In 1978 these 10 companies employed a combined total of 686,694 workers throughout the world, of whom 513,466, equivalent to 75% of the total, were employed in Britain. By 1982 the global workforce of these same companies had fallen by 23% to 530,275.
>
> This fall in the global workforce was accounted for exclusively by cutbacks in Britain, where the total workforce fell by 31% from 513,466 in 1978 to 353,508 in 1982 — a loss of 159,958 jobs in just five years. Meanwhile the overseas workforce of these companies rose by 2% from 173,228 to 176,767 in spite of the world recession. As a result of these changes, the British share of the global workforce of these companies fell from 75% to 67% between 1978 and 1982.[27]

Of course it might be argued that the relocation of production from Britain is greater than from elsewhere, given the country's specific economic problems. However we have already seen similar trends in West Germany, and Bluestone and Harrison give ample evidence of the relocation of capital from the United States.[28] It seems relatively uncontentious to state that capital is increasingly becoming internationalized and flexible.

There can be little doubt that banking capital enjoys the greatest flexibility. In the absence of government constraints, there is little to prevent its relocation to wherever the returns are greatest, as has been particularly noticeable in Britain since the abolition of exchange controls in 1979. Indeed a striking feature of the outflow of capital in this period has been the surge in portfolio investments — the purchase of shares and other securities issued abroad — by U.K. financial institutions, especially life assurance companies and pension funds. Nevertheless the internationalization and mobility of banking capital is probably best illustrated through a brief consideration of one of the key elements in the political economy of contemporary capitalist states, the Eurocurrency, or more specifically the Eurodollar, market.

The Eurocurrency market developed at the end of the 1960s and grewrapidly in the 1970s. From the late 1950s the U.S. government had begun to run a balance-of-payments deficit, paying out more than was received and doing so in dollars. Although these dollars could have been held in accounts in New York, or exchanged into other currencies, their owners chose to open dollar accounts in Europe and elsewhere to avoid U.S. political jurisdiction and control over interest rates.

In fact, Coakley and Harris identify three reasons for the growth of the Eurodollar market.[29] First, the Eastern bloc countries needed to hold dollars in order to trade but were reluctant to hold them in American banks for fear that the U.S. government might freeze their accounts in pursuit of some political objective. Second, and even more important, dollar holders wanted to avoid the controls that the U.S. government put on the rates of interest payable on deposits; the European banks attracted dollar deposits simply by paying higher interest. Third, the increase in oil prices in 1973 meant that the oil exporting countries, particularly Saudi Arabia, had huge amounts of dollars to invest. The great bulk of this money went to Europe, mostly to London, and into bank deposits rather than bonds, shares or property. This money was then lent by the banks mainly to governments but also to large corporations and other banks.

Why is this market important? First of all, the scale of it is immense: by 1982, it was running at U.S.$2,015 billion.[30] Moreover, the market is a very volatile one, indicating the flexibility of capital, particularly banking capital. Finally the importance, and size, of this market in any country is directly related to the extent of the controls imposed on it by governments. Its major centre is London, largely because of the absence of controls imposed on it by the British government, and the City of London owes much of its current status as perhaps the world's major financial centre to the Eurodollar market.

These characteristics of Eurocurrency dealings lead inevitably to two other particularly important points. The existence of this market inevitably constrains the autonomy of all governments whose trade currencies affect exchange rates and, as Coakley and Harris argue, "even though much movements of the exchange rate are not determined by the "real" economy's trade and investment flows, the cost of imports and exports is affected by them."[31]

They might also have added that exchange rate fluctuations are likely to affect interest rates and thus public sector spending and the general level of economic activity. Of course the existence of this market also has a particular importance for those countries in which the trading takes place and, although this point refers particularly to Britain, it is also significant when considering the political economy of the United States. If a government wishes to control its exchange rate it needs to control capital movement, a very difficult matter given the existence of a Eurocurrency market. What is more, as Coakley and Harris again point out:

> Apart from the question of control over foreign exchange activities [of the dealing banks], governments cannot tax their profits, impose reserve requirements upon them or issue directives concerning their lending activities without eroding the basis of their existence in London.[32]

While the financial sector enjoys great flexibility, the mobility of capital varies by sector manufacturing industry. Here again Frobel et al.'s work is revealing. They indicate that flexibility is lowest in agriculture, forestry, energy and mining. It is low but not as low in the stone, glass and ceramics industry, and the metal industry, and greatest in the chemical, electrical engineering and mechanical engineering industries.[33] Generally it seems clear, and not surprising, that companies involved in the resource and extractive industries, or fairly closely linked to these industries, find it most difficult to relocate production. Even so it is evident that three other factors have considerable effect on the flexibility of capital. First, different factors, and therefore different calculations, are involved in original location decisions as distinct from relocation decisions. Once a company is located in a particular country there are major costs involved in relocation, particularly if the firm is operating in a capital-intensive industry. Second, relocation is easier for labour-intensive than for capital-intensive industries, because of the costs of writing off plant or equipment in one country and moving or repurchasing it in another. The third point, relating to the size of a corporation, is worth rather more detailed discussion.

Large MNCs by definition operate in a number of countries and can move capital and production between countries with relative ease. Obviously, they can increase investment in their existing subsidiaries or create or purchase new ones. Moreover, there is no doubt that they can also move capital by trade between subsidiaries through what is known as transfer pricing. A large proportion of world trade in fact is trade between subsidiaries of MNCs. Indeed, Muller estimates that "somewhere between one-third and one-half of world trade consists of non-market transactions between multinationals from all home countries." In the United States, he claims, "more than 70 percent of total U.S. exports and more than 50 percent of imports are 'intrafirm subsidiary transfers' between subsidiaries of the United States and foreign multinationals."[34] In such circumstances firms are tempted to manipulate profitability in order to minimize tax liabilities. The process involved is easily described. One subsidiary either sells too cheaply to another, or buys at an inflated price from it. In either case the first subsidiary, located in a high-tax country, either takes a loss or breaks even while the second, located in a low-tax country, makes an exceptionally high profit.

It is almost impossible to assess the extent of transfer pricing. As two subsidiaries of the same firm are involved, and the amount of information any firm is required to disclose is limited, it is often only if and when a company is prosecuted that the process is revealed. However, Gaffikin and Nickson report a number of such cases[35] and, perhaps even more significantly, the OECD, and the EEC, have devoted a large amount of attention to developing means of controlling it.[36] At the least, transfer pricing is an important aspect of the increased mobility of capital and, what is more, it is a type of mobility that is difficult, if not impossible, for any government to restrict or control.

Capital held by large multinational companies, and particularly by big financial institutions, is more mobile than it has ever been. Moreover, such mobility is often encouraged by government, as it has been by the current Conservative Government in Britain. The Thatcher Government abolished exchange controls in 1979 in order to help increase the profitability of companies, profits which they hoped, expected, or at least claimed would be repatriated — an expectation that looks dubious given any knowledge of the behaviour of MNCs. The pertinent question is, in what ways does this flexibility act as a constraint on government? Does foreign investment occur at the expense of national investment by stimulating deindustrialization, increasing unemployment, and thus reducing government's policy options? Perhaps more to the point, how far does capital use its flexibility as a threat, or bargaining tool, against government in order to gain an advantage from government? Put another way, to what extent is the evident flexibility of capital reflected in the actions of capital in relation to government, or perhaps more specifically by the use of the threat of an investment strike as a sanction against government?

Investment Strikes and Incentives

To Lindblom and others, the structural constraint of capital results to a great extent from the potential or actual threat of an "investment strike." It is not always clear however what different authors mean by the term. One might see an investment strike as involving coordinated action between firms within one sector of the economy, or even within different sectors of the economy, to produce a united policy with which to confront government. Another might conceive of an investment strike as a threat most likely to be exercised by a single, very large company or institution. The empirical evidence suggests, as we shall see shortly, that neither of these types of action is likely to be successful, or even adopted. There is ample evidence, however, that large companies particularly in growth sectors can force governments into a situation analogous to a "beauty competition," with governments as the contestants and the firms as the judges. In this situation a company will announce, or otherwise make clear, its plans to invest in a new plant. Governments then compete for the privilege of having the plant in their country. A variation on this theme is provided if a company decides to invest in a country but the government wishes to influence its decision as to where it locates the plant, usually in order to sustain a regional policy.

McQuaid's thorough study of the relationship between big business and the American government denies the existence of investment strikes that involve coordination between companies.[37] He could find no examples of any such collusion being successful and cites two major reasons for this failure. First, he argues, the U.S. antitrust laws are sufficiently strictly operated to restrict such collusion. At the same time the divisions between different sectors of capital, and even between the interests of different firms within one sector, restrict collaboration. Thus, when some U.S. steel firms agreed to raise prices and so break the Kennedy Administration wage and price guidelines, their position was undermined when other firms refused to comply.

McQuaid also finds no evidence of industrial companies threatening an investment strike as a means of influencing government. Similarly, Webber denies the existence of any examples in West Germany,[38] while Story mentions none in France[39] and my own work suggests few if any examples in Britain. In fact, one example sometimes cited in the British context, the case of Chrysler, seems singularly inappropriate. In this case the British government gave aid to Chrysler for political reasons; certainly the Chrysler Corporation did not force the government to give aid and indeed appeared willing at first to give the corporation to the British government in order to reduce its problems and cut its losses.[40] Overall there are probably isolated examples of the operation of, or threat of, investment strikes, but such threats do not appear to play the major role assigned to them by structuralists.

There are however numerous examples of the type of beauty contest I referred to earlier. Harris, for example, cites the case of Ford Europe, which

> deliberately trailed its coat before successive European governments in order to stimulate their rivalries in offering concessions for a new car plant. Indeed, it laid down a minimum "asking price" — a subsidy of 35 percent of the proposed investment of 450 million dollars, exemption from duties due on imported equipment, subsidies for training the workforce, cuts in local taxes, guaranteed infrastructural provision, and loans at preferential interest rates from state banks.[41]

As *The Economist* commented at the time, "This is how one big company's careful gamesmanship shows up the structure of grants, loans, tax holidays, interest subsidies and other promises and caresses that underlie so much of Western Europe's big investment schemes these days."[42]

In fact, Harris goes on to indicate the scale of government incentives involved in these beauty contests when he points out:

> For Ford's Bridgend engine plant — costing £180 million — the company was originally said to have recouped some £100m from the British Government, or roughly £35,000 per job created in terms of public assistance; subsequently it emerged that the British Government had contributed £140 million to the final costs of the plant, or 78 percent of the total investment.[43]

Large companies thus do pressure governments into offering incentives for them to locate in their countries, but such pressure hardly appears to involve the threat of an investment strike. Rather, once a company has decided to invest in a particular region (e.g., western Europe, or the United States) it can make it known that it intends to invest and then stand back and wait for offers. This practice indicates, of course, major power as well as a very profitable piece of gamesmanship.

Despite such evidence, McQuaid's analysis seems to me to stress a more important point, namely that it is the need to maintain "business confidence" that is the major constraint on government in this area. In this regard the Kennedy Administration became increasingly concerned about the views of businessmen who disliked the Keynesian policies to which Kennedy was initially committed. In 1962, therefore, the Administration introduced new tax proposals to placate business. As McQuaid argues:

> [the view of business] came to have a powerful influence upon the way in which the Democratic administration's tax cut proposals were drawn up, legitimized, and eventually passed into law. Big businessmen clearly wanted Kennedy to act like a conservative Republican, and act like one he did, dressing his Keynesian program in every scrap of conservative clothing available.[44]

The crucial point is that concessions are made to preserve business confidence because the interests of business or capital are seen as compatible with, indeed to some identical with, the national interest. Here we return to what Lindblom calls the manipulation of volitions, or what a modern Marxist might call the hegemonic domination of capital.

The non-use of investment strikes by capital against government is not surprising. As we shall see in the next section, the location and relocation decisions of companies seem much more influenced by factors other than the availability of grants/incentives. What is more, as labour costs appear to be a major factor in location decisions, any threat of reduced investment is more likely to be used against trade unions than against government.

The Role of Incentives in Investment Decisions

I shall be concerned in what follows with three basic investment decisions: whether to invest at all; which international region to invest in, which I shall call the interregional decision; and the particular location of the investment within the region, the intraregional decision. The literature reviewed gives a fairly clear general picture of how decisions are reached, although with significant variations.

Demand factors are much more important than cost factors as far as the first two decisions are concerned, although I shall argue that cost factors, especially labour costs, may be becoming an increasingly important consideration in the interregional decision. However cost factors, especially labour costs and to a lesser extent government incentives, play a more important role in the intraregional decision.

The OECD Economic Policy Committee (EPC) recently produced a study dealing with the investment decisions of companies regardless of whether the investments considered were domestic or foreign, and this review is reported at some length in the OECD's later analysis of the importance of government incentives, *Investment Incentives and Disincentives and the International Investment Process*.[45]

The EPC reached three major conclusions:

- Expected output is by far the main determinant of productive investment.
- Investment incentives do have a direct impact on investment, although it is limited in comparison to the impact of expected market growth.
- In particular, if an investment incentive is a temporary one, it affects mainly the timing of investment expenditure, without a lasting significant effect on the level of capital stock, and does so particularly during periods in which demand expectations are favourable.[46]

The EPC review is based almost exclusively on studies using aggregate data and regression analysis. Studies which use a survey approach, however, asking company executives which factors influence their investment decisions, have reported similar results. Indeed Eisner and Lawler, in an article which reviewed survey-based studies of the importance of tax incentives in the United States and compared the results with those obtained by studies using aggregate data, found that:

> survey responses have indicated only modest effects of tax measures designed to stimulate, or discourage, capital expenditure. . . . Each dollar of loss or gain in taxes appeared to generate only minor compensating capital expenditure.[47]

Overall then, as far as the basic decision as to whether to invest is concerned, demand factors are clearly by far the most important. Similar results have been found by those studies which have examined the interregional investment decision. If there is sufficient profitable demand for a product in the United States, for example, then in many cases a company will invest there in order to meet that demand. Of course if cost factors mean that it is more profitable to supply a market from elsewhere, then a company may invest, or reinvest, at home or in a third country. The OECD study confirms this view at least in the period up to 1974: "A large number of studies . . . indicate that the foremost among determinants of inward foreign direct investment is the attraction of the market."[48]

However in this period, as far as cost factors are concerned, labour costs appear to be more important than government incentives particularly if we consider studies that concentrate upon developing countries. The OECD study claims that "while the evidence from general studies concerning the role of the supply of cheap labour has been weak, the results of some time series and cross-country analysis focussing on developing countries have pointed to a strong role for this factor."[49] Continuing, it argues: "In most available empirical studies, and in particular those concerning developing countries, host government incentives to investment appear to play a lesser role than the other factors [demand and labour costs]."[50]

Thus labour costs play an important role in interregional decisions, especially if it is feasible for production to be located in a developing country, and if labour-intensive industry and world markets are involved. Such circumstances may be becoming more frequent. Thus, while Frobel et al. show that most West German investment goes to developed countries, where a market for the products exists, they also indicate that an increasing amount of investment goes to newly industrializing countries (NICs) and particularly to free production zones.

Free production zones are industrial estates established by the governments of developing countries for TNC manufacturing plants that produce goods for export. These zones offer the TNCs cheap labour, stringent labour legislation, subsidies, and unrestricted repatriation of profits. As far as Frobel et al. are concerned, capital is relocating in developing companies when it can, that is, when transport and communication costs do not make it prohibitive to do so and when skilled workers are not required. It is relocating largely because of the high average number of hours worked and the low wages in these countries. For example, in 1979 the average number of hours worked in the garment and textile industry was 39 in West Germany, 37 in the United States, 48 in Hong Kong and 52 in South Korea. At the same time the hourly rate for a seamstress was DM10 in West Germany, DM9 in the United States, DM1 in Malaysia, and DM0.9 in South Korea.[51]

The picture is well summed up in a report cited by Frobel et al.:

> Despite significant advances, the technology of apparel production is still relatively simple and investment in fixed capital is low compared to most other industries. Lightweight and small, even 500 sewing machines can be transported more easily than a steel furnace or an auto-assembly line; an apparel plant can be dismantled and reassembled elsewhere in a very short time, leaving virtually no fixed capital behind. . . . The shift to predominantly unskilled workers has ended the industry's dependence on a dwin-

dling supply of skilled labour in the Northeast. . . . The functional separation of production from entrepreneurial tasks allows for the geographic separation as well. Certain functions performed by the jobber require skilled labour (designers, pattern markers, cutters etc.) and proximity to markets. Meanwhile the sewing and finishing stages of production, involving 95% of the total workforce, can be located in far-flung regions or countries.[52]

In essence the conclusions of Frobel et al. do not necessarily contradict the OECD analysis, for as we saw the OECD report argued that labour costs were more important for companies producing for a world market from developing countries. However the implication of the study of Frobel et al. is that labour costs are more important as a determinant of investment than the OECD credit, a fact reflected in the rapid growth of investment by transnational corporations in NICs, and that their importance is increasing.

This last point is particularly interesting as it appears to contradict the OECD's view. The OECD study certainly acknowledges that changes since 1974 have affected the situation:

And indeed, the apparent recently heightened cost sensitivity of international investment decisions in the present context of less buoyant market prospects, increased economic uncertainty and narrowing technological gaps among major firms, is an example of the important adjustments in the strategy of firms that have been progressively taking place since 1974.[53]

However the implication is that during this later period government incentives rather than labour costs have played an increasing role in interregional investment decisions. Indeed the study quotes favourably the views of BIAC (an international employers' association):

BIAC's contribution tends by and large to put more emphasis on the role of incentives and disincentives in international investment location decisions than the studies of a similar nature referred to above. This higher emphasis may stem from the fact that the evidence on which this contribution is based is more recent than that considered by these studies, the latter concerning mainly the pre-1974 period, or longer periods including that period, but not specifically the post-1974 context.[54]

While it appears true that cost factors have grown in importance in the post-1974 period, the OECD study probably places too much emphasis on government incentives and insufficient emphasis on labour costs in that later period.

Certainly the evidence I have already reviewed suggests that capital has become increasingly international and flexible. What is more, Gaffikin and Nickson's study of the English West Midlands gives ample evidence of the move of British multinationals to NICs. Their data on Dunlop, an integrated manufacturer of rubber goods, is particularly revealing. The sales of overseas subsidiaries as a share of Dunlop's world sales increased from 61 percent in 1977 to 67 percent in 1982. During the same period the profitability per employee increased substantially in Africa (from £1,000 to £2,444) and Asia/Australasia (from £955 to £3,400) while it fell dramatically in Britain (from a profit of £625 to a loss of £400 per employee).[55] This pattern both reflects, and has reflected upon, investment which has grown in overseas subsidiaries and fallen in Britain. As Gaffikin and Nickson say: "Dunlop's decision to increase its investment in the developing countries is based upon the realization that the company can obtain a much higher return on capital from the exploitation of cheap labour in those countries."[56] Indeed, this fact was clearly reflected in a television appearance by a senior Dunlop manager who said: "The thing you've got to be careful about when you talk is saying you've come here purely to exploit the natives. Well, that isn't really true because we're only an employer among many."[57]

Of course the work of Gaffikin and Nickson could be viewed as too particular, in that it deals solely with one area of Britain, or too superficial, in that its purpose is polemical rather than academic. However their findings are reinforced by the work of Andreff.[58] He shows that direct investments in LDCs grew from U.S.$32.8 billion in 1967 to U.S.$89.3 billion in 1978. Of this investment, 55 percent goes to the NICs, with no less than 15.1 percent being received by Brazil.[59] Andreff also indicates that while the overall rate of profit on investment abroad by U.S. multinationals in 1979 was 20.5 percent, it was 18.0 percent in developed countries and 29.4 percent in NICs.[60] There appears little doubt that a major reason for this higher level of profitability is low labour costs.

Despite all this it is when intraregional investment decisions are considered that cost factors become relatively more important than incentives. As the OECD study concluded, "incentives have a more important impact on the choice of location of investment at an intraregional [rather than an interregional] level."[61] It is at this level that the "beauty contests" identified earlier mostly operate.

Once again, however, the OECD study probably pays too little attention to labour costs, and here the work of Bluestone and Harrison is particularly relevant. They examine firms' decisions to invest in particular American states according to the incentives offered by those states. They identify ten factors that affect the investment plans and location decisions of companies, including transport costs, land costs, and government incentives/disincentives (involving the business climate, regulation, taxes and grants). There is little evidence, however, that government incentives play *any* important role in firms' location and investment decisions. In fact, Bluestone and Harrison claim that:

> location specialists find themselves in near-unanimous agreement on three points. First that investment inducements practically never do what they are

intended to accomplish. Second that even when they appear to entail no direct costs, they are enormously expensive in terms of foregone tax revenue. And third such subsidies end up being no more than windfall profits for the largest, most prestigious, and most powerful of all corporate enterprises.[62]

Thus, labour costs are perhaps the key factor influencing intraregional investment decisions. The available evidence on the differential pattern of investment in various U.S. states suggests that in the vast majority of cases firms invest in those states where unionization is less strong and wages are lower, regardless of the level of incentives offered. Indeed, Bluestone and Harrison quote with approval the conclusion of the *Wall Street Journal*: "Labour costs are the big thing far and away. Nine out of ten times you can hang it on labour costs and unionization."[63]

This review of the evidence on firms' investment decisions doesn't offer a great deal of support for the idea that government incentives are of sufficient importance to persuade firms to give up some of their privileges. They seem to play a role mainly after a company has decided to invest in a particular international region in effecting the intraregional location decision. Firms invest to protect or increase profitability, and in doing so they are most concerned with an assessment of demand. As far as costs are concerned, labour costs appear to have at least as much, and probably more, effect than government incentives on investment decisions.

Of course this immediately raises another question. If these conclusions are correct why do governments offer companies incentives on the present scale? One answer might be that governments are simply foolish, that they do not know that incentives play such a small role in firms' calculations. This seems unlikely, however, given the amount of expertise and information available to government. A second more plausible answer would be that because the stakes are so high — that is, given the high levels of unemployment and the possible effect they have on reelection chances — governments cannot afford not to offer incentives. After all, as we have seen, intraregional decisions are to some extent influenced by the level of incentives and in a given region many governments will be offering incentives. This situation was well summed up by a report of the Public Accounts Committee of the British House of Commons which said: "The Department of Industry pointed out [that] as virtually every country in the EEC offered a range of regional incentives, it was necessary to match what others were offering if mobile investment was to come to this country."[64]

In such circumstances, if a government does not offer incentives it will lose out to neighbouring governments unless it can offer relatively lower labour costs or more stringent labour legislation. Thus individual governments are in a weak position relative to large corporations. They can only hope to cooperate with one another to prevent or restrict "beauty contests" or bidding races. There have been efforts at such cooperation especially within the EEC, but they have not been notably successful.[65]

The Influence of Capital on Policy: The British Case

The previous section has indicated that capital enjoys a crucially privileged position in modern capitalist economies. Modern international
banks and corporations are highly flexible, and governments clearly
offer quite substantial incentives to attract capital investment from such
companies. However, international capital rarely uses its flexibility to
threaten government in order to extract incentives or concessions. This
is essentially because governments are not usually able to offer enough
inducement, in the form of grants or tax concessions, to make it worth
while for a company to invest if it wouldn't normally have done so. Thus
firms are more concerned with demand, and to a lesser extent with
labour costs, than with government incentives. The inference is that,
insofar as capital does exercise a constraint on government policy, it
does not do so in as simple a way as suggested by the structuralist
position.

In this section, I will develop this point by considering the capacity of
capital to influence government policy in those areas with which it is
most concerned. In fact, the section will raise two questions. Does
capital have significant influence over policy making in modern capitalist
economies? Insofar as it does exercise influence, how far does that
influence result from its structural position? The data presented deal
mainly with Britain, because space restricts the number of cases with
which I can deal in any detail. In any event, Britain does present an
interesting case for a number of reasons. First, it is a country in which
the economic crisis, measured in terms of almost every economic indicator, has been very deep, and one might expect a weakened capital sector
to have relatively little influence over government. Second, if most
authors are to be believed, Britain has a particularly strong trade union
movement; this fact again might lead one to expect capital to exercise
limited influence. Thus if I can find evidence of substantial influence by
capital over policy in Britain, where capital is relatively weak and
strongly opposed, then capital might be expected to be powerful elsewhere.

I shall concentrate on three areas of policy which are of particular
concern to capital and which have been particularly well researched in
Britain: industrial relations policy, wages policy, and industrial policy.

Authors who stress the dominant role of the trade unions in British
politics draw most of their material from studies on industrial relations
policy in the period 1960–80. Even in this area, however, the influence of
capital cannot be ignored. In the period immediately after World War II,
governments, particularly Labour governments, kept away from the
question of trade union reform, accepting it as a closed area. The pattern
changed in 1965, when the government appointed the Donovan Commission to investigate trade unions and employers' organizations. The Com-

mission's report in 1968 concluded that legislation was of limited utility in the field of industrial relations. However, despite this conclusion, the memory of the damaging strikes by the seamen in 1966 and in the docks in 1967 led the Labour Government to break with tradition, go beyond the report's recommendations, and move firmly into the area of industrial relations legislation.

Crouch sees the Labour Government's proposals, contained in the white paper "In Place of Strife," as a compromise between the managerial liberal collectivism of Donovan, and the state-corporatist proposals of industry and the Conservative opposition. He argues that the corporatist elements were designed as a "means of co-opting Labour's own organisations to assist the state and the employers in the control of labour."[66] In fact, the white paper proposed new measures for government intervention in the field of collective bargaining, including penal sanctions against offending trade unions and trade unionists. The proposal met with major opposition from within the trade union movement, the Labour party, the Parliamentary Labour Party (PLP), and sections of the cabinet led by James Callaghan. After a protracted struggle, the government was forced to withdraw its proposal and to accept the Trades Union Congress (TUC) assurances that it would deal with some of the problems voluntarily. While the efforts of the TUC in opposing the legislation were important, they were unlikely to have been successful without support from the PLP, although if such legislation had been passed they might successfully have opposed its administration.

When the Conservatives came to power in 1970 they were committed to trade union reform. The 1971 Industrial Relations Act was based upon a consultative document produced by the new Conservative government. The TUC was sent a copy of the green paper on October 5, 1970, and told that no consultation would be possible after November 13. Indeed, at a meeting between the TUC and Mr. Carr, the Employment Secretary, on October 13, the minister outlined the eight "basic pillars" of the new bill and declared them non-negotiable. The Government subsequently forced through its legislation, despite strong opposition from the Labour party inside Parliament, and the trade unions outside.

There can be no doubt that the 1971 Industrial Relations Act, together with the Code of Industrial Relations Practice which accompanied it, severely restricted the autonomy of trade unions and trade unionists. As Crouch argues:

In theory the Act marked a distinct increase in the monism of power in industrial relations by considerably reducing the circumstances in which workers could take industrial action and thereby exercise countervailing power. Certain constraints were also imposed on employers' powers in industrial conflict. . . . But it is clear . . . that the overall weight of the changes was to reduce workers' power to put pressure on employers.[67]

Although the trade unions failed to amend the legislation, they effectively restricted its implementation. As Michael Moran shows, the TUC advised affiliated unions not to register under the Act and not to cooperate with the National Industrial Relations Court (NIRC), and to attend its proceedings only when an action was brought against them.[68] The strategy proved so successful that by the end of 1972 the legislation was little used. Nevertheless, Moran makes an important point, which is worth emphasizing. The unions' opposition to the legislation was greatly helped by the fact that large companies and employers' organizations did not use its provisions for fear of damaging relations with employees.

During this period of confrontation, relations between the trade unions and the Labour party improved substantially. The trade unions sought and achieved a commitment from the party to repeal the Industrial Relations Act when it returned to power. Indeed, this commitment was a crucial element in the Social Contract between the TUC and the Labour party, and was fulfilled when the minority Labour Government put through the Trades Union and Labour Relations Act of 1974. This Bill, however, was emasculated by the Opposition in the House of Commons and the House of Lords. The trade unions could hardly be said to have made a positive gain; it was the trade unions' opposition to the administration of the original Act that was significant. Nevertheless, the Labour Government subsequently did make significant concessions to the trade unions in the field of industrial relations with the passage of the 1975 Employment Protection Act and the 1976 Trade Union and Labour Relations (Amendment) Act.

Thus for the first time unions were exercising a positive influence on policy. However, even here one or two qualifications need to be raised. Although the Amendment Act repealed the ban on the closed shops imposed by the 1971 act, it did little more than return the situation to the position prior to 1971. At the same time many employers favoured the establishment of closed shops as the basis of a more disciplined work force. Indeed, this legislative development cannot simply be viewed as a major concession to the trade unions against the wishes of capital. In addition, while the 1975 Employment Protection Act did improve the employment rights of trade unionists, and while the 1974 Health and Safety at Work Act brought about other improvements in workers' conditions, there is some evidence that the acts are being administered in a way that favours employers.

Boothman and Denham's analysis of the operation of the industrial tribunals is particularly relevant here.[69] Industrial tribuals have been operating in Britain for more than 15 years, and with respect to claims for unfair dismissal for over 10 years, and it is sometimes claimed that the legislation that established them represented a considerable gain for the TUC. However, Department of Employment figures indicate that in that 10 years there have been 3 million dismissals and only 40,000 claims for unfair dismissal (less than 1 percent). Moreover, 60 percent of these claims are resolved at the conciliation stage either because they are withdrawn or because a low cash settlement, under £200, is agreed. In addition, of the claims that are proceeded with, 70 percent are dismissed, and only 10 percent of the cases are ultimately deemed to involve unfair dismissal. Sixty percent of the compensation awards are less than £500 and only 1 percent are in excess of £4,000. In summary then, in only 4 in 10,000 of the cases brought do employers have to pay substantial damages. I have no figures on the costs to employers of defending themselves before the tribunals, but it is difficult in the light of this evidence to believe that employment protection legislation has been enormously expensive to employers.

Boothman and Denham's subsequent detailed empirical analysis involves a study of all reported cases of those decisions taken by tribunals on claims for unfair dismissal in connection with trade union membership or activities between 1974 and 1980. In particular they were concerned to analyze the justifications of their decisions given by the tribunals. Their conclusion was that "the content of discussions frequently suggested that the Industrial Tribunals' and the Employment Appeal Tribunals' theorizing may be subordinated to an ideological support for managerial prerogatives."[70] In other words, the decisions of tribunals are most often underpinned by a strong pro-management ideological background. As we shall see later, this conclusion rather neatly parallels the findings of Crouch in the area of wages policy.

Overall, then, it is evident that the trade unions have been successful in restricting the ability of governments to pass and administer legislation in the field of industrial relations. However, the legislation proposed in 1968–69 and the legislation passed in 1971 were designed to restrict the powers of the trade unions and strengthen the position of management. Subsequently unions achieved positive concessions from a Labour government in the 1960s and 1970s. In concluding, Crouch sees these developments either as a move toward corporatism, where unions are incorporated into the process in order to help control the work force, or as an increase in the power of the unions, to put them on a more equal footing with management. He regards the former analysis as more accurate, but in either case he still sees the unions occupying a subordinate position.

The subordination of the unions has been confirmed by legal developments since the election of a Conservative Government under Margaret Thatcher in 1979. The Thatcher Government has introduced three pieces of legislation that significantly restrict the autonomy of unions and thus strengthen the position of management in negotiations. The 1980 Employment Act restricted picketing and the closed shop, and removed maternity grants from workers in smaller companies. The 1982 Employment Act further restricted the closed shop and instituted changes in the legal provisions on strikes and trade union immunity. Subsequently the 1984 Trades Union Act has required secret ballots for the election of union officials and before a strike can be called.

Obviously the field of wages policy is one of the main areas with which both capital and labour have been concerned. After a major analysis of prices and incomes policy in Britain between 1945 and 1967, Dorfman concluded: "The most salient points about the TUC's performance since 1945 have been that its power has been limited and that it has had only negative influence on economic policy, especially wages policy."[71]

Indeed, although the Labour Government had committed itself to free collective bargaining in the 1966 election, and this policy had been endorsed by the unions, the TUC had to accept a statutory wages policy after 1966. Furthermore, Crouch argues that the activity of the National Board for Prices, which interpreted wages policy after 1964, was directed largely toward increasing control by management. He points out:

> The Board fully recognised that workers and management had distinctive and possibly conflicting interests. It thus accepted the rights of management and workers to see themselves at two "sides" of industry, but accepted this in such a way that management was the dominant partner since it was the party most completely identified with the common goal of increased productive efficiency.[72]

In this period, therefore, the incomes policy was imposed upon the unions by government and operated by the NBPI largely in the interests of management. Needless to say such developments were not opposed by management.

When the Conservative party subsequently came to power in 1970, it was committed to a reduction of government intervention in the economy and therefore to a voluntary prices and incomes policy. However, despite the introduction of tripartite and later multipartite talks on a voluntary policy, the government continued to listen to economists, notably with the Treasury, advocating statutory controls which were supported by capital. A statutory policy was introduced in 1972 and lasted until the February 1974 election. Once again the unions failed to achieve their main policy objective — free collective bargaining. Although the Conservative government wound up the NBPI, it established a Pay Board in its place. What is more, as Crouch argues, the Pay Board fulfilled a similar function: "It was clearly an attempt at re-establishing managerial authority by reducing the scope for workers' bargaining pressure . . . and sought achievement of this through strategies of involvement of unions and work-people in order to generate consensus."[73]

The unions failed to influence the Conservative government's policy, and that policy was hardly administered in their interest. However one union, the National Union of Miners, refused to adhere to stage three of the incomes policy. Against the background of the oil crisis and because of some inept political judgments, the Miners had succeeded in undermining the policy when Mr. Heath called a general election, which he lost.

The Labour party came back to office in 1974 committed to the Social Contract and to a voluntary incomes policy. Initially, the trade unions and the Labour party entered a loose agreement on wages policy. Subsequently agreement was reached on three phases in 1975, 1976 and 1977 which proved remarkably successful in restricting wage levels before the policy collapsed in the winter of 1978–79. However, the period from 1972 until 1978 was marked, as both Crouch and Panitch[74] argue, by the concerted attempts by governments to give tripartite planning machinery a substantive role in both policy formation and the control of organized labour.

When the Conservatives came to power in 1979 they were committed to free collective bargaining. However, the period since then has been marked by a major increase in unemployment, which has done a great deal to constrain wage claims in the private sector. At the same time the government has sought to control wages in the public sector by operating a "cash limits" policy. This means that the government can control wages indirectly, as we can see if we take its dealings with local authorities as an example. Here the government will allow a limited amount to cover wage increases in the annual grant it gives local authorities. The local authority will subsequently negotiate as an employer with the trade unions, but if it concedes higher increases than the government's norm, the excess has to be met from elsewhere in the authority's budget. Hence the government can claim to support responsible free collective bargaining while clearly restricting it.

The overall pattern again appears clear. The trade unions throughout the period would have preferred to see the reestablishment of free collective bargaining. Instead, they consistently saw the establishment of statutory, or "strong" voluntary policies which, as Crouch shows, have been operated in a way calculated to strengthen the position of management. This is hardly a record that suggests that the unions have more influence on wages policy than has capital.

So far we have considered two areas in which capital and labour are opposed and where one might have expected labour to exercise more influence. However, there are other areas in which it is evident that government is willing to make concessions to capital in order to encourage business confidence. Business confidence, of course, is a vague term, but governments' attempts to encourage it are often clearly reflected in policy decisions. The process is effectively illustrated in Marsh and Locksley's study of the power of capital in Britain, which presents a case study of industrial policy making.[75] In particular they show how the Labour Government's commitment to establishing or retaining business confidence led to the emasculation of the 1975 Industry Act.

In Opposition, the industrial policy subcommittee of the National Executive Committee (NEC) of the Labour party established a public enterprise working group to examine proposals to create a state holding company (a national enterprise board or NEB). The work of this group was underpinned by the ideas of Stuart Holland, then a lecturer at Sussex University but since 1979 a left-wing Labour MP. The policy they produced, which was subsequently approved after considerable debate and dispute in the committee, had two major radical elements. An NEB was to be established which would control the equity in the top 25 industrial companies, one major bank and two major insurance companies which it was planned to nationalize. In addition, all large companies were to be required to negotiate planning agreements with government about their plans for investment, employment, trade, and so on. These proposals, if enacted, would have significantly changed the nature of the British economic system, dramatically increasing the size of the public sector and restricting the autonomy of management in the private sector. The subsequent history of this proposal is revealing.

The proposal was enshrined in an Opposition policy paper entitled "The National Enterprise Board" published in April 1973. The document was subsequently considered by the NEC and included in the draft policy program which was presented to the 1973 Labour party conference. At the NEC meeting the so-called "25 companies clause" was the only one voted upon, but a proposal by the Chancellor of the Exchequer, Dennis Healey, to have it deleted was defeated. In fact this particular clause was to prove the first casualty because, although Holland's ideas were endorsed by the conference, opposition was mounting among the PLP leadership and particularly from the Prime Minister, Harold Wilson. Indeed, Wilson made his own view clear in the conference debate:

> My own view on the twenty-five companies proposal has been stated. I am against it, the Parliamentary Committee is against it. I will leave it with these words, that the Parliamentary Committee charged by the Constitution with the duty of sitting down with the Executive to select, from the Programme adopted by Conference, the items for including into the election Manifesto, entirely reserves its full constitutional rights on this matter, and there could be nothing more comradely than that.[76]

In fact Wilson got his way because the party manifesto published in January 1974 contained no specific reference to the takeover of 25 companies and only promised: "We shall create a powerful NEB with the structure and functions set out in Labour's Programme of 1973."[77]

The process of emasculation had begun but was to speed up after the election of a Labour Government. The initial moves seemed to suggest that radical legislation might result because Tony Benn and Eric Heffer, both strong supporters of the proposal, were appointed to the top two positions in the Department of Industry. In addition they immediately co-opted Stuart Holland onto a drafting committee established to produce a white paper. However, the situation changed rapidly. The major problem was that industry, particularly the Confederation of British Industry (CBI), the peak organization representing manufacturing industry, and the City strongly opposed the proposals. This opposition soon began to influence and then shape government thinking. Almost at once the Treasury produced a minute in which it argued that the NEB would inevitably be inflationary and too expensive to operate given the need to reduce public expenditure.[78] In response to this unrest Wilson took direct control of the Cabinet's public enterprise committee which was to consider the industry bill. At the same time the Chancellor obviously felt the need to attempt to reduce the CBI's fears when he told them: "the government has no intentions of destroying the private sector or encouraging its decay."[79] In similar vein at the Socialist International Conference in June, Wilson argued, "confidence demands that a clear frontier must be defined between what is public and what is private industry."[80]

Despite this, the CBI and the City were not reassured, and Aims of Industry (a proselytizing body for British industry) announced in July that it planned to spend up to £1.5 million on a pre-election campaign with the theme: "Say No to State Control." It was against this background that Benn's draft proposals were first circulated among, and then considered by, the Cabinet. Wilson's statement after that Cabinet meeting amply reflects the reasons for the modifications in policy which were made:

> The Cabinet have now agreed on the programme: I took charge of this operation several weeks ago, chaired all the meetings and the Cabinet on Friday accepted the draft which a small group of us put before it. . . . Above all, it meets my demand that it is clear and removes a great deal of uncertainty for business which has been created by public debate.[81]

The white paper entitled "The Regeneration of British Industry" finally appeared on August 15, 1974, reportedly after some 25 redrafts.[82] It was called by *The Economist* "a toned down electioneering version of earlier works"[83] and was certainly much less radical than the early proposals. There were two main differences between the white paper and the original policy paper. First, the NEB was no longer to hold equity in the top 25 companies but rather was to take over the government's current holding (for example in British Leyland) and also to hold equity in those companies assisted by government grants. In other words, it would operate in much the same way as did the old Industrial Reorganisation Corporation by aiding lame ducks and trying to encourage restructuring, but it would not be involved in the running of the profitable private sector. Second, the planning agreements, while still wide ranging, were to be voluntary rather than compulsory, and thus inevitably linked to the provision of government grants. Despite these changes however there was a new wave of protests from the Engineering Employers' Federation, the Aims of Industry, the Institute of Directors, and the CBI.[84]

When the bill was published at the end of January 1975, it followed broadly the content of the white paper but with one major change. Whereas the "Regeneration of British Industry" had devoted four pages to planning agreements, the bill dealt with them in one clause which guaranteed that firms voluntarily entering such agreements would not suffer a cut in their regional development grants.[85] In addition the NEB was given a limited initial finance of £700 million while the Secretary of State retained powers of tight control over the Board's investment decisions.[86] These changes had been worked out in the Cabinet's public enterprise committee and were thus strongly opposed by the party's left-wing MPs and union leaders.[87] Wilson's main aim throughout, however, was to preserve the confidence of the City and industry. Indeed, when he spoke at the CBI's annual dinner, he made it clear that industrial policy would remain under his personal direction and that he would be making all the appointments to the Board of the NEB.[88] Almost as if he felt the need to reemphasize his position, while the bill was in Standing Committee Wilson moved Tony Benn to the Department of Energy and replaced him with Eric Varley, a man with views on industrial policy similar to his own. The situation took on an almost comical aspect when Eric Heffer, who had resigned over the Common Market issue, led a number of left-wing Labour MPs who opposed the now emasculated bill in the later stages of its passage through the House of Commons.[89]

There is little doubt then that the bill was emasculated as it went through the policy-making process, but what does this tell us about the power of capital? Certainly we have seen that both the CBI and the City made direct representations opposing the proposals at all stages. Perhaps more significantly, however, the Prime Minister and the Chancellor consistently stressed the need to retain the confidence of both industry and the City. Indeed the preservation of confidence at a time when the pound was in trouble on the foreign exchanges was perhaps the major aim of the government. This appears to be another example of structural constraints at work — the interests of capital shaped government policy not mainly because of the direct representations by its agents but because their interests were identified with the national interest. As Coates says, the industrial policy changes were "part of the government's increasing concern to reassure private industry about its commitment to a healthy private sector, and about its willingness to subordinate its social programme to the gaining of greater industrial production."[90]

Assessment of the Structuralist Position

At the outset of the previous section I posed two questions about the influence of capital on government policy making. The case studies would suggest that capital does exercise significant influence over policy in Britain, and other researchers have confirmed this view after studying Germany,[91] France,[92] and the United States.[93] However, it is equally clear that in no sense is the government a simple agent of capital acting inevitably, consistently and completely in its own interests. In fact it is quite clear from this and many other studies that no general theory of the state is possible, and that one cannot expect a particular form of state, or particular policy outcomes, to be related in a straightforward and simplistic way to a particular pattern of economic relations. In other words the form and activities of the state are not simply determined by the dependence of the state on capital to ensure capital accumulation and economic prosperity.

Any analysis of the state must be historically specific and look at the precise nature of the relationships between capital and labour, and between both and the state. Lindblom in particular pays far too little attention to the relationship between capital and labour, concentrating upon the relationship between capital and the state as though in a sense it was independent of the relationship between capital and labour. However, Crouch's work in particular (and he is not a Marxist) indicates that the main consequence of the state's intervention in wages policy in Britain in the post-1945 period has been to reinforce both the dominance of management over workers and the strength of a pro-management ideology. The activities and actions of the state cannot be understood without an appreciation of the nature of capital/labour relations.

Overall, even the brief examination of three cases from one country presented here suggests that any analysis of the relationship between capital and the state has to be much more sophisticated than that presented by Lindblom and other structuralists. Clearly it needs to take account of the divisions that exist within capital, particularly those between domestic and international capital and industrial and banking capital. Lindblom however, fails to examine such divisions; yet it is clear both that they exist and that they affect the cohesion and influence of capital, and the reactions of the state. Indeed one factor in any understanding of the difference between capital/state relationships in Britain and those in France and Germany is the relative conflict between industrial and banking capital in Britain,[94] in contrast to their fusion in France[95] and West Germany.[96] At the same time any analysis also needs to take account of the differing degrees of organization and strength of labour in different countries. Historically labour has been organized, strong and relatively unincorporated in Britain and this situation again has influenced the activities of the state.[97]

While any analysis of the power of capital in modern capitalist democracies needs to be historically specific, nevertheless capital is clearly a crucial political force in such systems. What is more, the structuralists are right to emphasize that capital's power owes more to its privileged position in the economy than to simple interest group activity. However, many Marxists fail to appreciate that interest group activity does play some role, a pitfall which Lindblom at least avoids. Any analysis of the power of capital needs therefore to take account of this ideological dimension, the structural position of capital in the economy, and its interest group activity. Too much existing work ignores one or more of these aspects of the power of capital, which rarely uses direct threats of investment strikes or the like partly because it is seldom necessary to do so. The chief interest of capital — that is the creation of conditions in which continued and increased capital accumulation is possible — are most often seen as consistent with the national interest. To the extent that this is true, and of course in any historically specific analysis that is an open question, then this is the most important element in, and reflection of, the power of capital.

Notes

This study was completed in August 1984.

1. See R. Jessop, "The Capitalist State and the Rule of Capital: Problems in the Analysis of Business Associations," *West European Politics* 6 (April 1983): especially pp. 140–41.
2. C. Lindblom, *Politics and Markets* (New York: Basic Books, 1977). For a critique of Lindblom see D. Marsh, "Interest Group Activity and Structural Power: Lindblom's *Politics and Markets,*" *West European Politics* 6 (April 1983): 3–13.
3. Lindblom, *Politics and Markets*, p. 175.
4. Ibid., p. 179.
5. Ibid., p. 202.
6. Ibid., p. 178.
7. Ibid., p. 175.
8. Ibid., p. 349.
9. A. Campbell et al., *The American Voter* (New York: John Wiley, 1980), p. 135.
10. P. Converse, "The Concept of the Normal Vote," in *Elections and Political Order*, edited by A. Campbell et al. (New York: John Wiley, 1965), p. 15.
11. See D. R. Kiewiet, "Sociotropic Politics: The American Case," *British Journal of Political Science* (1981): 129–61, especially p. 152; D. A. Hibbs, "Economic Outcomes and Political Support for the British Governments among Occupational Classes," *American Political Science Review* (1982): 259–79, especially p. 269; D. A. Hibbs, "The Dynamics of Political Support for American Presidents among Occupational and Partisan Groups," *American Political Science Review* (1982): 312–32, especially p. 313.
12. See for example S. Kernell and D. Hibbs, "A Critical Threshold Model of Presidential Popularity," in *Contemporary Political Economy*, edited by D. Hibbs and H. Fassbender (Amsterdam: North-Holland, 1981), p. 65; M. Lewis-Beck, "Economic Conditions and Executive Popularity: The French Experience," *American Political Science Review* (1980): 306–23, especially p. 313.
13. See D. Hibbs and N. Vasilatos, "Macroeconomic Performance and Political Support in the United States and Great Britain," in *Contemporary Political Economy*, edited by D. Hibbs and H. Fassbender (Amsterdam: North-Holland, 1981), p. 36.
14. M. Mackuen, "Political Drama, Economic Conditions, and the Dynamics of Presidential Popularity," *American Journal of Political Science* (1983): 165–92, especially pp. 173–77.
15. Ibid., p. 187.

16. Data taken from British Gallup surveys.

17. B. Bluestone and B. Harrison, *Capital and Communities* (Washington, D.C.: The Progressive Alliance, 1980), pp. 104–5.

18. Ibid., chap. 2.

19. Ibid., p. 59.

20. F. Frobel, J. Heinrichs, and O. Kreye, *The New International Division of Labour* (Cambridge: Cambridge University Press, 1980).

21. F. Gaffikin and A. Nickson, *Jobs Crisis and the Multinationals* (Nottingham: Russell Press, 1984).

22. For an interesting critique of Frobel et al., see R. Jenkins, "Divisions over the International Division of Labour," *Capital and Class* 22 (1984): 28–57.

23. For a summary of the findings see Frobel, Heinrichs, and Kreye, *New International Division of Labour*, pp. 17–23.

24. Ibid., p. 21.

25. Gaffikin and Nickson, *Jobs Crisis*, pp. 54–58.

26. Ibid., p. 72.

27. Ibid., p. 71.

28. Bluestone and Harrison, *Capital and Communities*, pp. 50–58.

29. J. Coakley and L. Harris, *The City of Capital: London's Role as a Financial Centre* (Oxford: Blackwell, 1983), pp. 49–53.

30. Ibid., p. 52.

31. Ibid., p. 60.

32. Ibid., pp. 62–63.

33. Frobel, Heinrichs, and Kreye, *New International Division of Labour*, p. 194.

34. R. Muller, *Revitalizing America: Politics for Prosperity* (New York: Touchstone, 1980), pp. 25, 64.

35. Gaffikin and Nickson, *Jobs Crisis*, pp. 46–47.

36. Organization for Economic Co-operation and Development, *Transfer Pricing and Multinational Enterprises* (Paris: OECD, 1979).

37. K. McQuaid, *Big Business and Presidential Power* (New York: Morrow, 1982), especially chap. 6.

38. D. Webber, "A Relationship of 'Critical Partnership'? Capital and the Social-Liberal Coalition in West Germany," *West European Politics* 6 (April 1983): 61–86, especially pp. 71–74.

39. J. Story, "Capital in France: The Changing Pattern of Patrimony," *West European Politics* 6 (April 1983): 87–127.

40. See D. Coates, *Labour in Power* (London: Longmans, 1980).

41. Nigel Harris, *Of Bread and Guns* (London: Pelican, 1983), pp. 108–109.

42. *The Economist*, January 29, 1979, p. 73.

43. Harris, *Of Bread and Guns*, p. 109.

44. McQuaid, *Big Business and Presidential Power*, p. 216.

45. Organization for Economic Co-operation and Development, *International Investment and Multinational Enterprises* (Paris: OECD, 1983).

46. Ibid., p. 34.

47. R. Eisner and P.J. Lawler, "Tax Policy and Investment: An Analysis of Survey Responses," *American Economic Review* (1975), p. 209.

48. OECD, *International Investment*, pp. 38–39.

49. Ibid., pp. 39–40.

50. Ibid., p. 40.

51. Frobel, Heinrichs and Kreye, *New International Division of Labour*, pp. 136–37.

52. Ibid., p. 155.

53. OECD, *International Investment*, p. 43.

54. Ibid., pp. 42–43.
55. Gaffikin and Nickson, *Jobs Crisis*, pp. 115–21.
56. Ibid., p. 117.
57. Ibid., p. 119.
58. W. Andreff, "The International Centralization of Capital and the Re-ordering of World Capitalism," *Capital and Class* 22 (1984): 58–80.
59. Ibid., p. 75.
60. Ibid., p. 73.
61. OECD, *International Investment*, p. 52.
62. Bluestone and Harrison, *Capital and Communities*, p. 228.
63. Ibid., p. 188.
64. See OECD, *International Investment*, p. 53.
65. For a review of these attempts see J. Robinson, *Multinationals and Political Control* (London: Gower, 1983), especially pt. 2.
66. C. Crouch, *Class Conflict and the Industrial Relations Crisis* (London: Heinemann, 1977), pp. 161–62.
67. Ibid., p. 165.
68. M. Moran, *The Politics of Industrial Relations* (London: Macmillan, 1977).
69. F. Boothman and D. Denham, "Industrial Tribunals: Is There an Ideological Background?" *Industrial Relations Journal* (1981): 6–14.
70. Ibid., p. 10.
71. G. Dorfman, *Wage Politics in Britain* (London: Charles Knight, 1974), p. 145.
72. Crouch, *Class Conflict*, p. 108.
73. Ibid., p. 136.
74. L. Panitch, *Social Democracy and Industrial Militancy* (Cambridge: Cambridge University Press, 1976).
75. D. Marsh and G. Locksley, "Capital in Britain: Its Structural Power and Influence over Policy," *West European Politics* 6 (2) (April 1983): pp. 36–60.
76. For Harold Wilson's full views see *The Labour Party Annual Conference Report, 1973* (London: The Labour Party, 1973), pp. 160–70.
77. *Let's Work Together: Labour's Way Out of the Crisis* (London: The Labour Party, 1973), p. 6.
78. Details of the Treasury Minute in *The Times*, June 17, 1974.
79. Dennis Healy's speech reported in *The Times*, May 15, 1974.
80. Harold Wilson's speech reported in *The Times*, July 1, 1974.
81. *The Times*, August 5, 1974.
82. *The Regeneration of British Industry*, Command Paper 5710 (London: Her Majesty's Stationery Office, 1974).
83. *The Economist*, August 17, 1974, p. 73; see also *The Regeneration of British Industry*, paras. 8 and 23.
84. See *The Times*, August 29, 1974; September 6, 1974; September 20, 1974.
85. *Industry Bill, 1975* (London: Her Majesty's Stationery Office, January 1975), para. 21.
86. Ibid., paras. 8 and 10.
87. *The Times*, March 8, 1975.
88. *The Times*, May 21, 1975.
89. See D. Liston, "The Industry Act (1975) — A Personal Critique," *Poly Law Review* (1976): 42–48.
90. Coates, *Labour in Power*, p. 34.
91. Webber, "A Relationship of 'Critical Partnership'?"
92. Story, "Capital in France."
93. McQuaid, *Big Business and Presidential Power*.

94. See R. Jessop, "The Transformation of the State in Post War Britain," in *The State in Western Europe*, edited by R. Scase (London: Croom Helm, 1980).

95. Story, "Capital in France," p. 95.

96. Webber, "A Relationship of 'Critical Partnership'?" p. 79.

97. See D. Marsh and G. Locksley, "Labour: The Dominant Force in British Politics?" in *Pressure Politics*, edited by D. Marsh (London: Junction Books, 1983), pp. 53–82.

4

The State and Foreign Capital in the Advanced Industrial Capitalist Countries

LYNN KRIEGER MYTELKA

Foreign borrowing takes many forms, but the one that has attracted the most attention in the advanced industrial capitalist countries is direct foreign investment. This is partly due to the dramatic increase in U.S. direct investment abroad since World War II. More importantly, however, direct foreign investment has captured the public eye because, unlike bank loans or portfolio investment, it involves a measure of foreign control over the activities of domestic firms and this is believed to affect the autonomy of decision making in the economy as a whole.[1] Since economic and technological choices made in the private sector have wide ramifications for the distribution of gains within a society, the state, under certain circumstances, may be induced to intervene in the foreign investment process.

By mapping the changing patterns of direct foreign investment since 1960 and examining the policy response of various states, this study seeks to determine whether there is a link between investment flows and governmental attempts to regulate them. In the first section, we look at ten major countries in the Organization for Economic Co-operation and Development (OECD) as *recipients* of foreign investment. Behind this portion of the analysis is a set of hypotheses concerning the varied responses that states might make to changes in the level, sectoral concentration or costs of direct foreign investment. Where an economy has been highly penetrated by direct foreign investment, for example, yet such investment is perceived as vital to economic well-being, one would expect few attempts at regulation unless the costs of the foreign investment were seen by politically powerful groups in the society to be rising. Were the costs of direct foreign investment to remain at their previous level but economic conditions to worsen, these states, more-over, would most likely adopt incentives to increase the flow of foreign investment. Where the level or degree of sectoral penetration is increasing and foreign investment is not contributing effectively to the fulfillment of economic or social goals, then one might expect regulatory efforts to increase. Where rising unemployment and interest rates make job creation through domestic investment difficult, however, regulatory measures might well be relaxed so as to attract new foreign investment — whether or not such measures had discouraged direct foreign investment in the past. This is particularly likely in situations in which a regulatory thrust was initiated not by a government embarked on a socialist project but rather by one seeking a national solution to existing economic or social problems.[2]

In addition to looking at the ten major OECD countries as recipients of direct foreign investment, the first section examines changes in their role as capital *exporters*. These data are subsequently used to test the hypothesis that in major capital exporting countries states will tend to adopt liberal regimes toward incoming direct foreign investment for at least one of the following reasons: (a) those at the centre of policy making subscribe to a philosophy of economic liberalism; (b) the country is not a major recipient of direct foreign investment and thus policy makers face none of the concerns over loss of decisional or technological autonomy expressed where the economy is highly penetrated; or (c) because, in a pragmatic vein, decision makers simply fear retaliation in kind.

The second section of this paper documents the multiplicity of measures currently being taken by states in the major OECD countries to influence the foreign investment process. These policies range from explicit or implicit measures to channel the inflow of foreign capital to preferred sectors and regions, to regulate its contribution to the domestic economy, to induce an increase in the inflow of foreign investment, or to affect the terms on which domestic firms compete with foreign companies.

The next section presents case studies of Australia and France, both of which have relatively high levels of direct foreign investment, and each of which has adopted explicitly regulatory policies to channel foreign investment into desired activities and locations. Space considerations, however, preclude a similar study of countries, such as Belgium, which has a highly centralized system for channelling new investment through the use of inducements such as tax concessions and grants rather than regulatory mechanisms.

Despite the longevity of the inducement and regulatory mechanisms adopted by states in the advanced industrial capitalist countries, no systematic studies have been undertaken to determine the extent to which they have served to accomplish the goals used to justify their implementation, such as stimulating the inflow of new technology, increasing output, employment or exports, or promoting economic diversification and regional balance. This study is able to make a few qualified observations only with regard to the impact of regulatory activity on the inflow of new direct foreign investment. Quite obviously, in-depth analysis of the impact of state intervention on the foreign investment process, given current debates within Canada about the nature of a foreign investment review agency, must be undertaken. It is one of the conclusions of this paper that such an analysis be a first order priority.

Changing Patterns of Direct Foreign Investment

Over the past two decades real inflows of direct foreign investment (DFI) into the advanced industrial capitalist countries have risen steadily — doubling during the 1960s from an annual average of U.S.$3,976 million in the years 1960–62 to an annual average of $8,151 million during the period 1969–71 and more than doubling during the 1970s (Table 4-1). Figures on direct foreign investment inflows also demonstrate the increasing propensity among the ten major OECD countries covered in this study to invest in each other's markets. These ten countries absorbed over 60 percent of the world's total direct foreign investment inflow in 1970–72 and over 70 percent of this total in 1978–80.[3]

Among the ten countries, however, there have been considerable differences in the amount of direct foreign investment each has received. This variability across countries and over time is attributable to many factors. As part of their industrialization policies, Japan[4] and Sweden,[5] for example, have through legislation virtually excluded direct foreign investment since early in this century. The flow of direct foreign investment to these countries is thus quite low, although each has benefited from increased inflows of new technology through a variety of inter-firm agreements for joint product and process design and development, which do not, however, involve an exchange of equity.[6]

One of the most salient changes in the distribution of direct foreign investment among these countries, however, is the emergence of the United States as the principal host country. Clearly the size of the U.S. market is a factor. But prior to 1969 an overvalued U.S. dollar had served as a disincentive to European and Japanese firms which, having recovered from the destructive effects of World War II, might otherwise have invested in the United States.[7] As direct investment between members of the European Economic Community was fully liberalized for EEC firms as early as 1962, the flow of European foreign investment was directed primarily to the Community itself and from certain of these countries, notably France, to former colonial markets in Africa.[8] Changes in the exchange rate in the early 1970s coupled with growing protectionist pressures pushed a number of foreign firms to undertake major investments in the United States in this latter period. As Table 4-1

TABLE 4-1 Direct Foreign Investment Inflows: Three-Year Averages 1960–80 (millions of 1975 U.S. dollars[a])

	1960–62		1963–65		1966–68		1969–71		1972–74		1975–77		1978–80	
	$	%	$	%	$	%	$	%	$	%	$	%	$	%
Australia	652	16.2	859[b]	17.4	845	13.5	1,238	15.3	985	7.6	823	8.1	1,392	7.6
Belgium-Luxembourg	n.a.	n.a.	243[c]	5.1	329	5.3	474	5.8	868	6.8	977	9.5	1,053	5.8
Canada	1,005	24.9	574	11.8	1,027	16.3	1,138	14.0	911	7.0	484	4.8	887	4.8
France	374	9.3	568	11.6	446	7.1	679	8.3	1,420	11.1	1,460	14.2	2,228	12.2
West Germany	328	8.1	750	15.5	1,042	16.5	959	11.9	2,414	18.4	823	8.0	977	5.3
Japan	75	1.9	151	3.1	80	1.3	172	2.1	129	1.0	121	1.1	128	0.7
Netherlands	64	1.6	182	3.7	390	6.3	681	8.4	948	7.3	544	5.2	787	4.4
Sweden	87[d]	2.2	120	2.5	185	2.9	162	2.0	85	0.7	52	0.5	108	0.6
United Kingdom	856	21.2	874	17.9	675	14.4	1,190	14.7	1,876	14.5	1,607	15.7	2,841	15.8
United States	592	14.7	561	11.5	1,024	16.4	1,458	17.5	3,268	25.7	3,366	32.8	7,794	42.9
Total listed countries	3,976	100.0	4,434	100.0	6,265	100.0	8,151	100.0	16,118	100.0	17,303	100.0	18,197	100.0

Source: IMF, *Balance of Payments Yearbook: divers volumes* (Washington, D.C.: IMF).

a. Deflated using U.S. GNP implicit price index (1975 = 100) as published in OECD, *Main Economic Indicators: Historical Statistics,1960–79* (Paris: 1980) and OECD, *Main Economic Indicators* (Paris: Oct. 1983).

b. August of 1964 only.

c. 1965 only.

d. 1962 only.

n.a. = not available.

indicates, the U.S. share of real inflows of direct foreign investment from the major OECD countries rose from less than 15 percent in the 1960s to over 40 percent in the period 1978–80 and appears to be averaging close to 60 percent in the early 1980s (see the Appendix). At the same time, the stock of EEC direct investment in the Community rose from 35 percent of that of the United States in 1970 to 80 percent in 1978, with West Germany, the Netherlands and the United Kingdom emerging as the major capital exporting countries within the EEC and West Germany, France and Belgium becoming the principal recipients of intra-EEC direct investment.[9]

Finally it should be noted that for a number of these countries there have been dramatic break points in the inflow of direct foreign investment at different points in time (see Appendix and Table 4-1). In 1963–65, for example, while the inflow of direct foreign investment halved in Canada, it more than doubled in West Germany and almost doubled in France. In 1966–68, in contrast, the inflow of new direct foreign investment doubled in Canada, nearly doubled in West Germany but rose and/or fell elsewhere by far less dramatic amounts. The period 1969–71 was a break point for Australia when direct foreign investment inflows rose by 47 percent, but they declined to their previous levels in 1972–77, rising dramatically again in 1978–80. The effect of the oil price rise of 1973 and the increased liquidity of the Eurodollar market are evident in the 1972–74 period when new inflows of direct foreign investment surged from an annual average, in 1975 U.S. dollars, of $959 million in 1969–71 to $2,414 million in 1972–74 in West Germany, from $679 million (1969–71) to $1,420 (1972–74) in France and from $1,458 million (1969–71) to $3,268 million (1972–74) in the United States.

In order to appreciate the extent to which penetration of host markets by multinational corporations (MNCs) was maintained and in some instances increased during the 1970s, changes in the stock of foreign investment abroad and its sectoral location must also be examined. Changes in the stock of foreign investment may be financed not only by new inflows but by reinvested earnings and loans on the domestic market. For the major capital exporting countries, the average annual rate of increase in their stock of foreign investment abroad rose steadily during the global economic crisis from an average annual increase of 10.5 percent in the period 1967–71 to 11.2 percent in 1971–75 and 12 percent in 1975–78.[10] The growing stocks of capital abroad thus suggest that an important element in the ability of MNCs to adjust lay in their greater access to credit — mobilizing domestic resources in host countries and borrowing on international markets — and their access to the earnings of their subsidiaries in these host markets. "In the case of American firms, reinvested earnings represented an amount twice as large on average as the outflow of foreign investment from the United States in the period 1970–80. For British firms the ratio is 1.6."[11] Similarly, over 80 percent of the new foreign investment received by the United States went toward the acquisition of existing firms and not to the creation of new enterprises.[12] Multinational corporations have thus pursued a policy of adjustment similar to that of domestic firms; that is, they have tended to "shorten their time horizons" and reorient their investments toward restructuring and acquisitions.[13] This has had an impact on levels of industrial concentration and the degree of MNC penetration in key industries, as we shall see below.

Table 4-2 presents data on the stock of direct investment in selected OECD countries by economic sector. Although these data were available only to 1978, the trend away from investment in resource industries and

TABLE 4-2 Stock of Direct Investment in Selected Developed Market Economies, by Economic Sector

Host Country and Sector	1971–73[a]		1974–78[a]	
	U.S.$ Millions	%	U.S.$ Millions	%
Canada				
Total industry	27,857	100	42,903	100
Extractive[b]	10,601	38	14,564	34
Manufacturing	11,044	40	17,580	41
Services	6,212	22	10,759	25
Finance	3,120	11	5,443	13
West Germany				
Total industry	9,155	100	29,172	100
Extractive[c]	1,676	18	3,753	13
Manufacturing	5,792	63	12,261	59
Services	1,687	18	8,158	28
Finance & insurance	506	6	2,648	9
Italy				
Total industry	6,155	100	5,764	100
Extractive[d]	955	16	708	12
Manufacturing	3,337	54	3,315	58
Services	1,863	30	1,741	30
Banking & insurance	62	1	1,130	2
Japan[e]				
Total industry	851	100	1,920	100
Extractive	—	—	—	—
Manufacturing	756	89	1,539	80
Services	95	11	381	20
Netherlands				
Total industry	7,506	100	11,884	100
Extractive	—	—	—	—
Manufacturing	5,488	73	8,303	70
Services	2,018	27	3,581	30
Banking & insurance	425	6	773	7

TABLE 4-2 (cont'd)

Host Country and Sector	1971–73[a]		1974–78[a]	
	U.S.$ Millions	%	U.S.$ Millions	%
United Kingdom				
Total industry	13,827	100	22,277	100
Extractive[f]	4,084	29	6,811	31
Manufacturing	8,118	59	11,040	49
Services	1,625	12	4,426	20
United States				
Total industry	13,914	100	40,931	100
Extractive[f]	3,139	23	7,885	19
Manufacturing	6,722	48	16,289	40
Services	4,053	29	16,657	41
Finance & insurance	2,553	20	5,179	13

Source: United Nations, Centre on Transnational Corporations, *Salient Features and Trends in Foreign Direct Investment* (New York: 1983) Doc. No. UN/ST/CTC/14, pp. 48–50.

Note: The extractive sector includes agriculture, mining and petroleum unless otherwise indicated.

a. Years for Canada are 1971 and 1976; for West Germany, 1972 and 1978; for Italy, 1972 and 1976; for Japan, 1971 and 1977; for the Netherlands, 1973 and 1976; for the United Kingdom, 1971 and 1974; and for the United States, 1971 and 1978.
b. Petroleum and mining only.
c. Agriculture and petroleum; mining and quarrying are classified under manufacturing.
d. Agriculture, mining and petroleum.
e. End of March of the year following the one indicated.
f. Petroleum only; mining and agriculture, if any, are included under services.
— = very little or no investment of this type.

to some degree in manufacturing and toward the service sector (banking, information processing, insurance, commerce), which has become much more pronounced, was already evident then. Data on inward direct investment flows by sector for countries not covered in Table 4-2 largely confirm these trends.[14] Thus in Australia, annual net flows of inward direct investment into the primary products sector fell from an average of 37.5 percent in 1966–69, to 32.9 percent in 1969–72, to 13.3 percent in 1973–75 and to 5.4 percent in 1976–78. As in Canada, inward foreign investment flows, however, increased in the manufacturing and service sectors. However, much of the manufacturing activity, it should be pointed out, consisted of raw materials processing. In Belgium, where new inward foreign direct investment in manufacturing had represented between 86 and 92 percent of the total up to 1974, in the period 1975–79 it annually averaged only 56.1 percent of the total with the remainder going to the service sector. In France, the shift was somewhat less pronounced as the share of net flows of inward direct investment going to manufacturing declined from 45.9 percent in 1971–73, to 41.8 percent from 1974–76 and 35.4 percent in 1977–78, while the share going to services rose in these three time periods from 30.2 percent to 33.2 percent and up to 34.6 percent. The share of net flows of inward direct investment going to real estate also rose from 20.7 percent in 1971–73 to 20.9 percent in 1974–76 and to 25.3 percent in 1977–78.

Despite the general tendency of the share of new direct foreign investment in manufacturing to decline, as Table 4-3 demonstrates, there has been some evidence of increased concentration of foreign firms in the manufacturing sector. Partly because they "generally play only a relatively minor role in many of the crisis sectors . . ."[15] and partly because of their size, diversity, management, and access to technology, multinational corporations in a number of OECD countries were obliged to reduce employment to a lesser extent than were domestic firms. In Australia, Belgium, Canada and the United Kingdom this has led to a "growing penetration of multinational enterprises in the manufacturing industry . . . [as] the proportion of total manufacturing employment in enterprises with foreign ownership . . . increased, sometimes substantially, over the seventies. . . ."[16] Even more remarkable is the relatively steeper increase in the share of foreign firms in production in these and other OECD countries during this period. It is important to stress, however, that the degree of foreign control remains substantially different among these countries. Taking the number of foreign-controlled companies among the 50 largest corporations as an indicator of the relative importance of foreign ownership in the economy of OECD countries, we find that there are no foreign-controlled corporations at all among the top 50 firms in Japan, only one in Sweden, 2 each in the United States and the Netherlands, 7 in France, 10 in West Germany, 11 in the United Kingdom, and 16 in Canada.[17]

Two other observations with respect to the role of direct foreign investment in the advanced industrial countries need to be borne in mind as we examine the policy responses of OECD states toward inward direct investment. These are the contribution of direct foreign investment to economic growth and the cost of direct foreign investment inflows in relation to the longer term outflows of payments (dividends or other returns on the funds invested) from the host to the home country.

With respect to the advanced industrial countries, attempts to assess the impact of direct foreign investment are rendered especially difficult by the fact that "in relation to domestic capital formation . . . [direct foreign investment] is still quite small and there are so many other determinants of growth."[18] Nonetheless there are some important variations. Direct foreign investment contributed far more to the Canadian economy in the early 1960s than it has done during the years since 1963, when its contribution never rose above 4 percent of gross fixed capital formation and in several years (1976, 1981) was negative. Only in Austra-

TABLE 4-3 Share Represented by Enterprises or Establishments of Enterprises with Foreign Participation in Manufacturing

Country	Year	Cut-off Point	No. of Employees	Production	Profits	Assets
			(percentage)			
Australia[a]	1972	50	23.6	28.7	n.a.	n.a.
	1973	25	28.6	36.2	n.a.	n.a.
Belgium	1968	10	18.3	33.0	n.a.	n.a.
	1975	10	33.0	44.0	n.a.	n.a.
	1978	10	38.0	n.a.	n.a.	n.a.
Canada	1974	50	43.1[a]	51.1[a]	n.a.	53.9
	1975	50	44.3[a]	56.2	64.8	n.a.
	1977	50	n.a.	56.6	n.a.	n.a.
France[b,c]	1973	20	19.4	n.a.	n.a.	n.a.
	1975	20	19.0	27.8	29.4	n.a.
West Germany	1972	25	22.4	25.1	n.a.	n.a.
	1976	25	16.8	21.7[d]	n.a.	n.a.
Italy[e]	1977	50	18.3	23.8[d]	n.a.	n.a.
Japan	1973	25	2.0	3.8[f]	n.a.	n.a.
	1978	25	1.8	4.2	n.a.	n.a.
Sweden	1975	20	8.4	10.1	n.a.	n.a.
	1975	50	5.7	6.8	n.a.	n.a.
	1976	20	8.6	10.8	n.a.	n.a.
	1976	50	5.7	7.3	n.a.	n.a.
	1977	20	n.a.	n.a.	14.2	7.8
	1977	50	n.a.	n.a.	8.5	4.3
United Kingdom[a]	1971	50	10.3	14.2	n.a.	n.a.
	1973	50	10.8	15.3	n.a.	n.a.
	1975	50	12.4	18.7	17.9[g]	n.a.
	1977	50	13.9	21.2	22.5[g]	n.a.

Sources: OECD, *International Investment and Multinational Enterprises Recent International Direct Investment Trends* (Paris: 1981) Table 1, p. 38; OECD, Committee on International Investment and Multinational Enterprises, *Multinational Enterprises and the Structural Adjustment Process* (Paris: September 23, 1983) Annex, Table 9, p. 108.

Note: "Cut-off point" specifies the minimum percentage of foreign ownership for a firm to be included in the tabulations contained in this table; e.g., 50% implies that only firms with at least 50% foreign ownership are included.

a. Establishment-based data.
b. Including natural gas.
c. Excluding food industries.
d. Turnover.
e. Data on the basis of a survey of 1,079 corporations which represented on December 31, 1977, 2.4% of all corporations and 63.9% of total equity of existing corporations.
f. Sales.
g. Gross value added less wages and salaries.
n.a. = not available.

TABLE 4-4 Inflows of Direct Foreign Investment as a Percentage of Gross Fixed Capital Formation, 1960–81

	1960	1961	1962	1963	1964	1965	1966	1967	1968	1969	1970
Australia	7.1	4.2	6.5	6.5	6.6	n.a.	4.9	4.8	5.7	5.1	6.4
Belgium-Luxembourg	n.a.	n.a.	n.a.	n.a.	n.a.	2.3	2.1	3.3	3.5	3.3	3.5
Canada	7.1	5.4	4.6	2.4	1.9	3.5	4.5	3.9	3.2	3.5	4.3
France	0.8	1.1	1.3	1.1	1.5	1.2	0.9	1.0	0.5	0.8	1.3
West Germany	0.5	0.6	0.5	0.5	0.7	1.8	1.8	1.6	0.8	0.7	0.9
Japan	0.0	0.3	0.2	0.4	0.3	0.1	0.1	0.1	0.1	0.1	0.1
Netherlands	0.5	0.4	1.0	1.2	1.2	1.9	1.8	2.6	2.8	3.0	4.0
Sweden	n.a.	n.a.	0.9	1.4	0.6	1.3	1.9	1.3	1.3	1.7	1.1
United Kingdom	2.7	4.2	2.3	2.7	2.6	2.6	2.5	1.9	2.5	2.3	2.7
United States	0.3	0.3	0.3	0.2	0.3	0.3	0.3	0.5	0.5	0.7	0.8

	1971	1972	1973	1974	1975	1976	1977	1978	1979	1980	1981
Australia	7.4	6.6	0.8	7.2	2.1	4.8	5.0	6.5	5.9	6.6	6.0
Belgium-Luxembourg	4.7	3.8	6.2	8.4	6.6	5.5	7.7	7.8	5.8	6.9	6.9
Canada	4.0	2.5	2.8	2.5	1.8	-0.4	2.3	2.5	2.9	1.0	-4.0
France	1.0	1.1	1.7	2.5	2.0	1.2	2.2	3.0	2.3	2.6	1.9
West Germany	1.6	2.5	2.5	2.6	0.8	1.1	0.8	1.3	0.8	0.7	0.7
Japan	0.2	0.1	0.0	0.1	0.1	0.1	0.0	0.0	0.1	0.1	0.1
Netherlands	4.0	4.0	5.2	5.5	5.4	1.9	1.6	2.8	4.6	4.5	5.2
Sweden	0.8	0.6	0.6	0.6	0.5	0.0	0.5	0.4	0.6	1.2	0.8
United Kingdom	3.3	3.0	4.6	4.8	3.0	3.0	4.7	4.5	6.4	7.6	2.8
United States	0.2	0.4	1.1	1.8	1.0	1.5	1.1	2.0	2.6	2.3	4.4

Source: Calculated from DFI Inflows table, using gross fixed capital formation figures published in OECD, *National Accounts: Main Aggregates, 1950–78* (Paris: 1980), and OECD, *National Accounts: Main Aggregates, 1952–81* (Paris: 1983).
n.a.= not available.

lia, Belgium and the United Kingdom did foreign investment contribute more than 5 percent to gross fixed capital formation in the 1970s. This was a reflection, in part, of the severity of the global crisis, which was marked by a decreasing rate of productivity growth, increasing rates of inflation and unemployment, accelerated technological change, fundamental shifts in the structure of international competition, and the fall of domestic investment. Even then, as Table 4-4 reveals, this contribution only once rose above 8 percent.

Outflows of payments on direct foreign investment, however, rose steeply during this period (Table 4-5), generating concern in those countries that experienced structural balance of payments problems exacerbated by the impact of the economic crisis. It is important to remember, however, that policy responses to such difficulties will not be uniform, as the previous relationship of domestic capital to foreign capital, the intractability of existing economic structural problems, and prior policy initiatives all shape reactions to these new developments. Thus in Canada, pressures have risen for a liberalization of earlier foreign investment regulations in the hope of inducing new inflows of direct investment to offset increasng outflows.[19] In previously liberal Belgium, in contrast, greater attention is being paid to the need to obtain information from MNCs on proposed investment and disinvestment decisions, to devise industrial policy measures which stimulate domestic investment, including a greater role for state equity participation, and to safeguard workers' consultative prerogatives and income security in the face of plant closures.[20] Attention was particularly attracted in Belgium to the cost of direct foreign investment because the share of industrial incentives going to foreign-controlled enterprises was quite high: 52 percent in 1975, 43 percent in 1976, 53 percent in 1977, 35 percent in 1978 and 46 percent in 1979.[21]

Real outflows of direct foreign investment from the ten major OECD countries covered in this study trebled during the decades of the 1960s and 1970s — rising from an annual average of $9,107 million in 1960–66 to $16,307 million in 1967–73, $23,658 in 1974–80 and $28,507 in 1981 (Table 4-6). The postwar recovery and growth in the size of domestic firms, coupled with the imperatives of international competition, led West Germany, France, Japan and Canada to join the United States and the United Kingdom as major capital exporting countries in the 1970s. Although American DFI continued to rise, its relative share in total outflows by the major OECD countries fell from an average of 70 percent in the period 1960–68 to 47.8 percent in the years 1978–80, and there is some indication from Table 4-6 that the U.S. share had slipped below 25 percent by the early 1980s.

The increasing propensity of the advanced industrial capitalist countries to invest in each other's markets, the emergence of West Germany,

TABLE 4-5 Outflows of Payments of Direct Foreign Investment by Country, 1970–80

Country	1970	1971	1972	1973	1974	1975	1976	1977	1978	1979	1980
					(U.S.$ millions)						
Developed market economies											
Australia	307.0	361.1	391.9	588.9	635.0	707.8	766.6	749.5	791.3	972.9	959.2
Canada	635.0	770.3	684.0	897.7	1,202.6	1,323.4	1,259.6	1,466.4	1,909.3	1,936.7	2,081.1
Denmark	27.0	30.1	44.5	60.8	57.7	114.1	92.4	126.1	189.1	—	—
Finland	7.0	14.0	20.6	20.3	21.6	34.0	50.8	43.2	40.1	63.3	69.0
France	20.0	29.1	44.5	68.0	99.8	114.1	105.1	123.8	202.8	164.1	184.8
West Germany	771.0	929.8	912.0	1,299.4	1,791.9	1,396.3	1,512.4	2,556.9	1,652.6	2,596.9	2,577.0
Greece	3.0	5.0	6.5	14.3	12.0	12.1	—	—	—	—	—
Iceland	—	—	—	10.7	10.8	13.4	12.7	14.0	12.5	15.5	26.0
Japan	110.0	139.4	173.7	298.0	288.6	291.4	323.3	385.3	413.2	581.4	533.6
Netherlands	255.0	410.2	270.3	473.3	792.5	1,256.6	991.7	1,069.4	1,357.2	1,730.0	2,234.7
New Zealand	24.0	31.1	29.3	53.6	45.7	35.2	33.5	40.9	36.3	82.7	45.6
Norway	26.0	23.1	128.1	209.8	366.8	52.2	86.6	203.1	384.4	471.6	462.0
Portugal	—	—	29.3	31.0	33.7	—	—	—	—	—	—
South Africa	353.0	301.9	343.1	451.8	377.6	398.2	438.7	470.5	608.5	777.8	1,486.3
Spain	17.0	18.1	22.8	57.2	46.9	63.1	57.7	37.4	70.1	65.9	79.4
Sweden	32.0	41.1	42.3	63.2	299.5	65.6	68.1	119.1	77.6	67.2	106.7
United Kingdom	434.0	507.5	629.7	897.7	864.7	835.3	891.3	1,040.3	1,545.0	1,797.2	1,941.9
United States	441.0	620.8	694.9	703.4	264.6	1,056.3	1,431.6	1,260.9	1,615.1	2,403.1	3,175.7
Total of above	3,462.0	4,232.6	4,467.7	6,199.1	7,212.2	7,769.3	8,122.0	9,706.8	10,904.9	13,726.2	15,963.3

Source: United Nations, Centre on Transnational Corporations, Transnational Corporations and World Development, Third Survey (New York: 1983) p. 288.

TABLE 4-6 Outflows of Direct Foreign Investment, 1960–81 (millions of 1975 U.S. dollars)

	1960	1961	1962	1963	1964	1965	1966	1967	1968	1969	1970
Australia	39	40	27	20	n.a.	n.a.	58	97	102	194	154
Belgium-Luxembourg	n.a.	n.a.	n.a.	n.a.	n.a.	68	13	84	80	6	217
Canada	96	136	184	222	227	199	8	187	320	501	417
France	100	180	85	167	280	399	281	570	529	280	519
West Germany	269	341	479	380	397	450	508	419	613	805	1,214
Japan	143	171	139	217	100	132	177	198	339	302	494
Netherlands	174	165	193	240	253	253	424	480	533	730	722
Sweden	n.a.	n.a.	94	103	164	175	195	177	69	348	296
United Kingdom	1,296	1,161	1,054	1,254	1,283	1,476	1,275	1,240	1,516	1,870	1,822
United States	5,444	4,868	5,139	6,187	6,631	8,579	8,940	7,625	8,296	8,214	10,555
Total of above	7,561	7,062	7,394	8,790	9,335	11,731	11,879	11,077	12,397	13,250	16,410

	1971	1972	1973	1974	1975	1976	1977	1978	1979	1980	1981
Australia	138	159	246	272	162	256	225	194	244	341	357
Belgium-Luxembourg	240	225	322	525	236	335	417	466	1,027	144	77
Canada	321	515	918	910	896	827	1,352	2,079	1,823	2,112	3,668
France	526	757	1,124	857	1,578	1,569	1,000	1,695	1,560	2,133	2,955
West Germany	1,384	1,989	2,006	2,110	2,016	2,340	2,002	3,028	3,565	3,194	2,881
Japan	477	925	2,279	2,057	1,761	1,890	1,468	1,980	2,224	1,689	3,170
Netherlands	583	931	1,097	1,878	1,648	1,065	1,362	1,472	1,676	1,896	2,060
Sweden	233	336	355	467	436	568	661	348	475	437	540
United Kingdom	2,193	2,333	4,769	4,042	2,599	3,682	2,952	4,390	4,547	4,307	6,618
United States	10,089	9,849	13,698	9,956	14,242	11,347	10,680	13,442	18,422	13,126	6,181
Total of above	16,184	18,019	26,814	23,074	5,574	23,339	22,119	29,094	35,563	29,379	28,507

Source: IMF, Balance of Payments Yearbook, various years; deflated using U.S. GNP implicit price index (1975 = 100), as published in OECD, Main Economic Indicators; Historical Statistics, 1960–79 (Paris: 1980), and OECD, Main Economic Indicators (Paris: October, 1983).
n.a. = not available.

TABLE 4-7 Ratio of the Stock of Direct Investment Abroad
to the Stock of Inward Direct Investment
for the Major OECD Countries

	1967	1973	1978	Stock in 1978 Abroad	Stock in 1978 Inward
		(U.S.$ billions)			
Australia	0.074	0.049	0.101	1.1	10.9
Belgium-Luxembourg	0.929	0.579	0.490	4.7	9.6
Canada	0.193	0.237	0.315	13.6	43.2
France	2.000	1.517	1.000	14.9	14.9
West Germany	0.833	0.908	1.089	31.8	29.2
Japan	2.500	8.583	12.182	26.8	2.2
Netherlands	2.245	2.053	1.852	23.7	12.8
Sweden	3.400	3.000	4.615	6.0	1.3
United Kingdom	2.134	1.546	1.265	41.1	32.5
United States	5.717	4.917	4.120	168.1	40.8

Source: Computed from UN Centre on Transnational Corporations, *Salient Features and Trends in Foreign Direct Investment* (New York: 1983) Doc. No. UN/ST/CTC/14, Table 2, p. 34.

Japan and Canada as major capital exporting countries, and the emergence of the United States and France as capital importing countries have somewhat altered, although not entirely changed, the situation of each of the major OECD countries with respect to direct foreign investment. A summary measure of this change is the ratio of the stock of direct investment abroad to the stock of inward direct investment. Table 4-7 compares these ratios for the years 1967, 1973 and 1978. For Australia, Belgium and Canada there is a clear disequilibrium between domestic stocks and stocks abroad. Taking a more dynamic perspective by comparing the outflows (Table 4-6) to the inflows (Appendix), however, reveals that, while Australia and Belgium remain countries in which inward direct investment dominates outward investment, this ratio changed in the Canadian case from 0.138 (1960–62) to 0.857 (1972–74) and then shifted dramatically to 2.118 (1975–77) and 2.256 (1978–80) as outflows far exceeded capital inflows in those two periods.

Although the stocks of French, Dutch and British investment abroad exceed the stock of inward direct investment, the ratio of capital outflows to inflows reveals that inflows exceeded outflows in France throughout the 1970s, whereas the reverse was true for the Netherlands and the United Kingdom. For West Germany the ratio of stocks abroad of inward DFI hovered around the unity mark, but, in more dynamic perspective, the ratio of outflows to inflows moved from a range of 0.492 to 1.182 during the period 1960–74 to 2.575 in 1975–77 and 3.338 in 1978–80. In Japan this shift to capital exporting is even more dramatic (Table 4-7) with the take-off in direct foreign investment abroad coming in the period 1972–74, when the ratio of outflows to inflows rose from

2.471 (1969–71) to 13.563. As a recipient of direct foreign investment, Sweden remains of limited importance while its stocks of direct investment abroad have been increasing. In the next section we will examine the extent to which capital exporting is associated with a liberal approach to capital imports.

Policy Responses to Direct Foreign Investment

This section provides data on both explicit and implicit policies of the major OECD countries toward direct foreign investment. It covers, moreover, both regulatory and inducement policies designed to channel foreign investment into desired sectors or regions or to affect the amount, timing or location of inward direct investment.

Explicit regulatory policies are dealt with under four broad headings: authorization procedures and conditions of entry, both summarized in Table 4-8; sectors reserved to domestic investors, listed in Table 4-9; and other restrictions on foreign investment, noted in Table 4-10. Policies aimed at strengthening domestic firms vis-à-vis foreign corporations, including sectoral industrial policies and selective nationalization, are implicitly regulatory and are discussed in the body of the paper.

Explicit incentive policies, briefly summarized in the text, include the broad range of fiscal, financial and other investment incentive policies adopted on a seemingly nondiscriminatory basis to stimulate industrial restructuring or regional balance but generally acknowledged to have been used to favour new foreign investment in particular.[22]

Regulatory Policies

Only four of the OECD countries have no formal authorization procedures for inward direct foreign investment (Table 4-8) but each of these — the United States, the United Kingdom, Italy and West Germany — have a number of implicit mechanisms and policies which, in many instances, perform the same function.

In the United States, for example, a formal notification requirement for incoming foreign investment is used to impose reporting requirements on foreign firms. An Office on Foreign Investment in the United States then analyzes these data, and a Committee on Foreign Investment, established in 1975 under Treasury chairmanship, monitors the impact of foreign investment on the United States economy.[23] While this committee met formally only ten times from 1975 to 1981, under Congressional prodding it appears to have become more active in the past two years.[24]

In Italy, prior authorization is required for foreign investments in the finance sector and "major direct investments in Italy require approval by an interministerial committee. They are not screened, however, to sort

TABLE 4-8 Authorization Procedures for Inward Direct Foreign Investment

Country	Authorization Required for Some or All Inward Direct Foreign Investment (DFI)	Special Rules for Takeover Bids	Exchange Control Approval Required
Australia	Prior authorization required for certain investments; Foreign Investment Review Board (FIRB) reviews proposals on a case-by-case basis.	Special approval of Treasury or other relevant government dept. required.	Authorization of Reserve Bank required for all inward DFI.
Belgium-Luxembourg	Finance Ministry approval required for purchase of shares in public corporations by non-EEC firms (regional and general expansion law of 1970).	Approval required in case of bids by non-EEC nationals.	Approval of Belgium-Luxembourg Exchange Institute required for transactions over official foreign exchange market.
Canada	Foreign Investment Review Agency reviews two types of DFI (on case-by-case basis): i) foreign takeovers; and ii) establishment of new business in area unrelated to existing operations.		

France

Various decrees implementing the Foreign Economic Relations Act of 1966:

a) For non-EEC nationals, authorization of Ministry of Economy and Finance required, except in following cases:

   i) new DFI up to Fr5 million per calendar year in areas where investor is already active;

   ii) purchase or establishment of owner-operated handicraft or retail trade enterprise up to Fr5 million per calendar year; and

   iii) real estate enterprises.

b) For EEC nationals, prior notification only, except in the following cases, which require authorization of Ministry of Economy and Finance:

   i) sectors of activity that participate in administration of public authority;

   ii) investment affecting public order, health, security; and

   iii) investment obstructing application of French laws, regulations.

Have periodically been imposed.

TABLE 4-8 (cont'd)

Country	Authorization Required for Some or All Inward Direct Foreign Investment (DFI)	Special Rules for Takeover Bids	Exchange Control Approval Required
West Germany	None	None	None
Japan	Prior notification only (as of December 1980), except: i) four excepted industries (agriculture, forestry and fishing; mining; oil; leather and leather products); ii) subject to safeguard clauses if Minister of Finance, other competent Ministers feel Japanese interests adversely affected.	Consent of enterprise concerned is required.	
Netherlands		Special rules re mergers, acquisitions (relate to correct pricing of shares, prior notification, consultation with unions, government).	Authorization by Netherlands Bank — initial establishment only; foreign-controlled domestic enterprises are considered as resident for exchange control.

Sweden

Special permission of government required in following cases:

i) DFI in fields covered by 1916 National Resources Law;

ii) acquisition of real property (including hydro power) or claiming/working mineral deposits; and

iii) acquisition of more than 20 percent of voting rights and 40 percent of share capital in Swedish corporation (deemed "non-free" shares). In practice, permission is liberally granted.

Permission of Sveriges Riksbank required for all inward DFI.

TABLE 4-8 (cont'd)

Country	Authorization Required for Some or All Inward Direct Foreign Investment (DFI)	Special Rules for Takeover Bids	Exchange Control Approval Required
United Kingdom	Considerable review of incoming foreign direct investment by the Treasury.	Under Industry Act (1975) the government can prohibit transfer of control of important manufacturing enterprise to non-U.K. resident (never applied to date).	Authorization of Bank of England required. (Exchange Control Act of 1947).
United States	Notification, reporting requirements only. A Committee on Foreign Investment was established in 1975.	Some state regulations on foreign ownership of land (see Table 4-9).	

Sources: OECD, *Controls and Impediments Affecting Inward Direct Investment in OECD Member Countries* (1982); UNCTC, *National Legislation and Regulation Relating to Transnational Corporations* (1978); UNCTC, *Supplement to National Legislation and Regulations Relating to Transnational Corporations* (1980); Jean Boddewyn, *Western European Policies toward U.S. Investors* (New York: New York University, Bulletins No. 93–95, March 1974); Klaus W. Grewlich, *Direct Investment in the OECD Countries* (Netherlands: Sijthoff and Noordhoff, 1978); and A.E. Safarian, *Governments and Multinationals: Policies in the Developed Countries* (Washington, D.C.: British–North American Committee, 1983).

out those projects which are more desirable or to increase benefits. Direct investments are affected, however, by controls on capital and income flows."[25]

Similarly the United Kingdom, through its exchange control regulations, is able to screen incoming foreign investment. New investors are, in fact, required to apply

> to the Bank of England for permission to bring in capital and to borrow locally. . . . The Bank of England decides directly in the case of smaller investments but refers large and/or more sensitive ones to the Treasury's Foreign Exchange Control Committee which regularly assembles representatives of Treasury, the Department of Trade and Industry and other relevant units if necessary.[26]

In addition, investors are expected to contact the Department of Trade and Industry in order to satisfy them that the investment is "desirable" and that it "qualifies for the various incentives available."[27]

While West Germany thus remains the only country without explicit or implicit screening mechanisms, decisions of the Federal Cartel Office do set out certain broad limits to the expansion of multinational corporations, since multinational corporations tend to be the ones involved in many of the larger mergers in West Germany. "Both the other firm and the Cartel Office must be informed if a firm acquires 25 percent participation. Merger provisions apply explicitly to transborder combinations, and have been applied to deny such mergers."[28] Moreover, in the wake of a rash of direct foreign investments by Organization of Petroleum Exporting Countries (OPEC) governments in the 1970s, notably Iran's acquisition of a 25 percent interest in Krupp and the Kuwait government's purchase of a 14 percent share in Daimler-Benz, the West German government established "an informal notification system in which the banks and major firms report to the government any *impending* sales of companies or large blocks of shares to foreigners and . . . in a few cases the government encouraged German investors to buy the equity being offered for sale. . . ."[29]

In all other OECD countries some form of explicit state involvement in the inward foreign investment process occurs. In Australia, Canada, Finland, Greece, Ireland, Japan (prior to 1980), New Zealand, Norway, Portugal and Sweden, most inward foreign investment is subject to prior authorization. In the remaining OECD countries, under certain specified conditions, inward foreign investment is subject to authorization by central bank or ministerial authorities. Thus, when a takeover is involved (Belgium) or when the amount of the investment exceeds a specific threshold (Denmark, France) or where it might imperil national security or adversely affect local industry (Japan, post-1980), authorization is required.[30]

All of the OECD countries, moreover, have restrictions on entry of foreign direct investment into certain sectors (Table 4-9). For national security reasons defence industries, nuclear energy and utilities are prime candidates for closure to foreign investors. Financial institutions, especially banks, and communications media are also frequently closed to foreign ownership or closely regulated. In a number of cases, particular activities deemed vital to the national economy, such as resource extraction and processing, transportation, petroleum, steel, or automobile manufacture, may also be reserved for national investors — state or private.

A large number of OECD countries also restrict land ownership or the ownership of real estate by nonresident foreigners. This applies, for example, in Australia, Finland, New Zealand, Norway, Japan, Portugal, Spain, Sweden, Switzerland and a number of individual U.S. states where land is prized for its leisure value (beachfront property), its subsoil resources or its scarcity.

Access to local borrowing is another area in which a number of OECD countries discriminate against foreign investors (Table 4-10). There are no restrictions at all in Canada, West Germany, Japan, Netherlands, Switzerland, the United Kingdom and the United States. But there is some form of restriction in all the other OECD countries. Table 4-10 also reveals that several OECD countries require, as do France and Australia, or have required, as did the United Kingdom until 1979, exchange control approval for the repatriation of capital and profits. In addition, Sweden, Switzerland and some of the U.S. states require a certain proportion of nationals on the board of directors of foreign-owned firms.

Despite this plethora of regulations, in only four of the OECD countries — Japan, Canada, Australia and Italy — has a separate foreign investment act been enacted. In all other cases authorization procedures and investment restrictions were incorporated into central bank, trade, or other legislation. Only in Canada and Australia, moreover, were specialized foreign investment review agencies created, although in a number of countries (Belgium, for example), a high degree of centralization of the authorization process is evident.

In addition to explicit regulatory policies, a number of mechanisms have been designed to help domestic firms hold their own against possible competition or takeover by foreign firms. Such implicit regulatory policies include the kind of screening made possible by antitrust policy, as in Germany, specially designed industrial policies or credit facilities, and discriminatory practices in the bidding for government contracts. A few examples will demonstrate the range of such policies and the breadth of their practice within the OECD.

With specific reference to Australia and Canada, Grewlich notes that:

TABLE 4-9 Sectors Reserved to Domestic Investors

	Australia	Belgium	Canada	France	West Germany	Japan	Netherlands	Sweden	United Kingdom	United States
Public utilities										
Electricity	D	D		D			D		D	
Gas and other fuels	D	D		D			D		D	
Water	D	D							D	
Atomic energy				D						A
Municipal public services				D						
Transportation and Communications										
Aviation	B,D	D			B	A	B	B	C	A
Shipping		D				A	B	B		
Rail transport	D	D		D			D	D	D	
Road transport (bus)				B			D	B		
Telephone, telegraph, and telecommunications	D	D		D	D	D[a]	D	D		B[b]
Postal services	D	D		D		D	D	D	D	
Radio and TV broadcasting	B	D	C	B,D	D	A	D	D	B	C
Newspapers and magazines	B,C									

TABLE 4-9 (cont'd)

	Australia	Belgium	Canada	France	West Germany	Japan	Netherlands	Sweden	United Kingdom	United States
Primary industry										
Agriculture				C[c]		B				B[d]
Fishing						B				C
Forestry						B				
Mining			C[e]			B			D[f]	B[g]
Oil and gas			C			B				B
Distribution of selected primary products	D									
Banking, insurance, etc.										
Banking	A		B,C	C	C		C	A[h]		C
Insurance	B			C	D[i]		C	A[h]	B,C	C
Exchange dealings		A								
Customs brokerage										C

Other				
Alcoholic beverages				D
Employment services (labour exchange)				D
Explosives			D	
Leather and leather products		B		
Lotteries, etc.	D		C[i]	D
Tobacco		D	D[k]	
Retail sale of pharmaceuticals				
War materials			A	D
Salt industry		D		A

Source: OECD, *Controls and Impediments Affecting Inward Direct Investment in OECD Member Countries* (Paris: 1982).

A = excluded.
B = restricted.
C = special approval required.
D = public, private or mixed monopoly.
a. Telecommunications only.
b. Commercial satellite systems only.
c. Not applicable to EEC nationals.
d. Some state restrictions.
e. Northwest Territories only.
f. Coal only.
g. Selected minerals only.
h. Some exceptions (i.e., special permission).
i. Certain types of insurance only, by some *Länder* governments.
j. Casinos only.
k. Also includes matches.

TABLE 4-10 Other Restrictions on Foreign Investment

	Australia	Belgium	Canada	France	West Germany	Japan	Netherlands	Sweden	United Kingdom	United States
Local borrowing	X	X^a		X			X^a	X^a		
Repatriation of capital and profits	X^b			X^b				n.a.	X^b	
Taxation	n.a.		X			n.a.		n.a.		
Terms of establishment								X		X^c

Sources: OECD, Controls and Impediments Affecting Inward Direct Investment in OECD Member Countries (Paris: 1982); UNCTC, National Legislation and Regulations Relating to Transnational Corporations (New York: 1978); UNCTC, Supplement to National Legislation and Regulations Relating to Transnational Corporations (New York: 1980).

a. Long-term capital only.
b. Exchange control approval only.
c. Some states require that proportion of incorporators/directors must be U.S. citizens.
n.a. = not available.

Some governments have brought in policies having the effect of limiting the growth of enterprises under foreign control in certain important sectors by assisting domestic firms to reach a level of production and productivity enabling them to hold their own against external competition. The methods used include, for example, government support for research and development, financial assistance, and management training. . . .[31]

Thus in 1970 the Australian Industrial Development Corporation was created with a view to borrowing capital and lending the funds to Australian industrial firms and/or undertaking equity participation in such firms. Similarly the Canada Development Corporation was established in 1971 to help develop and maintain Canadian-controlled and -managed corporations.

Industrial policies geared to specific sectors and containing special measures to promote mergers and provide credits for research and development or for modernization have also been used to encourage domestic ownership or control. The French *plan calcul*, covering the computer industry, and the aeronautics and steel programs fall into this category.[32] U.K. undertakings that lacked the sectoral planning element, but nonetheless were clearly aimed at ensuring a domestic presence in a specific sector, include the government-sponsored merger of BMC and Leyland Motors, engineered by the British government to counteract the takeover of Rootes by Chrysler, as well as Ford's and General Motors' strong presence in the United Kingdom, and "favoured government purchases of British pharmaceutical and telecommunication products."[33] West German government encouragement to its domestic firms to purchase assets in companies threatened by takeover bids from foreign companies has already been noted. Nationalization has also been used to maintain a domestic presence in a sector dominated by multinational corporations, as the Italian state holding company IRI did in the case of two of the main national food processing and distributing companies in the late 1960s, and in the case of Innocenti steel.[34]

Lastly there are numerous examples of exceptions to treatment accorded domestic firms, especially in tendering for government contracts. In the United States, for example, "foreign-controlled firms are not eligible for the facility security clearance required to bid on U.S. defence contracts, except under special arrangements made on a case-by-case basis."[35] This covers, however, a wide variety of firms in the high-technology sector. Although such exceptions are permitted under OECD regulations by reason of public order or security interests, no similar justification can be offered in the case of a 1973 announcement by the Australian Prime Minister "that tenders for government contracts would be awarded to an Australian-owned enterprise in cases where Australian-owned and foreign-contolled firms would submit tenders which meet specifications and are equal in respect of price and availability."[36]

Incentive Policies

All the OECD countries have a wide variety of incentive programs designed to induce new investment to enter desired sectors and regions. Most of these programs are nondiscriminatory in nature, but quite a few have been used to favour direct foreign investment in particular. "Some of the most frequent of these policies comprise favoured tax treatment, export subsidies, 'location grants' within the context of regional policies, subsidised training of local labour, preferred access to local credit and possibly also protection against imports. . . ."[37] In Belgium, for example, the income of foreign managers and technicians qualifying as "non-residents having a dwelling in Belgium" is subject to favourable rates of taxation, and the "coordinating and supervisory" offices of foreign firms, if they are "auxiliary and preparatory" and not directly engaged in income-producing activities, are exempt from taxation.[38] Guarantees of obtaining foreign exchange at the official rate for repatriation of capital funds and for profit remittances are also offered to foreign investors in Belgium, and, in Italy, to foreign firms engaged in "productive investments."[39] In Switzerland, "tax concessions are available to foreign-owned companies which function principally as holding companies or which provide services to foreign affiliates."[40]

To alert foreign investors to their incentive policies, several European countries, notably Belgium, France, Greece, Ireland and the Netherlands, have specialized investment centres abroad or designated sections within their ministries at home designed expressly to negotiate fiscal and other concessions that might influence the amount and timing of the investment as well as its contribution to the host economy in terms of employment, exports, research and development or new technology. The DATAR, the Délégation à l'aménagement du territoire et à l'action régionale, for example, sponsors a French industrial development agency with offices in New York and other major foreign cities for this purpose. The Belgian industrial section of its consulate general in New York plays a similar role in negotiations with potential foreign investors.[41]

As the above review of regulatory and incentive policies illustrates, all of the advanced industrial capitalist countries have begun to pay greater attention to foreign investment and to negotiate with potential or actual investors. Considerable variation, however, exists in the kind of regulatory and incentive policies they have adopted. At one extreme we find West Germany and the Netherlands, which have few explicitly regulatory policies with regard to direct foreign investment. Like the United States, the United Kingdom and Belgium, however, they have a number of implicitly regulatory policies. Belgium and the Netherlands, moreover, have provided substantial incentives to foreign investors. France, Canada and Australia have each adopted explicitly regulatory policies, although only the latter two have created specialized foreign investment review bodies. Sweden and Japan (until 1980) have been most restrictive in their approach to direct foreign investment, but without the kinds of explicitly regulatory policies that have attracted so much attention to Canada and Australia. Correlating this information with the data on capital exporting from the first section of this paper reveals an absence of any significant relationship between capital exporting and regulation during the 1960–80 period. Although the United States and the United Kingdom are the two traditional capital-exporting countries, and each has maintained relatively liberal policies toward incoming direct foreign investment, Belgium and West Germany were not major capital exporters, and inflows of capital exceeded outflows of capital throughout much of this period. Yet they, too, are among that group of countries with fewer regulatory policies. At the other extreme, there is also an absence of correlation. Sweden, traditionally a capital exporter, has maintained highly restrictive policies on direct foreign investment. In Japan, where capital outflows increased dramatically in the 1970s, liberalization did begin in December 1980. This, however, is directly attributable to threats by the United States to close its market to Japanese goods, rather than to incoming Japanese investment which, in fact, it was seeking. Finally, as we shall see in the next section, while French liberalization may, in part, be a function of increasing pressure from firms engaged in exporting capital to liberalize the domestic economy from all state restrictions, such arguments cannot be made for Australian liberalization of its foreign investment regime since Australia did not emerge as a capital exporter in this period.

State Intervention in the Foreign Investment Process

In this section we will examine the changing policy responses of the state to direct foreign investment in the period 1960–80. As such responses are conditioned by (a) the pattern of direct foreign investment and its relationship to the realization of economic and social goals, as these are variously defined at different times; (b) the historical role of the state in the economy; (c) the nature of coalitions operating at the centre of the policy-making process and their orientation toward direct foreign investment; (d) the impact of changing economic and social conditions on the environment within which policies toward direct foreign investment are made; and (e) previous policy experience with respect to foreign investment, this analysis must be situated within the context of specific countries. Australia and France, both of which have relatively high levels of foreign investment and explicitly regulatory policies toward direct foreign investment, have been chosen as case studies here.

Australia

In the years immediately following World War II, economic and social policy was "strongly influenced by the near-invasion of Australia during the war"[42] and the massive unemployment of the Depression years.[43] This was particularly evident in three government policy initiatives: the "move to increase the self-sufficiency of the Australian economy via an expanded industrial base"; the decision, in 1949, to eliminate the potential strategic weakness of vast underpopulated areas by promoting large-scale immigration;[44] and the efforts expended to attract the overseas capital believed to be needed to support each of the previous initiatives.[45] This was also the year in which the Liberal–National Country (LNC) party coalition came to power, and this conservative government with its private enterprise philosophy would remain ensconced at the federal level until December 1972. With a rapidly growing population, a booming demand for housing, consumer durables and capital goods, and an open-door policy toward foreign investment, the Australian market became highly attractive to foreign firms. When in the 1960s the hitherto largely unsurveyed country revealed extensive deposits of iron ore, nickel, phosphate and bauxite, the inflow of direct foreign investment into mineral processing also rose dramatically.

Initially, "the colonial connection ensured easy entry by British firms, and helped to develop the derivative industrial structure that has remained a feature of the Australian manufacturing industry."[46] But U.S. direct investment in Australia was accelerating rapidly, increasing

> by 1071 percent between 1950 and 1967, compared with an expansion in total American direct investment abroad of only 403 percent during the same period. The growth of the American corporate commitment in Australia . . . was . . . substantially greater than the 405 percent increase in Canada, both areas of major American investment interest in the fifties and sixties. The level of U.S. corporate investment in Australia more than doubled between 1962 and 1967 alone.[47]

As early as 1954 the accelerated inflow of American direct foreign investment had called attention to the potential loss of Australian opportunities for participation in the high growth and profitability of new enterprises. In that year General Motors released its annual report revealing that the considerable profits earned by its Australian subsidiary would be entirely remitted abroad as all ordinary shares in this company were owned by Americans. This seeming unwillingness of foreign investors to allow Australians to participate in the equity of their ventures was sharply criticized in the press and by a small group of nationalists on the left.[48] But a full ten years elapsed before the state intervened and then it was a conservative coalition government which began the steady progression toward increased state intervention in the foreign investment process. This response had its roots in the increased penetration of foreign capital in the resource sector and the rising concern over balance-of-payments difficulties, generated in part, by the costs of foreign investment. Given the traditional openness of the LNC coalition to foreign investment, however, neither of these factors alone would have been sufficient to provoke the regulation of direct foreign investment. A trigger mechanism to catalyze nationalist sentiment was necessary, as we shall see below.

Throughout the 1950s and 1960s Australia continued to attract direct foreign investment — especially into the extractive sector, which emerged as the most dynamic sector in the economy during the 1960s and 1970s. By the late 1960s, there were only four other countries — Canada, the United Kingdom, West Germany and Venezuela — in which the book value of U.S. direct investment exceeded that in Australia.[49] In terms of the per capita U.S. dollar value of American direct investment, at the end of 1967 Australia was also near the top, ranking third with $204 behind Canada ($901) and Venezuela ($286) but well ahead of the United Kingdom ($112), West Germany ($58) and France ($39).[50]

With rapidly rising rates of new direct foreign investment, foreign ownership of Australian manufacturing and resource industries became pronounced. In 1965 it was estimated that the foreign share of the automobile, pharmaceutical and petroleum refining and distributing industries was over 95 percent, while 83 percent of the telecommunications industry, 80 percent of soap and detergents, 84 percent of the brown coal, and 75 percent of the silver, lead and zinc mining were in foreign hands.[51]

The costs of this high level of direct foreign investment were also rising. By the mid-sixties, "26–27 percent of total company income after tax was payable abroad" as compared with approximately 18–20 percent in the early fifties.[52] The rising rate of outflows of payments on direct foreign investment, coupled with Australia's import-dependent industrialization process and the major fluctuations in world prices encountered by its primary exports, helped generate three severe balance-of-payments crises during the 1950s and 1960s. Given the conservative orientation of the government in this period, however, balance-of-payments pressures led not to the regulation of capital outflows but to increased reliance on new foreign investment as a means to develop the mineral exporting sector.[53] Federal and state governments thus continued to provide lucrative incentives to attract new foreign capital into manufacturing and raw materials processing. In one instance the federal Department of Supply promised a foreign firm "duty-free admission for all imported materials if it agreed to manufacture locally" and, in another, the firm was promised "a premium above the price of imported goods for its output."[54] When

> Mobil oil decided to build its second Australian oil refinery, the South Australian government encouraged the company to build in that state by agreeing to provide not only access roads and railroad track but also housing, water and electricity. This was in addition to an undertaking that state preferences would be given to the products of the new refinery.[55]

At the same time, however, the need to meet rising Australian demand for participation in these industries obliged the government in 1964 to request that all new proposals for foreign investment in the minerals sector, and particularly in the Gove Peninsula bauxite deposits, include provisions for Australian equity shareholding.[56] Efforts to implement more thoroughgoing regulations were opposed by the Treasury at this time.[57]

It was thus with considerable shock that the conservative government of Prime Minister Holt greeted the U.S. "guidelines" policy on foreign investment adopted in 1965. Despite a background of balance-of-payments problems and sensitivity over the lack of participation of Australian capital in new minerals processing and manufacturing ventures, the first concrete step toward the regulation of inward foreign direct investment was, in fact, a reaction to this U.S. policy initiative. The response was contained in the government's official policy statement, *Overseas Investment in Australia*, published annually:

> Following the measures taken by the United States Government to restrict the flow of capital to a number of countries, including Australia, the Government requested that the Reserve Bank be consulted before overseas companies, or Australian companies in which there is a substantial overseas shareholding complete plans to borrow in Australia. . . . The general aim is to avoid overseas interests making too great use of Australian borrowings in substitution for funds that would otherwise be provided from overseas sources.[58]

Implicitly regulatory policies aimed at strengthening domestic firms vis-à-vis foreign corporations were the next order of business. In 1967 the Australian Resources Development Bank Ltd. and, a few years later, the Australian Industry Development Corporation, were set up with government financial backing in order to strengthen the capacity of Australians to undertake new investments.[59] These implicit policies were followed in September 1968 by a more explicit government intervention to ensure local equity participation. Following heavy stock market purchases of shares in a large Australian-owned life insurance company, M.L.C., Prime Minister John Gorton announced his government's intention "to amend the Companies Ordinance of the Australian Capital Territory (where the company was incorporated) to prevent that company and its accumulated stock of Australian savings falling under the control of anonymous and probably foreign interests."[60]

Three months later Gorton approached the Australian stock exchanges and requested that they change their listing requirements so as to permit companies to amend their articles of association in such a way as to ensure "that control of the company, exercised through the voting power of the shareholders, remains in Australian hands."[61] The stock exchanges reluctantly acceded to this request in January 1969. Then in 1971 the Gorton government appointed a Senate Select Committee on Foreign Ownership and Control to consider new measures to channel foreign investment and reduce its costs. A year later, the Liberal–National Country party under Prime Minister McMahon implemented the Companies (Foreign Takeovers) Bill of 1972.

This series of "nationalistic" measures implemented by a government ostensibly partial to free enterprise and an open door for foreign investment evoked considerable international furor. As in the case of the Andean group, whose members negotiated their regional regulations on foreign investment and technology transfer in the same period, international opposition to the Australian regulations took the form of threats to withdraw and/or withhold foreign investment.[62] Where the host market remains attractive for other reasons, however, there is usually little likelihood that such threats will be translated into action, and that indeed was the case in Australia. New inflows of direct foreign investment (Table 4-1) rose 47 percent in 1969–71 over 1966–68, and by 1972–73 foreign firms in the manufacturing sector accounted for 36 percent of the output and 29 percent of the employment (Table 4-3). The LNC government's response was not deemed adequate by the electorate.

In 1972 the first Labour government in two decades was elected on a platform which stressed the need to ensure a larger Australian share in new investment projects and the repurchase of foreign assets in Australia. The latter was particularly aimed at the rising foreign share in the resource sector. In January 1973 federal export controls were extended to all minerals, raw and processed. In March the Whitlam government halted the construction of natural gas pipelines by a private consortium pending establishment of a national pipeline authority. Over the next several months the government

announced decisions to establish a Petroleum and Minerals Authority "for exploration, production and refining" . . . to expand the Australian Industry Development Corporation . . . [to abolish] the subsidy for oil exploration . . . [and] existing tax concessions for mineral prospecting . . . and [to set up] a new treasury division on foreign investment and take-overs.[63]

Screening of new foreign investment under the Companies (Foreign Takeovers) Act was begun on a case-by-case basis in 1974 and was subsequently extended to the expansion of existing firms.[64]

By the early 1970s reduced levels of immigration and a low rate of natural population increase had sharply reduced the growth prospects of the domestic market in Australia.[65] "Even though certain parts of manufacturing were afforded increased protection . . . for example, the motor vehicle industry . . . this was not enough to arrest the increased pressure felt by local manufacturing firms."[66] Many of these firms were American and in early 1974 their views were published in Australia by the American Chamber of Commerce.[67] Unemployment had also begun to rise sharply in the mid-1970s and, despite two devaluations of the Australian dollar aimed at spurring exports and reducing imports, the high import content of Australian manufacturing industry was translated into high rates of inflation which raised domestic manufacturing costs above those of its export competitors — the Asian non-industrialized countries. Facing a stagnant domestic market and an inability to export competitively, Australian firms began to invest abroad, increasing the balance-of-payments disequilibria that had induced conservative governments in the past to favour new inflows of foreign investment. The elimination of subsidies and tax concessions for oil and mineral exploration, the increased effort to buy back Australian processing industries by the state and private Australian capital, and the stagnant domestic market, however, provided strong disincentives to new foreign investment, and in 1972–74 new inflows of direct foreign investment (Table 4-1) fell 20 percent from their high in 1969–71, although they remained above the 1966–68 and 1975–77 levels — both periods marked by liberalism toward incoming direct foreign investment.

By September 1975, following a political scandal which led to the dismissal of Dr. Cairns, minister for overseas trade, and the resignation of Mr. Connor, the minister for minerals and energy, both architects of the government's nationalistic policies, and in view of the declining rate of new inflows of direct foreign investment, the Labour government issued a new statement on policy toward foreign investment.

The statement explicitly recognized that 'Australia will, for the foreseeable future, continue to require foreign capital, including equity capital' for the development of its 'resources.' Only 'within this over-riding goal' and as 'a major longer term objective' did it declare itself in favour of 'the promotion of Australian control and the maximum Australian ownership compatible with our long-term capital requirements and our need for access to markets, advanced technology and know-how.'[68]

Three weeks later the Liberal and National Country parties issued their own statement concurring with the position now adopted by the Labour party. When the Australian Governor General engineered a mini coup d'état against the Gough Whitlam government, replacing it with a Conservative caretaker government in November 1975, many thought that Labour's foreign investment regulations would become a dead letter.

Although the Liberal–National Country party coalition government formed under Malcolm Fraser following elections in December 1975 did adopt a more encouraging attitude toward foreign investment, it did not entirely abandon the principle of regulation. The Foreign Takeovers Act of 1976 was implemented and a Foreign Investment Review Board (FIRB) was created, composed of one public sector and two private sector members to advise the Treasurer on foreign investment policy and to screen new investments and takeovers.

Not until the crisis deepened did the Conservative government move closer to its earlier open-door policy, placing even greater emphasis on attracting new direct foreign investment. Although no studies had been undertaken to determine the extent to which foreign investment regulations, rather than the elimination of subsidies, tariffs and tax concessions or the stagnant domestic market, were responsible for the continued decline in new inflows of direct foreign investment in the 1975–77 period, the LNC government, in view of its ideological predispositions against state intervention and in favour of direct foreign investment, decided to relax its foreign investment review process. In 1978 it proposed to treat "naturalizing firms" — that is, foreign companies with at least 25 percent local ownership and a majority of Australian citizens on their boards that pledged to increase Australian equity to 51 percent in the future — as Australian companies for investment purposes. This meant that they could undertake new investments without FIRB approval. The government also increased its level of effective rates of assistance — tariff protection and subsidies — to manufacturing industry. By 1980–81 net subsidies amounted to about 24 percent of manufacturing value-added.[69] Many of these incentives went to foreign firms, which continued to control over 90 percent of the automobile and petroleum industries, 78 percent of basic chemicals, over 50 percent of tobacco and nonferrous metal products, and considerable proportions of other industrial segments.[70] Australia ranked second only to Canada in the extensiveness of foreign ownership and control of its manufacturing sector.

As to raw materials, despite the concern evidenced in Australia over the need to ensure local participation in the raw materials processing sector, foreign penetration remained high. Foreign-controlled firms, for example, owned about half the reserves of crude oil, natural gas and natural gas liquids, 40–45 percent of the copper, lead, and silver refining, some 25 percent of the nickel and zinc refining, 66 percent of the alumina and aluminium smelting industry, and 40–45 percent of black coal mining.[71] Efforts by the Fraser government to expand aluminium smelting for export to Japan, moreover, were unlikely to alter this situation as the development of the aluminum industry depended entirely upon "the vertically integrated MNCs [Alcoa, Alcan, Alumax, Kaiser and Reynolds] not only to undertake the investment but also to establish world markets for the product."[72] In addition, as heavy electricity users, expansion of this and other minerals processing industries would require an estimated U.S.$1 billion in new investment in capital equipment for the electricity industry. Since these firms had negotiated "very low bulk electricity rates" there was criticism that too much emphasis on this sector represented "a real transfer of wealth away from the community" in subsidies and only limited job creation, since these industries were highly capital intensive. In March 1983, dissatisfaction with the existing government led to a return of the Labour party to power.

There is little doubt that the Labour party will attempt to tighten its control over the foreign investment review process and in particular seek to ensure that new investments and/or takeovers meet the key criteria of "net economic benefit" to Australia before approval. There is also little doubt that such efforts will evoke criticism from home country governments of major investing firms, especially where such governments, as in the case of the United States and the United Kingdom, are dominated by "free enterprisers." Within the context of the continuing crisis and in view of the relative inflexibility of the Australian economy, based as it is on a noncompetitive manufacturing sector and a foreign-dominated minerals exporting sector, the extent to which the Labour party can radically depart from the previous policy of relative flexibility in the application of foreign investment review procedures may well be circumscribed. In apparent recognition of these constraints, Prime Minister Hawke pointed out that while "majority ownership and control of our resources should be in the hands of the Australian people," Labour had "a very clear perception of the need for foreign investment."[73]

France

In contrast to Australia, the state in France has traditionally played a major role in the economy. Jean-Baptiste Colbert, finance minister to Louis XIV and the first controller general of France, for example, gave selective subsidies or interest-free loans to favoured industries, induced the introduction of new industrial processes from abroad by importing both machines and the skilled labour to man them, and sent inspectors to verify that products were being produced in accordance with the desired methods and the required quality standards.[74] Despite these proddings, over the next several centuries cartelization, with its absence of price competition, and protectionism in domestic and, later, colonial markets became distinguishing features of French capitalism; both were responses to the underlying weakness of the French industrial bourgeoisie.[75]

At the close of World War II French industry, for the most part, was both economically and technically inefficient.[76] Unlike the Netherlands and West Germany, generally regarded as relatively late industrializers among European countries, the size of the French labour force in agriculture remained high — 28.2 percent of the workforce in 1953, falling to 11.3 percent in 1973.[77] The relative lag in French industrialization was also reflected in the size of the French "traditional sector," that is, the class of small independent property owners engaged in small-scale, relatively labour-intensive production under family ownership and paternalistic management, many of whom were concentrated in industries associated with the first industrial revolution, such as the textile industry. Firms with over 1,000 employees, for example, employed 28.2 percent of the work force in Germany in the early 1960s but only 17.3 percent of the French work force. Firms with under 50 employees employed 36.4 percent of the French work force and only 27.1 percent of the work force in Germany.[78]

Throughout the postwar period the state played a central role in economic restructuring — manipulating macroeconomic fiscal and monetary levers and devising sectoral policies to stimulate industrial concentration, new investment in industry, and balanced regional development.[79] Not until the 1960s, however, did a number of large oligopolistic firms in key sectors emerge as viable interlocutors for the state in the shaping of French industrial policy.[80] Unlike its counterparts in Belgium, West Germany and the Netherlands, from the early 1950s onward, organized labour was pushed to the margins of the industrial planning process in France.[81]

Despite the centre-right coalitions that dominated French politics from 1958 to 1981, it is in the context of a state prone to direct intervention and a weak industrial bourgeoisie that one must interpret French response to the rising level of foreign penetration of the manufacturing sector in the 1960s and 1970s. The policy differences with Germany, where the pattern of direct foreign investment is roughly similar, are thus quite marked.

In the period to 1963, the response was highly liberal and indeed, as Premier Michel Debré wrote in July 1959, "If U.S. firms are going to set up plants in the Common Market, it is better, under any circumstances, that they choose France rather than her partners."[82] This attitude was, however, conditioned by the near bankruptcy of the French economy in 1957, the devaluation of 1959, French entry into the Common Market and the need, therefore, to pay even more attention to productivity than to merely increasing the volume of output.

Then, in 1962, 700 workers were laid off at the General Motors refrigerator plant at Genevilliers, a Paris suburb, and 800 of the 1,200 workers at a Remington Rand (USA) factory near Lyon were declared redundant.[83] Chrysler bought out Simca, Libby set up plants in Bas-Rhône, and General Electric attempted to purchase a controlling interest in France's only nationally owned computer firm, Machines Bull. All these events turned attention to the role U.S. firms had come to play in the French economy.[84]

By 1963 that role had, in fact, become significant. Gilles Bertin estimated that U.S. firms then controlled some 40 percent of the petroleum market, 65 percent of the production of farm machinery, 65 percent of the telecommunications equipment, 50 percent of the semi-conductors, 80 percent of the computers and 95 percent of the integrated circuits.[85] In response to these developments the government of Premier Georges Pompidou adopted a series of measures regulating incoming direct investment.

France, of course, was not unique in the degree to which its industrial sector had become penetrated by American capital in this period. In Germany, for example, after a long period of economic liberalism inspired by political considerations, the Commerzbank estimated that American-controlled investments in West Germany amounted to U.S.$2 billion in 1965, while the gross capital of all firms quoted on the West German stock exchange totalled only $3.5 billion in that year.[86] By that time, however, West German direct foreign investment in other EEC countries had increased considerably, and in the four-year period 1966–69, of some 776 requests for authorization reviewed by the French interministerial Committee on Foreign Investments, 298 (38.4%) were American, but 91 (11.3%) were German, 88 (11.3%) were British and 84 (10.8%) were Swiss.[87] One might expect, therefore, that the French and German responses to "*le défi américain*" (the American challenge) would be different.

While in 1967, in the midst of a serious economic recession, the German government blocked an attempt by Mobil Oil to take over the German firm Aral, demanding that its share be limited to 28 percent,[88] such direct interventions were infrequent and no legislation to deal with foreign investment was adopted. In France, where the state had a long tradition of intervention in the domestic economy and where the industrial bourgeoisie was relatively weak, a restrictive policy with respect to foreign investment was launched by the centre-right government of Premier Georges Pompidou in 1963. As in Australia, the French reacted to the 1965 U.S. guidelines that restricted capital exports by requiring that participants pay their contributions to a new foreign investment immediately and in cash. The use of French funds, moreover, was limited to less than half of the total financing.[89] This was followed in 1966 by a law, enacted by a decree in January 1967, which eliminated the use of foreign exchange controls for all financial operations except those linked to direct foreign investment. Rules for the review of all incoming foreign investments over one million francs were also established. The review process consisted of the submission of a preliminary declaration of intent to invest, which contained information on the investing firm and on the location, amount, and nature of its investment. The dossier was reviewed by an interministerial committee chaired by the Treasury within the Ministry of Economy and Finance and including representatives from the Ministry of Industry, the Ministry of Social Affairs, the Commissariat général du plan, and the DATAR.[90]

Despite the imposition of a foreign investment review process, new inflows of direct foreign investment rose in 1964 by 45 percent over the previous year and in 1965 remained well above the annual average inflow for the 1960–62 period (Table 4-1 and the Appendix). Nevertheless, General Motors' threat to switch its proposed investment from Strasbourg to West Germany, Ford's alleged shift of a proposed investment from Thionville to Belgium, and Phillips Petroleum's decision to locate its new refinery in the Benelux region rather than in Bordeaux frightened the Pompidou/Debré government into a relaxation of the foreign investment review process.[91]

"After 1966 the handling of applications became very liberal."[92] Within the Committee on Foreign Investment, the DATAR was most favourable toward U.S. investment since it was charged with creating new jobs in declining areas and could offer incentives for that purpose.[93] But no ministry or department actively supported "the acquisition of a French firm by an American investor. At best, such an acquisition is tolerated if no other 'French solution' is viable, but it has no real 'advocate' within the foreign investments committee."[94]

In the Sixth Plan, drawn up in the late 1960s and covering the period 1970–75, an even more pronounced liberalization with respect to foreign investment was envisaged.

> The Sixth Plan, by adopting a position of encouraging foreign investment without interference, differs significantly from its predecessor. This happens just when the major French industrial and financial groups have essentially done all they could to strengthen themselves and attain an international status. [Translation][95]

Neither the onset of restrictive policies nor the liberalization had much impact on the inflow of new direct foreign investment into France during the period 1950–75. From 1951 to 1958 the increase in foreign investment was rapid but it only represented an average contribution of 1 percent to gross fixed capital formation.[96] From 1958 to 1962, with no apparent change in French policy, which remained liberal throughout this period, foreign investment rose dramatically and came to contribute 6 percent of gross capital formation.[97] The downturn between 1962 and 1963 (see the Appendix and Figure 4-1) was a function of MNC divestment which preceded the policy shift of 1963. The restrictive policy adopted in 1963, however, was followed by a rapid increase in new inflows of direct foreign investment, while the liberalization in 1966 was followed by a decline in inward direct foreign investment in 1966 and again in 1968. Although the years 1970–75 marked a continuation of a relatively more liberal approach to direct foreign investment, continuity in policy cannot explain the dramatic increase in new inflows of direct foreign investment during this period in both France and West Germany — an increase linked far more to the intensification of intra-EEC direct foreign investment[98] and the increased liquidity following the rise in petroleum prices in 1973 than to new policies toward direct foreign investment.

With rising rates of new direct foreign investment inflows and reinvested earnings, by 1978 the stock of direct foreign investment in France had risen to U.S.$14.9 billion. Although the stock of direct foreign investment in West Germany amounted to U.S.$29.3 billion in the same year (Table 4-2), the penetration of foreign investment in the French industrial sector, measured as a percentage of total sector turnover in 1978, was considerably higher at 26.3 percent than Germany's 18 percent in 1980.[99] On an industry basis foreign penetration remained quite high; in the French computer industry, 72.6 percent of the turnover was foreign controlled, in petroleum and natural gas, 54.9 percent, agricultural machinery, 52.4 percent, chemicals, 47.5 percent, pharmaceuticals, 37.9 percent, and electronic equipment, 37.4 percent.[100] Foreign-controlled firms accounted for 21.3 percent of the employment in the electrical and electronics industry, 15.5 percent of employment in the chemical, pharmaceutical and plastics industries, and 11.2 percent of the employment in the machinery and equipment industry.[101] As the growth rate of GDP and productivity fell, inflation rose dramatically, and unemployment began its climb upward in the late 1970s, the French state evidenced its concern over French industrial competitiveness in a number of important documents, notably the Seventh Plan and the Commissariat général du plan's Berthelot Report.[102] Crisis-induced divestments such as Montedison's decision to close its Montefibre plant at Saint-Nabord in the Vosges in 1977, which brought workers into the streets, also focussed attention on the extensiveness of foreign control in industry and its consequences for employment in declining regions.[103]

Although the "discretionary" and "opaque" nature of the French system of controls on direct foreign investment permits "significant scope for varying policies on foreign direct investment when desired,"[104] a far greater emphasis appears to have been placed on implicit rather than explicit policies by the French government this time around. Both implicit regulatory policies are being used (in the form of sectoral or technological programs and, most recently, in a series of nationalizations) and implicit inducement policies that discriminate between domestic and foreign firms with respect to access to credit under a variety of newly created state funding mechanisms.

Since the 1920s, when the French state sought to preserve a share of the domestic market for domestically owned petroleum firms, and moving through the well documented history of the *plan calcul*, undertaken in 1966 to ensure a French presence in the computer industry,[105] the state

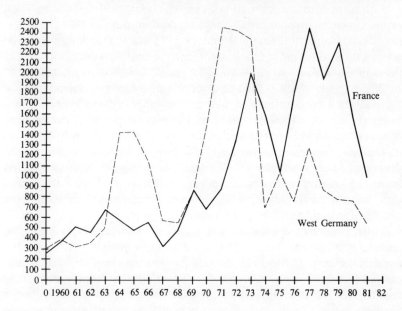

Source: See Appendix.

has periodically identified key sectors in which to strengthen national
firms without closing such sectors to foreign investment. In 1979 a
number of high-technology sectors were identified — offshore
petroleum, office automation, biotechnology, robotics, electronics and
energy-saving technology — in which national firms would be encouraged and a new Interministerial Committee for the Development of
Strategic Industries (CODIS) was created and provided with funds in
order to undertake this task.[106] Under the Socialist government of
President Mitterrand, leading firms in a number of these sectors, both
domestic and foreign-owned, were nationalized in 1982. By nationalizing
the Compagnie général d'électricité, Saint-Gobain-Pont-à-Mousson,
Péchiney Ugine Kuhlmann, Thomson-Brandt, Rhône-Poulenc,
Dassault, Matra and C.I.I.-Honeywell-Bull, 54 percent of the production in basic chemicals, 75 percent in artificial textiles, 36 percent in
office automation and *informatique*, 44 percent in electronics and 26 percent in electrical equipment, and 84 percent in the aviation industry now
fell under public ownership.[107] The ability of the French state to influence the direction of research, levels of employment, degree of internationalization, and rates of new investment in these firms was also facilitated by the nationalization of most of the remaining private banks in
France. Where the state now directly influences the leading firms in

these sectors, there is less need to regulate the activities of foreign firms in order to realize its economic and social goals.

With respect to inducement policies which implicitly favour national firms, two new mechanisms should be pointed out. In 1974 the Interministerial Committee for the Adaptation of Industrial Strictures (CIASI) was set up to aid firms in financial difficulty. CIASI, however, only assists those firms "*qui ne font pas partie d'un groupe industriel ou financier.*"[108] In this manner, CIASI is able to discriminate against all subsidiaries of multinational corporations as well as a number of large French firms. Similarly, CIDISE, the Interministerial Committee for the Development of Investment and Maintenance of Employment, created in 1979, has as its *critère déterminant* for funding "the independence of the firm: since diversified industrial groups — French or foreign — have privileged access to long-term financial resources (financial markets, eurocurrencies) and can easily mobilize their own resources across their different units" (translation).[109]

As the French case illustrates, many mechanisms are available to the state to regulate and induce new investment in industry. Although the approach taken by the French state has shifted from an overtly regulatory to a more implicitly regulatory one, and from inducement mechanisms that were nondiscriminatory in nature to those which favour smaller, nationally owned firms, such differences do not appear to account for the peaks and troughs in new inflows of direct foreign investment. Given the relative weakness of French industry vis-à-vis world leaders in dynamic sectors undergoing rapid technological change, a continued role for the state can be anticipated in the orientation of industrial development and, derivatively, in direct negotiations with foreign investors.

Conclusions

From the data and analysis presented in the preceding sections it is possible to draw a number of conclusions with respect to those factors that have induced states to intervene in the foreign investment process, the kinds of regulatory or inducement mechanisms they have adopted, and the impact of such regulations on the inflow of new direct foreign investment.

Among the OECD countries covered in this paper, only Japan and Sweden, both of which were relatively late industrializers, had long integrated the regulation of direct foreign investment into their industrial development strategies. Indeed, politically powerful forces in these societies, anxious to ensure the development of a strong domestic industrial sector, enacted legislation early in the century that excluded direct foreign investment from key economic sectors, encouraging technology imports through licensing and capital imports through bank lending or portfolio investment. It was not until inward foreign direct investment rose dramatically during the 1960s and 1970s, however, that other OECD states tended to become directly involved in the foreign investment process. The issues that figured heavily in public debates over the need for state involvement were national control over sectors deemed dynamic, strategic, or vital to the realization of economic and social goals; the rising costs of direct foreign investment, in terms of balance-of-payments disequilibria; growing technological dependence; and concern for possible loss of decisional autonomy.

Different states, however, responded to the stimulus of increased foreign penetration in substantially different ways, as the following examples demonstrate. In Germany and the United States, where the level of foreign investment remained low and/or the sectoral concentration appeared not to threaten domestic economic interests or social goals, state involvement took the form of monitoring incoming direct foreign investment. In the United Kingdom and Belgium, where the level of direct foreign investment was high and/or increasing, where it was concentrated in industries or regions deemed vital to national economic and social goals, and where historically the role of the state in the economy was limited, a variety of *implicit* regulatory or incentive mechanisms designed to attract and then channel direct foreign investment into preferred economic or geographical regions were implemented. In Australia, Canada and France, where the level of foreign investment was high, where the sectoral concentration appeared to threaten existing economic interests or social goals, and where the costs of direct foreign investment were perceived to have risen, both traditionally interventionist and non-interventionist states were induced to adopt *explicit* regulatory policies.

The exact conditions under which foreign investment became an issue and the precise mechanisms developed to deal with it were, however, unique to each country. They derived primarily from the historical role of the state in the respective economies, the nature of coalitions operating at the centre of the policy-making process and their orientation toward direct foreign investment, the impact of changing economic and social conditions, and previous policy experience with respect to foreign investment. The Australian and French cases discussed earlier in this paper are illustrative of the complex interaction among these variables.

In Australia, extensive foreign control of the dynamic extractive sector and serious balance-of-payments problems, partly attributable to the rising costs of direct foreign investment, laid the groundwork for the state's involvement in the foreign investment process. But the catalyst was a U.S. decision to encourage its firms to borrow abroad rather than to export capital. As those in power sought direct foreign investment as a supplement to domestic capital, the very rationale for their efforts was undermined. Given the traditionally limited role of the state in the Australian economy, only a ceiling on domestic borrowing by foreign firms was immediately imposed. Subsequent responses were cautionary and took the form of guidelines and directives. When these measures did not have the desired effect and a more interventionist Labour government came to power, an explicitly regulatory agency, the Foreign Investment Review Board, was created. Despite some relaxation of review procedures, the FIRB was retained by the conservative LNC coalition when it was returned to power.

In France, in contrast, it was the perceived loss of control, not over resources but over a strategic high-technology sector, that led a centre-right coalition to regulate incoming foreign investment and develop a sector policy with implictly regulatory content. Conforming to the country's long history of state intervention in the economy, an inter-ministerial committee was immediately struck and a review process initiated.

Although no studies were undertaken by the French or Australian governments to determine the impact of their regulations on either the inflow of new direct foreign investment or the extent to which such regulations served to promote the social or economic goals invoked to justify their adoption, threatened loss of new direct foreign investment led centre-right governments in France (1966) and Australia (1976) to relax existing regulations. Interestingly enough, an analysis of new inflows of direct foreign investment on a year-by-year basis over the period 1960–80 (see Figure 4-1) reveals absolutely no correlation between regulation and reduction in new foreign investment in either Australia or France. Increases in new direct foreign investment, more-over, occurred in periods characterized by regulation and in periods during which no policy changes intervened as well as in periods in which previous regulations were relaxed. In keeping with much of the economic literature on the foreign investment decision process, these results suggest that changes in the flow of direct foreign investment might be better explained by factors such as market size and dynamics, tariff, tax and other incentive policies, or relative factor proportions than by regulation.[110]

In sum, what this paper has demonstrated is the absence of any simple correlation between the changing pattern of direct foreign investment within an economy, or the growth of capital exporting by firms from a given country, and attempts by the state in that country to regulate the inflow of direct foreign investment or to relax such regulations. Similar stimuli will, it was argued, produce quite different policy responses in different countries, as these responses are shaped by a complex set of political and economic variables operating within a historically structured and conjuncturally specific context.

The literature lacks systematic analyses of the extent to which regulatory or inducement mechanisms have successfully attracted foreign investment or channelled it into sectors considered desirable. Clearly such studies are essential if policy alternatives are to be seriously evaluated.

Appendix

Direct Foreign Investment Inflows for Selected Developed Market Economies, 1960–82 (millions of 1975 U.S. dollars)

	1960	1961	1962	1963	1964	1965	1966	1967	1968	1969	1970
Australia	772	455	730	799	920	n.a.	770	775	991	945	1,249
Belgium-Luxembourg	n.a.	n.a.	n.a.	n.a.	n.a.	243	232	370	385	390	442
Canada	1,241	941	834	460	413	848	1,210	1,029	841	977	1,205
France	252	365	506	462	670	572	485	551	302	475	865
West Germany	300	373	312	346	495	1,409	1,424	1,132	572	551	828
Japan	11	108	105	181	191	81	50	73	117	106	131
Netherlands	48	44	99	128	156	262	262	409	499	519	747
Sweden	n.a.	n.a.	87	144	68	149	230	163	162	227	150
United Kingdom	700	1,213	656	796	883	944	904	742	1,046	960	1,182
United States	583	571	623	410	563	711	704	1,124	1,244	1,852	2,036
Total listed countries	3,907	4,070	3,951	3,727	4,357	5,218	6,270	6,367	6,159	7,003	8,835

	1971	1972	1973	1974	1975	1976	1977	1978	1979	1980	1981	1982
Australia	1,521	1,326	166	1,464	434	1,003	1,032	1,388	1,290	1,498	1,510	1,570
Belgium-Luxembourg	591	492	864	1,248	958	829	1,143	1,197	872	1,091	918	966
Canada	1,232	796	992	946	709	− 182	925	991	1,236	439	− 1,890	− 1,223
France	696	874	1,354	2,032	1,555	1,011	1,814	2,443	1,950	2,292	1,584	970
West Germany	1,499	2,459	2,436	2,347	692	1,022	755	1,289	854	789	769	530
Japan	278	207	−43	224	231	110	21	11	179	193	122	268
Netherlands	776	768	1,032	1,044	977	333	323	562	923	876	900	323
Sweden	110	86	87	83	80	4	72	60	86	177	116	108
United Kingdom	1,428	1,294	2,144	2,190	1,365	1,383	2,074	2,093	2,983	3,446	1,143	1,246
United States	485	1,216	3,367	5,222	2,635	4,130	3,333	6,611	9,117	7,655	14,301	6,335
Total listed countries	8,615	9,518	12,399	16,800	9,636	9,643	11,493	16,644	19,490	18,456	19,473	11,093

Sources: IMF, *Balance of Payments Yearbook* 1960–64 (Vol. 17), 1967–69 (Vol. 22), 1981–82 (Vol. 34), Part 1; except for France where 1965–66 = Vol. 20, 1963–67 and 1967–69 = Vol. 22. (Washington, D.C.: IMF) UNCTC, *Transnational Corporations in World Development* (New York: United Nations, 1983) p. 286 for 1970–80.

Notes: The dollar figures are deflated using the U.S. GNP implicit price index (1975 = 100), as published in OECD, *Main Economic Indicators: Historical Statistics, 1960–79* (Paris: 1980) and OECD, *Main Economic Indicators* (Paris: Oct. 1983). The figures for 1982 are estimates.
n.a. = not available.

Notes

This paper was completed in February 1984. The author wishes to thank Brent Copley for his assistance in researching this paper.

1. See, for example, the summaries and arguments presented in Neil Hood and Stephen Young, *The Economics of Multinational Enterprise* (London: Longman, 1979), especially chapt. 5; W.H. Goldberg, R. Neglandi, eds., *Governments and Multinationals: the Policy of Control vs. Autonomy* (Cambridge, Mass.: Oelgeschlager, Gunn and Hain, 1983), pp. 4–35; Charles Albert Michalet, "The International Transfer of Technology and the Multinational Enterprise," *Development and Change* 7 (1976); John N.H. Britton and James M. Gilmour, *The Weakest Link: A Technological Perspective on Canadian Industrial Under-Development*, Science Council of Canada Background Study No. 43 (Ottawa: Minister of Supply and Services Canada, 1978); and Robert Black, Stephen Blank, and Elizabeth Hansen, *Multinationals in Contention: Responses at Governmental and International Levels* (New York: The Conference Board, 1978).

2. See Black, Blank, and Hansen, *Multinationals in Contention*, p. 44; and Lynn K. Mytelka, *Regional Development in a Global Economy, The Multinational Corporation, Technology and Regional Integration* (New Haven: Yale University Press, 1979), chaps. 1 and 3.

3. United Nations, Centre on Transnational Corporations, *Transnational Corportions in World Development*, Third Survey (New York: 1983), Doc. No. ST/CTC/46, Table II.2, p. 19.

4. M.Y. Yoshino, "Japan as Host to the International Corporation," in *The International Corporation: A Symposium*, edited by Charles Kindleberger (Cambridge, Mass: MIT Press, 1970), pp. 345–69; Masuru Saito, "Introduction of Foreign Technology in the Industrialization Process: Japanese Experience since the Meiji Restoration (1968)," *The Developing Economies* 12 (June 1975): 168–86; Arnaud Dubois, "Le contrôle des changes et des investissements au Japan," *France-Japan ECO*, Chambre de Commerce et d'Industrie Française du Japon, No. 17 (1983).

5. Jan Erik Vahlne, "Foreign Direct Investments: A Swedish Policy Problem," in *Governments and Multinationals: the Policy of Control vs. Autonomy*, edited by W.H. Goldberg and R. Neglandi (Cambridge, Mass.: Oelgeschlager, Gunn and Hain, 1983), pp. 207–18; Goran Ohlin, "Sweden," in *Big Business and the State*, edited by Raymond Vernon (Cambridge, Mass: Harvard University Press, 1974), pp. 126–44.

6. See Marcel Bayen, *Characterisation des coopérations entre sociétés américaines et japonaises dans le domaine des technologies critiques* (Paris: Ministère de la recherche et de l'industrie, mars 1983), and Lynn K. Mytelka, "La gestion de la connaissance dans les entreprises multinationales," *Économie, prospective internationale* 20 (4e trimestre 1984): 74–33.

7. Centre d'études prospectives et d'informations internationales (CEPII), *Économie mondiale : la montée des tensions* (Paris: Economica, 1983), p. 242.

8. Jacques Pelkmans, "European Direct Investments in the European Community," *Journal of European Integration* 7(1) (Autumn 1983): 41–70, and Lynn K. Mytelka and Michael Dolan, "The Political Economy of EEC-ACP Relations in a Changing International Division of Labour," in *European Integration and Unequal Development*, edited by C. Vaitsos and D. Seers (London: Macmillan, 1980), pp. 237–60.

9. Pelkmans, "European Direct Investments," pp. 48–49.

10. Bernadette Madeuf and Carlos Ominami, "Crise et investissement international," *Revue Économique* 24 (September 1983): 926–70, Table 1, p. 935.

11. Ibid., p. 933.

12. CEPII, *Économie mondiale*, p. 243.

13. OECD, Committee on International Investment and Multinational Enterprises, *Multinational Enterprises and the Structural Adjustment Process* (Paris: OECD, 1983), pp. 19–20.

14. OECD, *Recent International Direct Investment Trends* (Paris: OECD, 1981). Data for Australia are from Table 16, p. 62, for Belgium from Table 18, p. 65, for France from Table 23, p. 72.

15. OECD, *Multinational Enterprises and the Structural Adjustment Process*, p. 69.

16. Ibid., p. 70.

17. Canada, Foreign Investment Review Agency, "Statistical Overview of Foreign Investment and FIRA" (Ottawa: FIRA, 1984) mimeo, Table 4.

18. John H. Dunning, "Technology, United States Investment and European Economic Growth," in *International Investment*, edited by J. Dunning (London: Penguin, 1972), pp. 377–411, p. 380.

19. Science Council of Canada, *Hard Times, Hard Choices: Technology and the Balance of Payments*, a Statement by the Industrial Policies Committee (Ottawa: Minister of Supply and Services Canada, 1981).

20. Daniel Van den Bulcke, "Export Activities of Multinational Enterprises in Belgium," in *Export Management: An International Contest*, edited by M.R. Ozinkota and G. Resar (New York: Praeger, 1982), pp. 149–73. D. Van den Bulcke, "Investment and Divestment Policies of Multinational Corporations in Europe," in *Investment and Divestment Policies of Multinational Corporations*, edited by D. Van den Bulcke, D.J.J. Boddewyn, B. Martens and P. Klemmer (Brussels: ECSIM, 1979), pp. 1–59; P.K. Mathew Tharakan and L. Soete, W.M. Schoofs, J.A. Busschaert, "Politique et processus d'adjustement en Belgique," in *Ajustement en vue des échanges* (Paris: OECD, Centre de Développement, 1975), pp. 105–40.

21. OECD, *Investment Incentives and Disincentives and the International Investment Process* (Paris: OECD, 1983), pp. 88.

22. A.E. Safarian, *Governments and Multinationals: Policies in the Developed Countries* (Washington, D.C.: British-North American Committee, 1983), pp. 67–72; Klaus W. Grewlich, *Direct Investment in the OECD Countries* (Netherlands: Sijthoff and Noordhoff, 1978), pp. 50–52; and Jean Boddewyn, *Western European Policies toward U.S. Investors* (New York: New York University, Bulletins No. 93–95, March 1974).

23. Fred C. Bergsten's Statement before the U.S. House Subcommittee on Commerce, Consumer and Monetary Affairs (1979) and Marc Leland's testimony in Hearings before the same committee in 1982 as cited in Safarian, *Governments and Multinationals*, p. 37.

24. Ibid.

25. Ibid., p. 44

26. Boddewyn, *Western European Policies toward U.S. Investors*, p. 19.

27. Ibid., p. 20.

28. Safarian, *Governments and Multinationals*, p. 43.

29. Ibid., pp. 43–44.

30. For a comparative review of this legislation see OECD, *Controls and Impediments Affecting Inward Direct Investment in OECD Member Countries* (Paris: 1982); OECD, *International Direct Investment: Policies, Procedures and Practices in OECD Member Countries* (Paris: 1979); United Nations, Centre on Transnational Enterprises, *National Legislation and Regulations Relating to Transnational Corporations* (New York: 1978); UNCTC, *Supplement to National Legislation and Regulations Relating to Transnational Corporations* (1980); and UNCTC, *National Legislation and Regulations Relating to Transnational Corporations* (New York: 1983), as well as works cited in note 22.

31. Grewlich, *Direct Investment in the OECD Countries*, p. 52.

32. Stephen Gohen and Peter A. Gourevitch, eds., *France in the Troubled World Economy* (London: Butterworth, 1982).

33. Boddewyn, *Western European Policies toward U.S. Investors*, p. 72.

34. Stuart Holland, "State Entrepreneurship and State Intervention," in *The State as Entrepreneur*, edited by S. Holland (London: Weidenfeld and Nicolson, 1972), pp. 5–44, p. 32.

35. Safarian, *Governments and Multinationals*, p. 38.
36. Grewlich, *Direct Investment in the OECD Countries*, p. 62.
37. Ibid., p. 50.
38. Boddewyn, *Western European Policies toward U.S. Investors*, p. 37.
39. Ibid.
40. Ibid.
41. Ibid., pp. 18–19.
42. Lawrence S. Welch, "Internationalization Pressure: A Post-War Australian Perspective," in *Export Policy: A Global Assessment*, edited by Michael R. Czinkota and George Tesar, (New York: Praeger, 1982), pp. 3–19, p. 3.
43. A.G.L. Shaw, *The Economic Development of Australia*, 7th ed. (Melbourne: Longman, 1980), p. 181.
44. Welch, "Internationalization Pressure," p. 3.
45. H.W. Arndt, "Foreign Investment," in *Australian Economic Policy*, edited by J.P. Niewenhuysen and P.J. Drake (Melbourne: Wilke, 1977), pp. 132–45.
46. Lawrence R. Welch and Finn Wiedersheim-Paul, "MNCs and the Australian Government: Some Emerging Policy Issues," in *Governments and Multinationals: the Policy of Control vs. Autonomy*, edited by W.H. Goldberg and R. Neglandi (Cambridge, Mass.: Oelgeschlager, Gunn and Hain, 1983), pp. 249–69, p. 250.
47. Donald T. Brash, "Australia as Host to the International Corporation," in *The International Corporation: A Symposium*, edited by Charles Kindleberger (Cambridge, Mass.: MIT Press, 1970), pp. 293–318, pp. 294–95.
48. Brash, "Australia as Host to the International Corporation," pp. 302–303, and Arndt, "Foreign Investment," pp. 134–35.
49. Brash, "Australia as Host to the International Corporation", p. 293.
50. Ibid., p. 295.
51. Ibid., p. 296.
52. Ibid.
53. Welch, "Internationalization Pressure," p. 6.
54. Brash, "Australia as Host to the International Corporation," p. 300.
55. Ibid.
56. Ibid., p. 303.
57. Arndt, "Foreign Investment," p. 136.
58. Brash, "Australia as Host to the International Corporation," p. 305.
59. Arndt, "Foreign Investment," p. 137.
60. Brash, "Australia as Host to the International Corporation," p. 308.
61. Ibid., pp. 308–309.
62. Mytelka, *Regional Development in a Global Economy*, chaps. 1 and 3.
63. Arndt, "Foreign Investment," p. 139.
64. Safarian, *Governments and Multinationals*, p. 10.
65. Welch, "Internationalization Pressure," p. 12.
66. Ibid., p. 15.
67. American Chamber of Commerce in Australia, "Summary of American Business Views," *Commerce* (January–February 1974): 11–14.
68. Arndt, "Foreign Investment," p. 140.
69. OECD, *Investment Incentives*, p. 74.
70. Welch and Wiedersheim-Paul, "MNCs and the Australian Government," p. 266.
71. Figures are from the FIRB annual report for 1982 cited by Safarian, *Governments and Multinationals*, p. 13.
72. Welch and Wiedersheim-Paul, "MNCs and the Australian Government," pp. 255–56.
73. "Hawke Is Dovish on Multinationals," *The Economist* (February 26, 1983), p. 74.

74. See, for example, Charles-Albert Michalet, "France," in *Big Business and the State*, edited by Raymond Vernon (Cambridge, Mass.: Harvard University Press, 1974), pp. 105–25, and Andrew Shonfield, *Modern Capitalism: The Changing Balance of Public and Private Power* (London: Oxford University Press, 1965) p. 77.

75. Lynn K. Mytelka, "The French Textile Industry: Crisis and Adjustment," in *The Emerging International Economic Order: Dynamics Processes, Constraints and Opportunities*, edited by H.K. Jacobson and D. Sidjanski (Beverly Hills, Cal.: Sage, 1982), pp. 129–66. See also Mytelka and Dolan, "The Political Economy of EEC-ACP Relations in a Changing International Division of Labour."

76. See, for example, Shonfield, *Modern Capitalism*; J. Sheahan, *Promotion and Control of Industry in Postwar France* (Cambridge, Mass.: Harvard University Press, 1963); and B. Guibert et al., *La mutation industrielle de la France du Traité de Rome à la crise pétrolière*, Tome I and II (Paris: Les Collections de l'INSEE, no. 31–32E, 1975).

77. On France see Christian Stoffaes, *La grande menace industrielle* (Paris: Calmann-Levy, 1978), p. 88; on the Netherlands, Arend Lijphart, "The Netherlands: Continuity and Change in Voting Behaviour," in R. Rose, *Electoral Behavior: A Comparative Handbook* (London: Collier Macmillan, 1974), pp. 227–68; and on Germany, Knut Borchardt, "Germany 1700–1910," in *The Fontana Economic History of Europe: The Emergence of Industrial Societies–I*, edited by Carlo Cipolla (London: Collins, 1973), pp. 76–160; and Georg H. Kuster, "Germany," in *Big Business and the State*, edited by Raymond Vernon (Cambridge, Mass.: Harvard University Press, 1974), pp. 64–86.

78. Yves Morvan, *La concentration de l'industrie en France* (Paris: Librairie Armand Colin, 1972), pp. 221, 285, 288.

79. See for more details, Stephen Cohen, *Modern Capitalist Planning: The French Model* (Cambridge, Mass.: Harvard University Press, 1969); John Zysman, *Political Strategies for Industrial Order: State, Market and Industry in France* (Berkeley: University of California Press, 1977); Suzanne Berger and Michael Piore, *Dualism and Discontinuity in Industrial Societies* (Cambridge: Cambridge University Press, 1980); and Cohen and Gourevitch, *France in the Troubled World Economy*.

80. Lynn K. Mytelka, "In Search of a Partner: The State and the Textile Industry in France," in *France in the Troubled World Economy*, edited by Stephen Cohen and Peter Gourevitch (London: Butterworth, 1982), pp. 132–50.

81. See Henry W. Ehrmann, *Organized Business in France* (Princeton: Princeton University Press, 1957); Ezra Suleiman, "Industrial Policy Formation in France," in *Industrial Policies in Western Europe*, edited by S. Warnecke and E. Suleiman (New York: Praeger, 1974); and George Ross, *Workers and Communists in France* (Berkeley: University of California Press, 1982).

82. Jean-Jacques Servan-Schreiber, *The American Challenge* (London: Pelican, 1969), p. 27.

83. Van den Bulcke, "Investment and Divestment Policies," p. 8.

84. Servan-Schreiber, *The American Challenge*, p. 28.

85. Ibid., pp. 23–24.

86. Ibid., p. 29.

87. Groupe de recherche de géographie industrielle, *Les investissements étrangers en France* (Grenoble: Presses universitaires de Grenoble, 1975), p. 128.

88. Servan-Schreiber, *The American Challenge*, p. 29.

89. Michalet, "France," p. 123.

90. Boddewyn, *Western European Policies toward U.S. Investors*, p. 20.

91. Servan-Schreiber, *The American Challenge*, pp. 27–28.

92. Michalet, "France", p. 123, and Servan-Schreiber, *The American Challenge*, p. 28.

93. Boddewyn, *Western European Policies toward U.S. Investors*, p. 20.

94. Ibid., p. 22.

95. "Le VIe plan prend, vis-à-vis de ces investissements, une position d'encouragement sans entrave, fort différente de celle du précédent; et ce, alors que précisément, les grands groupes industriels et financiers français ont, pour l'essentiel achevé ce qu'il

leur était possible de faire pour se renforcer et accéder à l'envergure internationale." Groupe de recherche de géographie industrielle, *Les investissements étrangers*, p. 11.

96. Ibid., p. 34.

97. Ibid.

98. Pelkmans, "European Direct Investments in the European Community."

99. Conseil économique et social, "Les investissements étrangers en France et français à l'étranger," *Regards sur l'actualité* 69 (March 1981): 19–28, p. 23.

100. Ibid.

101. Michel Delapierre, "La dimension productive : La structure des investissements directs" in *L'intégration de l'économie française dans l'économie mondiale*, edited by Charles Albert Michalet (Paris: Economica, 1984), pp. 77–102, p. 99.

102. *Strategy for Progress, Seventh Economic and Social Development Plan 1976–1980* (Paris: La Documentation Française, 1976); Commissariat Général du Plan, *Rapport du groupe chargé d'étudier l'évolution des économies du tiers-monde et l'appareil productif français* (Paris: January 1978).

103. Van den Bulcke, "Investment and Divestment Policies," p. 8.

104. Safarian, *Governments and Multinationals*, p. 24.

105. See, for example, S. Nora and A. Minc, *L'informatisation dans la société* (Paris: Éditions de Seuil, 1978).

106. "Trois nouveaux instruments de politique industrielle," *Regards sur l'actualité* 69 (March 1981): 28–38.

107. André Delion and Michel Durupty, *Les nationalisations 1982* (Paris: Economica, 1982), p. 191.

108. "Trois nouveaux instruments de politique industrielle," p. 28.

109. "L'indépendance de l'entreprise : en effet les groupes industriels diversifiés — français ou étrangers — disposent d'un accès privilégié aux ressources de financement à long terme (marchés financiers, euro-devises) et peuvent mobiliser aisément leurs ressources propres entre leurs différentes unités." Ibid., p. 32.

110. See, for example, R.E. Caves, *Multinational Enterprise and Economic Analysis* (Cambridge: Cambridge University Press, 1982); Charles Kindleberger, "The Monopolistic Theory of Direct Foreign Investment," in *Transnational Corportions and World Order*, edited by G. Modelski (San Francisco: Freeman, 1979), pp. 91–107; J.H. Dunning, "Explaining Changing Patterns of International Production: In Defence of the Electric Theory," *Oxford Bulletin of Economics and Statistics* 41(4) (November 1979): 269–96; Steven Hymer, *The International Operations of National Firms: A Study of Direct Foreign Investment* (Cambridge, Mass.: MIT Press, 1976); and Sanjaya Lall, ed., *The New Multinationals: The Spread of Third World Enterprises* (London: John Wiley, 1983).

5

The State and Industrial Decline:
A Survey

M.A. CHANDLER

In the last fifteen years, the response of the public sector to economic decline has become an issue of pressing political concern in almost all advanced industrialized states. In the face of continuing economic change and international pressures to reduce trade protection, all the advanced industrialized nations have been forced to deal with the problems of economic adjustment — some more willingly than others, some more effectively. Certainly in Canada, public assistance to ailing private sector firms and troubled industries is not new. Support for canals, railways, and the wheat pool are early testimony of assistance to failing private sector firms. Since World War II, both the federal and the provincial governments have given programmatic and ad hoc, firm-specific assistance to declining industries (Trebilcock et al., 1985, chap. 2). In Canada, the current management of decline has raised questions about past practices and has aroused debate over future directions and which instruments of policy should be used. In order better to inform that debate, this paper puts forward a comparative analysis of the role of the state in coping with economic decline and adjustment. The aim is first to array systematically the policies and instruments that have been employed in Europe and Japan. The second objective is to consider the political determinants of policy options by exploring the political forces that have shaped other nations' policies toward decline.

The Political Economy of Adjustment

Unlike the 1960s, which were characterized by economic growth and optimism in most industrialized nations, the 1970s and 1980s have brought high unemployment and inflation, low growth and fears of deindustrialization (Cox, 1982; Dahrendorf, 1982; Schmidt, 1983). Macro indicators of inflation, unemployment and economic growth all reflect the problems of the 1970s. Beyond these measures, the sense of economic crisis has been heightened by closures and threats of bankruptcy in many plants and firms (Dyson and Wilks, 1983, p. 1). The explanation for this stark economic downturn can be attributed to several factors: oil price hikes, competition from newly industrializing nations, and changing comparative advantage and market shares among developed countries (Denison, 1979). Exogenously induced change in its economic competitiveness has become a problem facing each advanced industrialized country; no nation has been spared the need to adapt to the changing world economic order. As national economic performance has deteriorated, economic problems have become political problems. The dislocations created by economic change are quickly taken up in the political process through the efforts of individuals to maintain their property rights (Hirsch and Goldthorpe, 1978). Losers — those likely to bear the burdens of economic change — try to insulate themselves through political action (Courchene, 1980; Reich, 1983a). The economic crises of the last decade have given rise to much debate about how to circumvent the damaging impact of the market (Dyson and Wilks, 1983, p. 5; Shepherd et al., 1983, p. 15). Zysman and Tyson point to the political problems that economic change provokes: how to reconcile the demands of those dislocated by international trade with the necessity of continued industrial adjustment (1983, p. 51). Acknowledging that in the 1970s and 1980s grave problems of adjustment have arisen that are political as much as economic, what have been the responses to these challenges? How have other nations sought to manage decline? What political factors have shaped each nation's response?

The problems of the 1970s were at first dealt with by macroeconomic measures. Broad budgetary and monetary responses could not resolve the structural problems that marked the period (Cox, 1982). Industrial policy as the term is generally used is quite distinct from macroeconomic policy; it refers to micro-intervention, which distinguishes among sectors. Industrial policy is defined as policy that tries to resolve problems in specific industrial sectors (Jenkin, 1983, pp. 19–20; Zysman and Tyson, 1983, p. 22). Curzon Price broadly defines industrial policy as any measure to promote or prevent structural change. She adds, however, that in recent years there is a new attribute — it is selective: "thus modern industrial policy aims at more than merely setting a general framework. It descends increasingly into the microeconomic sphere of economic decision taking that was formerly left to the price mechanism" (Curzon Price, 1981, p. 18). These micro-level interventions are structural; they are meant to affect the pace and development of industry (Green, 1981). In essence, there are three types of sectors — growth, transition and decline; each presents a different policy problem for the state.

In a growth sector, rapid increases in demand are accompanied by a quick evolution in the product and in its production and in distribution arrangements. The important problem for the firm is maintaining market share [in a growing market]. . . . For a government, the problem may be to assure the growth of national production so that imports do not capture the expanding demand and weaken the position of national firms.

A declining segment is one in which there are no possible significant changes in product or process by which firms can regain competitive position, and one in which demand for the industry as a whole is stagnant. An industry in transition is a mature industry undergoing basic changes in its production or production processes. . . . Whether an industry survives a transition period or slips until decline is irreversible depends upon both company choices and government policy. (Zysman, 1983, pp. 43–44)

Zysman argues that there are only a few sectors in which decline is inevitable (where no possible changes in product or process can bring the firm back to a competitive position). "Whether an industry is defined as being in decline or in transition is a political determination that cannot be made by simple marketplace measurement" (ibid., p. 45). This paper is concerned with policies toward firms and sectors that are not able to compete; at this point we beg the question of whether the difficulties are transitory or terminal, structural or cyclical. The question is: how have states responded to specific firms and industries that are not successful? How have they coped with the general problem of economic decline?[1] Magaziner and Reich note that there are three strategic choices facing every political community that confronts structural change:

A nation can ease the adjustment of capital and labour out of its declining businesses by assisting workers with retraining and relocating, by subsidizing the development of new businesses within the same region or community, and by helping firms to salvage those portions of declining businesses that are capable of becoming competitive on their own. A second choice is for a nation to protect declining businesses from foreign competition, to control cost-justified price increases, to prevent factory closings and relocations and to allocate government funds for the preservation of bankrupt companies. The third alternative is to do nothing and allow the market to work on its own, with resulting bankruptcies, unemployment and community or regional decline. (Magaziner and Reich, 1982, pp. 198–99)

Clearly the three "choices" really involve a broader range of possibilities: a laissez-faire approach toward declining firms may be accompanied by the extensive use of macroeconomic levers; the adjustment process may be slowed down rather than totally opposed; and policies to facilitate adjustment may be directed toward any of several agents — individuals, firms and regions.

To best develop a comparative perspective on the political responses to industrial decline in capitalist countries, this paper is divided into two sections. The first is mainly descriptive: it lays out when and how advanced industrialized nations have mobilized resources to deal with structural change. We draw on the experience of Britain, France, West Germany, Japan and the United States to present an analysis of the range of strategies that have been adopted. The emphasis is on depicting general strategic similarities across sectors within the same country.

The second section is devoted to the factors that have shaped the adjustment side of industrial policy. By appraising the circumstances that have moulded policy making in other political communities, we proceed to consider various policy options in light of the Canadian political process.

The State and the Market: Policies of Adjustment

No nation has been able to resist the pressures for firm-specific rescues; AEG Telefunken in Germany, Sasebo Heavy Industries in Japan, Chrysler in the United States and British Leyland in Britain bear witness to this. Textiles, coal, steel, and shipbuilding are among the mature or declining sectors that have posed major challenges of adjustment in each of the nations under review. The six states considered here have at some time provided assistance to ailing private firms and declining industrial sectors. Some policy making has been predominantly firm-specific; in other instances, the policy has been directed at the sector level. In some cases, the policy responses were routine and non-contentious; others sparked debate and controversy. In some cases, the purpose was to prop up a failing enterprise and to counter market forecasts; in other instances, the assistance facilitated rationalization and moderniza-tion — even at the expense of employment. Sometimes government played an interventionist role — inducing mergers to encourage rationalization, supplying capital for modernization, and ensuring a large and stable demand for products through public procurement. At other times, the state remained at the edge of the economy, isolated from the firm or sector. Even when the objectives appear to have been similar, a wide variety of instruments have been employed. In this section we shall provide a survey of the various responses of advanced indus-trialized states to economic decline, by examining the dominant strat-egies of Britain, France, West Germany, Japan, the United States and Canada.

Policy Patterns

The question of whether the state should intervene to promote adjust-ment is usually a contentious one. For some nations, firm failure, sec-toral decline or company bankruptcy are viewed as a necessary part of the economic system (Edmonds, 1983, p. 70). Thus, a consensus that some public action is required to cope with decline is not always the starting point of policy; state intervention as a response to economic crisis cannot be taken for granted. Among the nations considered here, Britain and the United States are examples of political systems where there is no consensus about the need to intervene to deal with economic decline (Coates, 1982; McKay, 1983b; Pollard, 1982); in these countries, there is as much debate over *whether* the state should act as there is in other nations over the *way* the state should respond. Recent writings in the United States (Thurow, 1980; Reich, 1983a, Magaziner and Reich, 1982; Zysman and Cohen, 1983) attest to the fact that there is no widespread agreement that the United States should have an industrial policy, let alone agreement over the nature of the state's involvement in structural change. This does not mean there is no policy debate in those nations — France, West Germany and Japan — in which there is more of a consensus. Indeed, there is evidence of considerable controversy; however, the issue is not whether policies to alleviate economic decline should be on the political agenda (McKay and Grant, 1983, p. 9).

Despite the accepted wisdom that Canadians are more willing to countenance state intervention (Hardin, 1974; Chandler, 1982), this predisposition cannot be interpreted as an automatic support for state-led adjustment. As will be argued in the next section, Canadian political culture may be supportive of *assistance* for those who must bear the costs of adjustment, but it cannot be said that there is concomitant acceptance of state-determined allocation of resources (Trebilcock et al., 1985, chap. 9). In this regard, Canada is similar to Britain and the United States — there is intense debate over whether the state should have an industrial strategy at all (Watson, 1983; Economic Council of Canada, 1983). Before we turn to the substance of policy, it must be recognized that the six nations analyzed here are divided into those states that still debate whether they should act and those for whom that question is not on the political agenda.

To present the policy patterns associated with each of the six nations, the scope and means of government policies toward industrial decline will be compared (Simeon, 1976). This will enable us to see national trends more clearly and understand what is distinctive about each of them. The scope of policy is defined as the range of matters in which governments are involved (Simeon, 1976, p. 559). In order to use the concept of scope to compare government policies toward declining industries and firms, we must specify what we mean by scope. The *extent* of intervention is in fact a multidimensional concept and cannot be indicated by any single measure — expenditure, for example. First of all, scope refers to the *range* of areas affected by public choice. However, the scale of intervention is not enough — it is also necessary to take into account the *depth* of intervention. To what extent does public replace private decision making? (Breton, 1974). Shepherd and Duchêne refer to the "heaviness" of intervention, in order to distinguish structural intervention, which replaces market forces, from environmental intervention, which changes the environment in which the market operates (1983, pp. 21–22). Differences in the depth of intervention are also brought out by John Zysman. In *Governments, Markets and Growth*, he argues that purposive industrial intervention, as opposed to the preservation of the existing economic order, requires that the state have its own view of industry, based on its particular definition of public purpose (1983, pp. 85–86). Besides *range* and *depth*, the *degree of integration* of the interventions can be a determining factor in deciding what is meant by *scope*. Are the public measures a collection of ad hoc actions, or are they part of a pattern within a coherent framework?

The means of policy refers primarily to the instruments or methods that the state employs in pursuing particular policy objectives. To compare the means of policy, we shall consider three characteristics of means: the purposes, the types of instruments, and the number or mix of instruments. The purpose of policy here refers quite simply to whether the policies are to *hinder* or *promote* adjustment. Obviously few states would say that they act consciously to prohibit change, but it is clear from the literature that there are significant differences in policy purposes. It should also be noted that a nation may use means that imply both purposes (Mahon and Mytelka, 1983). At this point, the emphasis is on the general purpose and direction of policy. There are many instruments available to advanced, industrialized nations that are striving to cope with industrial decline. These include: protectionist tariff and nontariff devices; tax concessions; direct subsidies; loans and loan guarantees; labour-related programs; regional aid; and nationalization. We shall not present a complete description or historical picture of the many ways in which each nation has dealt with decline, but rather shall examine the dominant approaches.

The United States

U.S. policy toward decline is the least interventionist of the six nations in our study. Data compiled by the Organization for Economic Cooperation and Development (OECD) show that the United States spends less than two percent of its gross national product on public subsidies to industrial enterprises. Mainstream ideology in the United States has consistently insisted that government should leave economic adjustment to market forces (Edmonds, 1983). Economic failures have traditionally been considered firm-specific problems. Given the severe ideological constraints on public sector intervention, assistance toward declining sectors has been predictably rare and haphazard. The few highly visible cases of "bailouts" (e.g., Lockheed in 1971 and Chrysler in 1979) resulted from administration requests to Congress to adopt emergency legislation authorizing assistance (Magaziner and Reich, 1982; Freeman and Mendelowitz, 1982). Public intervention is sharply differentiated from the usual activities of industry.

The scope of U.S. policy toward decline, therefore, has been limited in the breadth as well as in the depth of intervention. The pace and development of industry has been left to private decision making. When the U.S. government has intervened, its purpose has been to postpone or prevent adjustment. Therefore, it is not surprising that the few instances of government intervention reflect politically adept individuals trying to insulate themselves from those adjustment costs. The main instrument of U.S. "non-policy" (McKay, 1983b) is "industry-specific" protection (Krasner, 1978; Zysman and Tyson, 1983, chap. 1). In recent years, this protection has taken the form of "orderly marketing agreements" or "voluntary" quotas; such quotas have been applied to textiles, clothing, consumer electronics, footwear, steel and automobiles (Zysman and Tyson, 1983; Destler, 1980). Although some protectionist initiatives have been accompanied by proposals for reorganizing the industrial sector, there is no evidence of industries using the "breathing space" provided by protection to restructure (see various cases in Zysman and Tyson, 1983).

Besides protecting troubled industries by imposing import quotas, the United States often waives safety and health regulations. For example, both the Carter and Reagan administrations have exempted the steel and auto industries from compliance with costly environmental controls (Magaziner and Reich, 1982). U.S. labour market policies are another aspect of that country's response to decline. Unlike Japan and Western Europe, the United States has no regulations regarding plant closures and the obligations of employers who shut down factories (MacNeil, 1982). The U.S. 1974 Trade Act established a subsidy system to provide benefits for workers who lose their jobs as a result of foreign competition. Leaving aside such questions as whether it is trade competition or technology that makes industries less competitive, and whether those workers dislocated by international as opposed to domestic forces are worthy of assistance, the Trade Act has been criticized for its inefficiency. For example, J. David Richardson (1982) shows that almost 75 percent of the workers who received benefits returned to their former jobs. Instead of providing help for workers who have been laid off by a declining industry, the benefits go mainly to those who are temporarily unemployed. Moreover, among the workers certified as being eligible for assistance, only 4 percent were placed in new jobs and only 1 percent received benefits to help them find another job or to relocate. Besides, the firm subsidies under the Trade Act have not been considered a success either. The average grants (about $1 million per firm) are regarded as being too small to affect investor incentives (J. David Richardson, 1982).

In sum, the United States has relied on market-led adjustment. The impetus for assistance to declining industries comes from society, not the state (McKay, 1983b, p. 41). Various protectionist measures and a few rare interventions in a time of crisis have not been instituted because of any guiding framework. They are disparate measures adopted in response to specific political pressures (Edmonds, 1983, p. 87). When the United States has acted, it has employed a narrow range of instruments to forestall adjustment. When firms and industries have turned to government for help, the responses have been ad hoc, uncoordinated and half-hearted (McKay, 1983b).

Britain

Britain is an example of a liberal state that is committed to a market economy. It spends billions annually propping up declining firms and industries. British governments have provided assistance to a wide range of traditionally hard-pressed industries, such as steel, shipbuilding and textiles. However, given its poor economic performance, almost any industry is a potential candidate for decline, and therefore assistance (Gamble, 1981). Despite the large expenditures and numerous beneficiaries, British governments tend to intervene in a passive way — at the edge of the market. Much assistance has been directed to preserving jobs in declining industries and depressed regions, rather than toward the reorganization and adjustment of capital and labour (Grant, 1982). Even from 1972 to 1979, when Grant describes the approach as being a more interventionist "selective intervention,"[2] (1983, p. 49) the major thrust was largely reactive: to prop up industries in structural decline.

As Wilks observes (1983, p. 139), a major operating principle of British policy is to preserve the autonomy of the firm. The state does not lead industry or anticipate the need for sectoral adaptation. In the main, policy is ad hoc — a response to impending closures or bankruptcies. Why government intervenes to prevent some firms from going under and not others is more likely to be due to particular political pressures than to any consistent rationale (Wilks, 1983). Thus, the scope of British policy is based largely on an aggregation of ad hoc bailouts. It is an example of seemingly extensive public involvement that is, upon closer examination, a compilation of shallow, reactive and ad hoc interventions (Maunder, 1979; Green, 1981).

The relationship between government and the banks, labour, and business has tended to make British assistance to ailing firms and sectors more apparent than, say, the actions of French and Japanese governments, where closer organizational and functional ties between the state and other elements of society mean that state activities are often more indirect. The British government has not been able to use the banks as either an early warning system or a means of rescuing firms from collapse. The state sector in Britain does not have an extensive relationship with the business community, and so there is little of the consultative corporatist style that is so much a part of French and West German policy making (Blank, 1978; Gamble, 1981).[3]

Similarly, the fragmented labour movement in Britain makes the unions unlikely agents of private adjustment. Without the mediation of the banks, labour or industry, the government is left alone to meet demands for assistance and to act directly.

In order to preserve jobs even in the short term, Britain has often had to sacrifice long-term benefits (Green, 1981, p. 346). Successive British governments have employed various instruments to maintain employment in depressed regions and declining sectors, including: protection, subsidies, loans, and nationalization. The two main vehicles for subsidy assistance are the Regional Assistance Act, which provides regional development grants for industry and neutral aid to depressed regions, and the 1972 Industry Act. Sections 7 and 8 of the Industry Act are the basis for the selective intervention, in which billions of pounds are provided annually to keep ailing firms alive. Of the nations studied in this survey, Britain has been the most active subsidizer of declining firms. Yet this assistance has been criticized as incoherent and uncertain (DeCarmoy, 1978, p. 42).

The Employment Subsidy Scheme (1975) provides temporary assistance to maintain jobs in declining industries, such as textiles, clothing and steel (*The Economist*, January 14, 1978). Nationalizing lame ducks is another characteristic way in which the British try to stem decline. Once an industry has been nationalized, the government has usually adopted one of two courses, referred to as the "Chrysler" and the "British Leyland" options. In the case of Chrysler (U.K.), the funds were handed to the firm which was then left to develop its own recovery. In the case of British Leyland, there were more direct efforts by the government — the National Enterprise Board (NEB) to be precise — to effect the firm's recovery (Wilks, 1983). The Industrial Reorganization Corporation (1966–71) and the NEB, each established by Labour governments and intended to promote growth in workable firms, became vehicles for presiding over a series of bailouts (Grant, 1982). The changes brought by the Thatcher administration will be taken up later in this study; it should be noted here that the Tory Government has vowed, inter alia, to try to encourage labour mobility and adaptation, to impose tighter controls on subsidies for nationalized firms, and to stop propping up ailing firms (Curzon Price, 1981, p. 64).

West Germany

West Germany's response to economic decline has been quite different from that of U.S. or British governments. Expenditure-based measures of the size of the state do not provide an accurate picture of the scope of West German policy because they do not take into account two key elements of the German approach to economic problems. Unlike the banking systems in Britain and the United States, the German banks have been an integral element in assisting the German economy to adjust; they have lessened the need for active state-sponsored industrial policy (Zysman, 1983; Kuster, 1974). The central role of the banks has insulated government from the complex and detailed problem of monitoring and responding to the problems of major companies (Dyson, 1982a, p. 39). The other element of Germany's response to economic decline is the importance of social partnership or neo-corporatist collaboration among government, business and labour (Esser et al., 1983; Medley, 1982). German policies have sought to facilitate market trends; the term "social market" is used to describe the German approach: "It has been more limited in scope and more oriented to promoting a general industrial climate in which successful industries can flourish" (Grant, 1983, p. 75). Other observers concur that although German intervention is "at times critical and effective, nonetheless it is *light* not only in quantity, but also in its objectives, which tend to provide general support rather than to engineer specific strategic objectives in firms or industries" (Shepherd and Duchêne, 1983, p. 16). Since 1967, state intervention has been formalized by the Promotion of Economic Growth and Stability Act. Creating the best conditions for effective adaptation was one of the Act's major goals (Owen-Smith, 1979). In the 1970s there was a shift to a more anticipatory and active role by the state (Markovits, 1982). Measures for the strategic modernization of the economy concerned entire sectors and were based on lasting economic changes (Esser, 1983, p. 125). Selective intervention was undertaken by German governments, but always in concert with the banks, business, and labour. Individual industrial firms were not bailed out. In sector-wide intervention, the government's role has been to support measures of industry-led adjustment. (For case studies of individual sectors, see Esser et al., Fach and Dyson, 1983; Dyson, 1982a; and Markovits, 1982.) Recognizing the sometimes blurred boundaries between the public and private sectors in West Germany, the range of government responses to decline were fairly broad; their purpose was to promote stability and growth and to manage the exit of resources from declining sectors. There should be no doubt that this in no way implies the substitution of a "plan" in place of market determination. What distinguishes West German policy toward decline is its preference for corporatist devices. The repeated examples of intervention in which the economic and social consequences were dealt with in ways that would not detract from the adjustment process indicate a continuity that derives from shared beliefs rather than from a particular plan. Several observers of West German policy argue that the "social market" rule is now weakening and the country is turning more and more to heavier selective intervention as its economy is affected by unemployment and recession (Dyson, 1982; Emminger, 1982).

West Germany's industrial policies have emphasized the importance of being competitive and the need to speed up labour and capital adjustments to keep pace with market changes. The mode of decision making has been corporatist: banks, business and labour all participate with government (Hager, 1982). For example, crisis cartels including the various interests have been an important feature of managing adjustment in such difficult industries as coal and steel. The main instruments employed to promote sectoral restructuring have been concentration and mergers, tax concessions, and direct subsidies. In the case of the West German steel industry, since 1975 a major rationalization program led to the fusion of a new company, the reduction of the workforce (it was cut by 15 percent, or 50,000 jobs), a decline in production, state-aided capital investment, and regional aid for redundancies (Esser et al., 1983). Similarly, shipbuilding, another regionally concentrated industry, faced severe international competition in the 1970s. The aid program for the industry subsidized modernization and diversification. The workforce was reduced and the coastal states were given regional assistance. When Volkswagen underwent a crisis in the mid-1970s, the government did not subsidize the company directly. The measures worked out by the combination of the federal and state (*Land*) governments, the shareholders and the trade union were to provide for rationalization and modernization with a social program to ease the costs of adjustment for each worker. The only significant cash subsidy was paid for new investments in the region affected by the layoffs (Curzon Price, 1981).

Since 1974, total federal aid to various sectors has increased from DM5,741 million to DM8,623 million in 1980 (Grant, 1982, p. 75; see also Donges, 1980). Most of this growth was attributable to greater subsidies and loans, as distinct from tax concessions. Most industrial subsidies are provided either as regional investment incentives or as direct assistance to employees to encourage them to acquire new job skills. In all but a few cases (e.g., Krupp and AEG Telefunken), the West German government has allowed the bigger insolvent firms to fail, while at the same time subsidizing the re-employment of redundant workers (Trebilcock et al., 1985). Most regional aid is financed by both the federal and state governments. Assistance is distributed to regions, not to specific industries. Any industry-specific applications for aid must be approved and sponsored by a bank. The bank assumes the responsibility for administering the loan.

Labour market policies have also played a role in facilitating adjustment. West Germany provides far more generous unemployment benefits than the other nations surveyed here. Benefits are 68 percent of net pay earned during the 20 days before unemployment. Recipients who refuse to relocate or to participate in retraining may be disqualified. Wage subsidies are paid to firms as an incentive to create new jobs. Furthermore, a voucher program provides a subsidy for hiring and retraining workers unemployed because their plant has been closed down.

Magaziner and Reich point out that "labour market programs are an integral part of Germany's policy of accelerating economic modernization" (1982, p. 273). West German manpower policy is intended to promote the movement of labour out of declining sectors and into other parts of the economy. The emphasis is on training and relocation, rather than on income maintenance and compensation.

In sum, the thrust of West Germany's policies comes close to ideas incorporated in the OECD's concept of "positive adjustment." The approach is "essentially a commitment by governments not to shape industrial structures in a certain pattern, but to improve the conditions, notably factor mobility, that will allow the market to determine that pattern" (Hager, 1982, p. 236; OECD, 1978). In the rare cases when government has acted to shore up a firm (e.g., AEG Telefunken) or an industry (e.g., coal) there is evidence that the usual mediating institutions — the banks and labour-management — have failed. It should be noted that on the few occasions of direct rescue aid, the firms underwent substantial shrinkage and restructuring.

Japan

In terms of the usual measure of the size of government — expenditures as a percentage of gross domestic product (GDP) — Japan appears to have quite limited scope; in 1980, public expenditures constituted 33.1 percent of GDP (compared to an average of 40.3 percent in the OECD nations). This indicator, however, does not provide an accurate or useful measure of the scale of Japanese policy toward her declining industries. The links between business, government and the banks make the concept of distinct public and private sectors problematic (Hills, 1981). Government is not viewed as a separate force from the rest of society, and government policies are not viewed as rules imposed on industry (Vogel, 1979). It is assumed that it is appropriate for the government to participate in the shaping of industrial structure (Saxonhouse, 1979, p. 304).

"Japan's government and business leaders have long shared the assumption that the composition of the country's output must continually shift if living standards are to rise" (Magaziner and Hout, 1981; see also Patrick and Rosovsky, 1976). The restructuring of industry toward higher value-added, high productivity industries is the essential means of dealing with declining sectors. Through the practice of administrative *guidance*, the Ministry for International Trade and Industry (MITI) tries to bring about a shift in resources. Hills describes the system of advisory committees and conferences between government and business, which produce a series of indicative micro-plans (1983, p. 70). In depressed industries, MITI tries to promote much of the rationalization through a consensus with the industry.[4] The picture that emerges of Japanese policy is that of sector-specific policies, in which government agencies acting in consultation with industry use several instruments to facilitate market trends.

Is is impossible to understand Japan's approach to industrial decline without recognizing the role of the banks. Only about 20 percent of Japanese industrial investment is held in equity. The banks hold the rest in loans and are also able to hold equity in non-financial companies. Banks in Japan act as crucial conduits between government and individual companies. They are privy to early, detailed information about a firm's problems. Not only are the banks often able to deal with industrial difficulties before they become crises, these arrangements make the government's role more indirect and less visible.

Japanese industrial policies, with a few exceptions, have tried to promote rather than prevent adjustment. Although it is clear that the main thrust of public policy has been to promote the concentration and rationalization of depressed industries, there have been important brakes on the restructuring of several declining sectors (Allen, 1979; Hills, 1983; Kikkawa, 1983). MITI is the main agent in overseeing the contraction of industries in decline. Magaziner and Hout describe the many roles of the ministry: "broad policy architect, ad hoc working problem solver, formal regulator, regional policy arbiter, and informal administrative guide. In some industries it has a strong statutory authority, in others only a broad and sometimes weak influence" (1981, pp. 32–33). Although MITI acts as the coordinator of a broad range of instruments, the general assessment is that the ministry works with a light touch and much of its activity cannot be measured by cash expenditures (Magaziner and Hout, 1981; Kikkawa, 1983). To encourage growth and manage decline, MITI uses taxation, anti-trust, export and import controls, as well as subsidies and credit. Although there are numerous sector-specific combinations of instruments that MITI has used to stimulate growth, the way it has dealt with decline is quite consistent: rationalize the industry through concentration and deliberate restructuring, by scrapping excess capacity and reducing employment. Case studies of declining industries, including shipbuilding, aluminum smelting and textiles, portray a mixed record (Kikkawa, 1983; Hills, 1983). For example, since shipbuilding started to decline in 1973, Japan has sought to rationalize the industry by reducing its capacity and its labour force. An anti-depression cartel established in 1979 acted in conjunction with the sharply reduced rate of shipbuilding activity (Kikkawa, 1983, p. 241). Although the industry shrank from launching 17 million gross tons of ships in 1975 to 6.3 million tons three years later, and the labour force went from 163,000 in 1974 to 100,000 in 1978, the management of decline has not been a complete success (Magaziner and Hout, 1981, pp. 67–69). Shipbuilding is one of the very rare instances where the Japanese government prevented adjustment: the rescue of Sasebo Heavy Industries in 1978 stands as a stark example of political forces overriding the normal policy consensus.

Japan's labour policies encourage the advancement rather than the retardation of structural adjustment. Workers in troubled industries are designated for special benefits under the employment insurance system. The focus is on retraining and on wage subsidies for relocation. Typically, Japanese companies seek to retain their permanent employees and to shift them to other jobs within the firm. A prominent example of internal movements to avoid dismissal is Toyo Kogyo, the auto manufacturer, which shifted a lot of factory workers to the sales division during the period 1975–80. Obviously this kind of response is only possible in large firms.

Despite the rather blurred line between the public and the private sectors in Japan, bailouts of private firms or nationalization of failing firms are not customary parts of Japan's arsenal of instruments (Rohlen, 1979). Generally, ailing firms are left to collapse. Bankruptcy rates in Japan are four to five times higher than in the United States or Canada (Saxonhouse, 1979). Given the system of "administrative guidance" as well as the role of the banks, it is not possible to compare the number of bailouts in Japan with those in Britain or even France. Much of Japan's economic success has come from facilitating growth; its handling of decline is more uneven. The Structurally Depressed Industry Law, passed in 1978, was intended to provide a framework for dealing with those industries whose problems were more than cyclical. Although the legislation gives MITI a statutory basis for stabilizing uncompetitive industries, the ministry has not been able to bring about rationalization in such depressed sectors as shipbuilding, aluminum smelting and textiles (Magaziner and Hout, 1981; Kikkawa, 1983).

France

France contrasts with the other nations surveyed here both for its long history of direct state intervention and for its general distrust of the "market" (Green, 1983a, pp. 162–63). Between 1970 and 1984, French governments of varying political complexions have become involved in many sectors and firms in order to shape those industries' responses to economic change (Green, 1984). The government's control of the financial system, and thus of investment capital, heightens the state's capacity to intervene (Zysman, 1983; Cohen, Galbraith, and Zysman, 1982). The liberal rhetoric under the presidency of Giscard d'Estaing notwithstanding, throughout the 1970s and into the 1980s French governments have intervened heavily at the sector and firm level. The French state, well-informed about industrial conditions, has not been willing to remain at the edge of the market, but has engaged in structural intervention that clearly distinguishes between winners and losers (Dyson and Wilks, 1983).

Although France is the only one of these six countries with national planning, there is little evidence that the state's response to decline is part of a coherent, rational, and planned strategy (Green, 1981; Cohen, 1982). Green argues that, despite the use of broad, purposeful labels such as "industrial imperatives" or "strategic reinforcement strategy," the actions of successive French governments conform to a model of fire-fighting and crisis management rather than long-term strategic planning (Green, 1984, p. 142). This is not to suggest that the state simply acts in an ad hoc manner. France has developed important institutional mecha-nisms for coordinating industrial policy. Interministerial committees provide authoritative and centralized direction to policy. Industrial pol-icy has focussed on medium- and long-term growth in a number of key sectors.

The management of decline in France has been based on both prompt-ing adjustment through growth and restructuring and the protection of French firms (Mahon and Mytelka, 1983). Of the six countries surveyed in this paper, France has been the most directly interventionist. It has sought to create "national champion" firms to compete internationally (Zysman, 1977); it has subsidized the restructuring of failing firms and declining sectors, and has eased workers' burdens with redundancy payments and regional aid. France has employed a wide range of instru-ments in its efforts to cope with economic change. It is difficult to assess the actual number of bailouts that have occurred because the primary means of giving aid is for the government banks to forgive debts or to subsidize additional finance (Zysman, 1983). Since the mid-1970s, direct intervention has been more selective than previously (Green, 1984; Volkman, 1983). The major difference between France's treatment of declining sectors and firms and Britain's is that French assistance has generally been tied to rationalization and restructuring. Under Giscard d'Estaing, very radical rationalization sometimes took place; large com-panies were merged and large industrial groups abandoned some of their traditional activities (Green, 1984, p. 148). A common procedure in sector-wide rationalization has been to hone the sector down to two competing firms (e.g., Ugine and Sacilor in steel and Renault and Peugeot-Citroën in automobiles). The impact of the rationalization shows up in aggregate measures. From 1974 to 1981, bankruptcies increased by 70 percent and the industrial labour force declined more rapidly in France than in any other advanced industrialized country (ibid., pp. 148–49).

French manpower policy is directed toward full employment. The receipt of unemployment benefits is not contingent on participation in a training program, as it is in West Germany and Japan. Firms are limited in their ability to discharge workers; those that have been bailed out generally employ skilled workers who belong to well-organized trade unions. The socialist Mitterrand government has invited more direct participation by workers and union groups in its deliberations about bailing out particular firms.

The concept of a sector plan and state-to-firm contracts, which began with the steel industry in 1978, has become a prevalent mode of French industrial assistance. All the policies and instruments are combined in a single package in return for certain developmental obligations which the firm undertakes. The support of "lame duck" private firms is also carried out in a unique fashion. Bailouts are not automatic even if the firm is large; Boussac textiles, for instance, with 11,000 workers was allowed to fail. Before a firm is rescued, it is subject to a great deal of scrutiny. If a rescue ensues, it is a joint public/private venture based on an assessment of the firm's financial and industrial viability (Green, 1983a, pp. 176–77). It is interesting to contrast the French reaction with that of the British when they are confronted with a firm's financial crisis. In Britain, the response typically has been to buy time, to provide subsidies as a stopgap measure. (For cases in which rescues have been accompanied by restructuring, see Young, 1974.) In France, the state uses the crisis to force a restructuring (Cohen, 1982, p. 24).

The technique most associated with the Interministerial Committee for the Adaptation of Industrial Structure (CIASI) — the state agency that processes requests for rescues — is to encourage a healthy firm, through cash subsidies and credit, to acquire the ailing company. Control of credit through state-owned banks is another element of France's industrial policy (Zysman, 1983). The French have also used rationalization — the steel industry is a prime example — as a way of coping with decline. Protection through quotas, tariffs and preferential public procurement continue to be employed in France (Shepherd and Duchêne, 1983; Green, 1983a; Mahon and Mytelka, 1983).

The question of coordination and integration, like so many other aspects of French industrial policy, cannot be answered unambiguously. Agencies like CIASI and CODIS (the Interministerial Committee for the Development of Strategic Industries) were established to coordinate policy and they have done so. CIASI has been the central clearing committee for all rescue requests; CODIS is a cabinet-level committee that has centralized the previously dispersed industrial policy functions. The strategies put forward by CODIS are indicative, not mandatory, but they represent an attempt to develop a coherent industrial policy. Despite CODIS's emphasis on industries of the future, the troubled textile industry was added to its list of strategic areas. "Le Plan," which is so often associated with French industrial policy, had little impact during the 1970s (Estrin and Holmes, 1983a). Curzon Price notes that the major importance of the planning exercise was not that it directed anyone but that it brought government and industry together (1981, p. 44). The general characterization of the country's industrial policy is that France is a highly interventionist state whose policies have not always been part of a coherent national strategy (Cohen, 1982; Green, 1983b), but whose policy instruments toward a specific sector or firms have been effectively coordinated.

An analysis of the scope and means of the management of decline in Britain, France, West Germany, Japan and the United States reveals five distinct national approaches to the problem of economic change. These are not necessarily static approaches. Shepherd, for example, points out that British policy is becoming more realistic and more efficient. He depicts a scaling-down of technological ambitions and more acceptance of the need to trim excess capacity (Shepherd and Duchêne, 1983, p. 18). Shepherd's judgment that British industrial managers are also learning and becoming more realistic is disputed by Dyson, who argues that there is little indication of a change in attitude (ibid., p. 63).

In some cases, the primary emphases of particular national approaches have altered over time. For example, Japan's initial use of micro-level instruments to support promising sectors has been largely replaced by more macro-level instruments (Kikkawa, 1983). Although changes in the party in power may have initially brought about changes in policy, the distinctive national patterns have prevailed (Coates, 1982; Green, 1981; Hager, 1982). U.S. governments have consistently refused to use the powers of the state to accelerate adjustment; American interventions to preserve uncompetitive industries and firms have been ad hoc, non-institutionalized responses to short-term political pressures. British practice provides numerous examples of intervention. Although they are far more common, the interventions are similar to those in the United States in their focus on muting market signals rather than hastening adjustment to market forces. Saving jobs and shoring up depressed regions appear to be as much the objectives of British governments as national economic growth. The quotation attributed to Samuel Brittan is most apt: the British government does not steer the economy — it just bails it out!

West German governments have relied on the market to set the parameters for their industrial policies. However, here the market is not treated as an autonomous force that imposes outcomes on society. Through the concerted efforts of government, business, labour and the banks, West Germans are able to shape their economy (Dyson, 1980).

The picture of French policy making is more *dirigiste* than the German. Although there is some disagreement about the extent to which France's policy has been coherent, there is no disagreement that, within certain international and domestic constraints, the French try to steer major parts of their economy, and are not averse to sometimes bailing it out.

The Japanese system also takes its cues from the market. But here too there is a unique response: the market is not treated as an alien force that must not be interfered with lest it be distorted. The Japanese government tries to play a guiding role in channelling resources and providing various kinds of assistance to both growing and declining firms.

Canada

Where does Canada fit into this survey? How do the scope and means of Canada's involvement in economic adjustment compare to the other five countries? Besides Canada's historic practices of subsidizing the railroads, canals, and so on, there are numerous examples of aid to latter-day "roads and bridges." In 1979–80, available data show that the federal government spent $865 million and the provinces $333 million on trade and industry (Jenkin, 1983, pp. 152–53). These figures under-estimate the level of financial participation. If we include off-budget items like loan guarantees, the picture is much different. In a recent study, the Economic Council of Canada estimated that as of March 31, 1980, federal and provincial government loans and investments out-standing under programs of assistance to industry in the private sector equalled $6 billion (1982, p. 17). As of March 1980, there were 28 agencies, boards and divisions at the federal and provincial levels to provide loans, investments and loan guarantees (ibid.).

The seemingly broad range of Canadian involvement is similar to Britain's, where the depth of the state's participation in economic adjust-ment is not very great. The assistance is generally to firms rather than sectors.[5] Although there have been omnibus assistance programs like the Enterprise Development Program (EDP) and the Ontario Develop-ment Corporation, there is little indication that these have consisted of more than an aggregation of government subsidies to failing firms. For example, the 1982 Auditor General's Report found little evidence of a coherent set of guidelines for EDP boards to follow in granting funds or when monitoring to see if the terms were being observed (1983, p. 227).

The scope of Canadian policy is broad, it is not confined to any set of sectors, and it is not limited to any particular region. The dual focus on national economic growth and regional development provides a base for assistance to the industrialized heartland and to the less developed hinterlands. The degree or depth of intervention is fairly shallow, and assistance to private sector firms usually follows what is described as the "Chrysler model" in Britain. The cash is handed over and the company is left to adjust. Even when a firm has been bought out and joins the public sector, there is still little evidence that the government is asserting a lot of control. Canadair is a case in point. Senior civil servants on Canadair's board of directors provided neither government direction for the corporation nor gave the government useful information about the firm (*The Globe and Mail*, February 5, 1983).

The last element in the consideration of "scope" is the degree of integration and the extent to which separate actions are part of a general policy or framework. Michael Bliss concludes that there is no pattern to the confusing collection of Canadian subsidies to private firms (1982). Similarly, in a recent study of business bailouts, the authors affirm that although there are several factors explaining government rescues, there is no coherent industrial policy framework that links these various rescues (Trebilcock et al., 1985). Again Canada is closest to Britain. With the possible exception of textiles under the Canadian Industrial Renewal Board (CIRB) and the attempted restructuring of the fisheries processing industry, there is no consensus on the need for state involvement to help deal with economic decline (Watson, 1983); nor is it conditional on restructuring or modernization (Trebilcock et al., 1984). Specific political pressures are the best explanations of intervention to assist failing firms.

Much of Canadian intervention has tended to prevent or postpone adjustment. To this end, Canadian governments at the federal as well as the provincial levels have responded with tariff and non-tariff protection for troubled industries, loans, loan guarantees and direct subsidy for failing firms as well as public ownership of lame ducks (Morici et al., 1982). In the early 1970s, Canada's tariffs were generally higher than the other nations surveyed here (Economic Council of Canada, 1975a, p. 17). As in other nations, above-average protection is given to many of the sectors generally regarded as being in decline, e.g., textiles, furniture, leather products, shipbuilding. Unlike Japan and the three European nations studied here, Canada does not encourage mergers and market concentration.

Labour market adjustment programs provide income maintenance to displaced workers, as well as some training and relocation assistance. Although Canadian unemployment benefits compare favourably with those in other advanced industrialized states, the country's training and relocation programs, so crucial to mobility and adjustment, are less successful (Glenday et al., 1982; Saunders, 1984).

General industrial programs like the EDP provide assistance (mainly loans and loan guarantees) to failing firms. In addition, certain programs, like the Shipbuilding Industry Assistance Program, assist specific industries. In manufacturing, the main beneficiaries are shipbuilding, clothing and textiles, aerospace and defence (Canada, Department of Industry, Trade and Commerce, 1979). Although there have been programs like the Automotive Adjustment Program, which, inter alia, provided supplementary benefits and retraining subsidies to laid-off workers, and the Labour Adjustment Benefits Act (1982), which provides supplementary benefits for workers in an industry designated as undergoing significant economic adjustments, most Canadian adjustment assistance is to firms.

Two recent programs, the Industrial Regional Development Program (IRDP) and the Canadian Industrial Renewal Program (CIRP) should be noted, IRDP because it is now the major vehicle for non-sectoral adjustment policies and CIRP because it represents a significant change in approach. On July 1, 1983, the Industrial and Regional Development Program came into existence as the core federal program for the delivery of direct assistance to private sector firms. On its establishment, IRDP subsumed several former assistance programs and is now available to firms in all regions of Canada. The level of assistance for a firm depends on its location. The Canadian Industrial Renewal Board (CIRB) was established in 1981; it administers a program to assist the domestic clothing and textile industries to restructure and modernize. The selective approach of the Board is a shift away from assistance based on the needs of a particular firm or group of workers. The CIRB in general concentrates on long-term planning for the entire sector.

Besides the instruments employed at the federal level, it should be noted that the provinces are also coping, both individually and in concert with Ottawa, with declining industries (Davenport et al., 1982; Morici et al., 1982, chap. 6; Jenkin, 1983). In sum, federal and provincial governments have sought to preserve sectors through protective tariff and non-tariff barriers. Direct financial assistance through grants, loans and loan guarantees have usually left adaptive measures to the judgment of the particular firm. Even when the aid was conditional, it is not clear that the state could force the firm to meet the conditions — cf. the Chrysler and Massey-Ferguson rescues (Trebilcock et al., 1985). Furthermore, Canadian governments have been willing to take an equity position in assisted firms.

Explaining Policy

The second part of this paper surveys the determinants of policy — not to derive a theory of economic adjustment, but to impose some order on the various explanations that have appeared in the literature and to apply them to Canada. Much of the analysis of economic decline has been left to the economists. As a group, they have been largely critical of state interventions toward failing firms and declining sectors (Watson, 1983). Although economic analysis may be able to explain why a firm, sector, or economy is declining, it is not able to explain why the state intervenes — or what factors shape the state's choice of policy instruments. As David McKay notes in a recent critique of economic analysis, economists ignore the role of the state (1983a, p. 112).

We are concerned here with explanations of the political phenomena. This is not to suggest that there is no economic component or that economic factors are not important; however, government's efforts (or lack thereof) to deal with economic decline must be conceptualized as political response. The actions, economically justified or not, are the result of the operation of political forces.

The state of the economy is an important starting point in any analysis of public policy. Such characteristics as the degree of openness, the extent of regional and industrial concentration, and the level of resource endowments are attributes that shape the kinds of adjustment problems likely to arise, but the state of the economy may impose constraints on the policies that can be adopted. To explore the links between the state of the economy and industrial adjustment is beyond the scope of this analysis; however, an appreciation of the relevance of the economy should be a precaution against inappropriate comparisons. For example, the dynamic West German economy has been able to absorb unemployment in the textile industry and has thus been able to pursue employment-shedding restructuring and to support market principles as a basis for policy. The state of the British economy did not present the same possibilities (Shepherd, 1983, pp. 38–46; Grant, 1982). Even when there are important economic forces at work, it is necessary to consider how political factors transform economic conditions into political problems. Moreover, variations in economic performance, which are not always explained by differences in factor endowments, have led to a lot of interest in how political factors affect economic growth. The analysis of the state and economic decline has tended to fall into two broad categories, depending on which of the policy determinants receives the major emphasis. Most of the work of political scientists has emphasized the role of either *ideas* or *institutions* (broadly defined) in the determination of adjustment policies (Simeon, 1976; McKay, 1983a).

Ideas

Concern with the role of ideas in policy making may focus attention either on broad, nationally held cultural values or on more narrowly held ideological beliefs. Political culture refers to the shared beliefs and values that characterize a political community. As Simeon notes, a stress on dominant ideas is most useful in understanding the "more gross differences in the patterns of policy in different countries" (1976, p. 573). He goes on to say: "Ideas do not provide complete explanations. They tend to be general and thus to account for broad orientations rather than the specific details of policy." Political ideas here act to set broad constraints on policy makers. Political ideas have been used to explain observed differences in nation states, as well as to explain a consistent pattern within a single jurisdiction (King, 1973). Two recent comparative studies draw a similar conclusion. McKay and Grant find that the pursuit of a coherent industrial strategy depends in part on a "broad acceptance among political elites of the need for government to play an active role in helping industry adapt to change" (1983, p. 9). And in *Politics, Policy and the European Recession*, Andrew Cox unequivocally states the importance of collaboration between government, industry and labour:

"Clearly the message for the declining economies is that unless they can generate the incorporatist and consensual relationships between business, finance and labour which have been generated in the relatively prosperous nations, then the prospects for the 1980s are bleak" (1982, p. 30).

Shared Beliefs

The notion that there is a necessary role for the state in the economy sets West Germany, France, and Japan apart from the other nations in this survey. Esser, Fach, and Dyson refer to the confined terms of debate about economic policy in Germany (1983, p. 107). Dyson states:

> The nature of German economic argument is only to be understood against the background of an intellectual tradition of political economy that has given key place to the concept of state. This tradition has fostered the public regarding attitudes, a deep sense of interdependency and social responsibility even in the exercise of private economic power. (1982a, p. 61)

The French political system also shares this view of the state and economic life. "The open use of state power at home and abroad to achieve economic ends has been a continuous theme" (Zysman, 1977, p. 257). In France, intervention is both accepted and expected; there is a consensus about industrial development (Green, 1981, p. 347). Gourevitch describes the shared beliefs:

> The economic ideology which came increasingly to dominate French decision-makers — private and public, elite and mass — was a kind of growth oriented statist Keynesianism: growth was the goal; left to itself, the market would not provide the right incentives; the state had to intervene, not to displace the market, but shape it; the instruments of intervention included management of demand through fiscal policy, restructuring of industries by a variety of techniques (mergers, credit controls, taxation, subsidies), indicative planning, stimulated technological change, and a 'calibrated' open commercial policy through the coal and steel community, the EEC, and GATT. (1982, p. 3)

France is the only one of the nations surveyed here which has rejected the idea that the market is a dominant force. Green explains that "[French] governments have tended to guide the pace and direction of industrial change." This predilection for "administered industrialization" can be explained partly by the deep-rooted belief that market forces are blunt and ineffective tools of resource allocation (1983a, p. 161).

The Japanese consensus is described by Magaziner and Hout:

> The Japanese do, however, share a remarkably common view of the legitimacy of national government as guide and mediator. . . . Japanese historical tradition . . . grants to government a legitimate role in shaping and helping to carry out industrial policy. Japanese businessmen share with government leaders and officials a sense of the importance of co-ordinated

national development and are generally amenable to and in fact expect government intervention to advance this goal. (1981, pp. 4, 29)

In the United States there is a consensus, but it acts to constrain and limit the actions of the state. Public sector interventions to cope with market failures are treated as reluctant exceptions (McKay, 1983b, pp. 46–47). As Edmonds points out, although Americans are wary of any government intervention, in fact extensive intervention does take place. However, with regard to industrial policies, he observes:

> The historical ideological restraint that makes politicians, government officials and legislators reluctant to interfere too dogmatically or pervasively in private enterprise is matched by an equal resistance in private industry to government interference. Indeed, even where it is unavoidable, such as in the defence industrial sector, there is an instinctive feeling that the situation is unnatural and not conducive to efficiency. The American corporate executive distrusts his state and turns to it only as a last resort. (1983, p. 75)

In Britain, there is no consensus on the need for state involvement. Peter Maunder opens his essay "Government Intervention in the Economy of the U.K." with the observation: "The extent to which the state ought to intervene and influence private industry at the micro level continues to be an active political issue" (1979, p. 130). Similar views are stated by Grant and Wilks: "One of the distinguishing characteristics of the industrial policy debate in Britain is that the question of whether government should or should not have an industrial policy is itself highly contentious" (1984, p. 16). Comparing Britain and France, Diana Green points to the difference in beliefs and values, noting that state intervention is an accepted and expected feature of French political and economic life. In Britain, however, state intervention has always been a disputatious issue (1981, p. 334). The debate over adjustment policy is predicated on a classical view of the market and the totally separate state (Gamble, 1981).

Partisanship and Ideology

Political partisanship is another factor in the determination of policy. Political culture tends to be associated with general direction or scope of intervention; partisanship is linked not only to the direction, but also to the means by which the state acts. Political culture is obviously consistent over time, whereas partisanship can vary because of the party in power. Dyson and Wilks suggest that even when competing political partisans are out of power, they can influence the climate of opinion toward ailing firms and sectors (1983, pp. 253–54). Explanations based on party ideology are, however, more likely to occur when the reins of government shift from a political party at one end of the ideological spectrum to a party at the other. In Japan there has been no such variation; although there has been some analysis of the policy views of the Liberal Democratic party (LDP) (Pempel, 1982, chap. 2), the stress is more on the LDP as a broker party which reflects the social consensus. In the United States, the different bases of support for the Democrats and Republicans may translate into different policies. It is possible that identifying the nature of a party's constituency in the United States may help in trying to predict which political pressures are likely to result in protection. Evidence from the Chrysler case, however, indicates that, in that instance, party was not a salient factor in the bailout decision (Freeman and Mendelowitz, 1982). In West Germany, where the Social Democratic party (SPD) was replaced by the more conservative Christian Democrats (CDU) in 1982, France where the Gaullists were replaced by the Socialists in 1981, and Britain where the Tories and the Labour party have alternated too, the impact of party ideology has received some attention.

In West Germany the coming to power of the CDU was not seen as a major turning point in the process of industrial adjustment. Throughout the 1970s, the SPD had followed a social market approach in keeping with widely held views of the importance of competitive market forces (Markovits, 1982; Dyson, 1982b). The impact of ideology may well come from the rise of the Green party or other ginger groups who protest the material values that underpin German policies toward modernization (Chandler and Siaroff, 1984). Esser, Fach and Dyson conclude that these challenges are unlikely to change the basic approach to industrial adjustment but they may lead to less flexibility and adaptability in the German policies of adaptation (1983, p. 126).

The French case is more problematic. On the one hand, commentators like Diana Green stress the continuity of the French approach.

> Although state intervention in industry is a long-standing tradition in France, it is not ideologically motivated. . . . The traditional étatist mode of economic change and industrial management was not displaced or eliminated by the neo-liberal Giscardian regime of 1974–81. Similarly the arrival of the Socialist government of President Mitterrand in 1981 does not appear to have resulted in a radically different approach to crisis management. (1983a, pp. 161–62)

Other commentators focus on the changes brought in by a new government. For example, Hayward argues that the Socialist victory in 1981 led to changes in the goals of the French state as well as in the choice of instruments (1982, pp. 135–38). Similarly Cohen points to three policy changes: greater concern about unemployment, more efforts toward income redistribution, and an attempt to increase social control of the economy (1982, p. 181). Each change has direct implications for France's policies of adaptation and economic adjustment.

The British political system is often characterized by abrupt policy shifts; however, these so-called "U-turns" seem to take place within a government as much as between administrations. There is little doubt that there is genuine policy disagreement between the two major political parties. "The debate within and between parties has been couched in unreconcilable terms of common ownership and planning versus the free market and liberty" (Grant and Wilks, 1984, p. 24). But doctrinaire rhetoric aside, Coates and others provide ample evidence that Conservative and Labour governments were pulled to similar positions from different starting points (Coates, 1982, pp. 147–52; Grant, 1983, chap. 3; Green, 1981). For example, the U-turn of 1972 resulted, inter alia, in the Tories' 1972 Industry Act, which became a major element of Labour's subsequent industrial policies. The election of the Conservative party under Margaret Thatcher in 1979 once again brought to the fore the question of party ideology. Elected on a platform that promised a return to market discipline, the Thatcher record reflects the intractable problems and political pressures that confront any British government. There has been no dramatic reversal in policy; British Leyland and the British Steel Corporation continue to receive heavy public subsidies, regional assistance is still provided, and the National Enterprise Board survives (Curzon Price, 1981, pp. 62–63; Grant, 1983, pp. 78–99). Wyn Grant sums up the approach of the Thatcher government as the "trimming of industrial policy." Sir Keith Joseph, the Minister of Industry, explained, "We have not changed our diagnosis of the aims. Some unprecedented factors have made the transition stage more difficult" (Grant, 1983, p. 97). At this point, it seems that, compared to its predecessors, the Thatcher Government has been less susceptible to pressures for protection, but whether there is a longer term strategy for adjustment is not clear.

The Views in Canada

Questions of industrial strategy are currently prominent on Canada's public agenda. The issue is often stated in first principles. Should government intervene? Free trade or protection? Certainly there is no shared starting or fundamental point of agreement. Anyone surveying the question of Canadian industrial strategies must be struck by the lack of consensus.[6] Despite extensive public intervention in the economy, current debate focusses on *whether* the state should intervene. This conflict is inextricably related to two other questions: which level of government makes the policy and what the objectives should be (Jenkin, 1983; Tupper, 1981; Thorburn, 1984). These questions add a second dimension — regionalism — to the initial issue of state intervention. The interweaving is referred to by Michael Jenkin:

Perhaps even more important, however, has been the manner in which the character of economic development has profoundly affected the nature of regional conflict. . . . As a result, different patterns of economic development and interests have evolved, with provincial governments becoming a

natural focus for those interests. . . . the direction in which industrial policy is evolving elsewhere, with its emphasis first on sectoral, and now on
firm-specific action, poses special problems for a country with territorially
diverse interests. The decision to support, or indeed, to rationalize a particular form of industrial activity, especially at the firm level, inevitably has
territorial implications when economic activity is so regionally specialized.
Support for one industry or one firm is seen as support for one region or
province rather than another. It is in this sense that it has become virtually
impossible to discuss industrial policy in Canada without immediately
addressing the problem of regional economic competition and its political
manifestations — federal-provincial and interprovincial conflict. (1983,
pp. 25–26)

Although this problem of the interrelationship between industrial strategy and regional developments is often addressed in institutional terms
(and will be discussed in the next section), it is important to see that it
also bears on the formation of a consensus in regard to industrial
strategy. As a nation, Canada has not come to grips with the trade-offs
implied in pursuing both objectives.

The lack of a general framework or policy for industrial adjustment
leaves governments more vulnerable to sector- and firm-specific calls for
protection from the market. Canadian governments, federal and provincial, have responded to those demands by imposing tariffs and other
forms of protection, as well as firm-specific bailouts, but these tariff
barriers are cited by those who oppose state-led adjustment to demonstrate the folly of public sector intervention in the economy (Watson,
1983; Tupper, 1981). And so the debate continues.

Party ideology or partisanship does not seem to be significant in
determining Canadian adjustment policies. The major federal parties are
categorized as broker parties: both at times espouse the virtues of a free
market and at other times intervene directly in the economy. At the
provincial level, there have been efforts by every governing party to
encourage and shore up its industrial sectors (Jenkin, 1983; Thorburn,
1984). Although the provinces have created non-tariff barriers
(Trebilcock et al., 1983), have lobbied Ottawa for tariff protection for
their industries (Mahon and Mytelka, 1983; Molot, 1977), and have bailed
out failing private-sector firms (Trebilcock et al., 1985), no provincial
government has put forward a program to guide restructuring and modernization. Quebec, which does set forth a general development policy,
still favours protection as the main instrument in dealing with "the less
competitive sectors" (Quebec, 1979, p. 161). Given the federal system,
there are few incentives for a province to bear the social and political
costs of restructuring adjustment when the costs of protecting declining
industries will be shared by the rest of the country.

What can we conclude from this review? Although Canada has a long
history of state intervention and currently government expenditures
constitute over 40 percent of the gross domestic product, there is little

evidence of a consensus on whether Canada ought to have an industrial strategy; moreover, even among the proponents of state-led adjustment, there is no agreement about the true objectives of the strategy or how it could be formulated and implemented. The fragmentation of opinion is further reflected in the lack of consensus within government (French, 1980), within industry (Tupper, 1981), and within labour (McBride, 1983).

Institutions

The way institutions behave is the basis for a second major approach to an explanation of how policies come about (McKay, 1983b). Variations in organization and the distribution of authority are related to differences in adjustment policies. This approach includes explanations that focus on the process of decision making. Simeon points out that institutional (and process) characteristics may influence the scope as well as the means of policy (1976, p. 575). It should be noted that these structures and institutions may also be the consequences of policy choice.

Although each nation has its own institutions and processes for dealing with economic decline, a number of characteristics or dimensions that have been found to be empirically and logically related to policy choice emerge from the literature. Before putting forward a framework of analysis (rather than an explanation of any one country's policies or any particular sectoral or firm-specific response), we shall consider the state's organizational characteristics, the workings of national financial systems, and the organization and role of the private sector as they shape adjustment policy.

Organizational Structure and Process

One of the most common ways in which political scientists study economic adjustment is to describe the various agencies that formulate and implement policy. These agencies may vary in the degree of centralization of policy making, the degree of interagency coordination, and the institutional stability over time. For example, the French Inter-ministerial Committee for the Adaptation of Industrial Structure (CIASI)[7] included ministers and top-level public officials and bankers. The committee met weekly to deal quickly and efficiently with the problems of failing firms (Green, 1983a, pp. 176–77). The French CODIS (Interministerial Committee for the Development of Strategic Industries) is another example of a highly centralized structure. The Committee, made up of key economic ministers, was established in 1979. It is chaired by the prime minister and has no separate budget. Its purpose is to steer the development of strategic industries and to coordinate the various instruments of intervention. Japan's MITI (Ministry of International Trade and Industry), established in 1949, also exemplifies centralization and coordination. MITI has wide-ranging responsibilities but, although it has a comprehensive perspective, it is not unconstrained.

While it is clear that its impact varies across industries and that it comes under the aegis of the Ministry of Finance and the Fair Trade Commission, there is little doubt that MITI is the "focal point in industrial policy determination, lending it continuity and consistency" (Magaziner and Hout, 1981, p. 33).

The British agencies are quite different from the French and Japanese. There is no centralized coordinator reviewing industrial policy and anticipating economic crises. There have been numerous changes in the institutions responsible for industry; the relevant policy-making powers have shifted from the Ministry of Technology to the Department of Trade and Industry (1970–74) to the Department of Industry. Non-departmental responsibilities have also moved from the Industrial Reorganization Corporation (IRC) to the National Enterprise Board (NEB) to the current British Technology Group (BTG). As Wilks notes, in Britain "the more closely an institution becomes involved directly with selective intervention, the more vulnerable it has become to destabilizing change or even threat of abolition" (Wilks, 1983, p. 135).

Although these structural features clearly seem to hinder the emergence of a coherent industrial strategy, an even more basic implication can be drawn from the above discussions. The key quality of a nation's institutional organization is the extent to which the arrangements leave decision makers susceptible to demands for protection and efforts to prevent rather than promote adjustment. For example, Hills punctures the myth of an omnipotent MITI. She lays out the circumstances in which MITI has not been able to guide adjustment, when domestic and international pressures have led to dominance of the short term over the long (Hills, 1983, pp. 71–79; Saxonhouse, 1979, pp. 317–19). The West German system of social partnership has meant that, despite numerous redundancies, the unions have supported the modernization strategy in return for a role in formulating restructuring plans. Thus, even in the case of large-scale crises, like Volkswagen in 1974 or the steel industry since 1975, there have been no *effective* demands to rescue rather than adjust. Crisis cartels, including labour, management and government, have been the response to specific industrial crises.

France has been characterized by its "closed" public management — a bureaucratic elite who are relatively insulated from political pressure. Organized labour has been weak and unable to help shape the direction of adjustment, nor can it provide support for broad economic and political initiatives or sustain corporatist arrangements that characterize the political economy of West Germany. However, it must also be noted that in the bailouts that occurred during the 1970s as well as under the Mitterrand government, in each rescued firm the workers belonged to well-organized unions (Green, 1983a; Hayward, 1982). At the level of the industry rather than the individual firm, the highly unionized textile and steel industries (80 percent are unionized, compared to an average rate in France of 25 percent) have concluded special agreements for labour adjustment.

In Britain there is little insulation from demands for protection. First, there is no overall plan to judge the merits of rescuing a firm or sector. Second, response to dramatic crises comes from cabinet: each case is treated on an ad hoc basis and, as Wilks aptly concludes, "each is argued from first principles and each decision [is] unpredictable and taken ultimately on political criteria" (1983, p. 129).

Except for the strong ideological bias against state intervention to prop up market failures, the U.S. pattern is quite similar to the British. There is no agency charged with providing a supervisory role on industrial policy. Moreover, as Zysman and Tyson (1983) and Reich (1982) argue, there is no political coalition in support of adjustment based on restructuring and modernization. Demands for protection from the industry are dealt with by Congress in a political manner.

The Banking System

The capacity of the state to cope with adjustment problems is also related to circumstances outside the structure of specific government institutions. The role of the banks and the financial system are generally other elements in the institutional analysis of industrial strategy. The general hypothesis is that "structural differences in national financial systems contribute to the differing capacities of governments to intervene in the industrial economy" (Zysman, 1983, p. 285).

At least four factors determine the impact of the financial system on adjustment. First, the degree to which industrial finance depends on bank loans (as opposed to equity); second, the extent to which the banks may hold equity in non-financial firms; third, the capacity of the banks to exert discretionary power over the allocation of credit; and, fourth, the capacity of the state to exercise leverage over the banks (Zysman, 1983).

Since the banks are now more directly involved in firm financing, they are more likely to have early and reliable information about problems a company may be experiencing. The closer the relationship between troubled companies and the banks, the less likely that the government will be directly involved in rescues. Moreover, with the closer involvement of financial institutions, restructuring and reallocation within the troubled firm or sector are facilitated without the more usual mode of adjustment — laying off workers. Differences among financial systems create important variations in the ability of the state to control credit as an instrument of policy. Using credit allocation, it is possible to discriminate among firms and sectors without having to create a legislative vehicle or an administrative agency (Zysman and Pontusson, 1980, p. 41). In the cases of Japan, France, and West Germany, evidence indicates that the working of their financial systems was an important factor in generating adjustment policies (Zysman, 1983; Hager, 1982;

Owen-Smith, 1979, pp. 176–78; Esser, Fach and Dyson, 1983, p. 125; Suzuki, 1980).[8] In Japan, France and West Germany there are close links between industry and the banks. Moreover, the concentration of the financial institutions means that the banks exercise a great deal of power through credit allocation. In contrast to Japan and France, the West German banks are independent of the government.

At the same time, it is true to say that the capital market system in the United States and Britain acts as a separate domain from industry and government. Industry is not so dependent on long-term debt (and thus the banks) and the banking industry is far less concentrated than its counterparts in West Germany, Japan and France. Furthermore, because of the autonomy of the banking system, the state is not able to manipulate the allocation of credit through the banks. This has several implications for economic adjustment. Because the information readily available to Japan, French and West German banks (and governments) is lacking in the United States, and Britain, there is little early warning that a firm or sector is in trouble. Financial regulations, especially in the United States, are such that it is difficult for the banks to play the rescuing role they do in other nations. So without the banks playing a mediating role, demands for assistance must be addressed to government. Then the choice is to rescue or not, whereas in the case of the other three nations there are more varied and subtle instruments available to the banks and to government working through the banks (Zysman, 1983, chaps. 4, 5; Grant, 1982; Blank, 1978; Maunder, 1979, p. 139).

The Private Sector
The organization of the private sector and the relationship between the public and private sectors are additional aspects of institutional arrangements, broadly defined, that are associated with differences in the management of industrial decline. To explain this relationship between the public and private sectors, we must go back to the organization of interests within the private sector (Katzenstein, 1978). In those nations where there is concerted action between business and government or among business, labour and government, interests in the private sector are more centralized. Those nations (Japan and West Germany) in which business is represented by encompassing organizations are more likely to be given support for policies designed to promote economic adjustment. More narrowly organized business interests are far more likely to try to shield themselves from the costs of competitive adjustment (Olson, 1982). In their analysis of industrial policy among OECD nations, McKay and Grant conclude that good communications between political/bureaucratic and economic spokesmen are one of the prerequisites of a coherent industrial strategy (1983, p. 9). The relationship between business and government is important to policy making on at least two counts. Continuous communication means a steady flow of information

to decision makers; obviously, micro-level intervention for adjustment is impossible without adequate information. Second, consultation and collaboration is crucial to political feasibility. Heavy social costs often associated with restructuring present less of an obstacle if decision making is shared with the private sector. The cases of Japan, West Germany and France once again set them apart from the United States and Britain. In each of the first three, business interests are built into the policy process. Whether it is through the system of committees and conferences in Japan, the social partnership and crisis cartels in West Germany, or the participation of industry in identifying the priorities of the industrial strategy and the joint ventures between public and private capital in France, there are countless indications of the closeness of industry-government relations in the three nations. In each case, the state does not act in isolation in its efforts to cope with economic decline and adjustment.

Differences in labour organization also determine the state's ability to adjust to economic change. The institutionalization of labour's participation in the adjustment process and the dominance of trade unions in the export sectors within the labour movement are important features of West Germany's response to industrial adjustment. Although nationally organized labour is not a strong force in Japan, the corporatist role of labour at the level of the firm is an important feature of that country's approach. In West Germany, the broadly based labour movement provides flexibility and support. Workers are not left to bear the burdens of firm failure nor must they stand in absolute opposition to layoffs because a firm is in decline. In Japan, the close labour-management relations at the level of the firm means that labour can provide flexible support when a company is restructuring.

In France, too, organized labour has been weak at the national policy level. There are few cases where labour presents a united front to champion policies that will enhance its mobility and standing. Even in those firms or sectors where there are strong trade unions, French labour-management relations have not instituted a flexible system like the Japanese that can facilitate positive adjustment (Zysman, 1983, p. 164).

It is in Britain, the most unionized (50 percent of the workforce) of the nations surveyed here, that labour has the most negative impact on economic adjustment. The trade union movement is fragmented and has not been able to mobilize support for industrial policies of general benefit. At the firm level, further fragmentation has obstructed the internal flexibility often necessary to assist a declining company.

The relationship between labour, business and government varies a great deal across the systems surveyed here. Only in West Germany is labour a regular participant in the policy process (Markovits, 1982; Gourevitch et al., 1984; Lange et al., 1981). In Britain, despite such efforts as establishing tripartite Sector Working Parties as part of Labour's industrial strategy in 1975, British policy institutions and processes do not include industry or labour. It is generally acknowledged that because the public and private sectors are insulated from one another, British decision making suffers significantly. First, it is reactive rather than anticipative (Wilks, 1983). Second, little support is built up for industrial policies. Instead of medium- to long-range adjustment policies drawn up after consultation with industry, the government gets involved at the last minute in desperate efforts to save jobs and shore up depressed regions.

Although there is little disagreement that there is a difference between business-government relations in the United States and Britain and the more corporatist arrangements in France, West Germany and Japan, this is not to say that there is no conflict in the latter three or that the consultative process always promotes adjustment (Hills, 1981; Saxonhouse, 1979; Curzon Price, 1981). The point is that there is a qualitative difference in the government-business relations in the two sets.

Canadian Institutions

Comparing Canadian institutional arrangements with those of the other five nations helps to explain observed differences in policy. Perhaps even more importantly, examination of the institutional settings sheds some light on the transferability of other nations' policies. Policies cannot be borrowed summarily from other political systems; the only realistic way to consider the adaptation of policies is through an adequate understanding of the national contexts that shape policy.

The most significant characteristic of Canada's institutional structure is the federal division of power (the impact of federalism on Canada's industrial policies is discussed at length in Alan Tupper's paper, no. 10 in this volume). Constitutionally, both levels of government have powers that allow them to respond to the problem of industrial decline. As we have noted in the first section, the policies toward declining industries in Quebec and Ontario (the provinces where the problem is most severe) (Jenkin, 1983, chap. 4) are directed toward preserving the uncompetitive industries through protectionist measures and ad hoc rescues of failing firms (Faucher et al., 1984). Whenever these provinces have established agencies to guide the provincial economy, such as Quebec's Office de planification et développement du Québec or Ontario's Board of Industrial Leadership and Development to foster industrial development, the focus has been on subsidies and support to encourage growth rather than on restructuring to manage decline. Despite the provincial organizational structures created to deal with industrial policy, the results are no different from those at the federal level. There is no institution charged with and able to put together sectoral policies for restructuring declining industries. Although Ottawa and the provinces have cooperated in saving firms like Chrysler, Massey-Ferguson, and Cooperative Farm Implements, there is no federal framework or guideline that might give direction to the provinces in coping with their declining industries. Often, in these joint efforts, the provinces have carried out rescues to maintain employment; they have not seen them as vehicles for restructuring. For example, Ontario demanded that job guarantees be part of the conditions for the rescues of Chrysler, and Newfoundland's dispute with Ottawa over the rescue of the fish-processing sector focussed, inter alia, on the province's objection to the unemployment that would accompany restructuring.

Current federal-provincial arrangements have not been an adequate way of helping to integrate regional concerns into a single policy for national economic adaptation and growth (Jenkin, 1983; Thorburn, 1984; Tupper, 1981). What is necessary, as Michael Jenkin has pointed out, is "not a fusion of regional and industrial development policy but rather an institutional device which could more effectively tailor industrial policy to regional specifications without losing sight of the overall national strategy" (1983, p. 180). The machinery of government at the national level has not been able to do this. As Thorburn says, although the Departments of Industry, Trade and Commerce and of Regional Economic Expansion worked closely together, there was "always a problem with conflicting objectives between IT&C and DREE in that the former is concerned with the competitive position of Canadian industry and its long-term survival vis-à-vis international competition, whereas DREE is concerned with creating jobs in depressed areas" (1984, p. 78).

In addition to these departments which, as the agencies closest to the firms, are likely to be sympathetic to their requests, two other federal ministries are involved in industrial policy: the Department of Finance and the Ministry of State for Economic Development (MSED) (Aucoin and Bakvis, 1983). Both were potentially able to take a broader view of industrial development than either IT&C or DREE. However, as Richard French explains, the Department of Finance is unlikely to be the centre of a *dirigiste* industrial policy. The "ideological" bias of the department is non-interventionist and market-oriented; it is intellectually sceptical about state-led adjustment and about picking winners and losers. It favours reliance on the market rather than the state as the agent of change and, if necessary, opts for industry-neutral assistance as opposed to more sector-specific intervention (1980, pp. 109–17).

The MSED was unlikely to fill the primary policy position for several reasons. First of all, its main task was integrative — to bring together existing policies and to get departments to cooperate in the development of economic policy. Its job was not to pick and choose to develop a coherent policy, but to work out a consensus (Aucoin and Bakvis, 1983) with the other departments of government. When MSED became MSERD (the Ministry of State for Economic and Regional Development) in 1982, it officially took up the concern of regional as well as national economic development.

Given their constituencies, intellectual traditions and organizational mandate, no one federal department or ministry is likely to be the prime actor in the development of state-led positive adjustment and restructuring. Each may have a basis for supporting incremental assistance from government to the private sector, but no agency is likely to bring forward a coherent strategy of adaptation that will encourage growth sectors, and yet help to move certain resources away from declining sectors. The direction of policy that is more likely to emerge follows Zysman's description of "industrial preservationism," in which subsidy or protection is used to "mute market signals and relieve the need for change" (1983, p. 85).

Decline and dislocation have arisen in Canada as they have in all other industrial nations. The absence of broad policy agreement and technical yardsticks that ensue from shared objectives means that rescue decisions are likely to be made according to more than economic criteria. This means that policy probably will be influenced by the arguments of the political interests in each individual case.

Although the Canadian banking system is as highly concentrated as those in Europe (five banks account for 90 percent of total assets) the banks' relationship to government and industry and their role in adjustment policy are more like the financial systems in the United States and Britain. Although they are highly regulated, Canadian banks are sufficiently independent that the government cannot control credit to guide investment, as happens in France. Nor are they deeply involved in companies so that they act as early warning systems to anticipate problems, as they do in Japan, or can formulate and monitor rescues, as is the case in West Germany. Given the nature of its links to government and industry, the Canadian banking system does not serve as an instrument for state-led adjustment (Zysman, 1983), and the banks do not act on their own to lessen the demand for state intervention.

The relationship between the public and private sectors also differentiates Canada from France, West Germany and Japan. We have seen that a sharp distinction is made between the state and the private sector in Canada. Now the question is to what extent do the two consult and collaborate? The general assessment is that there is little discussion, planning and joint action between government and industry in Canada (Molot, 1977; Rotstein, 1972, p. 131; Jenkin, 1983). When government has sought to consult with the private sector, as occurred in the Tier I and Tier II exercises in 1977 and 1978, the results were shopping lists and "wish lists," rather than sector-based strategies of adjustment (Brown and Eastman, 1981). There is little demand from the business world for comprehensive industrial adjustment. Similarly, the labour unions do not emphasize industrial adjustment policies but rather have sought to "socialize" the costs of adjustment: through job creation measures, aid to communities hard hit by factory closures, and extended unemployment benefits. The point is not whether Canada is or should be more corporatist, but that neither management nor labour organizations are likely to be sufficiently broadly based to call for national or sectoral adjustment policies. The typical strategy has been to lobby for narrow forms of assistance and protection.

In Canada, neither industry nor labour interests are organized in the encompassing, centralized and hierarchical manner associated with more corporatist policy making (Schmitter and Lembruch, 1979; for indicators of interest-group activity associated with corporatism, see Wilson, 1983). There are 216 unions in Canada, of which only 16 have over 50,000 members. Bargaining takes place at the level of the firm. The fragmentation of the union movement, as well as the ambivalence toward corporatism within the labour movement, creates an unlikely foundation for corporatism (McBride, 1983; Panitch, 1979). Producer groups are also fragmented. Here, the impact of federalism is apparent. Most groups are organized on a regional and a national basis, but differences in the views of the regional and national offices often limit the national body's effectiveness in dealing with Ottawa (Molot, 1977). Another aspect of Canada's political economy that lessens the likelihood of cohesive producer representation is the extent of foreign ownership and branch plants. As Molot points out, the interests of subsidiary companies may well be different from their Canadian counterparts (ibid., p. 14).

In sum, Canada's institutional structures, banking system and public–private sector relationship decrease the probability that a state-led adaptive capacity will be developed. Organization at the federal level, the absence of adequate federal-provincial arrangements, and the autonomous banking system make it less likely that restructuring policies will be supplied; the fragmented organization of private-sector interests makes it unlikely that such policies will be demanded.

Comparing Britain and France, Diana Green spells out four prerequisites for coherent, state-led adjustment (1981, p. 346):

• a common, non-ideological view of the role of the state;
• a determination to use public funds as efficiently as possible, i.e., in order to achieve clearly defined industrial aims;
• government-industry relations based on some sort of common approach to industrial development, which presupposes a greater sensitivity on the part of government to industry's needs, as well as greater awareness on the part of the business community of the "national interest"; and
• coordination at the highest political levels.

From the material reviewed here, it is apparent that Canada does not meet these conditions. There is no shared view of the role of the state.

Other objectives to do with regionalism and the federal division of power constrain efficiency; industry-government relations are not on an ongoing, consultative basis, and policy making is fragmented.

The large number of "firm-specific" bailouts can also be traced in part to Canada's political institutions. Federal-provincial arrangements have not helped to integrate regional concerns into a single policy for national economic adaptation and growth; the division of powers means that declining firms or sectors have at least two avenues for presenting their demands for assistance. Moreover, in light of regional and federal-provincial conflicts, firm-specific crises have been politicized, making it probable that non-economic objectives are part of the calculus of decision making. Decisions to rescue are ad hoc and reactive: they are often a political response to firm failures that threaten jobs. There are no mechanisms in place at the federal level or in the realm of federal-provincial relations to sustain state-supported restructuring.

Conclusions

A survey of the policy patterns and major political determinants of policy in advanced industrialized nations begs more questions than it answers. Important exceptions to each nation's major policy thrust had to be omitted here in order to focus on the dominant strategies. Besides, explaining the treatment of any single industrial sector or the rescue of a particular firm probably requires more attention to situation-specific factors than the broad attributes emphasized in this paper.

In drawing on the experience of other nations, it is necessary to separate the effects of one stream of industrial policy from other elements. When comparing policies, political scientists have tended to use aggregate figures of unemployment, productivity, and segment of the workforce in manufacturing as measures of success or failure. These indicators, however, are a result of many policy decisions, not just restructuring, tariff protection, and so on. It is difficult to isolate judgments about the management of decline from an overall evaluation of economic and industrial policy. However, aggregate measures of economic performance, as well as more impressionistic material, consistently reveal a similar ranking. Japan and West Germany are ahead of the other four countries, France is in the middle, followed by the United States, with Britain always at the bottom (Cox, 1982; Magaziner and Reich, 1982; Hager, 1982; Dyson and Wilks, 1983). Even with agreement on the ranking of national adaptability to changes in the international economy, we cannot infer that some policies or methods are superior. The effects of policy are confounded because strong economies like West Germany and Japan are better able to absorb redundancies created in restructuring than are weaker economies like Britain (Grant, 1983). So, one cannot assume that the same policy or instrument would be equally successful in a different context. (See the essays in Dyson and Wilks (1983) for evaluations of the policy process.)

A typical study of impact focusses on a single nation and its treatment of one or more sectors (Maunder, 1979; Dyson, 1982a). These sector analyses, across nations or within a single country, can be quite useful. But it is worth noting that a recent collection of sector studies in Europe and Japan concluded that, in fact, it was easier to generalize by country than by industry (Shepherd et al., 1983, p. 15). The sector approach is often more detailed and can facilitate better understanding of the inter-action between the political system and the economic and social context (Shepherd et al., 1983; Cohen and Gourevitch, 1982; Zysman and Tyson, 1983). Furthermore, the sector approach permits observation of varia-tion within a single nation. For example, on the basis of aggregate economic measures and experiences in the steel and auto industries, Japan is justifiably considered to be adjusting to changing economic conditions quite effectively. However, in the fields of shipbuilding (since the mid-1970s) and aluminum smelting, MITI has not been able to guide each industry through restructuring. There is no agreement within these industries or with government; the industries want protection, and pol-iticians have responded to local demands for help (Magaziner and Hout, 1981). Appreciation of these "deviant" cases helps in understanding the general pattern of policy making in Japan.

Studies that emphasize the subsequent economic success or failure of the industry or the firm are certainly necessary for evaluating policy; but they may often ignore the trade-offs between economic growth and other values, such as regional development. Moreover, a single focus on effectiveness may be blind to the equity implications (for example, whether some groups in society are more likely than others to bear the burdens of adjustment). Some analyses of the two more successful nations (Japan and West Germany) have raised the equity issue. For example, it is argued that in Japan, women and older workers are less likely to have job security, and in West Germany that "concerted action" ignores the interests of less-skilled workers (Dyson, 1982a; Esser et al., 1983). Similar matters have been explored with regard to which workers are likely to benefit from protection in the United States (J. David Richardson, 1982; for Canada, see Glenday et al., 1982). These questions of impact require careful consideration in Canada. First, Canadians wish to know what works! But, equally important, they need to understand the economic context of the success and also the social as well as the economic costs.

In depicting the approaches employed by the six nations under review, it is clear that coping with economic decline is a complex problem. No nation that has achieved any success in managing decline has ignored the social effects of industrial contraction. Nor have they expected the affected workers and regions simply to bear the costs of adaptation without recourse to political action. In France, West Germany and Japan, the more successful states to deal with decline, there is much evidence that state-led or encouraged restructuring has been accompanied by assistance to hard-hit regions and redundant workers. If anything distinguishes Britain, Canada and the United States from the other three countries here, it is the way in which they respond to the social costs of economic change: Britain, Canada and the United States tend to shield workers and regions *from* change rather than support them *through* change.

Awareness of the experience of other industrialized nations may bring out several misconceptions, which detract both from fruitful policy debate and from Canada's ability to grapple effectively with the economic and social problems of decline. Myths have developed, which falsely limit the options open to Canadian decision makers and seriously constrict their ability to cope. Three such fallacies can be dealt with here.

"Canada is not Japan." The argument here is a familiar one; it is a variant on the national character thesis. First, it acknowledges that each nation has a distinct economic, political and social system. Unfortunately, the next step is to attribute policy outcome (success or failure) to "Japaneseness," a surrogate for the many factors that comprise the Japanese system. However, it is the many factors that must be abstracted to assess the determinants and the effectiveness of policy. Any comparison will be fruitless if there is no effort to isolate the sub-systemic factors that explain policy. The implication that policy adaptation is impossible because nations are "different" is an unacceptable substitute for analysis.

"Corporatism is alien to the free market." The liberal corporatism described by Lembruch refers to a "special type of participation by large organized social groups, especially in economic policy making. . . . the distinguishing limit is the high degree of co-operation among these groups themselves in shaping public policy. . . . Liberal corporatism rests on the premise that there exists strong interdependence between the interests of conflicting social groups in a capitalist economy" (1979, pp. 52–55). Consultation and collaboration have been shown to be important elements in the successes of France, Japan and West Germany. Yet certainly the latter two and France under the neo-liberal Giscardists could hardly be considered "anti-market." The expectation of negotiation and the sense of interdependence is what differentiates more corporatist modes from the pluralistic. Neither negotiation nor interdependence is antithetical to a market economy or a democratic state. More pluralistic modes of politics have led to situations in which all participants seek to insulate themselves from the costs of economic adjustment; the outcome may be the result of competing forces. Whereas more consultative modes yield no single big loser, the outcome may be more rationally determined by the various participants.

"Doing nothing is the only way to facilitate market trends." None of the nations surveyed here, no matter how committed they are to the market, have been able to ignore the political pressures raised by economic change. In some cases, this meant dealing with narrowly defined interests seeking direct protection; in other instances, the demands came from a broader collectivity, which was seeking to spread the burdens of displaced labour through compensation and retraining, or to internalize business losses through support for modernization and restructuring. We have seen that in those political systems that refuse or are unable to facilitate the mobility of labour and capital, the people or interests who will be adversely affected by competitive adjustment are most likely to try to shield themselves. Embracing the false dichotomy between letting the market work and protection has needlessly structured the debate over industrial decline and has obscured the complexities of policy making.

Notes

This paper was completed in August 1984.

1. It should be noted that, throughout this paper, "decline" is used in a general sense to refer to uncompetitive firms and sectors. It is not meant to convey the more specific, terminal quality of the Zysman (1983) definition.

2. According to Grant, "selective intervention" refers to micro-economic measures that discriminate among firms and industries. The approach is based on voluntary cooperation between business and government (1982, p. 18).

3. When the Labour party came to power in 1964, however, it did attempt to develop corporatist deliberative bodies under the aegis of the National Economic Development Council (NEDC) (Grant, 1982).

4. Hills notes that where there has not been consensus, e.g., in shipbuilding, MITI's influence has been quite limited (1983, p. 73).

5. The textile industry and the fisheries are two important exceptions.

6. The profound differences are well represented by the reports and studies of the two major federal advisory bodies: the Science Council and the Economic Council (see Jenkin, 1983). For examples of the differences in academic writing, see Watson (1983) and Thorburn (1984).

7. Established in 1974, the CIASI was replaced by the Socialists with CIRI (Interministerial Committee for Industrial Restructuring). Although CIRI is very similar to its predecessor, the Socialists have added six regional committees.

8. This should not be taken to mean that the financial systems are the same in all three nations. The banking systems in France, West Germany, Japan, Britain and the United States, and their links with the state, are lucidly described in Zysman (1983).

Bibliography

Abonyi, A., and M. Atkinson. 1983. "Technological Innovation and Industrial Policy." In *The Politics of Canadian Public Policy*, edited by M. Atkinson and M. Chandler. Toronto: University of Toronto Press.

Adams, F.G., and Lawrence Klein, eds. 1983. *Industrial Policies for Growth and Competitiveness*. Toronto: D.C. Heath, Lexington Books.

Adams, Roy J. 1982. "The Federal Government and Tripartism." *Industrial Relations* 37: 606–16.

Allen, G.C. 1979. "Government Intervention in the Economy of Japan." In *Government Intervention in the Developed Economy*, edited by Peter Maunder. London: Croom Helm.

———. 1980. *Japan's Economic Policy*. London: Macmillan.

———. 1981. *The Japanese Economy*. London: Weidenfeld and Nicolson.

Allen, K. 1979. *Balanced National Growth*. Toronto: D.C. Heath, Lexington Books.

Alt, James. 1979. *The Politics of Economic Decline*. New York: Columbia University Press.

Anderson, J., and M. Gunderson. 1982. *Union-Management Relations in Canada*. Toronto: Addison-Wesley.

Ashford, D. 1981. *Policy and Politics in Britain: The Limits of Consensus*. Oxford: Basil Blackwell.

Atkinson, M., and Marsha Chandler, eds. 1983. *The Politics of Canadian Public Policy*. Toronto: University of Toronto Press.

Aucoin, Peter, and H. Bakvis. 1983. "Organizational Differentiation and Integration: The Case of Regional Economic Development Policy in Canada." Paper presented at the Canadian Political Science Association, June.

Bacon, R., and W. Eltis. 1978. *Britain's Economic Problem: Too Few Producers*. 2d ed. London: Macmillan.

Bendick, Marc, Jr. 1981. "National Industrial Policy and Economically Distressed Communities." *Policy Studies Journal* 10: 220–35.

Berger, S.D., ed. 1981. *Organizing Interests in Western Europe*. New York: Cambridge University Press.

Biggs, Margaret A. 1980. *The Challenge: Adjust or Protect?* Ottawa: North-South Institute.

Birnbaum, Pierre. 1981. "State, Centre and Bureaucracy." *Government and Opposition* 16: 58–73.

Blackaby, F., ed. 1978. *British Economic Policy, 1960–1974*. New York: Columbia University Press.

———, ed. 1979. *De-industrialization*. London: Heinemann.

Blais, A., and P. Faucher. 1981. "La politique industrielle dans les économies capitalistes avancées." *Canadian Journal of Political Science* 14: 3–35.

Blank, S. 1978. "Britain: The Politics of Foreign Economic Policy. In *Between Power and Plenty*, edited by P.J. Katzenstein. Madison: University of Wisconsin Press.

Bliss, Michael. 1982. *The Evolution of Industrial Policies in Canada*. Study prepared for the Economic Council of Canada. Ottawa: Minister of Supply and Services.

Boltho, A., ed. 1982. *The European Economy: Growth and Crisis*. London: Oxford University Press.

Bratt, Harold A. 1974. "Assisting the Economic Recovery of Import-Injured Firms." *Law and Policy in International Business* 6: 1–36.

Breton, A. 1974. *A Conceptual Basis for an Industrial Policy*. Study prepared for the Economic Council of Canada. Ottawa: Information Canada.

Brittan, S. 1978. "How British Is the British Sickness?" *Journal of Law and Economics* 21: 245–68.

Brown, C.J.F. 1980. "Industrial Policy and Economic Planning in Japan and France." *National Institute Economic Review* 93: 59–75.

Brown, D., and J. Eastman. 1981. "The Limits of Consultation." Ottawa: Science Council of Canada.

Burton, John. 1979. *The Job Support Machine: A Critique of the Subsidy Morass*. London: Centre for Policy Studies.

Canada. 1983. *Report of the Auditor General, 1982*. Ottawa: Office of the Auditor General.

Canada. Department of Industry, Trade and Commerce. 1979. *Doing Business in Canada: Federal Incentives to Industry*. Ottawa: Minister of Supply and Services Canada.

Carter, Charles, ed. 1981. *Industrial Policy and Innovation*. London: Heinemann.

Caves, R., and Lawrence Krause, eds. 1980. *Britain's Economic Performance*. Washington, D.C.: Brookings Institution.

Chandler, A., and H. Daems, eds. 1980. *Managerial Hierarchies*. Cambridge, Mass.: Harvard University Press.

Chandler, M. 1982. "State Enterprise and Partisanship in Provincial Politics." *Canadian Journal of Political Science* 15 (4): 711–40.

Chandler, William, and A. Siaroff. 1984. "Post-materialist Politics in Germany and the Rise of the Greens." Paper presented at meetings of the Canadian Political Science Association in Guelph.

Coates, David. 1982. "Britain in the 1970s: Economic Crises and the Resurgence of Radicalism." In *Politics, Policy and the European Recession*, edited by A. Cox. London: Macmillan.

Cohen, S. 1982. "Informed Bewilderment: French Economic Strategy and the Crisis." In *France in the Troubled World Economy*, edited by S. Cohen and P. Gourevitch. London: Butterworth.

Cohen, S., and P. Gourevitch, eds. 1982. *France in the Troubled World Economy*. London: Butterworth.

Cohen, S., J. Galbraith, and J. Zysman. 1982. "Rehabbing the Labyrinth: The Financial System and Industrial Policy in France." In *France in the Troubled World Economy*, edited by S. Cohen and P. Gourevitch. London: Butterworth.

Coombes, D. 1982. *Representative Government and Economic Power*. London: Heinemann.

Corden, W.M., and G. Fels, eds. 1976. *Public Assistance to Industry*. Boulder, Col.: Westview Press.

Corrigan, Richard. 1983. "Choosing Winners and Losers: Business, Labor and Political Leaders are Searching for a U.S. Industrial Policy." *National Journal* 15: 416–43.

Courchene, T. 1980. "Towards a Protected Society: The Politicization of Economic Life." *Canadian Journal of Economics* 13: 556–77.

Cox, A. 1981. "Corporatism as Reductionism: The Analytic Limits of the Corporatist Thesis." *Government and Opposition* 16: 78–95.

———, ed. 1982. *Politics, Policy and the European Recession*. London: Macmillan.

Curzon Price, Victoria. 1981. *Industrial Policies in the European Community*. London: Macmillan.

Dahrendorf, R., ed. 1982. *Europe's Economy in Crisis*. London: Weidenfeld and Nicolson.

Davenport, P., C. Green, W.J. Milne, R. Saunders, and W. Watson. 1982. *Industrial Policy in Ontario and Quebec*. Toronto: Ontario Economic Council.

DeCarmoy, G. 1978. "Subsidy Policies in Britain, France and West Germany: An Overview." In *International Trade and Industrial Policies*, edited by S.J. Warnecke. London: Macmillan.

de la Torre, José. 1981. "Decline and Adjustment: Public Intervention Strategies in the European Clothing Industries." Brussels: European Institute of Business Administration.

Dell, E. 1973. *Political Responsibility and Industry*. London: Allen and Unwin.

Denison, Edward. 1979. *Accounting for Slower Economic Growth: The U.S. in the 1970s*. Washington, D.C.: Brookings Institution.

Destler, I.M. 1980. *Making Foreign Economic Policy*. Washington, D.C.: Brookings Institution.

de Vos, Dirk. 1982. "Governments and Micro-Electronics: the European Experience." Ottawa: Science Council of Canada.

Donges, J.B. 1980. "Industrial Policies in West Germany's Not So Market-Oriented Economy." *The World Economy* 3: 185–204.

Dyson, K. 1977. *Party, State and Bureaucracy in Western Germany*. Beverly Hills: Sage.

———. 1979. "The Ambiguous Politics of Western Germany." *European Journal of Political Research* 7: 375–96.

_____. 1980. *The State Tradition in Western Europe.* Oxford: Martin Robertson.

_____. 1982a. "The Politics of Economic Recession in Western Germany." In *Politics, Policy and the European Recession,* edited by A. Cox. London: Macmillan.

_____. 1982b. "West Germany: The Search for a Rationalist Consensus." In *Policy Styles in Western Europe,* edited by J. Richardson. London: Allen and Unwin.

_____. 1983. "The Cultural, Ideological and Structural Context." In *The Industrial Crisis,* edited by K. Dyson and S. Wilks. Oxford: Martin Robertson.

Dyson, K., and S. Wilks, eds. 1983. *The Industrial Crisis: A Comparative Study of the State and Industry.* Oxford: Martin Robertson.

Economic Council of Canada. 1975a. *Beyond the Frontiers.* Ottawa: Minister of Supply and Services Canada.

_____. 1975b. *Looking Outward: A New Trade Strategy for Canada.* Ottawa: Minister of Supply and Services Canada.

_____. 1982. *Intervention and Efficiency: A Study of Government Credit and Credit Guarantees to the Private Sector.* Ottawa: Minister of Supply and Services Canada.

_____. 1983. *The Bottom Line: Technology, Trade and Income Growth.* Ottawa: Minister of Supply and Services Canada.

Edmonds, M. 1983. "Market Ideology and Corporate Power: The United States." In *The Industrial Crisis,* edited by K. Dyson and S. Wilks. Oxford: Martin Robertson.

Emminger, Otmar. 1982. "West Germany — Europe's Driving Force?" In *Europe's Economy in Crisis,* edited by R. Dahrendorf. London: Weidenfeld and Nicolson.

Esser, J., W. Fach, G. Gierszewski, and C.W. Vath. 1982. "State Intervention: Steel Crisis and Policy — a Comparison." *Inter-Economics* 6: 279–81.

Esser, J., and W. Fach, with K. Dyson. 1983. "Social Market and Modernization Policy: West Germany." In *The Industrial Crisis,* edited by K. Dyson and S. Wilks. Oxford: Martin Robertson.

Estrin, S., and P. Holmes. 1983a. "French Planning and Industrial Policy." *Journal of Public Policy* 3 (February): 131–48.

_____. 1983b. *French Planning in Theory and Practice.* London: Allen and Unwin.

Faucher, Philippe, André Blais, and Robert Young. 1984. "L'aide financière directe des gouvernements du Québec et de l'Ontario à l'industrie manufacturière, 1960–1980." *Journal of Canadian Studies* 18: 54–78.

Franko, L.G. 1979. "Industrial Policies in Western Europe: Solution or Problem?" *The World Economy* 2: 3–50.

Freeman, B., and A. Mendelowitz. 1982. "Program in Search of a Policy: The Chrysler Loan Guarantee." *Journal of Policy Analysis* 1: 4–18.

French, Richard. 1980. *How Ottawa Decides: Planning and Industrial Policy Making, 1968–80.* Toronto: James Lorimer for Canadian Institute for Economic Policy.

Gamble, A. 1981. *Britain in Decline: Economic Policy, Political Strategy and the British State.* London: Macmillan.

Glenday, G., G.P. Jenkins, and J.E. Evans. 1982. *Worker Adjustment Policies: An Alternative to Protectionism.* Ottawa: North-South Institute.

Gourevitch, P. 1977. "International Trade, Domestic Coalitions and Liberty: Comparative Responses to the Crises of 1873–1896." *Journal of Interdisciplinary History* (Autumn): 281–313.

_____. 1982. "Making Choices in France: Industrial Structure and the Politics of Economic Policy." In *France in the Troubled World Economy,* edited by S. Cohen and P. Gourevitch. London: Butterworth.

Gourevitch, P., Andrew Martin, George Ross, Stephen Bornstein, Andrei Markovits, and Christopher Allen. 1984. *Unions and Economic Change.* London: Allen and Unwin.

Grant, W. 1982. *The Political Economy of Industrial Policy.* London: Butterworth.

_____. 1983. "The Political Economy of Industrial Policy." In *Perspectives on Political Economy,* edited by R.J.B. Jones. London: Frances Pinter.

Grant, Wyn, and Stephen Wilks. 1984. "British Industrial Policy: Structural Change, Policy Inertia." *Journal of Public Policy* 3: 15–28.

Green, D. 1981. "Promoting the Industries of the Future: The Search for an Industrial Strategy in Britain and France." *Journal of Public Policy* 1: 333–51.

_____. 1983a. "Strategic Management and the State: France." In *The Industrial Crisis*, edited K. Dyson and S. Wilks. Oxford: Martin Roberton.

_____. 1983b. "Giscardisme — Industrial Policy." In *Giscard, Giscardians and Giscardism*, edited by V. Wright. London: Allen and Unwin.

_____. 1984. "Industrial Policy and Policy-making, 1974–82." In *Continuity and Change in France*, edited by V. Wright. London: Allen and Unwin.

Hager, W. 1982. "Industrial Policy, Trade Policy and European Social Democracy." In *National Industrial Strategies and the World Economy*, edited by John Pinder. Paris: Atlantic Institute for International Affairs.

Hardin, H. 1974. *A Nation Unaware*. Vancouver: J.J. Douglas.

Harrison, R.J. 1980. *Pluralism and Corporatism: The Political Evolution of Modern Democracies*. London: Allen and Unwin.

Hartle, D. 1980. "The Need for Adjustment and the Search for Security: The Barriers to Change." In *Developments Abroad and the Domestic Economy*. Toronto: Ontario Economic Council.

Hartley, K. 1977. *Problems of Economic Policy*. London: Allen and Unwin.

Hayward, J.E.S. 1972. "State Intervention in France: The Changing Style of Government-Industry Relations." *Political Studies* 20: 287–96.

_____. 1976. "Institutional Inertia and Political Impetus in France and Britain." *European Journal of Political Research* 4: 341–59.

_____. 1982. "France: Strategic Management of Impending Collective Impoverishment." In *Politics, Policy and the European Recession*, edited by A. Cox. London: Macmillan.

Hayward, J., and R. Berki, eds. 1979. *State and Society in Contemporary Europe*. New York: St. Martin's Press.

Hayward, J., and M. Watson, eds. 1975. *Planning, Politics and Public Policy*. Cambridge: Cambridge University Press.

Hills, Jill. 1981. "Government Relations with Industry: Japan and Britain — A Review of Two Political Arguments." *Polity* 14 (2): 15–24.

_____. 1983. "The Industrial Policy of Japan." *Journal of Public Policy* 3 (February): 63–80.

Hindly, B., ed. 1983. *State Investment Companies in Western Europe*. London: Macmillan.

Hirsch, F., and J. Goldthorpe. 1978. *The Political Economy of Inflation*. Cambridge, Mass.: Harvard University Press.

Hirsch, J. 1980. "Developments in the Political System of West Germany." In *The State in Western Europe*, edited by R. Scane. London: Croom Helm.

Hobsbawm, E. 1982. "The State of the Left in Western Europe." *Marxism Today* 26: 10.

Jenkin, M. 1983. *The Challenge of Diversity: Industrial Policy in Canadian Federalism*. Science Council of Canada. Background Study Study no. 50. Ottawa: Minister of Supply and Services Canada.

Jenkins, G. P. 1980. *Costs and Consequences of the New Protectionism: The Case of Canada's Clothing Sector*. Ottawa: North-South Institute.

Johnson, Chalmers. 1982. *MITI: The Ministry of International Trade and Industry*. Berkeley: University of California Press.

Jones, R.J. Barry, ed. 1983. *Perspectives on Political Economy*. London: Frances Pinter.

Jordan, A.G. 1981. "Iron Triangles, Woolly Corporatism and Elastic Nets." *Journal of Public Policy* 1: 95–123.

Kanthrow, Alan. 1983. "The Political Realities of Industrial Policy." *Harvard Business Review* 61 (September/October): 76–87.

Katzenstein, P.J., ed. 1978. *Between Power and Plenty*. Madison: University of Wisconsin Press.

_____. 1980. "Problem or Model? West Germany in the 1980s." *World Politics* (July): 577–98.

Kikkawa, M. 1983. "Shipbuilding, Motor Cars and Semiconductors: The Diminishing Role of Industrial Policy in Japan." In *Europe's Industries*, edited by G. Shepherd et al. London: Frances Pinter.

King, Anthony. 1973. "Ideas, Institutions and the Policies of Government: A Comparative Analysis." *British Journal of Political Science* 3: 291–313, 409–23.

Krasner, S. 1978. "United States Commercial and Monetary Policy: Unravelling the Paradox of External Strength and Internal Weakness." In *Between Power and Plenty*, edited by P.J. Katzenstein, pp. 51–88. Madison: University of Wisconsin.

———, ed. 1983. *International Regimes*. Ithaca: Cornell University Press.

———. 1984. "Approaches to the State: Alternative Conceptions and Historical Dynamics." *Comparative Politics* 16: 223–46.

Kreile, M. 1978. "West Germany: The Dynamics of Expansion." In *Between Power and Plenty*, edited by P.J. Katzenstein. Madison: Univeristy of Wisconsin Press.

Kuster, G. 1974. "Germany." In *Big Business and the State*, edited by R. Vernon. Cambridge, Mass.: Harvard University Press.

Lange, Peter, George Ross, and Maurizio Vannicelli. 1982. *Unions, Change and Crisis*. London: Allen and Unwin.

Lembruch, G. 1979. "Consociational Democracy, Class Conflict and the New Corporatism." In *Trends toward Corporatist Intermediation*, edited by P. Schmitter and G. Lembruch. London: Sage.

Litvak, I.A. 1981. "Government Intervention and Corporate Government Relations." *Business Quarterly* 46: 47–54.

MacNeil, Michael. 1982. "Plant Closings and Workers' Rights." *Ottawa Law Review* 14: 1–56.

Magaziner, Ira C., and Thomas Hout. 1981. *Japanese Industrial Policy*. Berkeley: University of California Press.

Magaziner, Ira C., and Robert B. Reich. 1982. *Minding America's Business*. New York: Harcourt Brace Jovanovitch.

Mahon, Rianne, and Lynn K. Mytelka. 1983. "Industry, the State and the New Protectionism: Textiles in Canada and France." *International Organization* 37: 551–81.

Markovits, A., ed. 1982. *The Political Economy of West Germany: Modell Deutschland*. New York: Praeger.

Martin, R.M. 1983. "Pluralism and the New Corporatism." *Political Studies* 21 (1): 86–102.

Maslove, Allan. 1983. "Loans and Loan Guarantees: Business as Usual versus the Politics of Risk." In *How Ottawa Spends Your Tax Dollars*, edited by G. Bruce Doern. Toronto: James Lorimer.

Matthews, R.A. 1971. *Industrial Viability in a Free Trade Economy: A Program of Adjustment Policies for Canada*. Toronto: University of Toronto Press.

Maunder, Peter, ed. 1979. *Government Intervention in the Developed Economy*. London: Croom Helm.

McArthur, J.B., and B.R. Scott. 1969. *Industrial Planning in France*. Cambridge, Mass.: Harvard University Press.

McBride, S. 1983. "Public Policy as a Determinant of Interest Group Behaviour." *Canadian Journal of Political Science* 16: 501–517.

McKay, D. 1983a. "The Political Economy of Economic Policy." In *Perspectives on Political Economy*, edited by R.J.B. Jones. London: Frances Pinter.

———. 1983b. Industrial Policy and Non-policy in the United States." *Journal of Public Policy* 3 (February): 29–48.

McKay, D., and Wyn Grant. 1983. "Industrial Policies in OECD Countries: An Overview." *Journal of Public Policy* 3 (February): 1–12

Medley, R., ed. 1982. *The Politics of Inflation: A Comparative Analysis*. New York: Pergamon.

Messerlin, P., and C. Saunders. 1983. "Still Too Much Investment Too Late." In *Europe's Industries*, edited by G. Shepherd et al. London: Frances Pinter.

Metcalfe, L., and W. Quillan. 1979. "Corporatism or Industrial Democracy?" *Political Studies* 27: 266–82.

Michalet, C.A. 1974. "France." In *Big Business and the State*, edited by R. Vernon. Cambridge, Mass.: Harvard University Press.

Middlemass, Keith. 1979. *Politics in Industrial Society*. London: André Deutsch.

Migué, Jean-Luc. 1979. *Nationalistic Policies in Canada: An Economic Approach*. Montreal: C. D. Howe Research Institute.

Molot, M.A. 1977. "The Domestic Determinants of Canadian Foreign Economic Policy: Beavers Build Dams." Paper delivered at meetings of the American Political Science Association in Washington, D.C.

Morici, P., A. Smith, and Sperry Lea. 1982. *Canadian Industrial Policy*. New York: National Planning Association.

Mottershead, P. 1978. "Industrial Policy." In *British Economic Policy, 1960–1974*, edited by F. Blackaby. New York: Columbia University Press.

Muller, Ronald. 1980. *Revitalizing America: Politics for Prospects*. New York: Touchstone.

Neufeld, E. 1982. "Industrial Policy in Canada in the 1980s." *Western Economic Review* 1: 14–33.

Ohlin, G. 1978. "Subsidies and Other Industrial Aids." In *International Trade and Industrial Policies*, edited by S.J. Warnecke. London: Macmillan.

Olson, M. 1982. *The Rise and Decline of Nations*. New Haven: Yale University Press.

Organisation for Economic Co-operation and Development. 1978. *Selected Industrial Policy Instruments: Objectives and Scope*. Paris: OECD.

_____. 1979a. *The Case for Positive Adjustment Policies: A Compendium of OECD Documents*. Paris: OECD.

_____. 1979b. *Collective Bargaining and Government Policies*. Paris: OECD.

Owen-Smith, Eric. 1979. "Government Intervention in the Economy of the Federal Republic of Germany." In *Government Intervention in the Developed Economy*, edited by Peter Maunder. London: Croom Helm.

Panitch, L. 1979. "Corporatism in Canada." *Studies in Political Economy* 1 (Spring): 43–92.

Parkin, F. 1971. *Class Inequality and Political Order*. London: Granada Publishing.

Paterson, W.E., and G. Smith, eds. 1981. *The West German Model*. London: Frank Cass.

Patrick, Hugh, ed. 1976. *Japanese Industrialization and Its Social Consequences*. Berkeley: University of California Press.

Patrick, Hugh, and Henry Rosovsky. 1976. "Japan's Economic Performance: An Overview." In *Asia's New Giant*, edited by Hugh Patrick and Henry Rosovsky. Washington, D.C.: Brookings Institution.

Peacock, A., in collaboration with Rob Brant et al. 1980. *Structural Economic Policies in West Germany and the United Kingdom*. London: Anglo-German Foundation.

Pearson, C., and Gerry Salembier. 1983. *Trade, Employment and Adjustment*. Montreal: Institute for Research on Public Policy.

Pempel, T.J. 1978. "Japanese Foreign Economic Policy, the Domestic Basis for International Behavior." In *Between Power and Plenty*, edited by P.J. Katzenstein. Madison: University of Wisconsin Press.

_____. 1982. *Policy and Politics in Japan*. Philadelphia: Temple University Press.

Pestieau, C. 1978. *The Quebec Textile Industry in Canada*. Montreal: C.D. Howe Institute.

Pinder, John, ed. 1982. *National Industrial Strategies and the World Economy*. Paris: Atlantic Institute for International Affairs.

Pollard, S. 1982. *The Wasting of the British Economy*. London: Croom Helm.

Presthus, R. 1973. *Elite Accommodation in Canadian Politics*. Toronto: Macmillan.

Protheroe, David R. 1980. *Imports and Politics*. Montreal: Institute for Research on Public Policy.

Quebec. 1979. *Challenges for Quebec: A Statement on Economic Policy*. White Paper. Quebec: Government of Quebec.

Ramseyer, J. Mark. 1981. "Letting Obsolete Firms Die: Trade Adjustment Assistance in the United States and Japan." *Harvard International Law Journal* 22: 595–619.

Reich, R. 1982. "Making Industrial Policy." *Foreign Affairs* 60: 852–82.

———. 1983a. *The Next American Frontier*. New York: Basic Books.

———. 1983b. "An Industrial Policy of the Right." *Public Interest* 73: 3–17.

Resa, Georg. 1980. "Government and Industry in the Federal Republic of Germany." *International and Comparative Law* 29: 87–111.

Richardson, J., ed. 1982. *Policy Styles in Western Europe*. London: Allen and Unwin.

Richardson, J., and A. Jordan. 1979. *Governing under Pressure: The Policy Process in a Post-industrial Democracy*. London: Macmillan.

Richardson, J. David. 1982. "Trade Adjustment Assistance under the US Trade Act of 1974: An Analytical Examination and Worker Survey." In *Import Competition and Response*, edited by J. Bhagwati. Chicago: University of Chicago Press.

Ritchie, G. 1983. "Government Aid to Industry: A Public Sector Perspective." *Canadian Public Administration* 26: 36–46.

Rohlen, Thomas. 1979. "Permanent Employment Faces Recession, Slow Growth and an Aging Work Force." *Journal of Japanese Studies* 5: 235–72.

Rotstein, A., ed. 1972. *An Industrial Strategy for Canada*. Toronto: New Press.

Saunders, C., ed. 1981. *The Political Economy of Old and New Industrial Countries*. London: Butterworth.

Saunders, R. 1984. *Aid to Declining Industries*. Toronto: Ontario Economic Council.

Saxonhouse, C. 1979. "Industrial Restructuring." *Journal of Japanese Studies* 5: 273–320.

Schmidt, M. 1983. "The Welfare State and the Economy in Periods of Economic Crisis: A Comparative Study of Twenty-three OECD Nations." *European Journal of Political Research* 11: 1–26.

Schmitter, P., and G. Lembruch, eds. 1979. *Trends toward Corporatist Intermediation*. London: Sage.

Science Council of Canada. 1979a. *Forging the Links: A Technology Policy for Canada*. Science Council of Canada Report no. 29. Ottawa: Minister of Supply and Services Canada.

———. 1979b. *The Politics of Industrial Strategy: A Seminar*. Ottawa: Minister of Supply and Services Canada.

Seers, D., B. Schaffer, and M. Kiljuner, eds. 1979. *Underdeveloped Europe*. Hassocks, Sussex: Harvester.

Shepherd, G. 1983. "Textiles: New Ways of Surviving in an Old Industry." In *Europe's Industries*, edited by G. Shepherd, F. Duchêne and C. Saunders, pp. 26–51. London: Frances Pinter.

Shepherd, G., and F. Duchêne. 1983. "Industrial Change and Intervention in Western Europe." In *Europe's Industries*, edited by G. Shepherd, F. Duchêne and C. Saunders. London: Frances Pinter.

Shepherd, G., F. Duchêne, and C. Saunders, eds. 1983. *Europe's Industries: Public and Private Strategies for Change*. London: Frances Pinter.

Simeon, Richard. 1976. "Studying Public Policy." *Canadian Journal of Political Science* 9 (4): 548–80.

Skocpol, Theda. 1982. "Bringing the State Back." Paper delivered at a conference on States and Social Structures, New York.

Smith, Gordon. 1976. "The Politics of Centrality in West Germany." *Government and Opposition* 11: 387–407.

Strange, S. 1979. "The Management of Surplus Capacity: Or How Does Theory Stand Up to Protectionism 1920s Style? *International Organization* 33: 303–34.

Streeck, W. 1983. "Between Pluralism and Corporatism: German Business Association and the State." *Journal of Public Policy* 3: 265–84.

Suzuki, Yoshio. 1980. *Money and Banking in Japan*. New Haven: Yale University Press.

Thorburn, H. 1984. *Planning and the Economy*. Ottawa: Canadian Institute for Economic Policy.

Thurow, L. 1980. *The Zero-Sum Society*. New York: Penguin.

Trebilcock, M.J., J. Whalley, C. Rogerson, and I. Ness. 1983. "Provincially Induced Barriers to Trade in Canada." In *Federalism and the Canadian Economic Union*, edited by M.J. Trebilcock, J.R.S. Prichard, T.J. Courchene, and J. Whalley. Toronto: University of Toronto Press for Ontario Economic Council.

Trebilcock, M.J., Marsha Chandler, Morley Gunderson, Paul Halpern, and John Quinn. 1985. *The Political Economy of Business Bailouts*. Toronto: Ontario Economic Council.

Tresize, P., with Yoshio Suzuki. 1976. "Politics, Government and Economic Growth in Japan." In *Asia's New Giant*, edited by Hugh Patrick and Henry Rosovsky. Washington, D.C.: Brookings Institution.

Tupper, A. 1981. *Public Money in the Private Sector*. Kingston: Queen's University, Institute for Intergovernmental Relations.

Usher, D. 1983. "The Benefits and Costs of Firm-Specific Investment Grants: A Study of Five Federal Programs." Discussion Paper 511. Kingston: Queen's University, Institute for Economic Research.

Vernon, R., ed. 1974. *Big Business and the State*. Cambridge, Mass.: Harvard University Press.

Vogel, D. 1978. "Why Businessmen Distrust Their State: The Political Consequences of American Corporate Executives." *British Journal of Political Science* 8: 45–78.

Vogel, Ezra. 1979. *Japan as Number One: Lessons for America*. Cambridge, Mass.: Harvard University Press.

Volkman, Larber. 1983. *The Political Economy of France: From Pompidou to Mitterrand*. New York: Praeger.

Von Beyme, K. 1978a. "The Politics of Limited Pluralism? The Case of West Germany." *Government and Opposition* 13: 267–87.

_____. 1978b. "The Changing Relationships between Trade Unions and the Social Democratic Party in West Germany." *Government and Opposition* 13: 399–415.

_____. 1983. "Neo-Corporatism: A New Nut in an Old Shell." *International Political Science Review* 412: 173–96.

Von Beyme, K., and Ionscu, G. 1977. "The Politics of Employment in Germany and Great Britain." *Government and Opposition* 12: 88–107.

Warnecke, S.J., ed. 1978. *International Trade and Industrial Policies: Government Intervention and an Open World Economy*. London: Macmillan.

Warnecke, S., and E. Suleiman. 1975. *Industrial Policies in Western Europe*. New York: Praeger.

Warren, J.H. 1978. "Canada's Role in the GATT Negotiations." *Canadian Business Review* 5 (2): 36–41

Watson, W. 1983. *A Primer on the Economics of Industrial Policy*. Toronto: Ontario Economic Council.

Williams, G. 1981. *Not for Export*. Toronto: McClelland and Stewart.

Wilson, F.L. 1982. "Alternative Models of Interest Intermediation: The Case of France." *British Journal of Political Science* 12: 173–200.

_____. 1983. "French Interest Group Politics: Pluralist or Neocorporatist." *American Politcal Science Review* 77: 895–910.

Wilks, S. 1983. "Liberal State and Party Competition: Britain." In *The Industrial Crisis*, edited by K. Dyson and S. Wilks. Oxford: Martin Robertson.

Wolfe, David. 1983. "Backing Winners? Constraints on Industrial Strategy in the New International Division of Labour." Paper presented to the Association of Political Economy in Montreal.

Wright, V., ed. 1983. *Giscard, Giscardians and Giscardism*. London: Allen and Unwin.

_____, ed. 1984. *Continuity and Change in France*. London: Allen and Unwin.

Yoffie, D. 1983. "Adjustment in the Footwear Industry: The Consequences of OMAs." In *American Industry in International Competition*, edited by J. Zysman and L. Tyson. Ithaca, N.Y.: Cornell University Press.

Young, S. 1974. *Intervention in the Mixed Economy*. London: Croom Helm.

Zysman, J. 1977. *Political Strategies for Industrial Order*. Berkeley: University of California Press.

———. 1978. "The French State in the International Economy." In *Between Power and Plenty*, edited by P.J. Katzenstein. Madison: University of Wisconsin Press.

———. 1983. *Governments, Markets and Growth*. Ithaca, N.Y.: Cornell University Press.

Zysman, J., and S. Cohen. 1983. "Double or Nothing: Open Trade and Competitive Industry." *Foreign Affairs* 61: 1113–39.

Zysman, J., and J. Pontusson. 1980. "Industrial Adjustment and Business-State Relations." British Social Science Research Council. Mimeo.

Zysman, John, and Laura Tyson, eds. 1983. *American Industry in International Competition*. Ithaca: Cornell University Press.

6

Ministerial Roles in Policy Making:
Vote Seeker, Shaman, and Other Incarnations

CONRAD WINN

All political history shows that the standing of the Government and its ability to hold the confidence of the electorate at a General Election depend on the success of its economic policy.

Harold Wilson[1]

"He'll sit here" [Truman would say about Eisenhower], tapping his desk for emphasis, "and, he'll say, Do this! Do that! And nothing will happen. Poor Ike — it won't be a bit like the army. He'll find it very frustrating.

Harry S. Truman[2]

I think Dick's [Richard M. Nixon] going to be elected President but I think he's going to be a one-term President. I think he's really going to fight inflation, and that will kill him politically.

Dwight D. Eisenhower[3]

I was expected to accept the unanimous recommendation of the Department, though of course there was always the possibility that I might reject it. Seldom, if ever, was I given the luxury of multiple-choice options on matters of major import.

Flora Macdonald[4]

You thought that if you had power, you could do what you wanted. But that is a fundamental mistake. Not even I can do what I like — perhaps I can manage about a third of what I'd like to do. If I had not raised my hand in the Politburo when I did for military intervention — what could have happened? You would not be sitting here. And possibly not even I would be sitting here!

Leonid Brezhnev[5]

I was appointed Minister of Housing on Saturday, October 17, 1964. Now it is only the 22nd but, oh dear, it seems a long, long time . . . already I realize the tremendous effort it requires not to be taken over by the Civil Service. My Minister's room is like a padded cell, and in certain ways I am like a person who is suddenly certified lunatic and put safely into this great, vast room, cut off from real life and surrounded by male and female trained nurses and attendants. When I am in a good mood they occasionally allow an ordinary human being to come and visit me; but they make sure that I behave right. . . . Of course, they don't behave quite like nurses because the Civil Service is profoundly deferential — "Yes, Minister! No, Minister! If you wish it, Minister!" — and combined with this there is a constant preoccupation to ensure that the Minister does what is correct.

Richard Crossman[6]

Introduction

Those things which are the most important to know are often the most unknowable. It is vital to know the impact of the cabinet on the economy because the cabinet in Canada, as in other liberal democracies, is the most powerful economic authority sanctioned by popular will.[7] Little, however, is known about the influence of the cabinet. Cabinet decision making is shrouded in secrecy. Observers know little in a systematic and verifiable way about the information and options that are conveyed to ministers, cabinets, and cabinet committees, or about the decisions that are conveyed back to the public service.

This study will argue that the knowability of the cabinet policy-making process is also limited by the multiple and sometimes contradictory roles filled by ministers. Ministers are far more than vote seekers. Moreover, vote seeking for ministers is far more complex an art than delivering benefits to potential supporters and taking for granted those whose votes can be taken for granted. Given the complexity of ministerial roles, it is even difficult to guess what ministers should do if they want to act in their own interest.

Because of cabinet secrecy, our most systematic and reliable information consists of the actual expenditures and programs of governments. By comparing expenditures, programs, and the distribution of benefits under the governments of different parties and under the same government but at different times, it is possible to make inferences about the motivations of ruling politicians. The major part of this study reviews the quantitative literature in political science on the outputs of governments to see what can be learned or inferred about the significance of cabinets for economic policy.

Politically minded people who live and work outside academe are more likely to have decided views about the influence of politicians on the state of the economy than those who live and work within its cloisters. Outside academe, both the liberal democratic left and the liberal democratic right believe that politicians make a difference. The non-Marxist left holds that liberal, social democratic, and socialist politicians protect, in varying degrees, the working and middle classes from exploitation by the rich and powerful. The parliamentary-minded right holds that left-wing politicians, or politicians in general, are responsible for the expansion of the public sector and for losses in efficiency and freedom which the right attribute to the growth of government.

Within academe, political scientists have conducted by far the most research on the behaviour of politicians and of the electorate. They have conducted studies of individual politicians and events, and they have studied the impact on policy of anticipated elections, of the election of new governing parties, and of the ascension of new leaders. Frustrated by cabinet secrecy, however, and awed by the complexity of politicians' motives, political scientists have shied away from writing in a theoretical or "cause-and-effect" way about the influence of politicians. Economists have been more forthright than political scientists in assessing the policy impacts of politicians, perhaps because they are accustomed to the simplicity required by mathematical analysis. A popular view among professional economists in North America appears to be that politicians are the main source of inefficiency in the economy. The ignorance or self-interest of politicians is thought to explain why governments regulate more vigorously and more widely than they need to in order to achieve their objectives and why the regulatory world is needlessly complex.

Trebilcock et al. express one version of this viewpoint of economists in *The Choice of Governing Instruments*.[8] According to the Trebilcock theory of political life, ruling politicians are concerned primarily with reelection and therefore with winning the allegiance of marginally affiliated voters, to whom extra material benefits are channelled. Where possible, politicians underrepresent the costs of policy by resorting to obscure resource-generating instruments such as the manufacturing tax ("fiscal illusion"), and they exaggerate the benefits of policy by selecting high-profile command-and-control instruments ("output illusion"). The successful politician is good at reallocating benefits from infra-marginal voters (i.e., committed partisans), to marginal voters and effective at disguising what is being done. Moreover, politicians are apt to ignore considerations of the general welfare that would weaken their reelection efforts.

The Trebilcock theory is a good one, within limits. It helps to explain the presence of fiscal illusion[9] and the importance of output illusion, namely, why governments resort to regulatory instruments of a command-and-control type when other less salient market interventions might be more effective. However, the theory presents an incomplete picture of what ruling politicians do and a false picture of how ruling politicians get reelected. Reelection is far more complex a matter than one of transfers to marginal voters; indeed, such transfers can backfire. The quest for reelection is itself a multivariate phenomenon; what is good for a minister's personal reelection may not be good for the party's. Much of what ministers and cabinets do to win reelection takes place outside policy making, and the resources of government that enhance reelection prospects are a small fraction of government resources as a whole. In any case, many of the policy impacts of ministers are not felt by voters and may even be unknown to specialized interest groups.

In the following section, the functions of a minister are broken down into nine roles. The next section reviews the literature on the political business cycle, which concerns the supply by governments and the demand by electorates for desired economic outcomes. This literature sheds some light on the extent to which politicians are concerned with reelection. The policy determinants literature, which consists largely of quantitative studies of the hypothesized political and economic sources of government expenditures, is then discussed. This literature sheds light on the extent to which cabinets are influenced by ideological and other nonelectoral considerations. Next is a review of the ministerial cycle literature, which explores the impact of leadership succession and ministerial tenure on the content of policy. This literature sheds light on the influence upon policy of the legitimation needs of rulers. Then the limits of quantitative data in explaining the motivations of politicians are discussed. The final section reviews in a cursory fashion some of the literature in the field of psychobiography. The purpose of this section is to remind readers that leaders have a capacity to influence the course of events for a variety of idiosyncratic motivational reasons that may be unrelated to electoral self-interest, ideology, or other structural factors.

The Nine Roles of Ministers

Nine roles and nineteen subroles of cabinet ministers, as delineated by the author, are listed in Table 6-1. Each role corresponds to a set of activities and objectives, and the various roles and subroles overlap to some degree. As vote seekers, the ruling politicians strive to secure personal reelection, the party's success in the large or small regions for which they are responsible, and the party's national success as a result of their efforts as spokespersons on a given topic. The politician also helps the party nationally in the subrole of party leader or subaltern. As MPs, regional lieutenants, and cabinet ministers, politicians strive for support among marginal voters. As a leader of the party, however, his or her foremost concern is the well-being and enthusiasm of party loyalists. Party activists can become alienated from their party as a result of efforts to appeal to marginal voters; they may prefer party purity to victory. Cabinet ministers with leadership ambitions have strong incentives to serve the needs of loyalists rather than marginals.

Ministers in the role of reformer may seek reform along the left/right spectrum, along the universalist/particularist spectrum, and/or in idiosyncratic ways. As ideologues on the left/right spectrum, politicians may choose between equality and inequality, or between big government and small government. As ideologues on the universalist/particularist spectrum, they may choose between the interests and traditions of the dominant ethnocultural group on the one hand and ethnic equality on the other.

Some ministers are communalists, representing the collective interests of a province, region, or ethnocultural group. Most politicians are at least part-time shamans, using their skills as entertainers and thespians to uplift spirits and banish foreboding thoughts.

TABLE 6-1 The Nine Roles of Ministers and Their Impact on Marginal Voters, Policy Outcomes, and Symbolic Outcomes

Role	Subrole	Benefit to Marginal Voters[a]	Policy Outcomes[b]	Symbolic Outcomes[b]
Vote Seeker	MP	+	+	+
	Regional lieutenant	+	+	+
	Cabinet member	+	+	+
	Party leader	−	+	+
Reformer	Left/right ideologue	N.A.	+	+
	Universalist/particularist ideologue	N.A.	+	R
	Idiosyncratic	N.A.	+	+
Communalist		N.A.	R	+
Shaman		N.A.	+	+
Governor	Departmental policy maker	N.A.	+	R
	Departmental personnel manager	N.A.	+	+
Mediator	Between citizens and bureaucracy	N.A.	R	R
	Between interest groups and bureaucracy	N.A.	+	+
Patriot	Nation builder or integrationist	N.A.	R	+
	Nation maximizer	−	+	+
Delegate	Good citizen	N.A.	+	+
	Peoples' representative	N.A.	+	+
Private Person	Party patronage options	N.A.	R	+
	Private sector career	N.A.	+	+

a. + indicates that benefits accrue to marginal voters; − that benefits accrue to infra-marginals; N.A. that the distinction between marginal and infra-marginal voters is not applicable.

b. + indicates that the given role calls for outcomes; R that these outcomes are not required.

Ministers are governors, mediators, and patriots. As governors, they are their departments' normal authorities on policy, and they are responsible for the conduct of personnel insofar as that conduct affects departmental morale. As mediators, ministers can help achieve reconciliation between the bureaucracy and individual citizens or interest groups. As patriots, they strive to reintegrate disaffected or alienated regions or subgroups and to maximize the national interest vis-à-vis foreign governments and foreign corporations. As delegates, ministers may see themselves as representatives of ordinary people and as good citizens. As private persons, ministers must maintain job options in the event of personal defeat. If a minister loses but the party wins, a patronage appointment remains possible, but a career in the private sector is the most likely means of making a living.

The formal separation of vote-seeking from non-vote-seeking roles is a heuristic device, designed to distinguish between the materially partisan and the other roles of the minister. The distinction can be criticized on the grounds that *all* the roles of ministers affect their and their party's ability to be reelected. This point has some validity; indeed, some clever ministers are constantly on the lookout for the electoral implications of everything they do. However, the primacy of electoral considerations must not be exaggerated. Many of the non-vote-seeking roles rarely, if ever, affect the electoral prospects of a minister or his party. For example, ministers' performance as departmental policy makers and personnel managers rarely affects their or their party's fortunes. Professional political scientists, not to mention the public, rarely have any useful information about the administrative performance of individual ministers.

Ministers have considerable freedom to ignore electoral considerations in what have been termed their nonelectoral roles. It is often impossible for them to foresee how the public will actually react to their behaviour in such roles. Identical acts by a minister may elicit different public evaluations depending on the climate of opinion at the time, the identity of the minister, the way in which the minister has portrayed his act, and the way in which the act has been reported. Few ministerial acts will in any case provoke as much pleasure or displeasure as the publicly known aspects of a minister's private life. Errors of policy making or departmental administration are apt to harm a politician less than a known history of psychiatric treatment, crime, or sexual abnormality. Above all, ministers retain considerable freedom to ignore electoral considerations in their nonelectoral roles because they can exercise an enormous influence over what is or is not reported in the media. It is now commonly accepted in the scholarly study of mass communications that most news is subsidized, that is, made possible by speeches, press conferences, briefings, leaks, or releases rather than through the exclusively self-financed efforts of investigative journalists.

For each of the ministerial roles and subroles listed, Table 6-1 indicates whether special benefits to marginal voters are necessarily required. The electoral self-interest theory of Trebilcock and other economists requires marginal voters to receive benefits whose costs are absorbed by all voters or by infra-marginal voters alone. The table also indicates whether each role or subrole entails policy outcomes and/or symbolic outcomes. Policy outcomes refer to government expenditures, government regulations, or other government actions. Symbolic outcomes are defined as changes in public perceptions of well-being which result from the ability of ministers to persuade or manipulate the public using their personal ministerial staffs but not departmental resources, transfer payments, or other interventions involving the public service.

Conforming to the Trebilcock theory, the table indicates that the vote-seeker subroles of MP, regional lieutenant, and cabinet member lead to special benefits for marginal voters. However, the vote seeking subrole of party leader and the patriot subrole of nation builder lead to reduced benefits for these voters. As party leaders, ministers must be concerned primarily with the morale of their own partisans. As nation builders, they may have to bestow special benefits on partisans of the opposition party since a disaffected region is frequently one dominated by opposition voters. On balance, only three of the subroles filled by ministers lead to benefits for marginal voters while two subroles actually function in the opposite direction. Taken as a whole, then, the various roles of ministers do not lead inexorably to government expenditure for the benefit of marginal voters.

Much theorizing about the policy impact of ministers assumes that ministers must resort to the policy process to achieve reelection and that ministers cannot get reelected by symbolic means. However, by virtue of their prestige and prominence, ministers have greater access than have Opposition MPs to the mass media, to campaign money, to valued speaking opportunities, and to other, nongovernmental ways of influencing public attitudes. As Harry Truman observed, the power of the executive is above all the power to persuade. To secure reelection, it may be helpful for ministers to direct government largesse to their constituencies in one form or another, but it is not necessary. Because of greater prestige, greater media exposure, greater usefulness as a mediator to interest groups located in the constituency, greater rhetorical, histrionic and other skills, and weaker opposing candidates as a result of the preceding advantages, ministers require less largesse for their reelection bids than do ordinary backbenchers in their party.

Ruling parties likewise lack a pressing need to transfer benefits to marginal voters as a means of securing reelection. Incumbent parties begin with a head start in voter support for a number of reasons. As rulers, ministers have greater salience in the minds of voters than those who sit in the Opposition front benches. As long as their electoral prospects are reasonably good, incumbent parties have an easier task recruiting strong candidates. Ruling parties are normally well funded and, as governors, ministers have much more media exposure than Opposition leaders. In our parliamentary system, ruling parties retain the initiative of calling elections when their popularity is high and when the best pretext is available. Governments can use their control over the legislative agenda to select the best occasions to expose discord within the Opposition or to otherwise embarrass it.

The Trebilcock theory — that ministers need to hide from all or parts of the electorate their electorally motivated allocations — is correct. Nevertheless, the theory exaggerates the importance of electorally motivated allocations, and ignores the pressures to reward partisans at the expense of marginals. Electorally conceived allocations are a dangerous way of seeking public support and can backfire if perceived as evidence of self-interest, corruption, or desperation on the part of the government. Electoral self-interest in policy making is similar to electoral corruption; it works, but only on a small scale, as illustrated in the case that gave us the word gerrymandering. In the early 1800s, Massachusetts Governor Gerry, from whom the concept derived, was a successful incumbent until his electoral malfeasance reached the extreme of redrawing the boundaries of so many constituencies in so many ways that one constituency acquired the shape of a salamander; hence, "gerrymander." Transgressing the bounds of what was culturally acceptable, Governor Gerry was repudiated even by "loyal" partisans.

In their many roles other than as vote seekers, ministers may require policy outcomes that do not conform with the economists' portrait of politicians as appealing primarily to marginal voters. It must be acknowledged that ministers do want to avoid situations that place them at the centre of controversy and which therefore alienate marginal voters. Some ministers delegate most of their departmental responsibilities to their deputies with the explicit proviso that the deputies answer personally for any departmental actions that embarrass the ministers or the party.[10] Some may avoid potentially frustrating portfolios, such as the Status of Women, that entail energetic pressure groups and divided public preferences.[11] Ministers, however, are not preoccupied with maximizing transfers to marginal voters, since elections are not held yearly. Preoccupation with allocating benefits to marginal voters is time-consuming when ministers have little time; it is wasteful when ministers need to distribute largesse within their own party; and it is electorally dangerous for reasons already discussed.

It is ironic that the economists' portrait of electorally motivated benefits should emerge in recent years because such allocations are less important to electoral success than they have been in the past. Patronage and other benefits to loyalist and marginal voters have become less effective and reliable means of reelection as a result of increases in the incomes, education, and professionalization of Canadians. In the age of television, theatrical skills have replaced money and organization as the basis of political success. Television has penetrated society with such intensity and has personalized political contests to such a degree that leadership selection, leadership style, and media manipulation have become the most important ingredients in electoral success. Party money is always important, but money is used today to elicit information about voters' perceptions, to develop effective media messages, to transmit these messages, and thereby to persuade. In Canada, money, liquor, and jobs are used less and less to "buy" votes.

Trebilcock and other economists are right to hold politicians responsible for fiscal and output illusions, but they commit a grievous error in attributing fiscal and output illusions to the vote-seeking roles of politicians only. Fiscal and/or output illusions are required by all the roles and subroles of ministers. For example, a left-wing ideologue needs to play down the fiscal costs of the welfare state in order to win greater acceptance for his policy changes. The right-wing reformer needs to play down the dislocation and other costs of privatization in order to secure greater acceptance for his changes. The communalist needs to exaggerate his interlocutive powers to his ethnic or regional community while understating them to outsiders. The shaman needs to play down the costs of everything and play up the benefits of everything. The nation-building patriot needs to persuade the disaffected of the value of special benefits targetted for their needs without encouraging those who are otherwise content to feel that it is profitable to become disaffected. The nation-maximizing patriot needs to galvanize public opinion as an instrument of international bargaining without arousing public spirit to the point where compromise is no longer possible. All or almost all the roles and subroles of ministers entail the orchestration of illusions in order to contribute to the public weal.

In the absence of illusion, the vote seeker would be defeated. The ideological reformer would provoke class warfare. The communalist would undermine his community. The shaman would see his society become dispirited. The governor's department would be demoralized. The nation-building patriot would witness regional alienation. Without the ability to create illusions the nation-maximizing patriot would risk negotiating from weakness or embittering inter-country relations. Politicians know that illusions are important for all their roles. By observing which political leaders are remembered in history and which are forgotten, politicians learn that they will be esteemed less for the policies they choose than for how noble and patriotic these policies are made to appear. Noble thoughts and patriotic sentiments are certainly illusions, capable of both beneficial and destructive uses.

In the role of private person, a ruling politician must give thought to career alternatives in the event of defeat or declining interest in political life. The prospect of financial gain cannot be a significant motivation for most politicians because of insecurity of tenure and because of declining opportunities for personal corruption or capital accumulation. Since a common fall-back occupation for a defeated minister is a partisan appointment, a minister who is concerned about his occupational future is likely to emphasize loyalty to his leader and party. A history of party loyalty also makes a personally defeated minister more useful to a firm anticipating the need for assistance from cabinet. However, firms that could benefit from the partisan ties of a defeated minister are more likely to be small than large. Because they are so important to the Canadian economy, large firms do not require ex-ministers in order to gain access to cabinet or the higher bureaucracy. In any case, they often have sufficient intelligence on government policy making as a result of their own public and corporate affairs staffs and as a result of keeping one or more law firms and lobbying firms on their payrolls. Hence, ministers do not have strong incentives to make major economic policy decisions with the view to enhancing future job prospects.

Of all the roles and subroles of the minister, the most important may be that of shaman. The shaman's job is to ward off evil spirits, to make people happy. The political shaman does so by conveying the illusion of, and therefore contributing to, the reality of a united, contented people. The shaman's methodology is not econometric analysis, but magic. Magic is of course the term of the outsider. Like a placebo which relieves pain in some cultures, magic is a method of changing a group's self-image, a method that only cultural outsiders perceive as irrational.

In their past roles as shamans, federal ministers have transformed the historical fact of the British conquest of New France into the myth of "two founding nations." As shamans, ministers transformed "O Canada" from a symbol of sectional alienation into a ritual of national solidarity. Outsiders might say that the effect of "O Canada" was magical because it exceeded any rational expectation. The hymn was originally commissioned as a French Canadian nationalist song by the proto-separatist Saint-Jean-Baptiste Society when the society was established in the early 19th century. In fact, the composer, Calixa Lavallée, was so anti-English that he emigrated to the United States; he fought in the Civil War, wrote patriotic American music, and established the American Music Teachers Federation, which he represented abroad as its president. Lavallée died in French Canada's American diaspora, but he was able to compose "O Canada" on one of his extended return stays in Quebec.

As shamans and in their other non-vote-seeking roles, ministers are acutely aware of the importance of national moods and collective feelings, in which they see themselves as relatively skilled. They know that steady increases in income, health, education, employment, and other attributes of a stable, growing economy contribute to a sense of well-being, and make it easier to fulfil their multiple roles. Ministers realize that they are not experts in producing economic miracles. They know that they are skilled, and are expected to be skilled, in producing attitudinal miracles out of whatever economic conditions happen to befall the country.

The economists' portrait of the vote-seeking minister as responsible for fiscal and output illusions is flawed. The nonelectoral roles of the minister demand illusion even more than the electoral ones. Indeed, the electoral needs of ministers act as a brake on the ministerial desire to create illusions; some such behaviour helps reelection, but too much may risk defeat. Voters have been known to punish politicians for failing to live up to illusions or for creating unfulfilled expectations. In the final analysis, the argument that vote seeking explains fiscal and output illusions cannot be reconciled with the fact that citizens in countries with elections are better informed and therefore suffer from fewer illusions than the inhabitants of countries without elections.

The study began by noting that cabinet secrecy renders impossible the direct observation of ministers in their economic policy-making roles. Without reliable information about cabinet decision making, academics are obliged to fall back on information about government policies under different rulers and different electoral conditions. This type of information is discussed in the following section.

The Political Business Cycle Literature

The opening quotation for this study was taken from British Prime Minister Harold Wilson: "All political history shows that the standing of the Government and its ability to hold the confidence of the electorate at a General Election depend on the success of its economic policy."

This is the core idea of a large and rapidly expanding scholarly literature whose main theme has been entitled the political business cycle or, more simply, "the business cycle." Many of the authors are economists, and virtually all the writing is statistical, employing variations of common multiple regression techniques and sometimes employing less common methods such as Poisson probability techniques or simultaneous equations. Most of this literature examines macroeconomic conditions, but the focus of the business cycle literature on macroeconomic considerations such as inflation or employment is a tradition or convention, not a logical requirement. Another main theme in the literature is "policy determinants," which deals with government expenditures and programs. The leading academic who fails to abide by the conventional distinction between business cycle and policy determinants is Edward Tufte. In *The Political Control of the Economy* Tufte focusses on the business cycle largely from a macroeconomic perspective[12] but also looks at social security payments and other expenditures as auxiliary means available to incumbents for augmenting their electoral support.

The political business cycle has two complementary components —

the demand for desired economic outcomes and the government's supply of these outcomes. If the evidence shows that voting behaviour is unaffected by economic performance and that voters do not punish incumbents for economic failure, cabinets would presumably face little pressure to achieve economic growth and little external incentive to foster it. If, on the other hand, electoral behaviour is influenced greatly by economic conditions, evidence to this effect would corroborate the often expressed views of politicians that their management of the economy greatly affects their chances of reelection.

Electoral Behaviour

The literature on the election side of the business cycle is huge and convincing, consisting of many dozens of articles and books on electoral behaviour at national and subnational levels in different time periods in the United States, the United Kingdom, New Zealand, Canada, West Germany and other liberal democracies. The literature contains studies which examine the impact of macroeconomic performance as measured by central agencies, as reported in the media, as perceived by voters, and as experienced in the personal economic lives of voters. The data sets used are varied: they may consist of aggregate election returns combined with official macroeconomic records, or they may combine periodic polling data with official macroeconomic measures. Sometimes they consist entirely of survey data based on national interview samples. In one instance, the economic variables reflecting economic conditions were based on the content analysis of economic reports in a national daily newspaper. Time series, national cross-sectional, and cross-national designs have been used. The varied data sets and modes of analysis used in the voluminous studies of electoral impact lend confidence to the conclusions reached by the researchers.

While voters do indeed punish incumbents for poor macroeconomic performance and reward them for good performance, the influence of macroeconomic performance varies from time to time and place to place. Furthermore, not all measures of performance are equally influential. Voters tend to punish or reward governments for events which they value highly and which they feel justified in attributing to government action or inaction. For example, U.S. voters are more likely to vote in response to their own or their family's economic situation. The following paragraphs review some of the more important and recent studies of electoral response to economic performance.

An important recent work is Kiewiet's *Macroeconomics and Micropolitics*.[13] From a quantitative study of voting in U.S. presidential elections, he concludes that support for incumbents is predicted by national economic conditions, particularly as perceived. He also concludes that perceived national economic growth is a better predictor than unemployment, which is an inconsistent predictor, and a much better one than personal economic conditions. Kiewiet corroborates the conventional wisdom about the policy motivations of voters, namely the fact that voters who say they are concerned about unemployment tend to vote Democrat and those concerned about inflation tend to vote Republican.

Precisely why voters are more affected by perceived economic conditions than by their own particular situations has puzzled researchers. Kiewiet suggests that many Americans have been socialized to an ideological interpretation by which they hold themselves responsible for their economic fortunes. Studies by Weatherford and by Jacobson and Kernell suggest an alternative explanation based on an intervening variable.[14] They suggest that strong candidates and political money are less available to incumbents when the economy is in decline.

Contemporary Political Economy, edited by Hibbs and Fassbender, is considered to be an excellent collection of quantitative studies of the electoral connection.[15] The chapter by Bruno Frey and Friedrich Schneider examines the electoral impact of macroeconomic change in the United States and West Germany and concludes that increased real income affects executive popularity much less than inflation does. A chapter by Samuel Kernell and Douglas Hibbs on the popularity of U.S. presidents corroborates the main outlines of the Frey-Schneider conclusion and indicates that inflation is a major predictor of presidential popularity, indeed a much stronger predictor than is unemployment. In another chapter, Paul Pertez contrasts the effects of macroeconomic changes on the popularity of different ruling parties in West Germany.[16] He concludes that either ruling party gains popularity as a result of reductions in unemployment, but that the Social Democrats gain more when they are in power than the Christian Democrats do when they form the government. He attributes the difference to voter perceptions of the SDP's traditional left-wing commitment to low unemployment. In a chapter on "the Impact of Economic Variables on Political Behaviour in France," Jean-Dominique Lafay concludes that prime ministerial popularity is affected by real wage rates, inflation, and unemployment. Unemployment affects prime ministerial popularity when it is lagged one year, which suggests the length of time French voters require to assimilate and act on this particular item of information.

In their book *Political Aspects of the Economy*, Borooah and van der Ploeg report the results of an intensive statistical analysis of voting and economic change in the United Kingdom.[17] Like the contributors to the above-mentioned anthology, Borooah and van der Ploeg find that the voters whose behaviour they have examined are greatly influenced by macroeconomic changes. In an interesting sidelight, they also report that voters living in constituencies experiencing higher than normal unemployment are especially influenced by macroeconomic changes.

Public Policy and Public Choice, edited by Rae and Eismeier, is another anthology containing important articles on the electoral component of the political business cycle.[18] In a chapter entitled "Economic and Fiscal Effects on the Popular Vote for the Presidency," William Niskanen presents the results of a regression analysis of macroeconomic indicators. His data analysis shows that a 10 percent per capita net increase of national product between presidential election years is associated with a 6.5 percent increase in votes for the incumbent. Unemployment rates have no effect but, interestingly enough, increases in real per capita public spending are associated with a modest decline in popularity, while tax increases are associated with a more substantial decline in popularity. The greater impact of increased taxes when compared with increased government spending lends empirical credence to the concept of fiscal illusion discussed earlier. In a chapter in the same volume, "Budgets and Ballots: The Political Consequences of Fiscal Choice," Eismeier reports the results of his statistical analysis of the impact of tax increases on the fortunes of U.S. state gubernatorial parties seeking reelection. Among ruling parties that had enacted increased taxes or had proposed to do so, as many as 45.1 percent were subsequently defeated. Among outgoing parties that had held the line on taxes, only 27.5 percent failed to win another term in office.

In a recent article in *Comparative Political Studies*, Robertson reports the results of a Poisson method of predicting the collapse of governments in eight European democracies over the period 1958–79.[19] As any adherent of the business cycle school of thought would anticipate, Robertson finds that the probability of cabinet collapse is greatly influenced by the presence of rising inflation or unemployment. Macroeconomic changes do make a difference, and cabinets reap the rewards or pay the price.

Still another anthology devoted to the electoral impact of macroeconomic variables is *Political Process and Economic Change*, edited by Monroe.[20] In a chapter on "Politics and Economics in Everyday Life," Donald R. Kinder and Walter R. Mebane, Jr. show that the average U.S. voter assesses incumbent presidential candidacies primarily according to how he or she perceives national economic conditions. Those few Americans who hold government responsible for their personal economic fortunes are especially likely to vote accordingly. In a chapter on "The Political Dimensions of Wage Dynamics," Martin Paldam, a major researcher in the field, concludes that 20–40 percent of the vote for incumbents in national elections is explained by economic change. Governments are indeed held responsible for unemployment, inflation, and real growth rates by voters, who have a one-year time horizon. The impact of economic change is relatively simple to measure and predict in two-party systems, but considerably more complicated in multi-party systems. In a chapter on "Economic Expectations, Economic Uncertainty, and Presidential Popularity," Kristen R. Monroe and Maurice O. Levi add a further dimension to electoral behaviour, the role of uncertainty about economic conditions. Public uncertainty about future rates of inflation is likely to diminish presidential popularity.

In a January 1984 article in *Comparative Political Studies*, Urspring confirms the thrust of the business cycle theory in an empirical study of voter preferences among New Zealanders. He also adds a few innovations; for example, he tests for the impact on attitudes to incumbents of the ratio of current account balance to gross domestic product (GDP). In his aggregate data analysis, he analyzes the impact of anticipated growth rate using real future growth rates as a proxy for survey data containing voters' reported growth predictions, finding that future growth rates do predict present party preferences in the aggregate. One of Urspring's concluding paragraphs deserves citation:

> The empirical results presented in this article show unambiguously that the inflation rate, the unemployment rate, and most probably the state of the balance on current account exerted a significant influence during the period 1970–1981. The basic hypothesis has passed its empirical test with a high degree of success, thus establishing this important politico-economic relationship for one more country.[21]

In a paper presented at the 1983 annual meeting of the Canadian Political Science Association, Richard Johnston reported the results of time series survey analysis, which shows that Canadian voters, too, are influenced by macroeconomic conditions.[22] Like voters in other countries, Canadians tend to punish the incumbents for poor performance but, like West German voters and seemingly unlike U.S voters, Canadians make policy distinctions among their political parties. The Canadian voters are apparently unlike U.S. voters in that their choices are strongly influenced by personal economic fortunes; in Johnston's language, they are "egocentric." Like German voters, Canadians act as if they perceive substantive policy differences among the parties. In 1980, the outgoing Conservatives lost disproportionate numbers of supporters to the Liberals among previous supporters who were unemployed or dissatisfied with their material conditions. The opposite, however, did not happen to the outgoing Liberals in 1979; voters did not seem to blame the Liberals as much for personal economic misfortune as they did the Conservatives.

Perhaps the biggest single gap in the study of the impact of economic change on electoral behaviour is accounting for voter information. Of the dozens of business cycle studies, less than half a dozen have mentioned how information may be acquired. The U.K. study by Borooah and van der Ploeg observed that voters in high unemployment constituencies are especially affected by macroeconomic change, a fact that suggests a role for personal observation and familiarity.

One study focusses specifically on media reporting. In an article in the January 1984 issue of the *British Journal of Political Science*, Mosley reports the results of a regression analysis of economic events as reported in the press on attitudes to the ruling party. Mosley concludes that a regression in which values of unemployment and inflation reported by the *Daily Mirror* are used as independent variables explains a greater part of the variance in government popularity than a regression in which the values of unemployment and inflation reported by the Central Statistical office are used as explanatory variables."[23] Apparently, economics reporting has a greater impact on electoral behaviour than have the economic events themselves; Mosley's study confirms the truism that events acquire meaning as a result of how they are interpreted. The study also shows that it is as important for vote-seeking politicians to learn how to influence the media as it is for them to learn how to influence the economy. This point is overlooked in the policy-making theories of Trebilcock and other economists, but was argued at the beginning of this study.

The preceding pages have reviewed a small portion of the empirical literature on the electorate's responses to macroeconomic change.[24] The common conclusion almost invariably is that national and/or personal economic fortunes influence voters in their assessments of incumbents qua incumbents or in their assessments of parties qua bearers of economic ideologies. The common politicians' view that the state of the economy makes a difference is robustly upheld. Given this condition and given the importance of the desire for election, politicians have palpable incentives to manage the economy and government expenditures so as to reflect well on them. Ruling politicians have electoral incentives to manipulate economic events and especially how these events are reported in the media.

Policy Behaviour

Two types of scholarly literature help answer the question of how cabinets affect policy: the portion of the business cycle literature that treats macroeconomic indicators as a dependent rather than an independent variable, and the policy determinants literature, which seeks to explain programs and expenditures. This distinction is not entirely clear-cut because the major work on the business cycle as a dependent variable, Tufte's *Political Control of the Economy*, straddles the two fields. The book explores three issues that are often thought to be distinct: (a) governments' timing of economic benefits for the purpose of reelection, (b) the adoption of economic policies that are consistent with the ruling party's ideological world view and that may also assist its reelection efforts, and (c) the relative impact of industrial structure, openness of the economy, parties and ideology, and other determinants of public policy.

Tufte explains that the hypothesis of a political business cycle is an old one, part of the "folklore of capitalist democracies." The purpose of the book is to provide empirical evidence that governments organize economic policy for their self-interest. In his words:

> It is hardly a novel hypothesis that an incumbent administration, while operating with political and economic constraints and limited by the usual uncertainties in successfully implementing economic policy, may manipulate the short-run course of the national economy in order to improve its party's standing in upcoming elections and to repay past political debts. In particular, incumbents may seek to determine the location and the timing of economic benefits in promoting the fortunes of their party and friends. (pp. 3–4)

Following the publication of Tufte's book in 1978, a business cycle literature emerged that treated macroeconomic change as a dependent variable.

Not all contributors to the business cycle literature agree that governments manipulate economic cycles for partisan advantage. In *Political Economics*, a serious book on the subject published in 1983, Alt and Chrystal express doubt that an electorally motivated business cycle exists:

> No one could read the political business cycle literature without being struck by the lack of supporting evidence. There must be some cases where politicians have undertaken electorally motivated interventions. It is difficult to imagine politicians not exploiting some extra information or other resources. But while this clearly happens, and happens particularly clearly in some cases, such cycles may be trivial in comparison with other economic fluctuations.[25]

My reading of the business cycle debate leads to the conclusion that much of it rests on different conceptions of the very nature of the debate. Both critics and advocates of election cycle theory are willing to examine many of the same indicators of the economic condition: unemployment, inflation, real income, government expenditures, transfer payments, and so forth. They differ, however, on how they define the issue. In the narrow view of the critics, any given economic indicator must vary consistently according to the electoral timetable in each of a cross-section of nations. For the business cycle theory to be valid empirically, we must find that, say, unemployment bottoms out in most of the election periods in most of the democracies: when a bivariate statistical analysis is conducted or, better still, when a multivariate analysis is conducted to control for extraneous variables such as population change, unemployment will be found to be at its lowest point during election periods. Advocates of business cycle theory define the issue more broadly, to permit almost any cycle of economic indicators that coincides with election timetables to be evidence of a cycle, and to permit the motivation and electoral needs of outgoing governments to be considered.

The narrow view of the critics adheres more closely to conventions of the scientific method while the broad view of the advocates constitutes a better political science. The critics' view is better in scientific method because it rules out the selective use of evidence, specifying rules that are followed with "blind" consistency and that allow the possibility of rejecting a research hypothesis. In this debate, their view is more scientific because it does not permit the researcher to make discretionary judgments about the needs and desires of outgoing governments to seek reelection.

The highest purpose of science, however, is not to follow rules blindly but to describe facts as they are. Politicians do not always have to worry about reelection; their degree of confidence in this regard can influence their economic policy decisions. The political meaning of unemployment or inflation or other macroeconomic indicators can vary from country to country and from one era to another. As noted above, U.S. voters are more likely than West German voters to reward governments for perceived national economic performance, while West German voters are more likely than are Americans to reward governments for their personal economic fortunes. The broad view of the business cycle debate reflects much more accurately the real nature of political life and is therefore inherently more scientific.

Nonetheless, even the broad view of the business cycle does not lead to the conclusion that the policy outcomes and economic circumstances in liberal democracies are substantially determined by electoral timetables. The electoral policy cycle is relatively modest even if one adopts a broad and generous view of permissible evidence. Overall, the empirical findings conform with the portrait offered earlier in this essay: ministers are indeed vote seekers, but vote seeking is only one of many different ministerial roles and motivations. The evidence that politicians are able to manage for electoral purposes the expenditures and programs of government is a little stronger than the evidence that they can control economic conditions in the society. If we assume that ministers do want reelection and that they understand the electoral consequences of general economic conditions, the empirical evidence suggests that ministers are able to exercise only modest predictable control over the economy at large.

A 1975 article by Nordhaus entitled "The Political Business Cycle" is customarily taken as the starting point in discussions of the business cycle that treat the economy as a dependent variable. Nordhaus' article examines unemployment in a cross-section of countries, but produces weak evidence:

> The overall results indicate that for the entire period a political cycle seems to be implausible as a description for Australia, Canada, Japan, and the U.K. Some modest indications of a political cycle appear for France and Sweden. For three countries — Germany, New Zealand, and the United States — the coincidence of business and political cycles is very marked.[26]

Tufte's *Political Control of the Economy* followed shortly thereafter. The book has made an impact on the political science profession at large but has been generally ignored or criticized by specialists. It was not welcomed by specialists because it mixes different kinds of evidence and makes at least one exaggerated and unfounded claim. Moreover, Tufte tends to employ simple bivariate analysis instead of multiple regression and is therefore less able to isolate the impact of extraneous variables.

Tufte's most criticized claim stems from his comparison of real income changes in election and nonelection years among a cross-section of 27 democracies over the period 1971–72: real income grew in 64 percent of election years but in only 49 percent of nonelection years. A valid criticism of Tufte's interpretation of this finding is that he does not control statistically for the ability of governments to call elections at will and therefore to choose election dates to coincide with economic cyles.[27] We cannot know from his data what proportion of the supranormal election year income peaks are explained by the timing of the cycle to coincide with the election and what proportion are explained by the timing of the election to coincide with the cycle.

Tufte's evidence of a political business cycle is, however, not limited to one data exercise. He finds that real income grew in three-fourths of the election years during the Truman, Kennedy, Nixon, and Ford administrations as compared to only one-fifth of nonelection years. Tufte excludes from his analysis the Eisenhower election years, in which real growth declined, because of documentary evidence that Eisenhower expected large electoral victories and interpreted his mandate from the outset as one of reducing government rather than reducing unemployment. Surveying unemployment rates, Tufte concludes that

> except in the Eisenhower years, the election-day unemployment rate has averaged about one percentage point below the rate twelve to eighteen months before the election and nearly two percentage points below the post-election unemployment rate twelve to eighteen months after the presidential election. (p. 21)

Tufte compares economic growth according to the political importance of each election year. He finds that real growth increases an average of 3.4 percent when an incumbent seeks reelection, 2.6 percent in midterm congressional elections, 2 percent when an incumbent does not seek reelection, and only 1.5 percent in nonelection years (p. 24). He reports empirical evidence of kyphosis or peaking of transfer payments in election years. Within election years, they peak just before the fall election date while in nonelection years they peak in December. Tufte finds evidence of election-year kyphosis primarily when the incumbent is popular in the polls. From this fact, he concludes that electorally useful transfer payment kyphosis is probably explained by the voluntary cooperation of public servants, who wish to ingratiate themselves with the anticipated victor (p. 44). He observes "windows" or delays whereby social security expenditure increases are timed for the immediate pre-election period and the increased revenues required to pay for the increases are scheduled for the post-election periods.

One legitimate criticism of Tufte's analysis is that it focusses on the presence or absence of a predicted change in income or social security transfer rather than on the magnitude of such changes, with the result that the small magnitude of some of these changes is overlooked. Tufte also ignores the accidental nature of the timing of some of these changes. For example, the economy was stimulated in 1964 as a result of a tax cut which came in the election year because of a delay caused by Congress; Congress had refused an earlier presidential request for a tax cut.[28]

Those who argue against the existence of a political business cycle are subjected to methodological criticisms at least as severe as those directed against Tufte. In an article published in *Public Choice*, Paldam reports the results of a failed test of the cycle.[29] From his statistical analysis, Paldam concludes that the cycle does not exist. However, Blais et al. have raised serious doubts about the validity of Paldam's procedure because he employed non-constant dollars and examined the pattern of all public expenditure and not just central government expenditure.[30] Blais et al. argue that any test of the cycle should be restricted not just to central government expenditures but to civilian expenditures of the central government. The magnitude of military expenditures is determined primarily on the basis of external considerations and should not be included in the design.

Several other works provide strong evidence of electoral factors in economic cycles. Ames studied the impact of domestic and international financial capacity, coups, and ideology upon economic cycles among Latin American countries during the period 1948–70. He reports strong evidence that central government expenditures rise to a peak in election years. However, unlike the pattern in other parts of the world, in Latin America central government expenditures do not fall immediately after the election period.[31] Frey finds that government expenditures, transfer payments, and number of government employees rise in election years in West Germany, that non-military expenditures and number of employees rise in election years in the United States, and that total government expenditures rise during election years in the United Kingdom.[32] In a study of economic change in Israel, Ben-Porath shows a systematic relationship between the timing of currency devaluations and the timing of elections.[33]

In Canada, Blais and his colleagues have conducted a major study of provincial government expenditures in Ontario and Quebec.[34] They report evidence of expenditure kyphosis in the fields of health, roads, and agriculture. They also report evidence that election years are more likely to be budget deficit years. Even the significant exceptions to the pattern make sense. For example, they find that the first budget year of Jean Lesage's Quebec Liberals was a year of expenditure. This expenditure kyphosis in a nonelection year makes no sense in terms of the theory of the political business cycle, but it makes a lot of sense in terms of the ideological goals of the Quiet Revolutionaries. According to the taxonomy of roles outlined at the beginning of this essay, Lesage and his colleagues were reformers, governors, and patriots before they were vote seekers. Indeed, they were so absorbed in nonelectoral roles that they forgot to redistribute riding boundaries to reflect urbanizing changes and were defeated electorally as a result.

The Policy Determinants Literature

The political business cycle literature is customarily distinguished from the policy determinants literature by the fact that the cycle literature focusses on the timing of expenditures while the determinants literature examines the content of government policy. As a result, the determinants literature presents additional information about how cabinets actually function. The determinants literature, like the business cycle literature, finds that the electoral position of a government affects what it does.

Electoral Motivations

Writing in the 1940s, the formidable American political scientist V.O. Key argued that the structure of electoral competition among parties influences what governments do. In *Southern Politics in State and Nation*, Key provides evidence that states dominated by one party tend to pursue conservative, financially regressive policies. States with competitive party politics implement more left-wing, redistributive programs. According to Key, governments respond to electoral threats by employing redistributive public expenditures in order to appeal to middle- and lower-income voters.[35] During the 1960s, Key's ideas were explored empirically by Hofferbert, Dawson, Robinson, Dye and others, applying correlational techniques to data on the U.S. states.[36] They found that party competition was a factor in policy output, albeit a less important factor than socio-economic variables such as urbanization, industrialization and per capita income.

The quantitative studies of policy in U.S. states became a model for Canadian studies of policy variation at the provincial level. A study of the diffusion of policy innovation by Dale Poel reports that provinces characterized by electoral maldistribution are slower to adopt innovations.[37] Mishler and Campbell find that provinces characterized by the institutional development of their legislatures are more likely to invest in health care services.[38] William Chandler provides evidence that provincial governments are more likely to augment health and welfare expenditures when confronted by a strong left-wing opposition.[39]

Additional Canadian evidence that parties and therefore cabinets matter has emerged from studies of specific policy domains. The domain for which there is the strongest evidence of a political input is road building: both Spafford and Foot have cited evidence that provincial expenditures on highways peaked at election times;[40] Blake's analysis of Local Initiatives Program (LIP) grants shows that opposition members were rewarded for their past cooperation;[41] a study of Department of Regional Economic Expansion (DREE) grants by MacNaughton and Winn shows that the distribution of such grants to industry was explained partly by the electoral volatility of the constituencies in which recipient firms were located.[42] However, most of the variation in the distribution of grants is attributed to strictly economic considerations.

To this point, the study has reviewed evidence from the business cycle and policy determinants literature which shows that policy is affected by the electoral dilemmas of governments. However, the modest evidence of electorally explained policy suggests that the short-term vote-seeking motivations of ruling politicians are a minor rather than a major or an exclusive component of their policy-making behaviour. Having reviewed the vote-seeking motivations of politicians, the study now turns to their ideological motivation.

Ideological Determinants

The political science profession is divided on the issue of whether, when, and how ruling parties differ ideologically in policy. Some studies conclude that government policies in certain domains are not affected by the ideology of the party in power. Other studies conclude that ideology does matter. The single most important cross-national issue is whether left/right ideological differences are translated into left/right policy differences. At the present stage of scholarship, a reasonable and fair-minded assessment is that the party in power is one of several factors that affect the size of the public sector in a national economy, but that income equality and social mobility are not necessarily affected by who rules.

In the Canadian literature, *Political Parties in Canada* is the main source of arguments to the effect that political parties do not make a systematic difference to policy. In a chapter on bicultural policy, Winn presents evidence that French Canada benefited in foreign policy, immigration policy, federal-provincial relations and other domains as a result of the rise of a separatist movement and not as a result of which party happened to be in power in Ottawa.[43] In a chapter on "Redistributive Policy," McCready and Winn argue that the distribution of income is left unaffected even when the New Democratic Party is in power.[44] Saskatchewan NDP governments apparently did not lighten the tax burden of the lower strata. Furthermore, the welfare state programs advocated or first implemented by the left do not exhibit redistributive income effects. In chapters on trade and resource policies and foreign policies, Weir and Stevenson present additional evidence in support of the null thesis.[45]

The prevailing view in the political science profession is probably that parties do make a difference and that cabinets of different partisan complexions adopt different policies. The thesis of party differences is not expressed energetically in any one work but is articulated in a smattering of specialized studies here and there. Chandler argues that the strength of left-wing opposition parties in provincial legislatures has had an impact on policy;[46] a recent article on resource policies concludes that the extent and kind of public intervention in this field is explained by the ideologies of the parties in power in a given province, especially in the period after 1979.[47] In another article, Coleman presents evidence that the ideologies of the two main provincial parties in Quebec explain the parties' differences on language policy.[48]

The lack of consensus in the Canadian political science literature about the impact of parties on government policy is parallelled in the cross-national literature. The first major cross-national study of policy output was Frederick Pryor's comparative study *Public Expenditures in Communist and Capitalist Nations*.[49] Writing in the 1960s, Pryor presented considerable evidence that social security and other expenditures in Communist and capitalist systems are remarkably alike, especially when level of economic development is considered. His central thesis was that social and other expenditures are influenced by a country's level of economic development rather than by the ideology of its leadership.

Pryor's null thesis, sometimes called a thesis of "convergence," has been corroborated in a few important respects. In a comprehensive cross-national study of social security expenditures using multiple regression, Harold Wilensky finds that the variable, social security expenditures as a proportion of GNP, is strongly correlated with GNP per capita, the relative size of the pensionable population, and the age of the social security system. Wilensky concludes that "economic level is the root cause of welfare-state development, but its effects are felt chiefly through demographic changes of the past century and the momentum of the programs themselves, once established."[50] Political system type and elite ideology do not contribute statistically to Wilensky's explanatory model. Scharf's analysis of the pension expenditures of Communist and Western systems concludes that the pension efforts of a government are largely explained by the size of the pensionable population and the use of hidden or indirect taxes. The author offers the following light-hearted advice to policy makers: ". . . I should like to recommend a simple formula for any government wishing to improve its social security performance: Reduce the number of pensioners and shift the bulk of social security financing to indirect taxes."[51]

Other studies have examined the impact of the ruling party's ideology on the growth of the public sector, income inequality, social mobility, and rates of unemployment and inflation. A frequently cited study by Cameron, "The Expansion of the Public Economy," presents some evidence that the public sector tends to expand when the Social Democrats or Labour are in power. Cameron acknowledges, however, that the link between ruling ideology and public sector expansion is not always clear.[52]

Jackman conducted a major cross-national study of income inequality during the 1970s. In *Politics and Social Equality*, Jackman reports finding no evidence that the strength of socialist/labour parties is statistically related to the pattern of income distribution once the strength of trade unions and various economic variables are considered. In a more recent study devoted specifically to the impact of socialist parties on income distribution, he appears to recant, but only a little. He finds some evidence that the top quintile of income earners experiences reduced incomes under left-wing rule, but no evidence that the bottom 40 percent of income earners benefits.[53] In *Political Control of the Economy*, Tufte also presents evidence that the top quintile of income earners is more likely to experience the effects of tax equalization under the left than under the right (pp. 95–96).

The magnitude of the top quintile's loss is, however, small. Income data are in any case notoriously suspect. Furthermore, it is difficult to estimate to what extent the apparent capping of the top quintile is the result of incomes policy or to what extent it is the indirect result of the expansion of the public sector. Public sector salaries tend to be depressed at the top end.

Parkin and Hibbs have conducted studies of the impact of ruling ideology on social mobility and unemployment rates. In *Class Inequality and Political Order*, Parkin suggests that social democratic/labour governments do not greatly affect the pattern of income distribution, but they do increase social mobility.[54] Left-wing governments enhance social mobility by means of institutional changes, particularly as a result of the democratization of education. In a statistical study of unemployment and inflation in 12 OECD countries, Hibbs presents some convincing evidence that left-wing governments reduce unemployment and right-wing governments reduce inflation. About half the variation in unemployment and inflation in his sample of countries over a period of 25 years is explained by the ideology of the ruling party. Every 10 years of socialist rule meant a decrease in unemployment of about 1.7 percent and an increase in inflation of about 0.8 percent.[55]

All in all, both Canadian and cross-national studies of policy determinants present moderate evidence that the ideology of the party in power and of its cabinet makes a difference. The strongest evidence is Hibbs's, on unemployment and inflation rates. Cabinets do appear to make a major difference to these two macroeconomic indicators. There is, however, only modest evidence that cabinets make a predictable and systematic difference to the size of the public sector and to patterns of income equality.

Explaining Modest Ideological Differences

Three types of explanation have been adduced to account for the relatively modest impact of cabinets: an explanation rooted in a political economy or neo-Marxist approach, an explanation based on bureaucratic theory, and an explanation based on a decision-making perspective. Expressing a political economy or neo-Marxist approach, William Coleman asserts that political parties do not differ markedly on important economic issues of the constraints of the capitalist economy. Left-wing and right-wing parties can, however, differ on non-economic matters: "The greater the distance between a given policy and the activities of the capitalists appropriating surplus and reinvesting to maintain and expand profits, the more ideologies and differences in clientele among parties are likely to have an independent impact on policy."[56]

According to bureaucratic theory, the organizational requirements of government departments for efficiency and predictability constrain politicians from bringing about rapid, unforeseen change. For reasons intrinsic to the nature of bureaucracy, year-to-year changes are incremental, as incremental as bureaucrats can manage. This approach is reflected in the classic writings of Lindblom and Wildavsky.[57]

The decision-making approach emphasizes the context in which politicians must reach decisions. Many decisions must be made hurriedly with insufficient information because of exigencies. Yet, some of the most important policy decisions require a considerable volume of technical information to be effective. Many welfare state or "great society" programs fail to achieve their redistributive objectives because they are hurriedly designed on the basis of incomplete and inadequate data. Once programs are in place their persistence is ensured by vested governmental and non-governmental interests. Most welfare state programs cannot achieve redistributive effects unless they are qualified by a means test or its functional equivalent. Left-wing politicians, however, usually consider means tests to be objectionable.

To summarize, the task of designing programs to achieve redistributive or other effects is exceedingly complex. Politicians do not have the time to cope with such complexities, nor do they have the personal partisan staff able to understand and explain complex technical issues. The technical complexity of government programs helps explain why transfer programs are less effective than income taxation in alleviating inequality between classes or the size distribution of income.[58]

From the perspective of bureaucratic theory and decision-making theory, the modest difference found between public sector growth rates and unemployment rates under left-wing and right-wing rule no longer seems modest. Given the constraints posed by bureaucracy and by decision making under stress, the empirical differences observed by Hibbs on unemployment, and by Cameron and others on public sector growth, even the modest evidence of differences in income inequality, seem very significant indeed. Given the greater technical complexity of policy initiatives undertaken for ideological rather than electoral reasons, the evidence suggests that the ideological roles of ruling politicians are more important than their vote-seeking roles.

Before turning to the impact of leadership succession on policy, it is important to ask if the bureaucratic and decision-making explanations of the modest ideological differences make sense. From what we know about the working lives of politicians, are politicians constrained by pressures from their decision-making environment? According to the testimony of former ministers, ministers work in a pressure-cooker environment in which they are inundated with paperwork and have little time left to consult external sources of advice. As noted in one of the opening quotations, Flora Macdonald observed that she was virtually never given the luxury of several options from which she could choose. In the same autobiographical essay, she noted that she was constantly overwhelmed with last-minute documentation. Richard Crossman described much the same phenomenon in Britain:

> Every Department wages a paper war against its Minister. They try to drown him in paper so that he can't be a nuisance. Every night, as you know, we receive our red boxes. When I get home to my house in London about ten or eleven at night from the House of Commons, there are one, two, three, four or even five boxes, which include not only the papers for next day's meetings but the decisions which I have to make that night before reaching the Ministry the next day. The first job you have to do is to prevent yourself becoming a slave of the red box.[59]

Because of constant time pressures, ministers, especially those with substantial departmental responsibilities, have little opportunity to acquire independent sources of advice or information. President Lyndon Johnson, considered by many as a person of remarkable personal intelligence, admitted that he read only one book during his presidency.[60]

The Ministerial Cycle Literature

The third body of scholarly literature to be reviewed can be termed the ministerial cycle literature. This body of written work is thin, consisting on the one hand of articles on the legislative or policy cycle of U.S. presidents and on the other hand of Bunce's work on the policy consequences of leadership succession. If it is true that the policy behaviour of ministers and cabinets follows observable cycles, such information may reveal how ministers affect policy. The precise ways in which government policy is affected by ministerial cycles may identify the motivations of ministers and the constraints under which they work.

There is a considerable body of literature on the policy cycles of U.S. presidents, but very little on the policy cycles of other chief executives or cabinets. Bunce's work, which includes *Do New Leaders Make a Difference?* and a number of articles, constitutes the main cross-national or comparative studies of ministerial cycles. In Bunce's work, the phenomenon of ministerial cycle is cast in the form of leadership succession. Bunce focusses on the first stage in the rule of new leaders. The common conclusion reached by Bunce in her cross-national work and by scholars examining policy cycles within U.S. administrations is that major policy initiatives and events are concentrated in the early period of each new leader.[61] New leaders give expression to their ideas early in their period of rule, and they tend also to experience more than their fair share of excitement. In the case of U.S. presidents, foreign crises are reportedly concentrated during the presidential honeymoon period.[62]

Bunce shows that major institutional and expenditure changes are most likely to occur shortly after a new leader takes office, and that this pattern holds true for both the United States and the Soviet Union and, in the former, for both Washington, D.C., and the state capitals. She finds that percentage changes in budgetary allocations to categories such as education, health, and welfare are greater after a new leader takes office. The longer the tenure of the preceding leader, the greater the observed increase in social expenditures under the successor. Brezhnev, and before him, Khrushchev, increased welfare outlays considerably. Krushchev took a special interest in agriculture with a view to increasing the availability of food. Under other new East bloc leaders, housing starts increased, consumer goods were made more available, and agricultural expenditures rose. Bunce interprets the observed increases in social expenditures under new leaders in the United States and the Soviet Union as evidence that new leaders are motivated by the desire to legitimate their new leadership. Her discovery of a succession effect in the Soviet Union as well as in the United States demonstrates the enormous importance leaders attach to securing the esteem of the mass public. Short-term legitimation must indeed be important to political leaders in general, if Soviet leaders, who need not fear electoral defeat, act as if the affections of the mass public were vitally important.

In terms of the taxonomy of ministerial roles outlined early in this essay, Bunce's evidence of the legitimating behaviour of new leaders is inconsistent with the vote-seeking roles of politicians. It is axiomatic in electoral strategy that politicians who peak too early meet defeat at the ballot box. Hence, the early peaking of successful new leaders, in and outside parliamentary democracies, must be evidence of something other than vote seeking. It suggests that ruling politicians see themselves as shamans, as nation-building patriots, and in other roles that entail the contentment but not necessarily the electoral support of the mass public.

The desire of political leaders to please the mass public constrains those leaders who contemplate programs of economic development that will involve unpopular short-term decisions. Given the apparent importance to leaders of public contentment, political leaders are unlikely to embrace unpopular policies. It is not a question of political cowardice or the inability of electoral democracies to provide leadership. Even new leaders in Communist systems worry to some extent about public contentment or legitimation and, like Western leaders, also increase social expenditures. Because of the almost fundamental need of political leaders for harmony or legitimation, longer-term economic plans for Canada will have to exclude as many unpopular options as possible, and politicians will have to devote considerable energy to winning public acceptance for unpopular plans that cannot be dropped. The concluding portion of this study will return to the question of how leaders can persuade the public to accept unpopular policies.

Statistical findings need to be tested against non-statistical information and against the observations of participants themselves. According to the ministerial cycle literature, policy changes are concentrated in the honeymoon period. This phenomenon makes sense according to conventional wisdom about the decreasing intellectual capital of ministers. Politicians learn what they learn before acceding to high office. We noted above that President Lyndon Johnson found time to read only one book during his period in office. It follows that, if the major policy changes take place in the honeymoon period, ministers do not require on-the-job learning in order to be effective. Accordingly, a minister does not need to know the details of organizational management nor the identity of his or her administrative friends and foes in order to be in command. In *The Myths of Cabinet Government*, Crossman suggests quite the opposite. He asserts that ministerial succession "provides a sharp temporary increase in the power of the Civil Service" because new ministers need time to become informed (p. xviii). Ministers can get their way only by working long and hard at the ministerial post. A minister who wants to control the department "could have very little time or energy to spare for anything on the Cabinet agenda except his own Department's affairs" (p. xix).

If Crossman is right, how then do we reconcile the budgetary changes that are concentrated early in a term with the executive's need to learn the details of administration in order to be effective? One explanation is that cabinets insist on significant budgetary changes early in their terms as a relatively simple way of asserting their dominance over the public service. Budgetary changes are relatively easy for ministers to understand, requisition, and monitor; the important non-budgetary changes are left until later in the term. Political scientists studying the political business cycle or the ministerial cycle have tended not to notice such late-term non-budgetary changes because they are difficult to measure.

There is, however, a more pessimistic way of reconciling the phenomenon of early term budgetary changes with Richard Crossman's claim that ministers need on-the-job learning in order to become effective. It is possible that ministers become less intent on imposing their views as time passes. Perhaps they learn to appreciate traditional ways of doing things, become worn out, or simply realize how important departmental support is to enable them to make a good impression in cabinet or on television. Perhaps they learn that they and their departments have an identical interest. As Crossman says, for a minister to be successful, he "needs the acquiescence, at least, of the Department in what he is up to, and for this he needs to be a success in the Department's eye" (p. 65). The pessimistic interpretation is that the minister fights a war with his department which he in the end loses. In Crossman's words, again:

> the battle is really for the soul of the Minister. Is he to remain a foreign body in the Department, inserting into the departments things they don't like, things he wants and the Party wants? Or is he to become *their* Minister, content to speak for them? There is nothing easier than being a departmental success. Nothing easier at all. (p. 63)

In summary, Bunce's data and Crossman's observations can be reconciled optimistically by emphasizing the desire of politicians to dominate their bureaucrats or pessimistically by concluding that politicians are co-opted. Neither interpretation supports the economists' view that politicians are mainly vote seekers. The optimistic view leads to the conclusion that politicians occupy the roles of governor (i.e., departmental policy maker) as well as shaman, nation-building patriot, and other non-vote-seeking roles. The pessimistic view of co-option rules out Trebilcock's theory of the primacy of vote seeking because authority over policy has been retained by the bureaucracy.

The Psychobiographical Literature and Idiosyncratic Motivations

A discussion of the personal motivations and dilemmas of ministers is an appropriate occasion on which to turn to the fourth and final bibliographic theme of this study, namely the literature on psychobiography. The psychobiographical literature is virtually endless, particularly if one considers all the biographies of politicians. Every political biography and many general political histories must be included under the rubric of psychobiography because of the explicit or implicit psychological interpretations embedded in these studies. Any biographical work that mentions the family, ethnic, occupational, locational or other origins of a politician thereby makes implicit assumptions about the psychological importance of these origins for the future electoral or policy-making role of the politician.

Modern psychology is post-Freudian and hence relatively recent. However, psychological interpretations of human behaviour are at least as old as the written word. Old as well as recent histories and biographies contain implicit psychological interpretations, some of which have become so accepted that they are no longer recognized as particularly psychological. For example, it is widely accepted that John Diefenbaker's opposition to apartheid in South Africa and his allegiance to Israel were related to his identification with ethnic underdogs, a product of childhood victimization because of his German family name.[63]

The very size of the psychobiographical literature is its most important attribute. The size of this literature is testimony to the enormous importance assigned by scholars, journalists, and their readers to the idiosyncratic role played by political leaders.

Because there is so much psychobiographical literature, it is only possible here to provide a sense of its dimensions and to suggest how it may be structured. Psychobiographical works are of two types: case studies and cross-sectional analyses. For each type of analysis, three types of causal links are explored. In some studies the personality or personal characteristics of leaders are seen as dependent variables: certain societies, political systems, or political circumstances produce certain kinds of leaders. In other studies, the personality or personal characteristics of leaders are seen as independent variables, as factors affecting policy outcomes. In still another type of writing, the causal connection is unclear; the scholar seems intent on finding different kinds of personality types or different ways to measure the personality dispositions of leaders.

One of the most lucid and provocative studies of leadership as both an independent and dependent variable is a study of birth order conducted by Louis Stewart, a political psychologist. Stewart conducted a wide-ranging quantitative study of British and U.S. chief executives to see whether first-born, middle-born, and last-born children were likely to rise to leadership positions under varying types of political circumstances. He hypothesized that the different experiences of dominance, accommodation and submission in a leader's family of origin affected the leader's adult skills and therefore influenced his likelihood of political success. His conclusion merits extensive citation:

> . . . we have identified four, more or less distinct, political situations: (1) international crisis and war, (2) peace and adjustment of internal affairs, (3) collapse of social functions and civil conflict, and (4) revolution. Corresponding to these are the four leadership styles, respectively, of the first-born, middle-born, only, and last-born son. . . . The first-born male has the

greatest experience of dominance and of successful intervention in the affairs of others. The middle-born son, starting life in a position of dependence and relative weakness, gains later on an opportunity for dominance, having the most experience in mediation. The last-born son is from the beginning to end in a position of dependence and relative weakness, probably harboring the greatest resentment toward all authority. . . . The only child, dealing entirely with "higher authorities" whose favours he need never share, is most at home in center stage and least vulnerable to peer rivalry.[64]

Beyond Stewart's study of birth order, the literature on leadership contains countless case studies on individual leaders. Many of the case studies examine the full causal sequence, beginning with the impact of childhood on the development of adult personality and concluding with an analysis of the impact of personality structure on adult political behaviour. Psychological case studies are important because, as the formative political scientist Harold Lasswell observed, politically active people may displace "private affects" or motives relating to family onto "public objects." For example, a regicide may be motivated by the killer's hatred of his father.[65] Wolfenstein has written about the revolutionary personality as an escape from Oedipal guilt.[66] Haberman has examined Quisling as a case study in pathology.[67] Gottfried has looked at *Boss Cermak of Chicago* as an example of psychosomatic response to stress.[68] George has examined "Power as a Compensatory Value for Political Leaders" while Browning and Jacob have considered power as a motivation.[69]

Among sane political leaders, Woodrow Wilson attracted considerable attention, initially by Freud himself and later by Alexander and Juliette George. The Georges' study of Wilson examines the full causal sequence, considering the impact of Wilson's relationship with his father on his personality structure and the subsequent impact of his personality on the unfolding of political events. As the Georges explain, "It is by relating Wilson's overt behaviour, which sometimes seems naive or unreasonable, to some of his emotional needs, which were given their particular hue by his upbringing as a child, that the inner logic of his actions becomes clear."[70]

Wilson had enormous difficulty tolerating criticism and needed to be surrounded by uncritical admirers. This trait was the root of an imbroglio at Princeton when he was university president and the root of his difficulties with Senator Henry Cabot Lodge over ratification of the Versailles Treaty. Wilson's inability to accept criticism, it is asserted, was the product of his unresolved, suppressed conflict with his father and of the emotional repressiveness of his home environment.

Among leaders with pathological motivations, Hitler has probably received the greatest attention. The politically minded psychoanalyst Erich Fromm treats Hitler as a case in his sweeping, and now classic, study *The Anatomy of Destructiveness*.[71] Fromm places Hitler in the context of an implicit theory of necrophilia or love of death. He traces patterns of anal-sadism in the behaviour and language of his subject, showing Hitler's anal-sadistic obsessiveness even in contexts such as mealtime where aggression, conflict, and death have no apparent relevance. The psychoanalytic explanation of behaviour by Fromm and others is based on the interpretation of nonobvious behaviour (e.g., symbolic language) in the attempt to identify psychological motivations. Unfortunately, we cannot be sure that Fromm's selection of imagery from Hitler's personal and public communications is representative of Hitler, that the selected imagery accurately reflects necrophilia, or that Hitler's supposed necrophilic tendencies are an adequate explanation of the violence of his regime.

One of the few scholars to relate imagery to personality structure and political behaviour in an objective or verifiable way is David Luck. In "A Psycholinguistic Approach to Leader Personality," Luck represents the results of the quantitative content analysis of the imagery of aggression, sex, and death among a selection of Communist and Fascist leaders.[72] Using a verifiable quantitative method, he shows important differences in the frequency of aggressive imagery, especially anal-sadistic and death imagery. Luck finds that Hitler ranks higher than Stalin, who ranks considerably higher than Lenin, Mao, and Liu. After reporting his quantitative findings, Luck compares the imagery scores in a convincing manner to accepted knowledge about the private lives and public conduct of the leaders in question.

Content analysis has been employed not only to explore the psychoanalytic explanations of leadership but also to test less abstruse and moot personality characteristics. Hermann, for example, performed a quantitative content analysis of the speeches of congressmen in order to explain their positions on foreign aid. Her data revealed that congressmen favourable to foreign aid were generally more optimistic and more complex intellectually than those who opposed it.[73] Several studies of American presidencies show that the personality characteristics of individual presidents can be used to predict their performance. For example, presidents with high needs for affiliation are likely be uncritical and undemanding of their immediate subordinates. High n-affiliation presidents had a higher number of appointees who were subsequently charged with malfeasance.[74]

Overall, the psychobiographical literature shows that politicians can be motivated by a variety of idiosyncratic features of their personalities. Among elected politicians, these personality-related motivations do not necessarily contribute to, and may even undermine, electoral self-interest. As a whole, the literature suggests that elected politicians are often driven by psychological considerations that are unrelated to electoral self-interest, ideology, or other conventionally imputed motivations of ruling politicians.

Little is known in a systematic way about how politicians differ from the population at large. In Canada, lawyers greatly outnumber professional economists and political scientists among politicians, a fact that suggests that the main role of politicians is not policy making. Legal training is better suited to the ministerial roles of shaman, mediator, and patriot than to departmental policy maker.

Legal training is also not well suited to the role of vote seeker if one assumes that effective vote seeking requires an understanding of public opinion. Knowledge of public opinion may not, however, be essential to electoral success. Kingdon's large-scale study of candidates for office in the United States found that victorious candidates are actually less knowledgeable about public opinion than defeated candidates.[75] From this fact, Kingdon inferred that vote seeking is a complex task involving media, financial, and other talents as well as an understanding of public attitudes. The complexity of vote seeking undermines the electoral self-interest theories of Trebilcock and other economists; securing reelection appears to be a far more complex task than transferring benefits to marginal voters, even if some such transferring takes place.[76] If vote seeking involves many skills and talents, it is reasonable to assume that ministers see policy making as only one of many methods of assisting their reelection. Ministers therefore experience far less incentive to frame policy primarily in terms of short-term electoral self-interest than if policy making were the only or main weapon in their electoral arsenal.

Conclusion

This study began by delineating the multiple roles occupied by ruling politicians — vote seeker, shaman, governor, patriot, and so forth. It was suggested that a government's reelection strategy is a complex process, far more complex than arranging greater benefits for marginal or infra-marginal voters. In fact, given their countless media and other campaign advantages, ruling politicians do not need to make great partisan use of transfer payments and other benefits; such tactics can even backfire. Although Trebilcock and other economists have sought to explain the presence of fiscal and output illusions in terms of the vote-seeking motivations of ruling politicians, this study has contended that fiscal and output illusions can also be explained by the many non-vote-seeking roles and motivations of politicians.

Scholarly works relating to the political business cycle, the determinants of policy, the ministerial cycle and leadership succession, and psychobiography have been reviewed. The evidence from this literature conforms broadly with the portrait of ministers as occupying many roles and being motivated by many considerations. Cabinets do apparently time some macroeconomic changes and some transfer payments for electoral gain, but evidence in this regard is modest. Furthermore, strong evidence exists that political leaders seek public satisfaction at times and in contexts that are unrelated to their own immediate electoral needs.

From the perspective of long-term economic policy making and industrial strategy, the most important characteristics of ruling politicians are their desire for public contentment and their limited influence over public policy. The desire for public contentment emanates from most of their roles and is reflected in legitimating efforts that often serve electoral purposes only in indirect and inefficient ways. The limited policy authority of ministers is reflected in the modest nature of the business cycle and especially in the fact that redistributive differences between left-wing and right-wing governments are moot.

The ability of ruling politicians to influence mass perceptions of economic conditions will affect their ability to adopt economic strategies promising long-term gain for short-term pain. In other words, the more skilled that ministers become in generating a mood of public purpose, the more discretion governments have in fostering policies of economic change that entail long-term advantage for the society as a whole at the cost of short-term advantage for some particular sectors. According to the logic of this utilitarian perspective, a necessary but insufficient condition for the adoption of dislocating industrial strategies is a cabinet with significant shamanist skills. The concluding paragraphs of this study will propose ways to increase the policy authority of ministers and to augment their shamanist skills. The first issue involves control over government output; the second involves symbolic leadership.

Strengthening Policy Leadership

From the autobiographical writings of Crossman and other former ministers, it is evident that departmental interests constitute one of the strongest impediments to cabinet control of policy. Ministers have strong personal incentives to identify with their departments and to give little thought to other departments or to cross-departmental coordination. They have few independent sources of information with which to countervail the advice from their own departments. Furthermore, they have little time or energy to evaluate departmental advice even when they possess independent information.

Ministers could increase their authority over policy making within their departmental mandate by increasing the qualifications of personal, "exempt" staff drawn from outside the public service.[77] Personal advisers of ministers could be paid as much as or more than deputy and assistant deputy ministers to compensate good people from the private sector and from universities for disrupted careers. Ministerial advisers would not be allowed to join the public service directly because such an opportunity would provide too strong an incentive for them to identify with the interests of a department or of the public service instead of with the interests of the minister and party. Barred from public service careers for a predetermined period, exempt staff might instead be offered generous severance payments upon departure from ministerial service.

Increasing the authority of ministers one by one is not the same as increasing the collective authority of cabinet. Cabinets can increase their overall policy-making power by increasing their capacity to coordinate government activities. Large-scale bureaucracies typically experience problems of uncoordinated or conflicting actions. For example, in the field of copyright, the Consumer and Corporate Affairs' Bureau of Intellectual Property has for years worked at cross-purposes to the Department of Communications.[78] The Canadian government office of tourism spends millions of advertising dollars annually to convince people to vacation in Canada, while Air Canada spends millions to convince Canadians to fly south in winter. Successive cabinets have been committed to national integration; yet very little of the federal government's huge outlays on education and culture are targetted to encourage study and communication across the language and provincial barriers that divide this country.

Only the cabinet can achieve coordination of government programs in different departments. To do so, it could employ temporary task forces consisting of partisan loyalists and outside experts; partisan loyalties would countervail the seductive powers of departmental interests. Like ministerial advisers, task force staff would come from outside the federal government and would be paid extremely well. To avoid co-option by departments, the task force staff would not be permitted to do work for any of the agencies whose work was being coordinated until a predetermined period of time had elapsed.

Strengthening Symbolic Leadership

Three rules of effective persuasion are suggested.

First, tell the truth. A prevailing maxim among policy makers is that the public must be protected from unpleasant truth. This unstated maxim explains why Canadian politicians and bureaucrats refused for years to admit that Canadian interest rates are largely determined by U.S. monetary policy. Canadian spokesmen ended up talking gobbledygook as a result. Yet, keeping Canadians confused is not an effective method of encouraging them to identify with the collective good.

Second, emphasize the long term. Long-term policies should be explained as primarily long-term development projects. The public imagination is often captivated by long-term dreams, as for example by John Diefenbaker's Northern vision. At the same time, cabinets should avoid adopting short-term panaceas. For instance, they may be tempted to appease dictatorial regimes in the hope of securing larger export markets. Ingratiating diplomacy, however, runs the risk of encouraging Canadian citizens to think cynically of their own short-term private gains instead of in terms of long-term collective goals.

Finally, provide role models. Symbolism is important. Ministers influence the mass public by their personal conduct — salary increases in inflationary times, use of perquisites, the conspicuous choice of goods and services (e.g., Canadian or foreign wine or vacations). To make the most effective use of ministers as role models, the cabinet should draw up relevant guidelines. In war, successful military leaders are found at the front. In peace, successful political leaders make the kinds of economic sacrifices they expect of their people.

Notes

This paper was completed in November 1985. André Blais' advice and encouragement were warmly appreciated at every stage of this project.

1. Harold Wilson, as reported in *Financial Times*, March 1968.
2. Quoted in Thomas J. Peters and Robert H. Waterman, Jr., *In Search of Excellence* (New York: Harper and Row, 1982), p. 7.
3. Dwight D. Eisenhower, 1968, quoted in Henry C. Kensky, "The Impact of Economic Conditions on Presidential Popularity," *Journal of Politics* 39 (1977): 764–73.
4. Flora Macdonald, "The Minister and the Mandarins: How a New Minister Copes with the Entrapment Devices of Bureaucracy," *Policy Options* (September–October 1980).
5. Leonid Brezhnev in private conversation, as reported by a former Secretary of the Central Committee of the Czech Communist Party. Zdenek Mlynar, *Mraz prichazi z Kremlu* (Cologne, 1978) quoted in Archie Brown, "The Powers of the General Secretary of the CPSU," in *Authority, Power and Policy in the USSR*, edited by T.H. Rigby et al. (London: Macmillan, 1980).
6. Richard H.S. Crossman, *The Diaries of a Cabinet Minister*, Vol. I, 1964–66 (New York: Holt, Rinehart and Winston, 1975), p. 21.
7. I concede the difficulty of identifying correctly the cross-national equivalent of the Canadian cabinet. In the Soviet Union, for example, the Politburo is usually the functional equivalent of the Canadian cabinet, but under Stalin the leadership of the secret police was frequently the real locus of authority. Even the liberal democracies provide many examples where non-office holders exercise considerable influence in policy making and even in appointments to cabinet. A classic example is Colonel House, who held no official post in Woodrow Wilson's cabinet; a majority of the appointees to Wilson's first cabinet were selected on House's advice. Moreover, during the Versailles negotiations, House exercised more influence than did cabinet members. See Alexander C. George and Juliette L. George, *Woodrow Wilson and Colonel House: A Personality Study* (New York: Dover, 1964).
8. M.J. Trebilcock, R.S. Prichard, D.G. Hartle, and Don Dewees, *The Choice of Governing Instruments* (Ottawa: Minister of Supply and Services Canada, 1982).
9. E.G. West and Stanley L. Winer, "Optimal Fiscal Illusion and the Size of Government," *Public Choice* (1980): 607–622.
10. This observation derives from conversations with several present and former ministerial aides, to whom I am grateful.

11. Hon. Monique Bégin, former minister of health, acknowledged upon her retirement from public life that she had in effect turned down the Status of Women portfolio for this reason.

12. Edward Tufte, *The Political Control of the Economy* (Princeton: Princeton University Press, 1978).

13. D. Roderick Kiewiet, *Macroeconomics and Micropolitics* (Chicago: University of Chicago Press, 1983).

14. M. Stephen Weatherford, "Evaluating Economic Policy: A Contextual Model of the Opinion Formation Process," *Journal of Politics* 45 (November 1983): 866–88; Gary C. Jacobson and Samuel Kernell, *Strategy and Choice in Congressional Elections* (New Haven: Yale University Press, 1981).

15. D.A. Hibbs and H. Fassbender, eds., *Contemporary Political Economy* (Amsterdam: North-Holland, 1981).

16. For a contending agnostic view on the business cycle, see ibid., Reiner Dinkel's chapter entitled "Political Business Cycles in Germany and the United States: Some Theoretical and Empirical Considerations."

17. Vani K. Borooah and Frederick van der Ploeg, *Political Aspects of the Economy* (London: Cambridge University Press, 1983).

18. Douglas W. Rae and Theodore J. Eismeier, eds., *Public Policy and Public Choice* (Beverly Hills, Cal.: Sage, 1979).

19. John Robertson, "Inflation, Unemployment, and Government Collapse: A Poisson Application," *Comparative Political Studies* 15 (January 1983): 425–44.

20. Kristen R. Munroe, ed., *Political Process and Economic Change* (New York: Agathan Press, 1983).

21. Heinrich W. Urspring, "Macroeconomic Performance and Government Popularity in New Zealand," *Comparative Political Studies* 16 (January 1984), p. 476.

22. Richard Johnston, "Economic Factors in Recent Canadian Elections: Some Survey Evidence" (Paper presented at the annual meeting of the Canadian Political Science Association, 1983). See also Lynda Erickson and Kristen R. Monroe, "The Economy and Public Support for the Canadian Government and Political Parties, 1954–1978" (Paper presented at the annual meeting of the Canadian Political Science Association, 1981); J.R. Happy, "Personal Experience and Government Responsibility for Economic Performance in Canadian Voting Behaviour" (Paper presented at the annual meeting of the American Political Science Association, 1984).

23. Paul Mosley, "Popularity Functions and the Role of the Media: A Pilot Study of the Popular Press," *British Journal of Political Science* (January 1984), p. 128.

24. Some other references worth noting are: W. F. Keech, "Elections," and D.A. Hibbs, "A Dynamic Analysis of Economic Influence on Political Support for British Governments among Occupational Groups," *American Political Science Review* (1972): 259–79; H.S. Bloom and H.D. Price, "Voter Response to Short-run Economic Conditions," *American Political Science Review* (1975): 1240–54; G. Kramer, "Short-Term Fluctuations in U.S. Voting Behavior, 1896–1964," *American Political Science Review* (1971): 131–43; S. Kernell, "Explaining Presidential Popularity," *American Political Science Review* (1978): 506–22; J.H. Kuklinski and D.M. West, "Economic Expectations and Voting Behavior in the United States House and Senate Elections," *American Political Science Review* (1981): 436–47; J.R. Hibbing and J.R. Alford, "The Electoral Impact of Economic Conditions: Who Is Held Responsible?" *American Journal of Political Science* (1981): 423–39; M. Paldam, "A Preliminary Survey of the Theories and Findings on Vote and Popularity Functions," *European Journal of Political Research* (1981): 181–99; Roy Fair, "The Effects of Economic Events on Voters for the President," *Review of Economics and Statistics* (1978): 159–73; D.R. Kinder, "Presidents, Prosperity and Public Opinion," *Public Opinion Quarterly* (1981): 1–21; K.R. Monroe, "Econometric Analysis of Electoral Behavior: A Critical Review," *Political Behavior* (1979): 137–75. For evidence that congressional roles are infrequently, if at all, affected by the business cycle, see John R. Owens, "Economic Influences on Elections to the U.S. Congress," *Legislative Studies Quarterly* (January 1984): 123ff.

25. James E. Alt and K. Alex Chrystal, *Political Economics* (Berkeley: University of California Press, 1983), p. 125.

26. William D. Nordhaus, "The Political Business Cycle," *Review of Economics* (April 1975) p. 186. Other early contributions were by M. Kalencki, "Political Aspects of Full Employment," *Political Quarterly* (October/December 1943): 322–31, and C.A.E. Goodhart and R.J. Bhansali, "Political Economy," *Political Studies* (March 1970): 43–106.

27. On this point, see Alt and Chrystal, *Political Economics*, p. 121. See also R. Winters et al., "Political Behavior Cycle," in *Handbook of Political Behavior*, edited by S. Long, vol. 5 (New York: Plenum, 1981). A lucid discussion of the problem of planned and unplanned elections appears in André Blais, Kenneth Roberts, and Richard Nadeau, "Dépenses gouvernementales et cycles électoraux au Québec et en Ontario, 1950–80" (paper presented at the annual meeting of the Canadian Political Science Association, 1983). This paper presents a lucid and logical review of other pertinent issues as well.

28. On these points, see Alt and Chrystal, *Political Economics*, p. 122.

29. Martin Paldam, "An Essay on the Rationality of Economic Policy: The Test Case of an Electional Cycle," *Public Choice* (1981): 287–307.

30. Blais and his colleagues also criticize D.K. Foot's analysis of the expansion of public employment in Canada for underestimating his own evidence in support of the political business cycle. See Blais et al., "Dépenses gouvernementales," pp. 15–16.

31. Barry Ames, "The Politics of Public Spending in Latin America," *American Journal of Political Science* 21 (1977): 149–77.

32. Bruno S. Frey, "Politico-Economic Models and Cycles," *Journal of Public Economics* 9 (1978): 203–20.

33. Yoram Ben-Porath, "The Years of Plenty and the Years of Famine — A Political Business Cycle," *Kyklos* (1975): 400.

34. Blais et al., "Dépenses gouvernementales."

35. V.O. Key, *Southern Politics in State and Nation* (New York: Knopf, 1951), pp. 298–314.

36. Richard I. Hofferbert, "The Relationship between Public Policy and Some Structural and Environmental Variables in the American States," *American Political Science Review* (March 1966): 73–82; Richard E. Dawson and James A. Robinson, "Inter-Party Competition, Economic Variables and Welfare Politics in the American States," *Journal of Politics* (May 1963): 265–89; Thomas R. Dye, *Politics, Economics and the Public: Policy Outcomes in the American States* (Chicago: Rand McNally, 1966).

37. Dale Poel, "The Diffusion of Legislation among the Canadian Provinces," *Canadian Political Science Review* (December 1977): 605–25.

38. William Mishler and David B. Campbell, "The Healthy State: Legislative Responsiveness to Public Health Care Needs in Canada, 1920–70," *Comparative Politics* (1978): 470–97. See also Allan Kornberg and William Mishler, *Influence in Parliament: Canada* (Durham, N.C.: Duke University Press, 1976).

39. William Chandler, "Canadian Socialism and Policy Impact: Contagion from the Left?" *Canadian Journal of Political Science* (December 1977): 755–80.

40. Duff Spafford, "Highway Employment and Provincial Elections," *Canadian Journal of Political Science* (March 1981): 318–27; D.K. Foot, *Provincial Public Finance in Ontario: An Empirical Analysis of the Last 25 Years* (Toronto: University of Toronto Press, 1977).

41. Donald Blake, "LIP and Partisanship: An Analysis of the Local Initiatives Program," *Canadian Public Policy* (Winter 1976): 17–32.

42. Bruce D. MacNaughton and Conrad J. Winn, "Economic Policy and Electoral Self-Interest: The Allocations of the Department of Regional Economic Expansion," *Canadian Public Policy* (Spring 1981): 318–27.

43. Conrad Winn, "Bicultural Policy," in *Political Parties in Canada*, edited by Conrad Winn and John McMenemy (Toronto: McGraw-Hill Ryerson, 1976).

44. Douglas McCready and Conrad Winn, "Redistributive Policy," in *Political Parties in Canada*, edited by Conrad Winn and John McMenemy (Toronto: McGraw-Hill

Ryerson, 1976). Elsewhere Winn has argued that welfare state reforms frequently have perverse, unpredicted distributive effects. See, for example, "Affirmative Action for Women: More Than a Case of Simple Justice," *Canadian Public Administration* (Spring 1985): 24–46.

45. John Weir, "Trade and Resource Policies," and Garth Stevenson, "Foreign Policy," in *Political Parties in Canada*, edited by Conrad Winn and John McMenemy (Toronto: McGraw-Hill Ryerson, 1976).

46. Chandler, "Canadian Socialism and Policy Impact."

47. "The Politics of Provincial Resource Policy," in *The Politics of Canadian Public Policy*, edited by Michael M. Atkinson and Marsha A. Chandler (Toronto: University of Toronto Press, 1983). For evidence that left-wing provincial governments spend slightly more on social welfare, see Marsha A. Chandler and William M. Chandler, "Parliamentary Politics and Public Policy in the Canadian Provinces" (paper presented at the April 1974 meetings of the U.S. Mid-West Political Science Association).

48. William D. Coleman, "A Comparative Study of Language Policy in Quebec: A Political Economy Approach," in *Politics of Canadian Public Policy*, edited by Michael M. Atkinson and Marsha A. Chandler (Toronto: University of Toronto Press, 1983).

49. Frederick Pryor, *Public Expenditures in Communist and Capitalist Nations* (Homewood, Ill.: Dorsey, 1968).

50. H. L. Wilensky, *The Welfare State and Equality: Structural and Ideological Roots of Public Expenditures* (Berkeley: University of California Press, 1975), p. 47.

51. C. Bradley Scharf, "Correlates of Social Security Policy: East and West Europe," *International Political Science Review* (1981): p. 71.

52. D.R. Cameron, "The Expansion of the Public Economy," *American Political Science Review* (1978): 1243–61. An additional source of difficulty in testing the impact of left-wing rule on public sector expansion is to disentangle left-wing rule from country size. The left has tended to be in power among the small countries of northern Europe. Robert Dahl and Edward Tufte present evidence that small countries tend to expand the size of their public sector, especially the civilian portion, as a means of insulating their economies and societies from the vagaries of international economic change. See their *Size and Democracy* (Stanford: Stanford University Press, 1973). For additional evidence of greater public sector growth under the left, see Frank Gould, "The Growth of Public Expenditures: Theory and Evidence from Six Advanced Democracies," in *Why Governments Grow*, edited by Charles Lewis Taylor (Beverly Hills: Sage, 1983).

53. Robert W. Jackman, *Politics and Social Equality: A Comparative Analysis* (New York: Wiley, 1975), and "Socialist Parties and Income Inequality in Western Industrial Societies," *Journal of Politics* (1980): 135–49.

54. Frank Parkin, *Class Inequality and Political Order: Social Stratification in Capitalist and Communist Societies* (New York: Praeger, 1971). For additional evidence on the income reduction of the top quintile, see Christopher Hewitt, "The Effect of Political Democracy on Equality in Industrial Societies," *American Sociological Review* (June 1977): 450–64.

55. Douglas Hibbs, Jr., "Political Parties and Macroeconomic Policy," *American Political Science Review* (December 1977): 1467–87.

56. Coleman, "Language Policy in Quebec."

57. Charles Lindblom, "Decision-Making in Taxation and Expenditure," in *Public Finances: Needs, Sources and Utilization* (Princeton: National Bureau of Economic Research, 1961), and "Science of 'Muddling Through,'" *Public Administration Review* (1959): 79–88; Aaron Wildavsky, *The Politics of the Budgetary Process* (Boston: Little, Brown, 1964).

58. J.C.M. van Arnhem and G.J. Schotsman, "Do Parties Affect the Distribution of Incomes?" in *The Impact of Political Parties*, edited by Francis Castles (Beverly Hills, Cal.: Sage, 1982).

59. Richard H.S. Crossman, *The Myths of Cabinet Government* (Cambridge, Mass.: Harvard University Press, 1972), p. 65.

60. James David Barber, *The Presidential Character* (Englewood Cliffs, N.J.: Prentice-Hall, 1977), p. 86.

61. On succession, see Valerie Bunce, *Do New Leaders Make a Difference?: Executive Succession under Capitalism and Socialism* (Princeton: Princeton University Press, 1981), and "The Succession Connection: Policy Cycles and Political Change in the Soviet Union and Eastern Europe," *American Political Science Review* (December 1980): 966–77. On term cycles in the U.S. presidency, see Stephen Hess, *Organizing the Presidency* (Washington, D.C.: Brookings Institution, 1976), pp. 20–24; and John H. Kessel, *The Domestic Presidency: Decision-Making in the White House* (N. Scituate, Mass.: Duxbury Press, 1975), pp. 9–10.

62. Stephen Hess, "Portrait of a President," *Woodrow Wilson Quarterly* (Winter 1977): 43–48.

63. For John Diefenbaker's response to childhood teasing, see his *One Canada* (Toronto: Macmillan, 1975), p. 15.

64. Louis H. Stewart, "Birth Order and Political Leadership," in *A Psychological Examination of Political Leaders*, edited by Margaret G. Hermann (New York: Free Press, 1977), p. 234.

65. Harold D. Lasswell, *Psychopathology and Politics* (New York: Viking, 1960), pp. 74–76.

66. E. Victor Wolfenstein, *The Revolutionary Personality: Lenin, Trotsky, Gandhi* (Princeton: Princeton University Press, 1976).

67. John Haberman, "The Psychopathology of an Abortive Leadership: The Case of Vidkin Quisling," in *Psychology and Political Leadership*, edited by Robert S. Robins (New Orleans: Tulane University Press, 1977).

68. Alex Gottfried, *Boss Cermak of Chicago* (Seattle: University of Washington Press, 1962).

69. Alexander L. George, "Power as a Compensatory Value for Political Leaders," in *Journal of Social Issues* (July 1968): 51–80; Rufus P. Browning and Herbert E. Jacob, "Power Motivation and the Political Personality," *Public Opinion Quarterly* (Spring 1964): 75–90. A useful comprehensive review of much of this literature appears in Glenn D. Paige, *The Scientific Study of Political Leadership* (New York: Free Press, 1977). A widely respected study of the way normal American politicians see their world appears in John W. Kingdon, *Candidates for Office: Beliefs and Strategies* (New York: Random House, 1968).

70. George and George, *Woodrow Wilson and Colonel House*, p. xxii. See also Arthur S. Link, *Wilson: The Road to the White House* (Princeton: Princeton University Press, 1947), pp. 90–91.

71. Erich Fromm, *The Anatomy of Destructiveness* (New York: Holt, Rinehart and Winston, 1973).

72. David Luck, "A Psycholinguistic Approach to Leader Personality," *Soviet Studies* (October 1978): 491–515.

73. Margaret G. Hermann, "Some Personal Characteristics Related to Foreign Aid Voting of Congressmen," in *Psychological Examination of Political Leaders*, edited by M.G. Hermann (New York: Free Press, 1977). See also her "Explaining Foreign Policy Behaviour Using Personal Characteristics of Political Leaders," *International Studies Quarterly* (1980): 7–46 and "Assessing Personality at a Distance: A Profile of Ronald Reagan," *Mershon Center Quarterly Report* (Spring 1983): 1–8.

74. See Hermann, "Some Personal Characteristics."

75. Kingdon, *Candidates for Office.*

76. MacNaughton and Winn, "Economic Policy and Electoral Self-Interest."

77. These issues are also discussed in Conrad Winn, "Cabinet Control of the Public Service," *Canadian Public Policy* (March 1985): 125–28.

78. Conrad Winn, "Department of Secretary of State," in *Spending Tax Dollars, 1980–1981*, edited by G. Bruce Doern (Ottawa: Carleton University, School of Public Administration, 1980).

7

The Bureaucracy and Industrial Policy

MICHAEL M. ATKINSON

At the core of the debate on industrial policy is the question of market allocation. Can we trust or expect the market to allocate resources in a manner that will ensure economic growth and political stability? Those who see near perfect markets operating in most spheres of economic activity are inclined to respond in the affirmative and proceed to outline those rare occasions on which the market might conceivably fail (Watson, 1983). Those less sanguine about markets either see market failure as a widespread phenomenon, or argue that market outcomes, no matter how efficient, are by no means compatible with important political goals (Jenkin, 1983).

The most important alternative to market allocation is hierarchy. Where markets allocate according to the price mechanism, hierarchies employ managerial directives. The choice between markets and hierarchies is not an either/or proposition, but the demand for industrial policy is, generally speaking, the demand for more hierarchy. Specifically, it is a demand that public bureaucracies respond to structural weaknesses in the economy with policies that would reorient priorities and manage the adjustment process (Warnecke, 1975; Zysman, 1983). These policies typically include measures that would permit public authorities to discriminate among industrial sectors or individual firms by offering preferential treatment — protection, subsidies, access to credit — to some while denying it to others.

Defenders of the market respond to such a demand by arguing that even if market processes are deficient, it does not follow that allocation by public bureaucracy would be preferable (Wolf, 1979). The mere assignment of public functions to bureaucracy is no guarantee that they will be performed in a "socially optimal" manner (Downs, 1967, p. 40). There is, in other words, such a thing as "non-market failure."

It is to the question of non-market failure that this paper is addressed (although seldom in those terms). Outlined below are three "images" of bureaucracy, each of which contains a fundamental critique. The content of each critique, its implications for industrial policy, and an assessment of its persuasiveness are included in each section. These critiques do not exhaust all of the objections that might be levelled against bureaucratic projects for industrial strength, nor does each of the images as presented do justice to the often subtle reasoning that underlies each approach (hence the term image). They do, however, summarize recent, important work in the area of bureaucracy and bureaucratic power. Those who find the concept of bureaucratic pathology inherently appealing should have no difficulty believing in the veracity of one or more of the arguments presented.

These images of bureaucracy are not entirely consistent with one another. No effort is made to identify the precise conceptual and empirical points at which they part company, but it will be evident, particularly in the case of Image II and Image III, that to endorse one entails rejecting, in the large part, another. On the other hand there are points of agreement, particularly the view that it is entirely reasonable to assume that bureaucrats are self-interested.

Finally, it should be noted that there is no literature on the bureaucracy and industrial policy per se. There are studies of particular bureaucracies engaged in projects of economic development (e.g., Johnson, 1982), but no body of research or set of propositions that purports to make a tight connection between the structure or behaviour of bureaucracies and the pursuit of a successful industrial policy. For that reason inference and extrapolation characterize at least some of the analysis offered below. To provide an anchor for the reader, the paper begins with a brief discussion of the salient features of industrial policy. This should help in any assessment of the relevance for industrial policy of these rather general critiques of bureaucracy.

The Nature of Industrial Policy

The term industrial policy is typically defined in a very broad manner with few limits placed on what might be meant by "industrial" and even fewer on what qualifies as "policy" (Adams and Bollino, 1983). William Watson, for example, includes under the heading "industrial policy" virtually any measure that involves a conscious attempt by government to alter the composition of a nation's inputs or outputs (1983, p. 2). Thus a wide range of policy instruments are all eligible for the designation "industrial policy." On the other hand the ultimate objective of industrial policy is more sharply defined, and that objective is increased (and if possible equitable) economic growth. Moreover the primary threat to growth is generally understood to originate in changing patterns of international production and trade (Zysman and Tyson, 1983). It is the perhaps conceited belief that selective intervention by the state can facilitate adjustment to these changes, and even create comparative advantage, that provides the intellectual sustenance for industrial policy. Thus, in spite of a very broad definition, the hallmark of industrial policy is selective intervention for economic growth.

There appear to be three circumstances in which selective intervention might conceivably be required (Zysman, 1983, pp. 42–46). The first of these is a situation of actual or anticipated *growth*. If the growth is actual, the role of the state may be limited to protecting an industry in the early stages, establishing backward and forward linkages and perhaps locating export markets. Where growth is anticipated and developments are genuinely new, the state may be called upon to provide a much broader range of financial support to perhaps a narrower range of recipients. The second situation is that of *transition*. In this case there is a demand for policies of positive adjustment to facilitate the movement of labour and capital or for measures to subsidize uncompetitive production in anticipation of a return to earlier levels of demand. Finally, in circumstances of industrial *decline* (a concept difficult to define precisely), rapid exit or massive protection are the only alternatives.

Many observers of public bureaucracies have expressed considerable scepticism about their capacity to intervene successfully in any of the above circumstances (e.g., Watson, 1983). Under conditions of growth, for example, it is not clear why bureaucratic decisions should be superior to market outcomes since there are no rules for "picking winners" in the volatile technologies and no theory from which such rules could be deduced (Grant, 1983). Critics are similarly sceptical of bureaucratic decision making in situations of transition or decline. Here they suspect that even if bureaucrats could devise plans to rationalize production, these would have to meet political as well as (or perhaps instead of) economic criteria. Business firms, they believe, are more than willing to avoid the rigours of the market by the exercise of political power.

This paper probes and evaluates the theoretical justification for these harsh indictments of bureaucracy. If it can be shown that these critiques are seriously flawed, then there is no particular reason for concluding that bureaucracies are *inherently* ill-suited for making selective interventions in the economy. But that will not be enough to persuade all students of economic policy. Even if bureaucracies have some virtues, these, they submit, are not likely to extend to the realm of industrial policy. WilliamWatson puts the argument this way:"Distributing pensions is something government is likely to do well; designing an industrial structure is not" (1983, p. 29).

What is the nature, what are the distinguishing characteristics, of industrial policy that make it particularly problematic for public bureaucracies? First, much industrial policy making is *not routine* and *requires specialized, technical knowledge*. The conditions that give rise to demands for industrial policy are frequently international in origin and can seldom be precisely anticipated. For this reason industrial policy is sometimes created under crisis conditions in response to unique circumstances (Dyson and Wilks, 1983). Even when they are planned, some industrial policy measures — forced mergers and public corporations — are enormous in conception and unlikely to be repeated. Sophisticated information systems and flexible, discriminating responses are necessary even for the more routine programs of selective financial assistance to industry. Those who subscribe to the first image of bureaucracy — as self-serving and inefficient — will find these features of industrial policy particularly disturbing.

Second, and directly related to the question of definition, industrial policy is *broadly based and hard to integrate*. In the bureaucracies of most advanced industrial countries a variety of departments and agencies monitor the performance of a variety of industrial sectors. Few departments of industry completely monopolize all of the policy instruments in play at any given time. If the capacity to make industrial policy is widely distributed because in the pursuit of their mandates all departments and agencies impinge in some manner upon the prospects of firms and entire industrial sectors, then drawing policy instruments together will be a particularly pressing requirement. Yet those who see bureaucracy as penetrated by interest groups and internally incoherent are likely to argue that coordination is precisely what cannot be expected. For these observers the diffuse quality of industrial policy makes it an especially difficult policy area for public bureaucracies.

Finally, industrial policy usually entails *visible winners and losers*. Of course, adjustment that is unanticipated and unplanned entails the same thing. However, when the state directs the process of investment, responsibility for unpleasant outcomes can no longer be transferred to impersonal market forces. Industrial policy therefore tests the capacity of the state to identify responsible actors. This aspect of industrial policy will be of particular concern to those who subscribe to Image III — the bureaucracy as technocratic and unaccountable. Weak systems of accountability are particularly offensive to democratic sensibilities where the security of workers and their families and the viability of communities are at stake. This is another way of saying that industrial policy is highly politicized. It raises issues that take us well beyond static efficiency considerations to questions of democratic practice and political stability.

There are, of course, other policy areas that share with industrial policy some of these distinguishing characteristics. It is not feasible to argue that bureaucracies are capable of anything *except* industrial policy because industrial policy is uniquely demanding. What can be said is that when industrial policy takes a state-led, "plan-rational" form (Johnson, 1982), in which public agents substitute their judgments for those of private firms across a broad range of industrial sectors, all of these features of industrial policy are present at once. Under these circumstances bureaucracies that are active economic players will be open to the charge that every one of the images outlined below applies to them. How serious (or believable) is this charge? Is it enough to dissuade the most committed industrial planner from launching projects of industrial policy?

We begin our review with the approach to bureaucracy from economics where efficiency considerations are paramount. Here great stress is laid on axiomatic reasoning and very little (until recently) on empirical studies. With the second and third images of bureaucracy the emphasis is reversed. What should impress the reader about these images is just how selective they are; selective in conceptualization and selective in evidence. It is difficult for any one of them to be completely convincing and yet each has a ring of truth.

Because of this, and to anticipate somewhat the conclusion, it is prudent to remember that all bureaucracies are located in a political, cultural and economic environment. Economic bureaucracies in particular confront different challenges depending on the pattern of industrial development a country has experienced (Kurth, 1979) and other features of the state's structure. By abstracting the phenomenon of bureaucracy from its environment we inevitably acquire a distorted impression. All three images apply to Canada, but in this paper it will be argued that Image I is of less importance than the other two, that Image II is more serious in the Canadian case but nonetheless tractable, and that the most vexing problem is the one captured by Image III. None of them is so serious as to undermine altogether the idea of industrial policy. This is partly because reform is possible and partly because the success or failure of bureaucracies is frequently dependent upon factors beyond their control.

Image I: Bureaucracy as Self-Serving and Inefficient

The idea that bureaucracies are chronically inefficient institutions is an old and worthy one. It has been popularized recently by authors such as Northcote Parkinson and incorporated, with varying degrees of sophistication, into the theory of public choice. Early theorists in the public choice tradition include Tullock (1965), who stipulated some rather straightforward first principles of bureaucratic behaviour and then related in anecdotal form a series of confirming instances, and Downs (1967) who, in encyclopedic fashion, showed how much of the folklore of bureaucratic behaviour — especially empire building — could be derived from some simple axioms of bureaucratic conduct. Neither of these authors produced rigorously testable hypotheses, but both alerted social science in general to the pending arrival of economists as critics of public bureaucracies. It is not an exaggeration to say that the first full-blown critique came in 1971 with publication of William Niskanen's *Bureaucracy and Representative Government*. In deference to this work, and the enormous influence it has had, we will treat it as representative of the attitude of many economists toward bureaucracy, remembering that Niskanen's critics have produced revised and persuasive alternative models.

The Content of the Argument

Economists distinguish themselves from many other social scientists by attributing to their subjects rational, self-interested behaviour (the so-called "self-interest axiom"). They are also distinguished by their preoccupation with efficiency, particularly allocative efficiency — the distribution of values in society that produces the largest social benefit. It is the observation that self-interested bureaucrats will neither behave efficiently nor produce efficient outcomes that constitutes the critique at the heart of Image I.

Although there are several models of bureaucratic behaviour based on numerous (sometimes contradictory) assumptions, two axioms stand out as particularly important for the economist's indictment. The first of these is that non-market outputs, a term understood to cover government services in general, are hard to define and hard to measure. The main reason is that they have no price attached to them and consumers do not pay for them directly. As a result consumers have difficulty signalling their preference for one service over another, or one form of delivery over another, except by communicating with politicians, a method held to be fundamentally inadequate (Wolf, 1979, p. 115). Thus real demand for services, while not entirely unfathomable, is very hard to discover because governments face virtually no markets whatsoever for their outputs (Downs, 1967, p. 30). It is hard to underestimate the importance of this for Image I.

The second assumption is that most government services are supplied by monopolies. Either the public sector as a whole is considered a monopoly or (somewhat more reasonably) most bureaus are taken to be the sole suppliers of their services (Tullock, 1976; Borcherding, 1977). The importance of the monopoly assumption is made manifest by the further assumption that monopoly bureaus will behave in a manner analogous to monopoly firms in the marketplace. The natural tendency of monopolists is to engage in monopolistic pricing or price discrimination. The monopoly status of bureaus aggravates the problem of evaluating output since no alternative suppliers exist. Moreover, monopolists in the public sector, it is argued, are granted the ultimate indulgence — shelter from the discipline of the marketplace, namely bankruptcy. As a result of this insulation bureaucrats are free to pursue non-pecuniary rewards such as long lunches and frequent holidays. It comes as no surprise then that studies show that unit costs for similar output are higher in public than in private firms and that public firms have the higher staff to capital ratio (Orzechowski, 1977).

What remains is to specify a bureaucrat's maximand and explore its implications. Put another way, how will bureaucrats extract their monopoly rents? Some suggest that bureaucrats will maximize the size of their bureaus. Bureaucrats in search of budget growth will evaluate the performance of any given service solely in terms of its contribution to an expanding budget (especially Niskanen, 1971). But bureaucrats may also insist on higher quality standards. A preference for new and even unknown technologies coupled with an apparently mindless opposition to what is simple and familiar manifests itself in what has been called "gold-plating" (Newhouse, 1970; Fallows, 1982). Still others argue that bureaucrats value their autonomy and will thus seek to maximize their discretion (Migué and Bélanger, 1974). This might account for bureaucratic energies devoted to the acquisition and retention of information. Finally, it should be noted that some scholars in this tradition do not limit themselves to a single maximand. In one of the earliest formulations Anthony Downs simply asserted that bureaucrats strive to maximize power, prestige, convenience and security (1967, p. 84), an attractive formulation that does not lend itself easily to any empirical test (Jones, 1975).

The Niskanen Formulation and Industrial Policy

Of the various proposed maximands it is fair to say that a bureau's budget has been the most popular. This has largely been due to the work of William Niskanen whose *Bureaucracy and Representative Government* has had a significant impact on the thinking of economists. In this book Niskanen develops a model of the bureau as a non-profit organization financed, in part at least, by grants from a sponsor, normally an elected official or an elected body. The relation between sponsor and bureau is one of bilateral monopoly: a single purchaser of services (the sponsor) faces a single seller (the bureau). In contrast to a profit-seeking firm that offers units of output for a price, the bureau offers a set of services in exchange for a budget.

Problems arise over demand for the bureau's output. Since that demand is communicated to the sponsor through the rather imperfect mechanism of the electoral process, actual bureau output is unlikely to match consumer demand (Niskanen, 1971, p. 27). Instead, bureaucrats are inclined to exaggerate demand so that they may press for a larger budget which they can, in turn, use to generate greater output. The result is an oversupply of services. Sponsors are at a distinct disadvantage in attempting to reverse this process since they are relatively poorly informed with respect to the bureau's production costs, information carefully guarded by the bureau. Moreover, it is not clear that the reelection of sponsors is tied to the total net benefits of any given service, so that incentives to reduce supply are rather weak. On the contrary, the rather narrow time horizons of most politicians encourage the premature adoption of inappropriate (read expensive) responses (Wolf, 1979, pp. 114–15).

The distorting effects of the bureaucratic provision of service do not end with the self-serving practices of bureaucrats. Those who own specific factors used in the production of services have a clear incentive to advocate higher levels of bureaucratic supply. The same incentive exists for those groups in society with a higher demand for a bureau's services and lower taxes. The budgetary review process, as described by Niskanen, is completely unable to cope with the effects of this informal coalition because too often the interests of budget reviewers and those of the coalition are broadly consistent (1971, p. 153). The problem here is not with bureaucrats and politicians per se but with institutions that somehow fail to harness personal interests to the public good. For Niskanen the most obvious bureaucratic alternative (there are, of course, market alternatives) is the introduction of competition among bureaus to break single-bureau monopoly power.

What are the implications of Niskanen's analysis for the conduct of industrial policy? At the heart of the analysis, of course, is the conviction that bureaucracies are, by nature, inefficient and that to entrust to bureaucrats any aspect of public policy is to expose it to the tyranny of oversupply. Thus we would end up receiving more industrial policy than we need supplied by more bureaucrats than necessary.

But even if the general argument were entirely true in the abstract, it is not clear that in reality it covers all of industrial policy. Niskanen intends the term "service" to apply to those activities provided to a sponsor by its bureau (1971, p. 45), but throughout his treatment of bureaucracy he makes it clear that the type of bureau he has in mind is supplying a service in a second, more typical, sense. This bureau is discharging a public activity on behalf of a client and as such can be considered a line or clientele department. Such bureaucracies are ubiquitous, of course, but how much industrial policy is likely to be supplied by such a department? Any program of subsidies would clearly qualify. Applicants could be assisted by bureaucrats to meet the program's criteria, and information pertaining to the success of the subsidies in meeting their objectives would be in bureaucratic hands. This is already the case in Canada with the Department of Regional Industrial Expansion's mega-program, the Industrial Regional Development Program. Other programs, such as those intended to facilitate the transfer of technology from government laboratories to industry, similarly appear vulnerable to the type of abuse Niskanen has in mind.

There are other industrial policy instruments, however, that cannot be construed as the provision of services. These include the most coercive of instruments such as restrictions on capital imports, forced mergers and the creation of public enterprises. It is not clear how bureaus charged with the deployment of such instruments can exaggerate demand for their "services." Undertakings of this sort are subject to debate at the highest political levels and are informed by ancient ideological divisions. Moreover, the results are relatively easily monitored, as illustrated by the outcry that has accompanied aerospace and electronics debacles in Britain and France. In cases of "heroic" industrial policy, the bilateral monopoly that Niskanen assumes characterizes all bureaucratic-political relations is not as readily evident. In fact, the possibility of bureaucratic-political alliance seems much more likely. Even Niskanen acknowledges that over time every bureau "will be constrained to supply the output expected by the sponsor" (1971, p. 42). For the major, highly coercive, industrial policy instruments the time frame may be very short indeed.

Ironically, industrial policy may be more problematic for the information bureaucrats do not possess, than for that which they do. The technical nature of industrial policy suggests to some that "the most serious difficulty industrial policy makers face is the virtually complete absence of the information they would need to put into effect the economist's solutions" (Watson, 1983, p. 99). In Canada this point has been made by the Economic Council of Canada in assessing the success of the government's aid-to-industry programs (1983). Even here, where program decisions can be considered routine, managers are forced to make complicated assessments about the likelihood of projects taking place without assistance and the chances of them succeeding with it. In a distributive policy environment with a program providing a considerable degree of discretion, there is no shortage of critics (e.g., Binhammer, McDonough, and Lepore, 1983; Canada, 1984). In nonroutine policy settings, where the future of entire industrial sectors is being planned, it is farfetched to suggest that bureaucrats have a monopoly on the information needed to make these decisions or a monopoly on the information needed to evaluate them. In short, the delivery of industrial policy, as Watson suggests, is not the same as the delivery of family allowance or unemployment insurance. This may give pause to the advocates of industrial policy, but not for the reasons implicit in Niskanen's analysis.

Finally, it is time to ask whether bureaus can always be counted on to seek ever larger budgetary allocations. Migué and Bélanger have argued that bureaucrats are in fact seeking to increase discretionary income and that, therefore, contrived increases in demand for a bureau's output will not result in greater supply. Beyond the level of output where marginal value equals marginal cost, the rents that bureaucrats can appropriate are a negative function of output and therefore of budget (Migué and Bélanger, 1974). Bureaucrats, they argue, should be content with simply increasing demand since this increases discretion. Moreover, it has been observed that bureaus that do succeed in increasing outputs can actually face reduced budgets as sponsors reward efficiency with fewer resources (Warren, 1975). In short, increased budgets are by no means widely sought, nor are they unmixed blessings. When they are granted, the reason is frequently that large expenditures, efficient or not, are precisely how sponsors wish to manage problems. Expenditures, after all, have a symbolic as well as an instrumental value (Edelman, 1967, chap. 2). It is the failure to appreciate this, and the significant differences among bureaus, that leaves Niskanen open to the charge that he has created "an ideal-type, a hypothetical, exaggerated, ahistorical bureau" (Wade, 1979, p. 355).

The Breton-Wintrobe Formulation and Industrial Policy

In a recent, important addition to the economic view of bureaucracy, *The Logic of Bureaucratic Conduct,* Albert Breton and Ronald Wintrobe seek to avoid the obvious shortcomings of earlier analysis by constructing a more complex and perhaps more realistic model of bureaucracy. In doing so, however, the authors also succeed in showing that the theoretical deficiencies of this literature make it almost impossible to reach any firm conclusions about the bureaucracy and industrial policy from the point at which the analysis begins.

Breton and Wintrobe offer a theory of the *supply* of public services. They conceive of bureaucratic life as essentially a trading process in which bureaucrats, whether in the public or the private sector, exchange the informal services they provide for policy characteristics (1982, pp. 25–26). These latter are particular features of policy, many of which are not required as a matter of logic, but are instead negotiable. In the case of subsidies, examples would include the question of precisely who is eligible, how they will be paid and so on. These features of policy and the perquisites of office (which are often policy characteristics as well) are considered the objects that bureaucrats seek to maximize. Thus Breton and Wintrobe reject the idea that bureaucrats maximize a specific objective function such as the size of their bureaus (p. 27). Moreover, they portray bureaucrats as suppliers of services not to some clientele but to superiors, some of whom will be politicians. Thus bureaucrats are involved in the policy process as contributors, not merely rent seekers.

They do, of course, expect to be paid. At the heart of the exchange relationship which characterizes subordinate-superordinate relations in bureaucracies lies the capacity of bureaucrats to engage in "selective behaviour." Bureaucrats have the capacity to behave efficiently, that is, at a rate that exceeds what formal rules imply; inefficiently, worse than the formal rules require; or formally, precisely as officially required. Thus for Breton and Wintrobe bureaucrats are efficient when they supply informal services that achieve the goals of their superiors. Efficiency then, is a term used in a rather special limited sense. Equally important, bureaucrats are not always inefficient as Niskanen would have it. They are, rather, selectively inefficient according to the payment received in the currency of policy characteristics and the risks involved in behaving inefficiently (1982, pp. 42–54).

The exchanges described above occur within networks which are treated as surrogate markets. But "whereas market exchange requires law-based property rights, network exchange requires trust-based property rights" (Breton and Wintrobe, 1982, p. 61). Trust is required because bureaucratic transactions take place over time and there are no institutions to enforce commitments. Individuals linked to one another by trust form a network which can be larger or smaller depending on such factors as educational homogeneity. The authors argue that as vertical trust increases, so does the capacity for efficient behaviour, whereas an increase in horizontal trust enhances the capacity for inefficient behaviour (p. 133). This distinction they put to excellent use in describing the practices of Japanese firms and, beyond that, the growth of the Japanese economy.

The final critical element in the Breton-Wintrobe formulation is the idea of bureaucratic competition. Departing once again from the earlier tradition, they argue that models of bureaucracy based on the presumed monopoly power of bureaucrats are seriously deficient. There is, they suggest, a market for managers characterized by a considerable amount of competition in both the public and private sectors. The authors note, however, that this type of competition — competition within bureaus — is imperfect. Fortunately, it is augmented by competition among bureaus. This latter type of competition, denied by other models of bureaucracy, is described as Schumpeterian competition and is equated with entrepreneurship. Once again, however, competition of this variety is no guarantee of efficient behaviour on the part of bureaucrats. This is because the ability to compete depends on a bureau's capacity for selective behaviour and this, by definition, can be used efficiently or inefficiently. In short, sponsors will seek to place limits on competition where it breaks down trust and hence the capacity of bureaucrats to supply informal services efficiently (1982, pp. 128–29). Some degree of monopoly may be necessary, after all, to promote innovative activity, a conclusion already reached in the context of the optimal market structure for innovation (Scherer, 1980).

While this model of bureaucracy represents an improvement over previous formulations, it is useful to recognize its limitations for either understanding or prescribing bureaucratic behaviour in the area of industrial policy. One of the objections to industrial policy, as we have seen, is that bureaucrats, acting in their self-interest, will distort the intentions of politicians and take decisions that are not the most efficient. All of this will result in an industrial structure less productive and less resilient than would have emerged under free market conditions. Breton and Wintrobe offer no information that would directly confirm or contest this perspective. As they quite candidly acknowledge, "the question of whether bureaucracies are efficient is separate and distinct from whether bureaucrats are efficient" (1982, p. 164). To know the former, they suggest, one must have a theory of the demand for public services, as well as the theory of supply which Breton and Wintrobe provide. And these theories must be made consonant with one another. At the moment no such integrated theory exists.

This does not mean that the theory Breton and Wintrobe provided cannot be used to outline some of the efficient and inefficient practices of bureaucracies and hence explain why some bureaucracies are more responsive to political direction than are others. In fact, these authors bring the economic study of bureaucracy a considerable distance simply by treating organizational structure as a factor of production (1982, p. 132), thus acknowledging that changes in both formal and informal structures can have an effect on the efficiency of bureaucrats. The image of public bureaucracies as chronically inept institutions, an image celebrated in the economics literature, is thus usefully discredited. Similarly the idea that private bureaucracies are uncontaminated by inefficient behaviour is also undermined. The authors argue that private sector bureaucrats, like their public sector counterparts, cannot expect to take home the profits of their activity. Instead, both are paid on the basis of their superiors' assessment of their performance (p. 94). Thus incentives to behave efficiently are not rooted in some final market-based criterion that must be met. Likewise, the idea that the outputs of private bureaus can be measured whereas those of public bureaus cannot is strongly contested on the grounds that an overall measure of profitability is of no assistance in assessing the contribution of a single bureau (p. 117; also Alchian and Demsetz, 1972).

What these analyses show is that while there may be consensus on the idea that bureaucrats are self-interested (a consensus that extends beyond the economics profession), there is no agreement on what this entails with respect to efficiency. The view that public bureaucracies exercise a monopoly in the supply of services and suffer certain special debilitating afflictions has been challenged. Public bureaucracies may still be cumbersome and hidebound but it is not clear that this is inevitable or that private, corporate bureaucracies are untouched by these problems.

Similarly, there is no consensus on just what bureaucrats wish to maximize. However persuasive, monocausal theories are always open to the shock of disconfirming instances. Thus Niskanen's hypothesis must survive the 1980s where bureaucrats are increasingly rewarded on the basis of their ability to restrict output and cut spending (Aucoin, 1981). If the utility functions of bureaucrats are this malleable, we should develop a healthy suspicion of theories that imply inherent and immutable pathologies.

Finally, this literature implies that industrial policy is no different from any other policy area and therefore requires no special treatment. For this reason there is no direct confrontation between this image of bureaucracy and empirical studies of industrial policy. For its adherents, none is needed. But to accept this judgment requires one to embrace the idea that regardless of the programs and policies adopted there will be little variation in the success of industrial policy projects that require extensive bureaucratic involvement. Ideology, culture and organizational form count for very little. Those who find such a position difficult to accept will conclude that this image of bureaucracy is one-sided and its implied consequences far from inevitable.

Image II: Bureaucracy as Penetrated and Incoherent

The state-led model of economic development envisages the state as an economic player pursuing specific industrial objectives on both a macro and a case-by-case basis. Bureaucrats not only have discretion in the application of regulations and the provision of credit, but use this discretion to achieve clearly articulated outcomes usually expressed in the form of a development strategy. The entire adjustment process is politicized and, most important for the bureaucracy, centralized (Zysman, 1983, p. 91).

Without necessarily questioning the advisability of such a strategy, an array of scholars have offered reasons to be deeply skeptical of its workability. They see bureaucracies as typically penetrated and captured by interest associations and in continual conflict with one another. As such, public bureaucracies cannot be expected to offer advice and implement policy in a manner that is anything other than incoherent. Certainly industrial policy, with its enormous demands, is quite beyond the competence of public sector bureaucrats.

The Content of the Argument

At its core this image portrays public bureaucracies as constellations of departments and agencies each intent on organizational survival and, if possible, aggrandizement. These bureaus pursue narrow, short-term goals that typically bring them into conflict with other bureaus for funding, clients or access. As such these bureaus are inherently incapable of considering broad allocative questions. Instead, complex decisions are broken down into simpler components where private, sectoral deals are easier to make. No correction is made for "sectoral decomposition" because of the tendency within bureaucracies to treat problems sequentially (Lindberg, 1977). Thus, if they are entrusted with the instruments of industrial policy, no overall consensus on appropriate direction will emerge. Outcomes will vary across sectors and over time. It is true that the bureaucracy can be counted on to supply some form of government in this area, but

> The government supplied will not go in any single direction, but in many dependent on the agency and its relationship to its clientele. For the same reason it will be nonconsensual and incoherent government. There would be no integrating ideology or philosophy, only a set of specific ideologies about specific problems. (Peters, 1981, p. 82)

Evidently this version of the pathology of bureaucracy shares some of the assumptions of Image I. Once again bureaucrats seek to maximize the interests of their bureaus and adopt policy positions or fashion ideologies that are consistent with those interests. But unlike the earlier interpretation of bureaucratic beheviour, there is no compulsion in Image II to identify a specific maximand. The mere fact that bureaucrats' policy preferences are dictated by a bureau's interest and little else is a sufficient condemnation. Moreover this version of bureaucracy does not envisage the relationship between bureaucrat and politician as central to the problem of bureaucratic government. The main problem lies in the relationship among bureaus (conflictual) and between bureaus and clientele interests (accommodating). This is a deadly combination producing among bureaucrats a restricted range of vision, an unwillingness to accept direction, and an inability to sympathize with other points of view.

This image of bureaucracy has had, in recent years, a decisive influence on students of foreign policy. Pioneered by Graham Allison under the title of the Governmental (or Bureaucratic) Politics model it portrays bureaucrats as "players who act in terms of no consistent set of strategic objectives but rather according to various conceptions of national, organizational and personal goals" (Allison, 1971, p. 144). These "various conceptions" are dictated largely by position in the bureaucracy. Each bureau has a well-defined interest which is an expression of career goals, formal responsibilities and agency ideologies. The bureau's interest gives rise to preferences in each decision situation. The bureaucracy as a whole is understood to consist of a host of autonomous agencies and independent departments each in pursuit of a parochially defined interest. Bureaucratic players interact with one another along regularized circuits ("action channels" in Allison's terminology) creating coalitions and bargains and engaging in bureaucratic battles. The outcomes of this strategic play are dictated by the relative power of each agency and the skill of the various players (in Canada see Nossal, 1979; Schultz, 1980).

The strength of the bureaucratic politics model lies in the fact that it articulates so well with the much older tradition of pluralism in the study of politics in general. In fact, Stephen Krasner has argued that "bureaucratic politics applies the logic of pluralism to policy-making within government" (1978, p. 27). Just as pluralists envisage society as comprising myriad groups each seeking influence but none holding a monopoly of power, so bureaucracies are understood to comprise separate agencies engaged in an interminable contest for power but unable to rule alone (Rourke, 1976).

Thus the pluralist version of society and the bureaucratic politics version of the state closely parallel one another, and when they are drawn together the distinction between state and society begins to fade. It soon emerges that some "autonomous" agencies or departments actually have a powerful clientele with whom they can potentially develop a common attitude toward policy. The nurturing of this clientele and the building of organized support for departmental programs becomes a preoccupation for bureaucrats (Long, 1966). In fact some departments apparently owe their existence to this presumed need for functional representation. Known as clientele departments, their basic raison d'tre has been to act as feedback agencies. They succeed in keeping the major combatants — producers and consumers, labour and management — apart while at the same time augmenting traditional forms of representation based on electoral constituencies. In its most advanced stage this form of government, described by Lowi as "interest-group liberalism," encourages the delegation of state powers to clientele groups. It is they, or their representatives, who interpret vague regulations and exercise extensive grants of discretionary authority (Lowi, 1979). Not only do these enfranchised clientele groups enjoy privileged access, but they also exercise considerable decisional latitude with respect to those very issues on which their interest depends.

Implications for Industrial Policy

If bureaucracy is as incoherent as this image suggests, there are devastating implications for the capacity of governments to conceive and execute policies of industrial adjustment. In the first place, the groups created and nurtured by this process will be producer groups bent on obtaining and preserving privileged treatment from the state. Once they succeed they become what Mancur Olson has called "distributional coalitions," whose main energies are devoted to rent seeking rather than productive activities. He has argued at length that the mere presence of distributional coalitions will stifle economic growth by establishing barriers to the movement of factors of production. The accumulation of these coalitions and the entitlements they have wrestled from indulgent bureaus eventually choke off economic growth altogether (Olson, 1982). Thus it is no accident, according to Olson, that countries such as Japan and West Germany enjoyed periods of unparallelled growth in the aftermath of World War II. The legacy of that conflict was the dissolution of distributional coalitions in each country and the preservation, at least in Japan, of the bureaucratic elite now unfettered by previous obligations (p. 378).

The second implication of Image II is that industrial policy making will lack a "centerpoint from which to shift the direction and priorities expressed in the routine accumulation of particular bargains" (Zysman, 1983, p. 311). The diffuse nature of industrial policy seriously aggravates this problem. Even in a parliamentary form of government there are multiple bureaucratic sites for elaborate bargaining. And once bargains are struck in a bureaucracy organized to support particular producer interests, no bureau can be entrusted with authority over the others. As Theodore Lowi has observed of the economic powers of the U.S. government:

> They seem flexible only because they are numerous. They seem rational only because they are specialized. . . . All of them exist separately and independently. There is hardly a scintilla of central control because no such control could ever be entrusted to any one of them. No governing institution possesses central control because in a liberal state a virtue is made of its absence. (Lowi, 1979, p. 83)

Similar lamentations come from Ira Magaziner and Robert Reich who describe the process of economic policy making in the U.S. as "decentralized and chaotic." The single most striking feature of American industrial policy, they argue, is the absence of a single office charged with overall responsibility for monitoring world markets, increasing industrial competitiveness and easing the burden of adjustment (1982, p. 258).

With a state bureaucracy that is both permeated by organized interests and lacking a centrepoint, we should expect an inadequate and/or inappropriate response to economic crisis. According to Theda Skocpol, just such a response was forthcoming from the U.S. federal government at the onset of the Depression (Skocpol, 1980). Whether or not the New Deal represented a break with orthodox economic thought, the U.S. administration was in no way equipped to impose on business and labour a new regulatory regime that would promote economic expansion. Although the administrative system had been largely freed during the Progressive era of the patronage control of the parties, its shape and content was still dependent on struggles between Congress and the President. In a polity based on divided sovereignty "no centrally co-ordinated, executive-dominated national bureaucratic state could emerge, not even during World War I" (p. 175).

As a result, the National Recovery Administration had to be created de novo. In a manner which has persisted undiminished to the present, the NRA, led by a former businessman, recruited heavily from the ranks of business. In this manner powerful corporations and trade associations were placed in charge of the new regulatory codes which they proceeded to employ to freeze the economic status quo. In a similar manner the Public Works Administration (PWA) also floundered for lack of autonomous administrative capacity. Charged with spending billions on public works projects, the Administration proceeded very slowly and conservatively, aware that their budget was many times in excess of the entire federal construction budget in 1930 (Skocpol, 1980, p. 177). Consequently, the impact of the program was much less than expected. If bureaucracy is sometimes used as a synonym for rigidity, the PWA experience suggests that the *lack* of an established bureaucracy by no means ensures flexibility.

It might be countered, of course, that since these are all U.S. writers developing U.S. examples, bureaucratic incoherence is a peculiarly U.S. phenomenon. It is unlikely to develop where constitutional arrangements provide for a fusion rather than a separation of powers. The United States, in short, is possessed of a remarkably weak state which, when it acts, does so by fits and starts followed by long periods of consolidation and policy drift.

This line of argument has been employed in the area of social policy (Leman, 1977), but it does not fit industrial policy quite so well. First, it appears to be in the nature of industrial policy that responsibilities should be dispersed. As was pointed out earlier, the lack of consensus on the meaning of either "industrial" or "policy" has encouraged broad inclusive conceptions that resist intellectual moulding and consensus. Thus even where constitutional principles do not discourage centralization of economic policy making, industrial policy making, which is by definition sectoral and selective, can nonetheless prove highly resistant to it. Second, where the locus of economic policy making is centralized, but in a bureau without strong links to business and labour, the result has been a significant downgrading of the whole idea of industrial policy. Under these circumstances debate over industrial policy can easily degenerate into a purists' battle between those who seek to preserve the sanctity of markets and those who believe in the creativity of hierarchy.

To some degree the experience of both Britain and Canada illustrates these developments. In Canada the undisputed centre of economic policy making is the Department of Finance (Phidd and Doern, 1978). Its primary concern has been demand management, and it has demonstrated steadfast loyalty to neoclassical economic orthodoxies. Nonetheless, the Department of Finance does not control all economic policy making. On the contrary, it watched in horror during the 1970s as a variety of centres of economic expertise were created in the federal bureaucracy, some of them specifically to defend consumer and producer interests, others to supplement the essentially short-to-medium-term orientation of the department's economic advice. But no department or agency has emerged to coordinate industrial policy in the manner that the Department of Finance conducts macroeconomic policy. The result has been classic disputes over the viability and appropriateness of industrial policy (French, 1980) and the absence of any coordinating core (Abonyi and Atkinson, 1983, pp. 114–15).

In Britain, arguments over industrial policy also tend to revolve around the stark choice between market and bureaucratic solutions. Here too the deep commitment of the Treasury to automatic, macroeconomic responses to changing economic circumstances has stood firmly in the way of industrial policy (Blank, 1978). As a result, old institutions are ill-placed to manage intervention when, as in the case of North Sea oil, it is forced upon them (Zysman, 1983, p. 203). Once again, it appears to be the nature of industrial policy that it cannot be conducted in the traditional arm's length fashion without the bureaucracy eventually coming to rely on business for information and direction. As for anticipating structural change, the British civil service appears incapable of acting with any effectiveness via sectorally oriented bureaus. The overall inclination seems to be to proceed on a case-by-case basis, not to reorient the economy but to relieve the immediate source of discomfort. In fact, the more able an agency becomes in selective intervention, the more vulnerable it becomes to reorganization or the threat of abolition (Wilks, 1983, p. 135).

Middlemas has located Britain's difficulties at the political apex arguing that "the structural problem is that industry as a whole has no thematic focus in cabinet to match the economic directorate [the Treasury]" (1981). But it is likely that the problem runs deeper still. The Fulton Report notwithstanding, there continues to be a "fundamental separation of the public service from occupations in industry" (Coombes, 1982, p. 69). Moreover, the training and traditions of the administrative elite in Britain have nurtured a strong antipathy toward economic intervention. This antipathy, John Armstrong has argued, is closely connected to the deficiencies of an Oxbridge-centred administrative education. Intervention is resisted because it would, in the first instance, reveal the inadequacies of this elite and, in the second, would inevitably entail the creation of an elite corps of technocrats whose very presence would disturb the rather comfortable homogeneity (some might say mediocrity) of the present administrative setting (Armstrong, 1973).

For writers in this tradition the incoherence of bureaucracy is not simply a matter of constitutional form. Incoherence may be more pronounced in the United States but it is certainly not confined to that country. The economies of all OECD countries are complex entities where decisions can frequently be managed only by breaking large issues into simpler components and treating these separately. This is all the more the case given the international dimension of industrial policy, which inevitably draws the interests of other nations into any economic calculations. This style of decision making has its advocates (e.g., Lindblom, 1965), but the point is that it is not the style envisaged in models of state-led growth.

The Persuasiveness of This Argument

Of the many lines of objection that might be offered to the view that bureaucracies are invariably divided, penetrated, and incoherent, two seem particularly important in the context of industrial policy. The first of these is that altogether too much emphasis is placed in this formulation on the role of bureaucracy in fashioning industrial policy, while insufficient attention is paid to the role of politicians. In the context of U.S. foreign policy, for example Amos Perlmutter (1974) and Jerel A. Rosati (1981) have argued that a preoccupation with bureaucratic conflict risks underestimating the role of the President and Congress. This argument is even more compelling in a parliamentary system where politicians have the constitutional means, if not necessarily the will, to bind bureaucrats closely to political objectives.

Put another way, the absence of a coherent industrial policy may have more to do with the absence of a political consensus than with an incoherent bureaucratic design. In fact, the "endemic and pervasive conflict" (Schultz, 1980) that bureaucratic politics theorists divine in most decision settings may itself be a response to a political vacuum or to intense ideological conflict. Moreover, bureaucratic conflict, where it does exist, is not necessarily the creation of bureaucrats. The problems of industrial policy are not equally tractable from state to state, and divisions within society over appropriate responses may be deep enough to leave both bureaucrats and politicians unable to fashion a politically acceptable alternative quite irrespective of organizational design.

Industrial policy in Britain is a case in point. Here industrial policy issues are highly politicized and subject to routine tests of ideological purity. Party conflict over economic policy is institutionalized so that neither labour nor industry can effectively be barred from the political stage. So salient and politicized are industrial policy issues in Britain that bureaucrats make a practice of retreating quickly to the safety of precedent and market-based assessments (Grant and Wilks, 1983, p. 25). Thus it is not only a recalcitrant bureaucracy or the presence of producer groups exercising policy vetos that has prevented Britain from fashioning and using instruments of industrial policy. Policy paralysis is also the result of "an inability to find terms on which to make a deal about the nature of state intervention" (Zysman, 1983, p. 209). This is aggravated in

Britain by divisions within the ranks of business and the decentralization of organized labour. As Katzenstein has observed, "the organizational fragmentation of Britain's private sector is striking" (1978, p. 310). Of course a reorganization of bureaucratic structures may change this, but the point of this objection is that it is not simply the form of the state that leads to coherent or incoherent policy, but the content of the debate and the presence of agreement or disagreement on whose interest shall be sacrificed and whose preserved (Gourevich, 1978).

The second line of objection to Image II concerns relations among bureaus themselves. Simply put, it is not immediately evident that bureaus must always be in conflict. Cooperation and coordination across formal bureaucratic lines is by no means unknown. In fact, the presence of informal networks (trust networks for Breton and Wintrobe, 1982) itself warns against a preoccupation with agencies and bureaus as isolates. Beyond that, Robert Goodin (1975) has argued that a conflict of interest among bureaus does not necessarily induce a behavioural conflict. Not all issues are zero-sum, and there are frequent opportunities for compromise, even in industrial policy situations where policy decisions are complex. More important, not all bureaucrats have the same stake in an issue, and for those whose stake is low, the benefits of engaging in a bureaucratic fight, even if it can be won, may not warrant the costs or the risks. Considerations such as these go some distance toward explaining why wholesale bureaucratic conflict did not characterize the selection of a new fighter aircraft in Canada even though the bureaus involved had different interests and (ultimately) different preferences (Atkinson and Nossal, 1981).

Stories of successful coordination within the realm of industrial policy may not abound, but they do exist. France, for example, its reputation for centralized direction notwithstanding, has had considerable difficulty in overcoming the problems posed by the multiplicity of compartmentalized agencies involved in the industrial policy process. The solution has been the creation of interministerial committees that have introduced a much needed measure of coordination to industrial policy (Green, 1983, pp. 173–81). These committees have been established to cope with problems of industrial decline, to pick winners by providing help for the strong, exceptional firms, and, perhaps most significantly, to engage in strategic planning by selecting areas in which France should strive to attain international competitiveness. They are important organizational innovations in themselves, and in addition these committees have established fast and flexible procedures to enhance their efficacy.

Most bureaucracies may in fact be organized anarchies, unclear about their objectives and irrationally committed to existing policy instruments. The present array of bureaucratic forces in Canada in the industrial policy field suggests that these qualities and the force of Image II apply to a considerable degree. This problem is tractable, in Canada and elsewhere, but only if industrial policy is given a place of prominence on the political agenda. The French example is instructive: "Coordination did not . . . become a reality until industrial problems were accorded political importance. . . ." (Green, 1983, p. 175). Too often bureaucratic drift is simply a product of political disarray (Self, 1972, p. 181; Goodsell, 1983; Coombes, 1982, pp. 68, 71).

Image III: Bureaucracy as Technocratic and Unaccountable

Could it be that the problem of bureaucratic government is not that it is weak and ineffectual, but that it is, instead, robust, autonomous and unaccountable? In recent years observers of bureaucracy from diverse academic perspectives, including sociology, public administration, and political science, have pointed to the rise of an insular bureaucratic elite capable of manipulating politicians and jealous of its exercise of public authority (Etzioni-Halevy, 1983). While doubtless exaggerated in this form, this characterization of bureaucracy poses a different kind of problem for the formation of industrial policy. Concern that industrial policy decisions will be unfair, incoherent and contradictory (Watson, 1983), in short excessively politicized, gives way to the fear that decisions will not be politicized enough (Kaufman, 1981). Developed in closed, secretive fashion and subject to some unknown professional standard, industrial policy falls into the hands of bureaucrats who possess not merely a monopoly of information, but a monopoly of skill (Bendix, 1945).

The Content of the Argument

The bureaucracy portrayed in Image II is dependent on social formations, especially interest groups, for information and cues about acceptable policy. In particular, those with financial and political resources have to be accommodated to the point of permitting them to exercise the powers of the state. Indeed, the division between state and society begins to melt away, and the state becomes merely the battleground on which societal conflicts are fought and the winners duly confirmed. The bureaucracy is always someone's handmaiden. In direct opposition to this view the third image of bureaucracy begins by reasserting the state/society distinction. It portrays state officials in general, and bureaucrats in particular, as singularly able to exert their will on society and leave their unique stamp on public policy. The problem is that ordinary political values, including the distributive implications emphasized in Image II, are no longer as evident. The prospect for industrial policy is that bureaucrats will make colossal errors of judgment yet escape responsibility.

This image of bureaucracy asserts that the authority possessed by the state is fundamentally different from the authority possessed by other social organizations. For one thing the state is a compulsory organization that claims control over territories and people (Skocpol, 1982, p. 16). It is the uniqueness of state power and the fact that it cannot be distilled into class or group relationships that allows the state/society distinction to be made and the image of autonomous bureaucrats to emerge. Scholars such as Trimberger (1978) and Heclo (1974) have documented the exercise of this autonomy: Trimberger by showing how bureaucrats used state power to reorient economic development in Japan, Turkey, Egypt and Peru; Heclo by detailing how bureaucrats in Britain and Sweden eschewed the status quo and successfully pressed on politicians and interest groups significant social policy innovations. Of course the idea that bureaucrats act on their own preferences was a critical element in Image I. But in the case of Image III public officials seek not only private goals but also other, more general, societal goals frequently described in terms of the public interest. Under these conditions the interests of state officials cannot be reduced to their immediate or long-term material gain, nor can they be said to represent a mere reflection and condensation of the contradictions of capitalist society (cf. Poulantzas, 1975).

Many of those who have spent a considerable time observing bureaucrats in Western democracies have arrived at a similar image of autonomous bureaucrats:

> Can there really be much doubt who governs our complex modern societies? Public bureaucracies are responsible for the vast majority of policy initiatives taken by governments. . . . In a literal sense the modern political system is essentially "bureaucratic" — characterized by the "rule of officials." (Putnam, 1975, p. 87)

But none of this tells us how this autonomy is achieved. According to one line of argument (closely allied to that in Image I) it derives from the growing importance of technical expertise in policy initiatives and the monopoly bureaucrats hold on this expertise. There are other factors, of course. Politicians do not have the time or the inclination to become well versed in the natural, managerial or social sciences, and parliaments are typically without the surveillance mechanisms or the resources that would permit a genuine review of "technical" decisions. Still, this image of the bureaucracy lays greatest stress not on the deficiencies of political institutions, but on the transformation of bureaucrats into technocrats and the consequent loss of political control which that entails.

Nowhere has the fear of technocracy been as pronounced as in France where a homogeneous elite, ostensibly trained in technical subjects at the École polytechnique and the École nationale d'administration, has occupied senior posts in all of the critical institutions of the Republic.

This elite, it is alleged, eschews ideological discussions in favour of "radical pragmatism" and concentrates exclusively on means, never looking beyond "the concrete realizations of the Constantine plan" (Cohen, 1977 pp. 46–48). But France represents merely the cutting edge. Even in the British civil service, renowned for its celebration of the enlightened "amateur," efforts have been made to improve the status of scientific and technical personnel (Putnam, 1976, p. 208). The impact on democratic values within bureaucracies has been striking. Working with data drawn from Britain, Germany and Italy, Putnam has confirmed that technically trained officials do place more emphasis on productivity and efficiency questions than on distributive issues and questions of social justice. Moreover, they tend to be impatient with "political" pressures, viewing these as primarily irrational and disruptive (Putnam, 1977).

But whatever the rhetorical appeal of this vision of a technocratic elite, the real threat posed by the transformation of bureaucratic elites probably rests more with their absorption into the political arena than with their rejection of it (Atkinson and Coleman, 1985). Observers of politicians and bureaucrats in Western democracies have drawn attention to a growing willingness on the part of senior bureaucrats to admit that political considerations need to be incorporated into ostensibly technical decision making. This gives rise to what Heclo, in the context of U.S. bureaucracy, has referred to as the politicization of bureaucracy and the bureaucratization of politics (Heclo, 1977, chap. 2). The barrier between politics and bureaucracy, so clearly drawn by Weber at the turn of the century, today can barely be found. Studies in a variety of countries all point to a convergence of roles and the establishment of a sense of mutual reliance and personal trust between bureaucrats and politicians. Heclo and Wildavsky have described a policy-making community in Britain where politicians and bureaucrats function, "sometimes in conflict, often in agreement, but always in touch and operating within a shared framework" (1974, p. xv). Suleiman has similarly described a "politico-administrative hierarchy" in France where traditional divisions between politicians and civil servants are breaking down (1974). In Canada, Campbell and Szablowski have concluded that "the distinction between bureaucrats and political participants in the policy process simply does not exist in many crucial decision-making settings" (1979, p. 201).

What is being described in these studies is the growth of a policy oligarchy. What are its foundations? The first of these is probably the technical nature of much policy discourse, a development discussed above, that forces politicians to rely more heavily on bureaucrats. Second, there is a growing similarity in the career paths of politicians and bureaucrats, especially in France (Dogan, 1979), the United States (Heclo, 1977) and Japan (Johnson, 1982). Third, there has been an increase in the use of coordinating institutions, or central agencies, charged with meeting the needs of politicians for usable knowledge at appropriate junctures in the policy process. In Canada, where this organizational innovation has enjoyed considerable popularity, the result has been the creation of a stratum of bureaucrats eager and able "to operate as effective political actors in the ministerial-bureaucratic milieu" (Campbell, 1983, p. 296). Fourth, while the claim of bureaucrats to participate in policy may rest on their expertise, it no longer seems plausible to expect bureaucrats not to care about the content of the policies they are enacting. To the degree that bureaucrats become mission-committed, traditional barriers between policy and administration begin to fade, and bureaucrats and politicians emerge as allies rather than foes (Goodin, 1982; cf. Image I).

Implications for Industrial Policy

Advocates of industrial policy should find this image of bureaucracy quite attractive. The idea that bureaucrats are becoming more profes-sionalized, more sensitive to political considerations and more tech-nically able bodes well for industrial policy where technical and political considerations must both be given weight. It comes as no surprise then that students of industrial policy argue that state-led strategies of adjust-ment will require bureaucracies with centralized power, autonomy from legislatures and technical competence (Zysman, 1983, p. 300). It is this type of autonomous state bureaucracy that can resist the demands of unwelcome interests and pilot state initiatives in the marketplace with some measure of confidence. These bureaucrats are by no means easy prey for rent-seeking producer associations. Moreover, where bureaucrats feel that they share with politicians responsibility for the conduct of economic policy, the prospects for industrial policy appear brighter still. Kenneth Dyson, in comparing Britain and Germany, attributes the superior performance of the German government to the convergence of organizational and policy skills at the apex of the politico-administrative hierarchy in Bonn (1977, p. 63).

Unfortunately, even if it were to be agreed (for the moment) that several states were on the threshold of developing a cohesive, cen-tralized, capable bureaucracy, it is not clear that all industrial policy goals would be well served. France is a case in point. The centralization of the state bureaucracy and its partial insulation from domestic pres-sures have offered an ideal opportunity for concerted action. The close connection between career senior bureaucrats and the Gaullist and Giscardian parties during the 1970s further narrowed the channels of influence and enhanced bureaucratic autonomy. Coordination of indus-trial policy was made vastly easier by the *grand corps* tradition, the recruitment of the top graduates from select schools which provided networks that virtually dissolved bureaucratic boundaries (Suleiman,

1974). Finally, the French state, because of its unique relationship to the banking community, possessed the capacity to direct public funds and private investment toward specific ends (Zysman, 1983, chapter 3).

Arguably the creative use of the state power has given France one of the most robust economies in Europe and a growth rate which, before 1973, rivalled that of Japan. Certain industries — oil and steel, for example — for a time profited from massive infusions of investment directed by a centralized administration. And yet, as Zysman has demonstrated, the same strategy failed miserably in the case of electronics. Here the rapid pace of technological development made central direction inappropriate. The tactics that had worked so well in the other sectors — the establishment of national champions with guaranteed markets and ready flows of capital — could not insulate the electronics industry in France from the rigours of international competition. Zysman draws the conclusion that the structure of the state bureaucracy should correspond to the structure of an efficient firm in the sector being organized (1977, especially chap. 7). Unfortunately the state bureaucracy, particularly, one might add, a centralized state bureaucracy, is seldom so malleable.

Quite apart from the appropriateness of state structure, the goal of state policy in the electronics industry, namely technological self-sufficiency, showed very little realism. Not only is this goal itself something of a chimera, but France had virtually no comparative advantage in the broad range of computer equipment targetted. Zysman accuses state officials in France of giving in to "simple insecurity" and national prestige considerations (1977, chap. 5). Others see the electronics experience as just one example of French industrial policy in the 1960s, a policy that in general paid no attention to comparative advantage (McArthur and Scott, 1969). In either event, all of the putative advantages of the type of bureaucracy embodied in Image III are no guarantee of success for strategies of state-led industrial growth.

If the bureaucrats of Image III are, for all of their expertise, still fallible, does the area of industrial policy pose any special accountability problems? Certainly the technical considerations attendant upon most industrial policy decisions would suggest so. Even routine disbursements under subsidy programs require careful calculation with respect to a firm's viability and the likelihood that a proposed investment would have occurred without the subsidy. Manuals are of limited assistance and, in any event, the rules are normally far from precise. Instead bureaucrats must know and respond to both technical and political considerations, a situation plainly anticipated by exponents of Image III. Listen to Chalmers Johnson describe the Japanese situation:

> One of the great strengths of Japanese industrial policy is its ability to deal with discrete complex decisions without first having to find or enact a law that covers the situation. Highly detailed statutes serve the interests primarily of lawyers, not development. (1982, p. 319)

One might observe, perhaps cynically, that political institutions like the Diet are also rather tedious and seldom serve the interests of development. In fact, Johnson concludes that in Japan both the legislative and judicial branches have been reduced to "safety valves" called upon when needed to discourage the numerous interest groups that, if catered to, would only distort the priorities of the developmental state (1982, p. 315).

The accountability implications of this attitude are rather ominous, but perhaps the fact that many industrial policy decisions are nonroutine and hence visible to politicians and constituents will be a mitigating factor. Certainly Aberbach and his colleagues have suggested that where issues are highly politicized the autonomy of public servants will be seriously reduced (1981, p. 250). Cases of massive industrial rescue would appear to bear this out. Yet technical questions are still important. Moreover, there is little to prevent politicians and bureaucrats from agreeing to the expedient of defining political problems as essentially technical ones.

But perhaps the most important implication of industrial policy for matters of accountability lies in the fact that it involves winners and losers and uncertain outcomes. Successful projects are seen as such only years later when most politicians and many bureaucrats are not around to claim credit. Closed plants and lost jobs on the other hand are immediate. For that reason, even if politico-administrative communities exist and politicians and bureaucrats are willing to use them to plan industrial change, there is no incentive to make the plans widely known. The covert nature of the system, plus the wide discretionary powers inherent in industrial policy, leave the autonomous state bureaucracy wide open to corruption, something that has occurred on occasion in Japan.

The Persuasiveness of This Argument

Do most countries possess technically competent, homogeneous, politically sensitive, centralized bureaucracies poised to assume the responsibility of fashioning and implementing an industrial policy? This is a difficult formula but there are certainly those who see it as a necessary, if not sufficient, condition for state-led policies of economic growth. And to the degree that this image of bureaucracy is approximated in real life, France and Japan are the favoured examples of just such a bureaucracy and just such a set of policies (Katzenstein, 1978; Zysman, 1983).

Unfortunately neither of these examples stands up entirely to sustained scrutiny. In France, for example, planning documents have acknowledged that the diffuse quality of industrial policy and (conventional wisdom notwithstanding) the fragmentation of bureaucratic authority have combined to thwart ambitious across-the-board industrial policies. The 5th Plan made precisely this observation in acknowledging that "too great a dispersion of administrative centers of decisions in particular constitutes an obstacle to rapid decisions which are often called for . . ." (cited in Estrin and Holmes, 1983, p. 135). The incoherent character of French industrial policy during the heyday of state guidance is a picture painted by others (e.g., McArthur and Scott, 1969) who note that the coordination of state intervention was too loose to possibly have the intended dramatic effects. In addition, *dirigiste* industrial policy has not always enjoyed consistent political support. With the advent of the Socialists, the strategy of international challenge embodied in much of the rhetoric and reality of Gaullist policy had to compete with pressure to "reconquer internal markets" (Estrin and Holmes, 1983, p. 143). Thus even if a symbiotic relationship between politicians and bureaucrats in France has survived the change of power, and the *dirigiste* style remains, it is not clear that the content of French industrial policy will go unchallenged.

Just as important is the fact that the French bureaucracy does not appear to be immune from the kinds of internal conflicts portrayed in Image II as central to the bureaucratic experience. In fact, Vincent Wright has described the French bureaucracy as "particularly prone to internal tension and dissensions. It is characterized not by uniformity but by diversity and fragmentation" (1974, p. 48). Struggles between the Ministry of Finance and the spending ministries parallel experiences elsewhere, while rivalries among the various corps contribute yet another obstacle to coordination (Wright, 1978). To this is added the fact that the French pursuit of high technology has occasioned the development of sector-sensitive instruments which in turn have fostered clientele relations (Vernon, 1974, p. 13).

The Japanese experience has been similar. The rise of the major economic bureaucracies — the Ministry of International Trade and Industry (MITI) and the Ministry of Finance in particular — has been marked by numerous jurisdictional disputes and debates over appropriate policy. Johnson describes these disputes as "the very lifeblood of the Japanese bureaucracy" (1982, p. 320). They raise the question, however, of the degree to which Japanese industrial policy is either centralized or coordinated. Once again, the diffuse character of industrial policy has meant that a variety of agencies and ministries — Transport, Labour, the Bank of Japan, the Fair Trade Commission — have claimed at least some of the responsibility for industrial policy. Fierce loyalty to the organization, referred to by Breton and Wintrobe as vertical trust, can lead to "sectionalism of perhaps a more rigid kind than in other bureaucracies" (Trezise with Suzuki, 1976, p. 787). The practice of rotating ministers, on the other hand, has done nothing to strengthen cabinet control. Moreover, it is this bureaucracy, and particularly MITI, that has, on occasion, bowed to local political pressures (shipbuilding), applied rules without discrimination (export incentives), offered familiar but inappropriate prescriptions (cartelization of the cotton textile and apparel industry), and lavished attention on industries that had little potential for dynamic growth (coal) (Tresize and Suzuki, 1976).

None of this means that Japan has not adopted a state-led economic development strategy under the direction of an exceptionally talented economic elite. But this system of bureaucratic rule is not immune from the debilitating effects of competition and bureaucratic infighting. It is partly this, but also the presence of other distinctive Japanese institutions, including *amakudari* ("descent from heaven") and *keiretsu* (the oligopolistic organization of industry), that has led some to wonder just how important the structure of the state bureaucracy has been (Hills, 1983, p. 70). MITI's influence, in particular, seems to be limited to industries in the "decline" or "growth" stage, while established industries — auto, steel and computers — escape much direction. MITI has also had its influence curbed with the internationalization of Japanese capital. This has reduced the leverage of the state, and the state itself has become subject to international pressure both to conform to the General Agreement on Tariffs and Trade and to restrain exports. Finally, even if the Japanese bureaucracy is given credit for the country's "economic miracle," it is not entirely clear that having achieved the status of "fastest of the followers" it can now become an industrial leader. As Zysman has observed, "state guidance may be more effective for organizing high growth catch-up than for trailblazing into the future" (1983, p. 315).

With these cautionary tales in mind we can have a final look at bureaucratic-political relations, the symbiosis that lies at the heart of Image III. This portrait, it will be recalled, draws considerable strength from the observation that politicians and bureaucrats have experienced a convergence of roles conducive to concerted action by the state, but threatening to democratic sensibilities. In what is arguably the most penetrating empirical assessment of this issue, Aberbach, Putnam and Rockman conclude that, while "contested territory" exists, there is still a division of labour between bureaucrats and politicians in Western democracies. Civil servants continue to prefer consensus and incremental adjustment while their political colleagues remain passionate, idealistic and ideological. Bureaucrats are more attentive to narrow, sectoral interests while politicians still think in terms of political principle and political advantage. Matters are changing in some realms — for example, civil servants appear to be increasingly important in the critical areas of planning, budgeting and coordination — but bureaucrats and politicians are not simply interchangeable, at least not yet (Aberbach, Putnam, and Rockman, 1981, chap. 1). This is very important for industrial policy. If politicians remain distinctive actors, possessed of a legitimacy ultimately denied to bureaucrats, it is unlikely that the latter (in all but the most exceptional cases) will be able to substitute a bureaucratic version of industrial development for one that has been fashioned by politicians.

Conclusions

Each of the images of bureaucracy presented here has sought to highlight a particular feature of bureaucracy that would limit its capacity to intervene in the marketplace on the side of economic growth. Many of the authors discussed have drawn their conclusions on the strength of their knowledge of a single bureau or a single country. For this reason, each of the images seems to have only limited applicability. This plainly reduces the usefulness of any single formulation and it is probably prudent to acknowledge that all bureaucracies are, to differing degrees, inefficient, incoherent and unaccountable. The elimination of all of these pathologies is, at best, a naïve wish, while the elimination of one of them might simply invite, in larger measure, the problems posed by the others. This prompts one conclusion about bureaucrats, one conclusion about politicians, and one conclusion about the images themselves.

About bureaucrats and bureaucracies it should be said that we are very far indeed from prescribing a single appropriate organizational design for purposes of industrial policy. As Zysman has shown in the case of France, what is good for one sector may be devastating for another. The same observation holds for different countries facing different problems. Some time ago Alexander Gerschenkron pointed out that the institutional needs of early industrializers such as Britain differed markedly from those of later industrializers such as France and Germany, while the needs of these latter countries could not be equated with those of even later industrializers such as Korea and Brazil (1962, chap. 1). If there are no single trajectories of industrial development, it would seem rash indeed to insist upon a single organizational formula.

This does not mean that the structure of the bureaucracy and the composition of the politico-bureaucratic hierarchy will have no impact on the success of state-led development strategies. It merely cautions against simple formulae and high expectations. Most important, the bureaucratic design should not be monolithic. Inasmuch as industrial policy is essentially sectoral in design, every consideration should be given to the industrial organization of the sector and, crucially, to the precise goals that are sought by the state with the instruments available. The absence of any example of unqualified bureaucratic success under all conditions offers a strong case for flexibility in organizational design. The diffuse and technical nature of industrial policy provides whatever further inducement is needed.

The second conclusion pertains to politicians. What Images II and III show (more by their weakness than their strength) is that even able bureaucrats armed with all of the leverage that a centralized state structure offers cannot generate the consensus and vision upon which industrial policy depends. Only politicians can do that. Everywhere it has been employed, industrial policy has occasioned controversy and conflict, but it appears to have worked well only where politicians have either negotiated or imposed a consensus among producer groups on the extent and aims of state action. Where this has not been accomplished, as in Britain, only part of the responsibility can be laid at the door of "inappropriate" political-bureaucratic institutions. These latter may facilitate the formation of governing coalitions, but they cannot substitute for them.

Finally, can bureaucrats themselves be trusted to deliver the industrial policy desired by politicians? According to Image I, bureaucrats will first of all suit themselves. Yet there is no convincing evidence that in suiting themselves bureaucrats will not, in fact, meet the political objectives set for them. Because Image I does not allow for bureaucrats to seek a maximand in which the public interest is served, it imposes by fiat a premature closure on the matter. The pathologies described in Image I should, of course, be resisted but there is no reason to believe that such resistance is bound to fail.

According to Image II, even if bureaucrats wished to provide their services efficiently, industrial policy would founder on the shoals of incoherence. But once again the evidence is far from conclusive. It is probably true that industrial policy poses particularly serious coordination problems, but the barriers to bureaucratic cooperation are not insurmountable. It is much more likely that where it exists bureaucratic incoherence is a reflection of political disarray. And without the requisite political leadership, bureaucrats can be excused for imposing their own objectives.

For adherents to Image III the answer is yes, bureaucrats can deliver industrial policy, but in so doing they are likely to escape responsibility for the outcomes. Bureaucrats in Canada are shielded by conventions of ministerial responsibility, but to that has been added a host of other means of spreading the risks associated with picking winners and declaring firms and sectors redundant. Chief among these is the expansion of the industrial policy process. While the first two images of bureaucracy concentrate on bureaucrats themselves and bureaucratic structure, Image III contains the view that a complete understanding of what Katzenstein has called the policy network can come only by examining the relations bureaucrats maintain with private sector actors. These relations are becoming more complicated, because of the need to accommodate an increasing number of interest groups, and more compartmentalized, because of a growing sectoralization of all forms of policy making (Richardson, 1982, p. 197).

Industrial policy thrives when it is based on what McKay and Grant call "a broad acceptance by private investors of the need for government intervention" (1983, p. 1). Bureaucrats who have the qualities described in Image III can be relied upon to cultivate this broad acceptance and to create small sector-specific policy communities far away from the partisan battle. This may be the only way in which industrial policy can achieve a measure of success in Canada. Thus, rather than become preoccupied with the bureaucratic weaknesses that lie at the centre of our first two images, it is the problems associated with bureaucratic strength that should command the attention of industrial policy advocates.

Note

This paper was completed in August 1984.

Bibliography

Aberbach, Joel D., Robert D. Putnam, and Bert A. Rockman. 1981. *Bureaucrats and Politicians in Western Democracies*. Cambridge, Mass.: Harvard University Press.

Abonyi, Arpad, and Michael M. Atkinson. 1983. "Technological Innovation and Industrial Policy: Canada in an International Context." In *The Politics of Canadian Public Policy*, edited by Michael M. Atkinson and Marsha A. Chandler. Toronto: University of Toronto Press.

Adams, F. Gerard, and C. Andrea Bollino. 1983. "Meaning of Industrial Policy." In *Industrial Policies for Growth and Competitiveness*, edited by F.G. Adams and L.R. Kleins. Lexington, Mass.: D.C. Heath.

Alchian, A.A., and H. Demsetz. 1972. "Production, Information Costs, and Economic Organization." *American Economic Review* 62 (December): 777–95.

Allison, Graham T. 1971. *Essence of Decision*. Boston: Little, Brown.

Armstrong, John A. 1973. *The European Administrative Elite*. Princeton: Princeton University Press.

Atkinson, Michael M., and William D. Coleman. 1985. "Bureaucrats and Politicians in Canada: An Examination of the Political Administration Model." *Comparative Political Studies* 18 (April): 58–80.

Atkinson, Michael M., and Kim Richard Nossal. 1981. "Bureaucratic Politics and the New Fighter Aircraft Decisions." *Canadian Public Administration* 24 (Winter): 531–58.

Aucoin, Peter. 1981. *The Politics and Management of Restraint in Government*. Montreal: Institute for Research on Public Policy.

Bendix, Reinhard. 1945. "Bureaucracy and the Problem of Power." *Public Administration Review* 5: 194–209.

Binhammer, H.H., L.C. McDonough, and G. Lepore. 1983. *Government Grants to Private Sector Firms*. Ottawa: Economic Council of Canada.

Blank, S. 1978. "Britain: The Politics of Foreign Economic Policy: The Domestic Economy and the Problem of Pluralist Stagnation." In *Between Power and Plenty*, edited by P. Katzenstein. Madison: University of Wisconsin Press.

Borcherding, Thomas E. 1977. "The Sources of Growth of Public Expenditures in the United States." In *Budgets and Bureaucrats: The Sources of Government Growth*, edited by T.E. Borcherding. Durham, N.C.: Duke University Press.

Breton, Albert, and Ronald Wintrobe. 1982. *The Logic of Bureaucratic Conduct*. Cambridge: Cambridge University Press.

Campbell, Colin. 1983. *Governments under Stress*. Toronto: University of Toronto Press.

Campbell, Colin, and George Szablowski. 1979. *The Superbureaucrats*. Toronto: Macmillan.

Canada. 1984. Task Force on Federal Policies and Programs for Technology Development. *Report*. Ottawa: Minister of Supply and Services Canada.

Cohen, Stephen. 1977. *Modern Capitalist Planning*. Berkeley: University of California Press.

Coombes, David. 1982. *Representative Government and Economic Power*. London: Heinemann.

Dogan, Mattei. 1979. "How to Become a Cabinet Minister in France." *Comparative Politics* 12 (October): 1–25.

Downs, Anthony. 1967. *Inside Bureaucracy*. Boston: Little, Brown.

Dyson, K.H.F. 1977. *Party, State, and Bureaucracy in Western Germany*. Beverly Hills, Cal.: Sage.

Dyson, Kenneth, and Stephen Wilks. 1983. *Industrial Crisis: A Comparative Study of the State and Industry*. Oxford: Martin Robertson.

Economic Council of Canada. 1983. *The Bottom Line*. Ottawa: Minister of Supply and Services Canada.

Edelman, Murray. 1967. *The Symbolic Uses of Politics*. Chicago: University of Illinois Press.

Estrin, Saul, and Peter Holmes. 1983. "French Planning and Industrial Policy." *Journal of Public Policy* 3 (February): 131–48.

Etzioni-Halevy, Eva. 1983. *Bureaucracy and Democracy: A Political Dilemma*. London: Routledge and Kegan Paul.

Fallows, James. 1982. *National Defense*. New York: Vantage Books.

French, Richard D. 1980. *How Ottawa Decides: Planning and Industrial Policy Making, 1968–80*. Toronto: James Lorimer for Canadian Institute for Economic Policy.

Gerschenkron, Alexander. 1962. *Economic Backwardness in Historical Perspective*. Cambridge, Mass.: Harvard University Press.

Goodin, Robert E. 1975. "The Logic of Bureaucratic Back Scratching." *Public Choice* 21 (Spring): 53–67.

————. 1982. "Rational Politicians and Rational Bureaucrats in Washington and Whitehall." *Public Administration* 60 (Spring): 23–41.

Goodsell, Charles. 1983. *The Case for Bureaucracy*. New York: Chatham House.

Gourevich, Peter. 1978. "The Second Image Reversed: The International Sources of Domestic Politics." *International Organization* 32 (Autumn): 881–912.

Grant, R.M. 1983. "Appraising Selective Financial Assistance to Industry: A Review of Institutions and Methodologies in the United Kingdom, Sweden and West Germany." *Journal of Public Policy* (October): 369–96.

Grant, Wyn, and Stephen Wilks. 1983. "British Industrial Policy: Structural Change, Policy Inertia." *Journal of Public Policy* 3 (February): 13–28.

Green, Diana. 1983. "Strategic Management and the State." In *Industrial Crisis*, edited by K. Dyson and S. Wilks. Oxford: Martin Robertson.

Heclo, Hugh. 1974. *Modern Social Politics in Britain and Sweden*. New Haven: Yale University Press.

————. 1977. *A Government of Strangers: Executive Politics in Washington*. Washington, D.C.: Brookings Institution.

Heclo, Hugh, and Aaron Wildavsky. 1974. *The Private Government of Public Money*. Berkeley: University of California Press.

Hills, Jill. 1983. "The Industrial Policy of Japan." *Journal of Public Policy* 3 (February): 63–80.

Jenkin, Michael. 1983. *The Challenge of Diversity*. Study prepared for the Science Council of Canada. Ottawa: Minister of Supply and Services Canada.

Jenkins, Bill, and Andrew Gray. 1983. "Bureaucratic Politics and Power: Developments in the Study of Bureaucracy." *Political Studies* 31: 177–93.

Johnson, Chalmers. 1982. *MITI and the Japanese Miracle*. Stanford: Stanford University Press.

Jones, J.C.H. 1975. "The Bureaucracy and Public Policy: Canadian Merger Policy and the Combines Branch, 1960–71." *Canadian Public Administration* 18 (Summer): 269–96.

Katzenstein, Peter J., ed. 1978. *Between Power and Plenty*. Madison: University of Wisconsin Press.

Kaufman, Herbert. 1981. "Fear of Bureaucracy: A Raging Pandemic." *Public Administration Review* 41: 1–9.

Krasner, Stephen D. 1978. *Defending the National Interest*. Princeton: Princeton University Press.

Kurth, James. 1979. "The Political Consequences of the Product Cycle: Industrial History and Political Outcomes." *International Organization* (Winter): 1–34.

Leman, Christopher. 1977. "Patterns of Policy Development: Social Security in the United States and Canada." *Public Policy* 25 (Spring): 261–91.

Lindberg, Leon N. 1977. "Energy Policy and the Politics of Economic Development." *Comparative Political Studies* 10 (October): 355–82.

Lindblom, Charles E. 1965. *The Intelligence of Democracy*. New York: Basic Books.

———. 1977. *Politics and Markets*. New York: Basic Books.

Long, N. 1966. "Power and Administration." In *Public Administration and Policy*, edited by P. Woll. New York: Harper and Row.

Lowi, Theodore. 1979. *The End of Liberalism*. 2d ed. New York: Norton.

Magaziner, Ira, and Robert Reich. 1982. *Minding America's Business*. New York: Random House.

McArthur, J.B., and B.R. Scott. 1969. *Industrial Planning in France*. Cambridge, Mass.: Harvard University Press.

McKay, David, and Wyn Grant. 1983. "Industrial Policies in OECD Countries: An Overview." *Journal of Public Policy* 3 (February): 1–12.

Middlemas, K. 1981. "The Chamberlain Touch in Government." *Daily Telegraph*, March 16.

Migué, J.L., and G. Bélanger. 1974. "Towards a General Theory of Managerial Discretion." *Public Choice* 17 (Spring): 27–43.

Newhouse, J.P. 1970. "Toward a Theory of Non-Profit Institutions." *American Economic Review* 60: 64–74.

Niskanen, William A. 1971. *Bureaucracy and Representative Government*. Chicago: Aldine.

Nossal, Kim Richard. 1979. "Allison through the (Ottawa) Looking Glass: Bureaucratic Politics and Foreign Policy in a Parliamentary System." *Canadian Public Administration* 22 (Winter): 610–26.

Olson, Mancur. 1982. *The Rise and Decline of Nations*. New Haven: Yale University Press.

Orzechowski, William. 1977. "Economic Models of Bureaucracy: Survey, Extension and Evidence." In *Budgets and Bureaucrats: The Sources of Government Growth*, edited by T.E. Borcherding. Durham, N.C.: Duke University Press.

Perlmutter, Amos. 1974. "The Presidential Political Center and Foreign Policy: A Critique of the Revisionist and Bureaucratic-Political Orientations." *World Politics* 27 (October): 87–106.

Peters, B. Guy. 1981. "The Problem of Bureaucratic Government." *Journal of Politics* 43: 56–82.

Phidd, Richard W., and G. Bruce Doern. 1978. *The Politics and Management of Canadian Economic Policy*. Toronto: Macmillan.

Poulantzas, Nicos. 1975. *Political Power and Social Classes*. London: New Left Books.

Putnam, Robert D. 1975. "The Political Attitudes of Senior Civil Servants in Western Europe." In *The Mandarins of Western Europe*, edited by M. Dogan. New York: Halsted Press.

———. 1976. *The Comparative Study of Political Elites*. Englewood Cliffs, N.J.: Prentice-Hall.

———. 1977. "Elite Transformation in Advanced Industrial Societies: An Empirical Assessment of the Theory of Technocracy." *Comparative Political Studies* 10 (October): 383–412.

Richardson, Jeremy. 1982. "Convergent Policy Styles in Europe." In *Policy Styles in Western Europe*, edited by Jeremy Richardson. London: George Allen and Unwin.

Rosati, Jerel A. 1981. "Developing a Systematic Decision-making Framework: Bureaucratic Politics in Perspective." *World Politics* 33 (January): 234–52.

Rourke, F. E. 1976. *Bureaucracy, Politics and Public Policy*. 2d ed. Boston: Little, Brown.

Scherer, F.M. 1980. *Industrial Market Structure and Economic Performance*. 2d ed. Chicago: Rand-McNally.

Schultz, Richard J. 1980. *Federalism, Bureaucracy and Public Policy: The Politics of Highway Transport Regulation*. Montreal: McGill-Queen's University Press.

Self, Peter. 1972. *Administrative Theories and Politics*. London: George Allen and Unwin.

Skocpol, Theda. 1980. "Political Response to Capitalist Crisis: Neo-Marxist Theories of the State and the Case of the New Deal." *Politics and Society* 10: 155–201.

———. 1982. "Bringing the State Back In." Paper presented to a conference on States and Social Structures, Mount Kisco, New York, February.

Suleiman, Ezra. 1974. *Politics, Power and Bureaucracy in France: The Administrative Elite*. Princeton: Princeton University Press.

Trezise, Philip H. with Yukio Suzuki. 1976. "Politics, Government and Economic Growth in Japan." In *Asia's New Giant*, edited by Hugh Patrick and Henry Rosovsky. Washington, D.C.: Brookings Institution.

Trimberger, Ellen Kay. 1978. *Revolution from Above: Military Bureaucrats and Development in Japan, Turkey, Egypt and Peru*. New Brunswick, N.J.: Transaction Books.

Tullock, Gordon. 1965. *The Politics of Bureaucracy*. Washington, D.C.: Public Affairs Press.

———. 1976. *The Vote Motive*. London: Hobart.

Vernon, Raymond. 1974. "Enterprise and Government in Western Europe." In *Big Business and the State*, edited by Raymond Vernon. Cambridge, Mass.: Harvard University Press.

Wade, L.L. 1979. "Public Administration, Public Choice and the Pathos of Reform." *Review of Politics* 41: 344–74.

Warnecke, Stephen J. 1975. "Introduction." In *Industrial Policies in Western Europe*, edited by Stephen J. Warnecke and Ezra N. Suleiman. New York: Praeger.

Warren, Ronald S. 1975. "Bureaucratic Performance and Budgetary Reward." *Public Choice* 24 (Winter): 51–58.

Watson, William G. 1983. *A Primer on the Economics of Industrial Policy*. Toronto: Ontario Economic Council.

Wilks, Stephen. 1983. "Liberal State and Party Competition: Britain." In *Industrial Crisis*, edited by K. Dyson and S. Wilks. Oxford: Martin Robertson.

Wolf, Charles. 1979. "A Theory of Non-market Failure: Framework for Implementation Analysis." *Journal of Law and Economics* 22 (April): 107–40.

Wright, Vincent. 1974. "Politics and Administration under the French Republic." *Political Studies* 22 (March): 44–65.

———. 1978. *The Government and Politics of France*. London: Hutchison.

Zysman, John. 1977. *Political Strategies for Industrial Order*. Berkeley: University of California Press.

———. 1983. *Governments, Markets, and Growth*. Ithaca, N.Y.: Cornell University Press.

Zysman, John, and Laura Tyson. 1983. *American Industry in International Competition*. Ithaca, N.Y.: Cornell University Press.

8

The Effects of Business-Government Relations on Industrial Policy

ANDREW B. GOLLNER

> Give me good politics and I shall give you good economics.
> Baron Joseph Dominique Louis,
> Minister of Finance under Louis XVIII

The objective of this paper is to present a set of conclusions, drawn from a comparative review of the literature, on the question: what kinds of business-government relations are conducive to what kinds of industrial policies? The countries examined were: Canada, the United States, the United Kingdom, France, West Germany and Japan.

The review explored the literature along a number of distinct boundaries. It surveyed four general "macro" theories — pluralism, elitism, corporatism and Marxism — each of which claims, on very different grounds, that business-government relations in any society are the products of that society's prevailing social structure and ideology. The review also looked at some "meso" or middle-level theories of financial systems, of state structures and of economic development and at how each of these claims to explain the prevailing relationship between business and government concerning industrial policy. Finally, the review also examined some "micro" theories that derive their explanation from some of the internal characteristics of the parties involved (e.g., the failures or successes of business leaders to be socially or politically responsible, the failures or successes of government decision makers to be responsive to the realities of the market system).

The barriers to definitive conclusions to the questions raised in the first paragraph are enormous. Many writers subscribe to the view that of all the forces at play in industrial policy making, "the most important of all is the relationship between government and industry."[1] Paradoxically, very few authors actually support this position with detailed empirical analyses. A shortage of data is only one of many barriers to theory building in this area. A greater obstacle is the fact that the data at our disposal are frequently contradictory, and are sharply fragmented along ideological lines. Scholars diverge widely over the nature of industrial policy and whether or not it merits governmental application. On a country-by-country basis, opinions on the content of industrial policy are equally divided. Industrial policy is deeply and diffusely embedded in the overall policy domains of most societies. Boundary-setting between it and other policy realms is probably one of the most hazardous analytical tasks today. Robert B. Reich, a well-known U.S. analyst of industrial policy, neatly sums up the disarray that characterizes much of the industrial policy literature today:

> Industrial policy is one of those issues that seems to have gone from obscurity to meaninglessness, without any intervening period of coherence. Indeed, it has a sort of Rorschach quality these days, in whose ink spots people see their fondest hopes or direst fears.[2]

The business-government relations literature projects an equally kaleidoscopic image. As Murray and McMillan observe, "the vast bulk of the literature in the field is written in a normative vein from recognizably partisan positions."[3] The current state of the art is one of "ignorance and partisan speculation."[4]

While some common threads can be discerned in the analytical jungle described above, the conclusions of this review are tentative. They are put forward as working hypotheses that may serve as benchmarks in the construction of a future theoretical synthesis.

The literature suggests that a logic of institutions underlies industrial policy. This paper postulates that there are three critical factors that shape both the patterns of business-government relations found in a particular country and the type of industrial policy being pursued. These factors are:

- the level of business confidence in the state as entrepreneur;
- the perceived economic payoffs to dominant business interests from industrial policy; and
- the capacity of government to design, coordinate and implement complex and penetrative policy packages.

This paper will now examine the causes and consequences of these factors.

Approaches to Industrial Policy

Industrial policy is viewed in this paper as a purposeful government attempt to influence industrial investment and production decisions. The objective of these attempts is to *assist* industry in coping with environmental change.[5] Industrial assistance may be set up as a shield, protecting industry from external forces; it may also be constructed to help industry adapt to its external environment (if need be by winding down); and finally, it may also be designed with the aim of helping industry chart entirely new directions for itself.

There are many possible approaches to industrial policy. Some writers distinguish between targeted and non-targeted approaches.[6] Others draw a distinction between interventionist and non-interventionist[7] or *dirigiste* and laissez-faire[8] industrial policies. Analysis of the various typologies generated in this area suggests that industrial policies fall into any one or a combination of the following three types.

The situational approach   This is an ad hoc approach to industrial policy, and is the one most frequently applied. In the course of its application, policy makers may focus their attention on a *specific firm/industry* (e.g., financial aid to Chrysler Corporation or to Massey-Ferguson), a *specific policy instrument* (e.g., subsidies) or a *specific industrial sector* (e.g., transportation). In each of these three specific cases, the policy makers' focus is situational. Assistance is usually random and often at odds with other government objectives or policy instruments. The overwhelming driving force of situational industrial policy is political expediency of one type or another. Least important are considerations of economic efficiency, rationality or congruence with broad national economic objectives. Industrial policy in Canada, the United States and the United Kingdom since 1945 has frequently been dominated by this approach, although various elements of this approach are also to be found on a much smaller scale in West Germany, France and Japan.

The reallocative approach   Reallocative industrial policy[9] is an attempt to overcome the inevitable economic irrationalities produced by the situational policy approach. Its goal is to facilitate the rapid reallocation of investments from the least efficient to the most efficient sectors of industry in order to improve national industrial competitiveness or efficiency. It emphasizes the necessity of taking a broad look at the overall economy and at other government objectives *prior to* the selection of the appropriate industrial objectives. Governments utilizing this approach have essentially three choices. (a) They can identify industrial winners and losers and target their aid accordingly.[10] (b) They may focus their efforts on reindustrialization.[11] (c) They may also follow the path of industrial "triage."[12] In whatever form, the reallocative approach aims to maximize efficiency/productivity using primarily financial incentives. Whether any of these choices can deliver the desired policy objectives in practice is of course an entirely different question. Industrial policy in France and Japan has utilized this approach at times, but not in the main. Rare glimpses of it may also be seen in Canada and Britain.

The structural approach   Structural industrial policy, like the reallocative approach, recognizes the necessity of reviewing overall government objectives prior to the selection of industrial objectives. The key difference between the reallocative and structural approaches is that the former aims to optimize industrial performance according to one criterion, efficiency/productivity, while the latter pursues a number of objectives simultaneously. Structural industrial policy takes a very broad perspective; it is designed to foster a balanced economic structure through the coordinated use of a wide assortment of policy instruments. In addition to subsidies, the state may use regulation, direct control, suasion, economic leadership, etc. to advance its industrial policy goals. Jarboe's conceptualization of structural industrial policy is instructive. "The structural approach seeks the optimal mix of industries, not the optimal industry . . . its focus is the creation and maintenance of a balanced structure of production." [13]

Structural industrial policy making begins by identifying those industries that best serve a nation's core economic objectives (e.g., economic growth, job creation, exports). It may also entail an a priori ranking of industries according to level of impact upon the economy. Once strategic industries are thus identified, they receive preferential treatment to enable them to attain or maintain high levels of self-sustaining economic viability (as, for example, with Japan's nurturing of its microchip industry).

Structural industrial policy need not, indeed should not, entail massive state intervention in the economy. It works best when the state restricts its economic "meddling" and concentrates merely on the "commanding heights." Again, as Jarboe observes, "By concentrating on strategic industries, the entire structure of the economy can be affected, while avoiding the problems associated with the overwhelming complexity of the economic system." [14]

It is now appropriate to turn to the question of whether these specific industrial policy approaches require specific patterns of business-government relationships, and if so, what kinds of businessgovernment relationships are conducive to what kinds of industrial policy.

Business-Government Relations and Industrial Policy

The relationship between business and government is conceptualized in this paper as the degree of influence each party has over the other regarding the design and implementation of industrial policy. ("Each" is misleading in that neither business nor government is a homogeneous entity that speaks with a single voice. To put it another way, homogeneity, or lack thereof, varies greatly from issue to issue. Obviously, the relationship of interest here is the interaction that takes place between the key players or concerned fractions of both communities over industrial policy.)

Only three general types of relationships between business and government are possible. In one type, business is dominated by government. In a second, business is in the preponderant position. In the third case, there is a relative balance between the two sectors. Murray and McMillan have drawn a rather more complex typology by further subdividing each of these three relationship types according to the level of agreement or consensus that is found between the parties on specific policy options.[15]

The literature leads us to conclude that structural and reallocative industrial policies are generally found in societies where governments are in a dominant position vis-à-vis business as far as the design and implementation of industrial policy is concerned. (This dominance may or may not be antibusiness.) Conversely, situational industrial policies are found in those societies where business and government are in balance, or where business has a dominant influence over the design and implementation of industrial policy.

But this conclusion, instructive as it may be, is not a sufficiently strong guide to policy makers. What they really need is information about the forces that combine to produce the different kinds of business-government relations.

As stated earlier, three interdependent variables seem to play a particularly important role in shaping both the patterns of business-government relations and the industrial policies of societies. These are:

- the level of business confidence in the state as entrepreneur;
- the perceived economic payoffs to dominant business interests; and
- the capacity of government to design and implement complex, penetrative policy initiatives.

These principles will be illustrated briefly with examples drawn from the countries under review.

The notion that only "strong" states can pursue structural industrial policy and that "weak" states are only able to sustain situational policies is a frequent theme in the literature.[16] The argument is that since structural industrial policy involves a high level of policy coordination, a harmonious utilization of a wide array of policy instruments and a deep penetration of business decision-making processes, it cannot be applied with any hope of success by states that are identified as weak.[17] The accumulation of strength, or the demonstration of weakness by the state appears to be a composite of a number of inputs. It appears, first of all, that the level of business confidence in the state as an entrepreneur is critical. In Japan, France and West Germany, this confidence level tends to be quite high, whereas it is quite low in Canada, the United States and the United Kingdom. The obvious question is, why do confidence levels differ?

One immediate explanation is derived from history. In Japan, France and West Germany, the three countries that pursue structural industrial policy, traditions of state intervention run very deep. In these three countries, the state is *not* perceived by business leaders as an entrepreneurial upstart but as a legitimate and respected economic partner. The Lockean version of the social contract, with its emphasis on the virtues of limited government, is conspicuously absent from their political cultures.

The nature of the dominant economic sector at the time of a country's first major industrialization drive is also of some significance here.[18] When the textile industry was the leading sector, societal demands for state intervention and policy coordination were relatively weak, since private enterprise could muster on its own the needed factors for successful development. Thus, for example, industrialization in Britain could unfold with relatively little state involvement during the 18th and 19th centuries. In contrast, when steel, railways and heavy industry were the dominant sectors, the challenge of industrialization could no longer be met by private entrepreneurial effort alone, and required an active state involvement. As Zysman sums up, "By this logic, present-day relations between business and the state in an early industrializer such as Britain are dramatically different from those in a latecomer such as Japan because of the different ways in which each country resolved the problems of the initial stage of industrialization."[19] Vogel's paper on why business distrusts the state in the United States also supports the above thesis:

> The American bourgeoisie regards state officials with a sort of contempt; they are newcomers to American institutional life whose later arrival testifies to their inexperience and irrelevance to economic development . . . the mistrust of the state by businessmen is a function of the state's previous role in industrial development: the greater the state's previous role the greater the state's leadership and direction, the greater the cohesiveness between present business and governmental elites.[20]

The impact of industrial policy on the leading business sectors is another critical part of the equation. Until relatively recently, the governments of France, Japan and West Germany were able to pursue reallocative and structural industrial policies because these approaches did not pose a threat to dominant business elites. For example, the collaboration of large segments of the French financial community with the Nazis and with the Vichy regime during World War II ensured that the collaborators would be divested of their equity in and control over France's most significant financial institutions. These institutions subsequently became the chief instruments of the French state in the pursuit of its industrial policy.

In West Germany, *Strukturpolitik* was pursued by policy instruments quite different from those used in France. Nevertheless, the power vested by the postwar German state in the newly created banks helped to ensure that the dominant industrial elite of postwar Germany would benefit rather than suffer from the selected policy approach. The German economy was particularly amenable to structural industrial policy after the war. "Germany . . . required the least transformation of its industrial structure [after World War II]: its industries were well suited to the markets that began to emerge during the postwar boom."[21] And as Schonfield puts it, business resistance to *Strukturpolitik* was non-existent: "they built upon the familiar structural foundation and plan, much of it invisible to the naked eye, as if guided by an archeologist who could pick his way blindfold about some favorite ruin."[22]

In sharp contrast to the above, dominant business interests in Canada, the United States and Britain perceive few economic pay-offs and many economic costs from structural industrial policy. As Richard French and others have shown, in Canada, for example, efforts to introduce a reallocative or structural approach have always been derailed, "politicians apparently backing off when it appeared that adopting any specific policy would likely bring down upon them the wrath of the champions of the industries omitted from the list of those to be targeted."[23] Business opposition to structural industrial policy in Canada (as in the United States) is particularly well stated by the Business Council of National Issues:

> We do not believe that a comprehensive national industrial strategy is either feasible or necessary . . . the management of business by public officials makes little sense. . . . The federal government's . . . attempt to plan for and direct major economic change does not inspire confidence in the ability of government to develop effective and detailed directives for industrial development.[24]

In the case of Britain, successive British governments, Labour and Conservative, have attempted to institutionalize structural-type approaches to industrial policy since 1945. The very first efforts, in 1945, were rejected by business leaders as unacceptable statist intrusion into the marketplace. Business resistance was particularly strong among the ranks of the British financial community.[25] With minor differences, this corporate opposition persists up to the present time.

In short, in Canada, the United States and the United Kingdom, the introduction of reallocational or structural versions of industrial policy threatens to undermine the currently individualized and unfettered access of dominant business elites to industrial aid, and generally to reduce their preferential economic status. Thus, the dominant business elites in these countries are opposed to reallocative and structural policy options because they see themselves victimized rather than assisted by them.

It should be mentioned here that the earlier corporate elite support for coordinated structural policy in France, West Germany and Japan has significantly diminished recently. Indeed, by the end of the 1970s structural industrial policy was seriously diluted by large doses of situational industrial policy, especially in France and West Germany. Rather than undermining the argument presented above, recent erosions of the structural profiles of West German or French industrial policy help to illustrate our case. As Zysman explains:

> The political task [these countries confront] . . . in trying to sustain growth has changed. . . . The central difference is that politically entrenched interests will have to be confronted directly rather than finessed. . . . [These countries] must now confront politically entrenched producer interests. . . . In the 1980s . . . the political problems of industrial adjustment have changed. . . . In the fast-growing countries postwar expansion was linked to a structural shift of labor out of agriculture, a transformation that is now complete. Consequently these countries (France, Japan, and Germany in this study) must now displace powerful and entrenched industrial interests in order to accomplish the sectoral shifts and reorganization of production essential to continued growth.[26]

In short, the capacity of governments to launch and implement complex and penetrative policy initiatives such as structural industrial policy is clearly a function of the level of business confidence in the state as entrepreneur and of the perceived corporate costs/benefits of such approaches. There are some additional factors, however, that may increase or decrease governmental capacity to pursue complex policy initiatives. The location of a society on a continuum between pluralism and corporatism appears to be particularly relevant.

It is by now almost conventional wisdom that whereas a pluralistic society is most amenable to situational industrial policy, structural industrial policy is the natural descendant of corporatist business-government relations. The third approach, reallocative industrial policy, tends often to be described as apolitical, that is, above both the adversarial and the fused politics of the pluralist-corporatist dichotomy.[27]

It is held that corporatism is the model most suitable for negotiating, planning and implementing those comprehensive and difficult decisions that define the structuralist or reallocative policy approach. Indeed, there are many who will argue that corporatism is an essential prerequisite for structural or reallocative industrial policy.[28] By default then, societies tending toward pluralism will be more likely to apply situational industrial policy.

While Japan comes closest to the corporatist model in our sample, the other two structuralist countries, France and Germany, share more characteristics in common with corporatism than with pluralism.

Canada, Britain and the United States stand in stark contrast to the above, and are seen as countries far removed from the corporatist paradigm at the macro or national level. The United States is identified by virtually all writers as the country with the most limited corporatist tendencies and thus therefore the furthest removed from structural policy. In Canada, as Atkinson and Coleman,[29] Panitch[30] and others have argued, macro-level corporatism is almost non-existent. A similar causal pattern holds true in Britain, as Fox[31] and Cox[32] argue in separate studies.

The capacity of government to launch complex, penetrative policies is also conditioned by the level of elite homogeneity or elite interpenetration between business and government. These levels are the highest in Japan, France and West Germany and are lower in the cases of Canada, Britain and the United States.

Japan offers perhaps the best illustration of the thesis that the acceptability and success of structural industrial policy is highly dependent on business-government elite homogeneity or elite interpenetration. In Japan, through the practice of *amakudari* (literally meaning "descent from heaven") senior government officials tend to move on to become presidents of strategic corporations after they have fulfilled their public sector mandates. And afterward, when they come to negotiate with government officials on behalf of their private sector units, their government contact points tend to be people who were previously their subordinates in government. As Chalmers Johnson writes:

> In 1974, the president of New Japan Steel, the nation's largest profit-making enterprise, was Hirai Tomisaburo, MITI's vice-minister between 1952 and 1953; the executive director of the Tokyo Electric Power Company, the world's largest privately held utility, was Ishahara Takeo, MITI's vice-minister between 1955 and 1957; the executive director of Toyota Motor Company was Yamamoto Shigenobu, MITI vice-minster between 1966 and 1968; and the vice-president of Arabian Oil was Ojimi Yoshihisa, MITI vice-minister between 1969 and 1971.[33]

Elite interpenetration helps to create mutual trust and confidence between business and government. It enhances policy coordination, and thus removes an important barrier to structural or reallocative policies.

The nature of a country's financial system also affects the capacity of governments to undertake structural industrial policies. Having examined the industrial policies and financial systems of France, Japan, West Germany, Britain, and the United States, Zysman found that where capital markets are the major source of industrial investment, governments are denied the necessary political leverage to enter into and control the industrial decisions of private corporations.[34] To put it another way, the domination of capital-market-based industrial financing in Britain, Canada and the United States sharply curtails the domination of government, and does not enable the state to engineer anything other than situational industrial policy.

Conversely, Zysman found that

> selective credit allocation is the single discretion necessary to all state-led industrial strategies . . . credit-based financial systems with state-administered prices [such as in Japan and France] will facilitate intervention and ease the political problems of mustering support for state-led industrial promotion.[35]

Conclusions

This paper distinguishes between three general approaches to industrial policy, and argues that the choice between these distinct approaches is largely a function of the relationship between business and government. Structural and reallocative industrial policies appear to require a pattern of relationship wherein government can dominate the design and implementation of industrial policy. Situational industrial policies are found in those societies where domination by the state is curtailed.

The paper has argued that the degree to which one party or the other dominates the design/implementation of industrial policy is conditioned by three interdependent variables. These are the level of business confidence in the state as entrepreneur; the extent to which dominant business interests see themselves suffering or profiting from industrial policy; and the capacity of government to launch and implement complex, penetrative policy initiatives.

In societies where structural or reallocative policies are the mainstream approach, the level of business confidence in the entrepreneurial state is high. Dominant business elites in these societies — i.e., in Japan, West Germany and France — appear to profit from structural industrial policy, and, in all three cases, governments have had a high capacity to launch and implement complex, penetrative policy initiatives. In societies where situational industrial policy is the mainstream approach — as in Canada, Britain and the United States — the salience of the above variables is substantially lower.

The conclusion to be drawn from the above is that there is indeed a logic of institutions. The three industrial policy approaches cannot be easily transported across cultural/political boundaries. This statement is not intended to deny political choice, but rather to draw attention to the political conditions under which transplants may flourish or decay.

This paper makes no value judgments as to whether Canada should or should not institute a structural industrial policy approach. Its message, rather, is that this or any other industrial policy requires a parallel political strategy. Whatever its economic merits, structural industrial policy is a high-cost political commodity. To be economically successful, structural industrial policy needs to be sustained by the political "props" outlined in this paper. Without those props, the economic wisdom of structural industrial policy quickly evaporates.

Notes

This paper was completed in December 1984.

1. R. George, *Targeting High-Growth Industry* (Montreal: Institute for Research on Public Policy, 1983), p. 47.

2. Robert B. Reich, from his address at a seminar jointly organized by the National Foreign Trade Council Foundation and *Business Week*, Washington, D.C., October 18, 1983.

3. V.V. Murray and C.J. McMillan, "Business-Government Relations in Canada: A Conceptual Map," *Canadian Public Administration* 26 (Fall 1983), p. 608.

4. Ibid., p. 609.

5. This conceptualization is closely related to one presented by Kenan Patrick Jarboe, "Industrial Policy in America: Concepts and Politics," Ph.D. dissertation, University of Michigan, 1983.

6. George, *Targeting High-Growth Industry*.

7. Paul Davenport et al., *Industrial Policy in Ontario and Quebec* (Toronto: Ontario Economic Council, 1982).

8. Christopher Beckman, *Strategies of Industrial Adaptation: A Review of the Debate*, Executive Bulletin, No. 25 (Ottawa: Conference Board of Canada, 1983).

9. The following writers are well-known advocates of this approach: G. Schwartz and P. Choate, *Being Number One: Rebuilding the U.S. Economy* (Lexington, Mass.: Lexington Books, 1980); I. Magaziner and R. Reich, *Minding America's Business* (New York: Harcourt Brace Jovanovich, 1982).

10. See C. Lester Thurow, *The Zero-Sum Society* (New York: Basic Books, 1980), pp. 80–81.

11. See, for example, Amitai Etzioni, "Reindustrialization of America," *Science* 209 (1980), p. 4459. Also Glen Williams, *Not for Export* (Toronto: McClelland and Stewart, 1983). This by and large is the main thesis of Canadian economic nationalists.

12. Felix Rohatyn is a well-known advocate of this approach in the United States. See "Reconstructing America," *The New York Review of Books* 28 (1981), p. 3, also Jarboe, "Industrial Policy in America," pp. 144–47.

13. Jarboe, "Industrial Policy in America," pp. 153, 165.

14. Ibid., p. 155.

15. Murray and McMillan, "Business-Government Relations in Canada," pp. 595–97.

16. See Peter Katzenstein, ed., *Between Power and Plenty: Foreign Economic Policies of Advanced Industrial States* (Madison: University of Wisconsin Press, 1978); Stephen Krasner, *Defending the National Interest* (Princeton: Princeton University Press, 1978).

17. See also Stephen Cohen, "France: Industrial Policy in the Entrepreneurial State," *Journal of Contemporary Business* 11 (June 1982), p. 103.

18. Alexander Gerschenkron, *Economic Backwardness in Historical Perspective* (Cambridge, Mass.: Harvard University Press, 1962), and also James Kurth, "Political Consequences of the Product Cycle," *International Organization* (Winter 1979), and his essay in the 1982 special issue of *Industrial Organization*.

19. John Zysman, *Governments, Markets and Growth: Financial Systems and the Politics of Industrial Change* (Ithaca, N.Y.: Cornell University Press, 1983), p. 290.

20. David Vogel, "Why Businessmen Distrust Their State: The Political Consciousness of American Corporate Executives," *British Journal of Political Science* 109 (January 1978), pp. 59, 76.

21. Zysman, *Governments, Markets and Growth*, pp. 251–52.

22. Andrew Schonfield, *Modern Capitalism* (London: Oxford University Press, 1965), p. 240.

23. Richard French, *How Ottawa Decides: Planning and Industrial Policy Making, 1968–80* (Toronto: James Lorimer for Canadian Institute for Economic Policy, 1980), pp. 129–32.

24. Business Council on National Issues, *National Priorities* (Ottawa: BCNI, 1983), pp. 32–38.

25. Wyn Grant and Stephen Wilks, "British Industrial Policy: Structural Change, Policy Inertia," *Journal of Public Policy* 3 (1) (1983): 13–28, and Michael Moran, "Finance Capital and Pressure Group Politics in Britain," *British Journal of Political Science* 112 (October 1981): 381–404.

26. Zysman, *Governments, Markets and Growth*, pp. 24, 26, 53.

27. Jarboe, "Industrial Policy in America," pp. 203–205.

28. See, for example, J. Badaracco and D. Joffie, "Industrial Policy: It Can't Happen Here," *Harvard Business Review* 61 (November–December 1983): 96–105, or A. Kantrow, "The Political Realities of Industrial Policy," *Harvard Business Review* 61 (September–October 1983): 76–86.

29. Michael Atkinson and Norman Coleman, "Corporatism and Industrial Policy," (November 1983), p. 6, mimeo.

30. Leo Panitch, "Corporatism in Canada," *Studies in Political Economy* (Spring 1979): 43–92.

31. Allan Fox, "Corporatism and Industrial Democracy: The Social Origins of Present Forms and Methods in Britain and Germany" (London: Social Science Research Council, 1978).

32. Andrew Cox, "Corporatism as Reductionism: The Analytical Limits of the Corporatist Thesis," *Government and Opposition* 16 (1) (1980): 78–95.

33. Chalmers Johnson, *Japan's Public Policy Companies* (Washington, D.C.: American Enterprise Institute, 1978), p. 10. See also Boston Consulting Group, *Business Strategies for Japan* (Tokyo, 1970).

34. See Zysman, *Governments, Markets and Growth*.

35. Ibid., pp. 76, 80.

9

The Role of Trade Unions in Industrial Policies, 1945 to 1984

STEVEN B. WOLINETZ

This is an essay on unions and industrial policy. The juxtaposition of these two topics reflects both the importance of trade unions in Western economies and the salience of the debate on industrial policy underway in a number of countries today. In virtually every Western democracy, there are individuals or groups arguing that effective response to shrinking industrial bases and a changing international economic order requires the adoption of industrial policies designed to support existing industries and ensure that they remain competitive. The questions with which this essay deals are the following. If industrial policies are adopted in one form or another, what role are trade unions likely to play in their formulation and operation? Are trade unions likely to be supportive of industrial policies, and to what extent are they likely to be involved in their formulation and development?

Such questions do not lend themselves to easy answers; or, if they do, the simple answers are rarely worth having. In order to discuss the question in greater depth, we must examine the ways in which trade unions have been involved in the industrial policies that have been in place in postwar capitalist economies. This essay will do so by means of a critical review of the existing literatures on industrial policy and on trade unions and public policy. The paper will show that *direct* trade union involvement in industrial policy is limited, particularly when compared to trade union participation in macroeconomic or incomes policies in countries such as the Netherlands or Sweden. When unions are involved in industrial policy, it is typically either as participants in commissions organized to oversee the reorganization or phasing down of industries, or as members of defensive coalitions seeking protection for declining industries. Instances in which trade unions are able to initiate or veto policies are rare and occur only when trade unions wield considerable market or political power. This pattern reflects both the predilections of employers and policy makers and the difficulties which trade unions encounter when they attempt to inject themselves into industrial policy discussions on terms which they would regard as favourable. This in turn conditions trade union attitudes toward industrial policy. Because trade unions typically lack sufficient market or political power to determine the content of industrial policies, some unions may prefer not to participate lest they compromise their positions or be seen to endorse policies which their members reject.

Before we proceed, a number of remarks about our approach are in order. First, the paper is a critical review of the literature. With the exception of the discussion of the Netherlands, which draws on original research, the analysis is based on examination of secondary materials. Second, although the focus is unions and industrial policy (which we define as selective or discriminatory aids to industry, such as tariffs or import quotas, subsidies, loans or loan guarantees, tax breaks, procurement policies, support for research and development), the essay draws on literatures on the politics of postwar economic policy, the domestic sources of foreign economic policy, and trade union involvement in politics. There is very little literature which deals directly with trade unions and industrial policies.[1] The literature on trade unions in politics focusses largely on relationships between the unions, business and government. There is considerable emphasis on the participation of trade unions in bipartite and tripartite advisory structures, and the ways in which these affect relationships between unions and their members. However, the emphasis is largely on macroeconomic policy and the circumstances under which trade unions accept wage restraint; there is virtually no mention of industrial policies.[2]

Equally, the literature on industrial policy has little to say about trade unions.[3] Part of the literature is polemical and argues for or against industrial policy as a cure for the ills of different national economies.[4] Another portion is descriptive; it outlines the industrial policies in place in different settings and considers their international ramifications, but tells us little about the politics of industrial policy. Instead, the tendency is to assume that industrial policies result from coalitions, of ailing firms, local representatives, and trade unions, enlisted to bolster demands for subsidies or protection; however, the ways in which such coalitions come together are rarely examined.[5] The remaining literature tells us more about the politics of industrial policy, but says little about trade unions.[6]

In the absence of any detailed literature on trade unions and industrial policy, our analysis must be based on a synthesis of related literatures and an examination of trade unions and economic policy in several countries. We will begin by examining the role of trade unions in postwar economic policy and then consider the extent to which trade unions were involved in or able to influence industrial policy.

Unions and Industrial Policy in the Postwar Period

Trade union participation in postwar economic policies varies considerably. At one extreme, we have countries such as France and Japan, in which trade unions were virtually excluded from policy processes and predominant policy coalitions.[7] At the other, are countries such as the Netherlands, Sweden or Austria, in which trade unions participated extensively in the formulation and implementation of economic policies. In between, we find cases such as Britain, Canada, and the United States. In Britain, trade unions were included to some extent in policy processes, but lacked control over them. In Canada and the United States, trade unions remained outside of policy processes but could exercise influence through lobbying. If we consider the postwar period as a whole, there is relatively little trade union involvement in industrial policy. Among the countries we have mentioned, only France and Japan engaged in regular attempts to intervene selectively in the economy; however, unions were systematically excluded. Elsewhere, once postwar power relationships were clarified, there was relatively little industrial policy on the agenda until the decline of older industries became a problem in the 1960s and 1970s.

The relatively minor role which trade unions played in postwar industrial policies reflects the balance between capital and labour at the end of World War II and the terms of the compromises or settlements which emerged. In most Western European countries, labour movements and parties of the left emerged from the war in a relatively strong position. The postwar strength of the left is best understood against the backdrop of war and depression.

Before the war the prevailing view among politicians, right or left, was that little could be done to regulate the economy or manage the business cycle; except in Sweden, the dominant economic policies in most countries were liberal, and entailed minimal intervention in the economy. After the war this changed: reflecting both the severity of the Depression and the experience of the war, voters gravitated toward the left. At the same time, politicians and bureaucrats realized that levels of unemployment prior to the war were now not only unacceptable, but politically dangerous. Reflecting both the new mood and the shifting political balance, as well as the availability of new techniques — countercyclical policies had seemingly worked in countries as diverse as the United States, Sweden, and Nazi Germany — policy makers committed themselves to ongoing intervention in order to ensure full employment and minimal levels of welfare (Salvati and Brosio, 1979; Gourevitch, 1984; Apple, 1980).

The new commitments did not dictate either the form or extent of intervention, or the shape of postwar economies. Immediately following the war, parties of the left such as the British Labour party hoped to use their increased strength in order to implement sweeping changes, including the nationalization of the means of production. Other socialist parties hoped to do the same, or at least to introduce more extensive planning. In contrast to attitudes in the 1950s, there was little faith in the ability of capitalist economies to provide the jobs or the minimum levels of welfare which policy makers now deemed essential (Bornstein, 1984; Gourevitch et al., 1984).

The initial impetus toward nationalization and planning did not have the impact that many expected. Although many parties of the left were in power in the immediate postwar years, either their support ebbed or else the left divided, denying many parties the strength required to implement the more sweeping elements of their programs. In Britain, the Labour party succeeded in nationalizing many weaker industries, establishing the National Health Service, and broadening the foundations of the welfare state, but lost power in 1951 and did not return to government until 1964. Although the Conservatives accepted all of Labour's nationalizations except for iron and steel, Labour's drive toward socialism was halted.

In Scandinavia, Social Democratic parties were strong enough to extend social welfare measures but were unable to implement planning. In the Netherlands, Socialists' hopes for a democratically planned economy were dashed by their coalition partners. In Germany, Social Democrats were confined to the opposition at the federal level until 1966. In France, deep divisions between the Socialists and the Communists limited the circumstances under which the left could govern and effectively precluded implementation of any program of reform. This meant that the form of postwar intervention was determined either as a result of compromise among several parties or by parties of the centre or the right (Bornstein, 1984; Gourevitch et al., 1984).

International factors also influenced the shape of domestic economies. The outbreak of the cold war led to the Marshall Plan, which provided funds to finance postwar reconstruction and recovery and laid the foundations of a postwar economic order based on free trade and international competition (Maier, 1977). Recovery in turn reduced the need and desire for selective intervention and produced a shift toward macroeconomic management. As recovery proceeded, and countries approached full employment, policy makers settled on demand management and counter-cyclical policies as their principal tools for managing the economy. Sustained growth and the postwar economic miracle further reduced interest in selective measures (Gourevitch et al., 1984).

With the exception of France and Japan, the predominant policy coalitions did not exclude labour, but rather limited the terms of its participation. In France and Japan, policy coalitions reflected alliances among the state bureaucracy, large industries, and agriculture (Zysman, 1983). Elsewhere, trade unions were integral elements of postwar coalitions, but the terms of the postwar social bargains confined their participation to social policy and the broad outlines of economic policy. Investment decisions were the prerogative of capital.

For their part, unions were expected to support government policy, maintain labour peace, and, in some countries, participate in incomes policies intended to facilitate economic management and ensure the profitability of investments. In exchange, unions gained full employment, expanded social welfare, and a voice in some government policies (Salvati and Brosio, 1979; Apple, 1980; Gourevitch et al., 1984). However, except in circumstances in which either capital or the state had reasons to include trade unions, this rarely extended to industrial policy. We can explore this by examining the way in which the postwar bargain unfolded in different countries. France, the Netherlands, Sweden, and Britain are relevant for our discussion.

France: Dirigisme *without Trade Unions*

France, along with Japan, stands out not only for the exclusion of trade unions from predominant policy coalitions, but also for its regular recourse to selective industrial policies. Following World War II, France established a small but strategically located planning apparatus, the Commissariat du plan, in the upper echelons of the bureaucracy. By drawing on connections within the bureaucracy, as well as ties to leading firms, French planners were able to set interrelated targets for economic growth, and orchestrated incentives, such as tax relief plus financial support, that encouraged compliance with goals laid out in the plan (Zysman, 1983). The character of French planning has changed over time. Earlier plans concentrated on building the infrastructure required for a modern industrial economy. Later, the focus shifted to building internationally competitive firms. Under Giscard d'Estaing, the emphasis was on allowing the market to guide investment decisions (Estrin and Holmes, 1983). Successive plans have become less comprehensive. However, French planning and French industrial policies have retained a *dirigiste* character even when the central thrust was supposed to have been to allow the market to run its course; policy makers typically prefer intervening in support of selected firms rather than by more general aids to industry (Green, 1983). A second element of consistency has been the role of trade unions; they have barely been involved.

The negligible role of trade unions in French planning and industrial policy reflects the ideological divisions of French politics and the distance between interest groups and the French state. Although French trade unions initially supported the Plan, and tripartite consultative structures complemented the activities of the Planning Commission, French planning developed as an alliance between planners and business (Zysman, 1983). Trade unions have been at best minor participants in the Plan's Modernization Commissions (Cohen, 1977). This reflected the ideological posture of the French trade unions: neither the Communist CGT nor the Christian Democratic CFTD wanted to endorse the existing system by participating in the planning process (Cohen, 1977). Nor was their participation desired. French policy makers have frequently scorned interest groups of all stripes, preferring instead to shape policy without the interference of partial interests. This has been particularly true of the planning process: rather than consulting with the Patronat (the employers' association) planners preferred dealing with selected firms (Shonfeld, 1965). The virtual exclusion of unions under the Fourth Republic continued under the Fifth. Governments of the right, in power from 1958 to 1981, had little inclination to include trade unions in national policy processes or industrial policy decisions. Thus, restructuring in sectors such as textiles or steel has taken place without active union participation; in their comparison of the French and Canadian textile industries, Mahon and Mytelka (1983) report that trade unions played a negligible role in the reorganization of the French industry.[8]

The Netherlands: Incomes Policies as a Substitute for Industrial Policy?

In contrast to France, trade unions in the Netherlands are closely incorporated into policy making. The position of trade unions reflects the terms of a wartime bargain between capital and labour, in which both agreed to cooperate in impending reconstruction, the resolution of interwar debates, and the requirements of the policies pursued. Reflecting the openness of the Dutch economy, there have been few attempts to shelter industries from foreign competition; instead, the emphasis has been on building industries which could compete in world markets. Dutch policy makers combined counter-cyclical policies with incomes policies. Recourse to incomes policies meant involving trade unions. Although this gave unions voice in the economic and social policies, trade unions have been less directly involved in industrial policy. This reflects the terms of the wartime settlement: unions gave up claims to co-determination, leaving control of investment in private hands (de Hen, 1980; Windmuller, 1969).

Postwar economic policies in the Netherlands stem from interwar debates on the need for industrial policies and the desire of two major political groupings, Catholics and Socialists, to establish differing forms of "public industrial organization" (tripartite regulatory boards) in order to govern different sectors of the economy. Following the war, the Socialists and Catholics came to power in a series of "Red-Roman" coalitions which governed until 1958. Initially, Socialists hoped to use the proposed system of tripartite regulatory boards, capped by economic and social councils, as devices for planning and regulating the economy. However, Socialist designs were blocked by the Catholic party. Although the Catholics also favoured public industrial organization, they rejected more *dirigiste* schemes and insisted on the creation of regulatory boards from the bottom up, i.e., by agreement among the trade unions and employers' associations in each sector. Reflecting their electoral strength and pivotal position, the Catholics gained control of the Ministry of Economic Affairs in 1946. This permitted them to shape both the system of public industrial organization that was finally created in 1950 and postwar economic and industrial policies in effect during the 1950s (de Hen, 1980; Wolinetz, 1983a).

The 1950 Law on Public Industrial Organization established the Social and Economic Council (SER) as a tripartite body, with equal representation from trade union federations, employers' associations, and Crown members, appointed by, but independent of, the government. The Social and Economic Council was to serve both as an official advisory organ to the cabinet and as the capstone of a system of sectoral regulatory bodies to be established on the request of trade unions and business associations active within a given sector. In practice, however, sectoral boards were created only in the weaker sectors of the economy, and the advisory role of the SER proved to be far more important than its regulatory role. The former gave trade union federations a voice in social and economic policies, but not in the regulation of individual sectors of the Dutch economy (Windmuller, 1969; Wolinetz, 1983a).

At the same time, the Catholic party used its control of the economics ministry to carry out the active industrial strategies advocated in the 1930s. These involved promotion of industry, financial facilities, subsidies, and encouraging industries to locate where jobs were needed (de Hen, 1980), supplemented by regular recourse to incomes policies. Incomes policies were jointly administered by the Foundation of Labour, a bipartite structure created by trade union federations and employers' associations during World War II, and the Board of Government Mediators, which had been granted special powers to regulate labour relations under a 1945 emergency decree. Incomes policies were an important instrument among a battery of tools designed to achieve economic growth, full employment, price stability, and a favourable balance of payments. By holding wages to the bare minimum, policy makers hoped to marshall the resources needed for the reconstruction of basic industries (de Vries, 1978). Later, incomes policies became a device for providing Dutch industries with a competitive edge. By restraining wages, policy makers established the Netherlands as a "cheap island" among more expensive producers. This facilitated exports and created an attractive climate for investment (Windmuller, 1969; Wolinetz, 1983b).

Implementation of incomes policies required the consent of the Dutch trade union movement. This was obtained by incorporating the unions into the policy process. Trade union federations participated in the bipartite, "privately" established Foundation of Labour, which advised the government and worked with the Board of Government Mediators in the determination and administration of incomes policies. As a result, national trade union federations were involved in both the determination of wage guidelines and the review of collective agreements to ensure conformity with national wage policies (Windmuller, 1969). Although the Social and Economic Council superseded the Foundation of Labour in its advisory role in 1950, the trade union federations continued to be heard through the Council, and the Foundation continued to be involved in wage policies. Guided incomes policies, which held wage increases to the cost of living through 1956, continued well into the 1960s. However, labour market pressures made the maintenance of incomes policies increasingly difficult (Windmuller, 1969).

Thus far, we have traced what was in practice an indirect role for Dutch trade unions in support of industrial policies. In the aftermath of war, when the need for cooperation in the reconstruction of the economy was apparent, trade unions were willing to accept wage restraint. Co-operation continued despite initial disappointments because the trade union movement gained a voice in government policy, the expansion and elaboration of the welfare state (actively promoted by the postwar centre-left cabinets) and, for a time, full employment. Following the postwar reconstruction, the Ministry of Economic Affairs retreated from "active" to more "passive" industrial strategies (de Hen, 1980). However, since the mid-1960s, the decline of older industries has resulted in renewed recourse to industrial policies.

More recent developments in the Netherlands reflect earlier policies. Postwar policies restrained wages in order to provide jobs for a growing population. However, by the mid-1950s, the Dutch were approaching full employment. This made it difficult to contain wage drift or maintain incomes policies. In the early 1960s, wages shot up. "Black wages," which were supplementary payments offered by employers in order to attract labour, were widespread and there was considerable unrest at the base. Trade union federations, increasingly annoyed by requests for continued wage restraint, raised their demands in order to maintain control of their followers. Labour market pressures forced employers' associations to accede, resulting in a series of wage explosions in 1963, 1964, and 1965 (Windmuller, 1969; van Doorn et al., 1976). This increased the cost of labour and altered incentives to invest. Prior to the wage explosion, relatively inexpensive labour costs had encouraged invest-ment in labour-intensive industries; afterward investments tended to be more capital-intensive (van Doorn et al., 1976).

Changes in labour costs coincided with shifts in the international economy. Industries such as textiles, clothing, and shipbuilding were increasingly threatened by foreign competition. Both the openness of the economy and membership in the European Economic Community (EEC) precluded recourse to protection. Instead, the government offered subsidies in order to maintain employment and sponsored restructuring programs designed to restore competitiveness (Langdon, 1980). Commissions appointed to oversee restructuring plans typically included representatives of both firms and trade unions. In addition, a number of the restructuring plans were brought under the aegis of a special restructuring agency, the Netherlands Restructuring Company (NEHEM), which included representatives of unions and management on its governing board and sectoral committees (Wassenberg, 1982). Although the trade unions found their participation in such commissions a source of frustration, and eventually withdrew from both the NEHEM and a number of sectoral commissions, evidence derived from investigations carried out by Stephen Langdon (1980; 1981) indicates that the trade unions were able to exert considerable influence in the reorganization of the Dutch textile industry in the 1970s.

Langdon's work, part of a larger study on industrial change and cooperation between first and third world countries, shows that the Federation of Dutch Trade Unions (FNV) and particularly its largest affiliate, the Industriebond or Industrial Union, played an important role in the reorganization of the cotton-spinning industry, the restructuring of textile finishing, and in preventing the shutdown of ENKA-Breda, which dominated the synthetic fibre market in the Netherlands.

In the cotton-spinning industry, the threatened closure of a large non-integrated producer precipitated government involvement which resulted in the reorganization of the industry in 1974 and 1975 under a single firm, Spinnerij Nederland. Representatives of trade unions, employers' associations and the government participated in a restructuring commission which devised a plan for the reorganization and modernization of production. Trade union representatives were instrumental in securing special "transfer list" provisions for workers who were laid off. These required the new company to pay redundant workers full wages for one year, provided that they sought work or underwent retraining, and also included special retirement benefits for workers 57.5 years or older. Government representatives initially rejected those provisions but later acceded because the 1,700 to 1,800 jobs affected were in a single area, Drente, where the principal industry was textiles. Union demands were reinforced both by shopfloor reactions and the possibility that union representatives might withdraw from the restructuring commission; this had already occurred in a number of other industries. The government in office at the time, a Socialist-led centre-left cabinet, was also sympathetic to the unions and anxious to preserve employment (Langdon, 1980, pp. 32–39).

In a second instance, the reorganization of synthetic fibre production, AKZO, a subsidiary of the multinational ENKA, announced the closure of its Breda plant. In August 1972, workers occupied the plant. The firm withdrew its plan and worked out a new scheme in conjunction with the employee council. This reorganized production in the Netherlands and Germany, spreading the impact more widely than the original company plan. Government support for the workers was a factor in the withdrawal of the initial plan. The decision to involve the employee council thus provided an opening for the firm's workers and the trade unions (Langdon, 1980, pp. 46–52).

In a third case, cotton weaving and finishing, trade unions and factory councils were involved in reductions in capacity. Although neither the government or union roles, nor the reorganization, were as extensive as in cotton spinning, the unions were able to secure special transfer list provisions. In this instance, however, the firms affected were not concentrated in a single region, and each firm's employee councils had to approve, and not merely consider, reorganization plans. Although the government initially resisted the extension of the transfer list provisions, both a large demonstration in The Hague and the desire to maintain the cooperation of the trade unions tipped the balance toward the trade unions (Langdon, 1980, pp. 40–45). However, this victory was only temporary: finishing and weaving firms were slow to carry out planned reductions in capacity. In 1980, this resulted in the failure of several firms, and layoffs in both the weaving and finishing industry and in the spinning industry. By this time a centre-right cabinet, opposed to selective aid, was in office, and the government refused to aid the firms or finance special transfer list provisions for redundant workers. As a result, the unions withdrew from the sectoral commission and began advocating protection (Langdon, 1981, pp. 773–75).

Although recourse to tripartism involved Dutch trade unions in restructuring, trade unions found their participation to be a frustrating experience. Although in some instances the unions were able to ensure that displaced workers were offered alternative employment or other compensation, in other instances the unions were unable to prevent layoffs. Participation in NEHEM (Netherlands Restructuring Company) was equally problematic, because the Ministry of Economic Affairs was reluctant to grant NEHEM much autonomy, and, because firms were frequently reluctant to share information with each other, NEHEM's sectoral committees frequently bogged down (Wassenberg, 1982; Wolinetz, 1983a). By the late 1970s, trade unions had withdrawn from a number of commissions. Difficulties in sectoral commissions paralleled developments at the national level: trade union federations and employers' associations found it impossible to agree on central wage bargains in the Foundation of Labour, and growing disagreements reduced the prestige and influence of the Social and Economic Council (Wolinetz, 1983a).

Both the difficulties of NEHEM and the overall experience of restructuring in the 1970s have coloured trade union attitudes toward recent debate on industrial policy in the Netherlands. In 1980, the Netherlands Scientific Council for Government Policy issued a report on the future of Dutch industry which highlighted declining industrial employment in the Netherlands, stressed the impact of product cycles, and urged greater government involvement in industrial policy, in particular in the promotion of research and development and innovation. The vehicle for this was to be an expert commission, without representatives from either labour or management. The Scientific Council report led to the appointment of a top-level commission, the Advisory Commission on Industrial Policy under G. Wagner, a former managing director of Royal Dutch Shell, to make recommendations on industrial policy. This commission did, however, have indirect representation (i.e., representation by trusted individuals, but acting in their own right rather than as the representatives of specific organizations) from unions and employers. The trade union movement monitored the activities of the Wagner commission and of its successor, the Advisory Commission on the Progress of Industrial Policy (also headed by G. Wagner), but expressed little interest in *direct* involvement in the determination of the proposed industrial policy. This was particularly evident in the Social and Economic Council's report on the Scientific Council's proposal. Although the trade union federations and employers' associations wanted to be informed of developments, neither side relished direct involvement or responsibility for industrial policy (Wolinetz, 1983a).

The posture of the trade unions reflects both the direction of the Wagner commissions and the risk of being too closely involved in industrial restructuring. In contrast to the Scientific Council's report, the recommendations of the first Wagner commission emphasized the necessity of positive adjustment and freeing up market forces, stressed the importance of developing a new industrial élan, and recommended the establishment of a fund to finance innovative projects (Netherlands, 1981). In a later report, the follow-up commission argued for the de-indexation of wages and complete government withdrawal from wage regulation (Netherlands, 1982). Because the emphasis is on market-led recovery, facilitated in part by limiting wage increases, there are few immediate or obvious benefits which trade unions can win for their members. Being involved in restructuring entails similar risks, because it usually involves layoffs. Although trade union officials may regard such layoffs as necessary, they are reluctant to be seen to be sanctioning reductions in employment without securing something in exchange: job preservation agreements, which trade unions have tried to secure through collective bargaining, or a voice in firms' investment and disinvestment decisions. However, employers have refused to concede either of these.

In the Dutch case, positions on industrial policy reflect the unravelling of the postwar social contract. Earlier postwar policies reflected a community of interest among employers and trade unions which is no longer present. Unions are reluctant to trust employers to invest in ways which would create jobs and desire greater control over firms. However, trade unions are in no position to enforce their will; it is difficult to organize workers to strike in order to preserve or expand employment when doing so might put their own jobs at risk. Nor do unions have the political power to enforce a different set of policies; parties of the left are too weak and divided and, even if they were stronger, it would be difficult to implement alternative industrial policies without the consent of business.

Sweden: Labour Market Policies and Industrial Policy

Sweden is a second example of a country in which the trade union movement has been incorporated closely into policy processes. As in the Netherlands, the government relied heavily on macroeconomic management and consensual wage regulation, but resorted to selective measures when confronted with industrial decline. Nevertheless, there are important differences. In the Netherlands, the socialist trade union federation, the NVV, and the party to which it was allied, the Labour party (PvdA), shared power with religiously based parties and trade union federations; as a result, both were forced to compromise on a number of issues. In Sweden, the Social Democratic party and the national trade union federation, the LO, did not face similar competition for the allegiance of the working class. Although it lacked a majority, the Swedish party was in a stronger position to place its stamp on policy.

The greater strength of the left in Sweden is reflected in the terms of the social bargain, and in postwar wage policies. Reflecting the limits of the Socialists' power in Sweden, the major policy innovations under the Socialists involved neither socialization of wealth nor planning, but rather the expansion and elaboration of social welfare policies, carefully orchestrated counter-cyclical policies, and "solidaristic" wage policies that forced wages up (Martin, 1979; 1984). Solidaristic wage policies were the LO's answer to the need for wage restraint in order to maintain international competitiveness: rather than endorsing wage restraint as a device for providing jobs, the LO developed its own version, the Rehn model (after the LO's chief economist), which insisted on uniformly high wages in all sectors of the economy. This squeezed weaker firms and encouraged the shift of resources into areas in which larger profits could be expected. Shifts in investment were in accord with the LO design: higher wages could be extracted from more productive industries. The government eased the resulting dislocation with active labour market policies designed to retrain workers. Manpower programs were supplemented by counter-cyclical measures (Martin, 1979; 1981; 1984; Esping-Andersen and Friedland, 1982).

The Swedish case reflects the policies of a strong, cohesive labour movement working through a dominant, kindred party and involves an indirect industrial policy administered through centralized wage bargaining. Neither the LO nor the Social Democrats were strong enough to socialize major industries; instead, the party and trade union federations worked within the capitalist system, and tried to shape it to their advantage. This was done as part of a social contract in which the Socialist government left capital to its own devices but, at the same time, implemented policies which effectively restructured the economy by encouraging investments which would provide workers with better-paying and more productive jobs. The specific content of investments remained in private hands; however, incomes policies and counter-cyclical policies influenced the thrust and timing of private investments (Martin, 1981, 1984; Pontusson, 1984). Individual workers were disrupted in the process, but the centralization of the trade union movement insulated leaders from rank and file pressures.

Swedish policies shifted in the 1960s and 1970s. In the early 1960s, the LO began to raise questions about the extent to which existing labour market policies could cushion workers from the impact of structural or technological change. Although there was no change in the LO's commitment to structural change, LO reports stressed the need for more "active" and "coordinated" industrial policies (Martin, 1984). In 1967, the ruling Social Democrats, smarting from losses in 1966 municipal elections, took up the theme and called for an "offensive industrial policy." By 1973, a number of instruments for selective intervention and support were in place: these included a state investment bank, a state holding company and a board charged with fostering technological development (Lundmark, 1983; Pontusson, 1984). The Social Democrats' original intent was to promote innovation. However, particularly under the bourgeois (i.e., non-Socialist) coalition which assumed office in 1976, rescues and bailouts predominated. By the late 1970s, older sectors such as textiles, glass, timber, steel, and shipbuilding were receiving assistance (Lundmark, 1983; Pontusson, 1984).

As in the Netherlands, trade unions played a role. In his examination of Swedish responses to crises, Lundmark describes government intervention in shipbuilding. This began in 1974, when credits were granted for expansion. In 1975, the impending failure of a Gothenberg shipyard forced deeper involvement. In order to prevent the bankruptcy, the government took over the yard. The Gothenberg yard was then merged with a second yard, with the government retaining a 50 percent share. Further crises led to the incorporation of other yards and the establishment of Swedyard as a publicly owned corporation. However, structural difficulties continued, forcing the government and Swedyard to consider reductions in capacity. Uncertain parliamentary support in 1978 and 1979 (a minority Liberal coalition was now in office) delayed the implementation of plans to close two shipyards, as well as a compromise plan which would have spread the impact over a larger number of yards (Lundmark, 1983, pp. 232–36).

Trade unions were involved in a number of phases in this process. According to Lundmark, the 1975 takeover of the Gothenberg yard resulted in part from trade union criticisms of the shipyard management. Representatives of the metalworkers participated in a ministerial commission, a royal commission and, after the change of government, a ministerial task force dealing with the troubles of the industry. The trade unions also enjoyed statutory representation on firms' boards of directors, and could also make their views known in parliament (which in this case was the final arbiter) through their ties with the Social Democratic party. These diverse channels of access allowed unions to follow developments and oppose less desirable restructuring schemes (Lundmark, 1983). However, it is difficult to assess how much influence this gave the LO or the metalworkers' union; divisions in the bourgeois coalition increased the leverage of the opposition Social Democrats. Moreover, although Lundmark's sketch suggests that the unions were influential, he asserts that the principal decisions were made by management and the government (Lundmark, pp. 253–37, 241) and notes that the unions "complained that the crisis measures were *fait accompli*" (p. 237). Similarly, Pontusson argues that the trade unions' role in restructuring was marginal:

> In general, industrial policy-making has pivoted on direct state-business relations, and by-passed corporatist structures of interest mediation. The tripartite sector councils set up in the late 1960's evolved into discussion clubs, without any real policy-making functions. . . . The most important industrial policy measures have been formulated and administered directly by the Ministry of Industry. The terms of state aid to industry have been worked out through negotiations between policy makers and corporate management. *To the extent that labor has at all participated in such negotiations, it has been represented by local unions, which have typically assumed the role of lobbying for their firms.* (Pontusson, 1984, pp. 13–14, emphasis added)

Pontusson's comments are of particular interest because they suggest that, as in the Dutch case, the presence of trade unions does not guarantee that they will be influential, and that industrial policy may divide local unions and national organizations.

Although market failures and the need for restructuring projected Swedish unions into sectoral discussions, aid for declining industries is not the main focus of LO views on industrial policy. The rescues and bailouts of the late 1970s reflected the actions of a narrowly based right-wing coalition anxious not to associate itself with unemployment (Lundmark, 1983; Pontusson, 1984). Selective aid conflicts with the view that industries should adapt to the market and opens the possibility of conflicts between the LO and local or sectoral unions — something which the LO has striven to avoid (Martin, 1984). LO thinking moved in a different direction and began to address problems of industrial democracy and sources of investment. Previous policies had assumed that investments would come largely from the private sector. However, solidaristic wage policies had encouraged not only the ongoing modernization of Swedish industry, but also concentration of ownership (Esping-Andersen, 1981). This led to growing concern with the sources of investment. As Andrew Martin points out, the question of whether investments were to come from the private or public sector remained unresolved in the Rehn model. In the 1960s, consideration was given to using pension funds for this purpose, in effect using the funds as an instrument of industrial policy, but this idea was not fully developed until the 1970s, when the LO introduced the Meidner Plan, which proposed to transfer shares of firms' profits into union-controlled wage-earner funds. These funds would have voting shares in firms and, over time, gain control over Swedish industry (Martin, 1981; 1984).

In its original form, the Meidner Plan represented a device to ensure investments and gain greater ownership and control over firms. Establishing the proposed wage-earner funds would provide a basis for ensuring public investment without necessarily provoking a flight of capital. In addition, it would also provide a rationale for accepting wage restraint in order to facilitate investment, without the benefits automatically accruing to capital (Esping-Andersen, 1981). However, the plan, as proposed, was not necessarily an instrument of industrial policy in the sense of providing selective aids to industry; what it would have done was provide a means for ensuring that some of the benefits of successful industrial policies accrued to workers and their unions (Martin and Ross, 1980). This could provide a basis for union participation in industrial policies even if these policies resulted in net losses of jobs. However, precisely because the Meidner Plan would have transferred control over investment to unions, employers and the bourgeois parties opposed it. The compromise version which has been passed greatly dilutes the potential for union control (Martin, 1984; Bornstein, 1984).

Britain: Trade Unions at Arm's Length

The case in Britain is both similar to and different from that in the Netherlands and Sweden. Britain emerged from World War II with widely shared commitments to full employment and the expansion and elaboration of the welfare state in order to ensure minimal levels of subsistence. It adopted Keynesian techniques in order to manage the economy. Over time, as the British were confronted with the decline of major firms and industries, selective intervention became more and more prominent. However, trade union involvement in industrial policies has been far less extensive than one might imagine, particularly when one considers the purported strength of the British trade union movement and its connections with the Labour party.

In order to understand the lack of trade union involvement in British industrial policy, it is useful to examine the evolution of postwar economic policy. Britain emerged from World War II with a strong trade union movement and a Labour government. After a brief period in which the Labour party nationalized certain industries and attempted to plan the economy, the British settled on macroeconomic management as the best means to guide the economy and ensure full employment. However, there was a continuing tension between the Treasury's attempts to manage the domestic economy and the role of the pound sterling as a reserve currency. Maintaining the value of the pound worked to the advantage of British finance capital, which invested heavily overseas, but complicated the Treasury's attempts to manage the economy. Expansive policies invariably led to a surge of imports that produced balance of payments deficits, requiring restrictive measures to ease pressures on the currency. In turn, restrictive measures led to increased unemployment and pressures for expansion (Blank, 1977). Successive rounds of "stop and go" led to a search for alternative solutions. In the 1960s, Conservative and Labour governments attempted to enlist trade unions and employers' associations in a program of national economic planning. In 1962, the Conservatives established the National Economic Development Committee (NEDC), a tripartite structure with equivalent sectoral Economic Development Committees (EDCs or "Little Neddies"), and an autonomous planning structure, the National Economic Development Office (NEDO). The Conservatives' planning exercise was barely underway when Labour returned to power in 1964. In order to give greater political direction to the process, the Labour government brought the NEDO under the control of the newly established Department of Economic Affairs (Shonfeld, 1965; Leruez, 1975). Nevertheless, the exercise was anything but a success. Neither the NEDC nor its sectoral counterparts proved able to give direction to individual firms. Nor did Labour pursue the expansive policies which would have added impetus to the plan. Instead, targets were ignored and economic planning, like much of Labour's 1964 and 1966 programs, was impaled by the refusal of the Wilson government to devalue the pound until 1966. This meant that economic policies remained caught in the pattern of stop and go which planning was supposed to end (Lereuz, 1975; Blank, 1977; Hall, 1984).

The planning experiments of the mid-1960s were superseded by controversial attempts on the part of both parties to regulate trade unions in order to reduce strike rates, and by increased recourse to selective industrial policy. Impetus for selective measures came in part from the desire to modernize Britain's aging industrial base and in part from the need to rescue firms in order to maintain employment. Selective measures, which dated back to the 1950s, when the government promoted reorganization of textile mills, increased under the Labour government in the late 1960s. In office from 1970 to 1974, the Conservatives, led by Edward Heath, initially rejected selective aids, but found themselves compelled to make a U-turn in 1972 in order to rescue Rolls-Royce from bankruptcy. The 1972 Industry Act expanded existing regional assistance programs and permitted extensive assistance to firms outside of assisted regions as well. The Labour party returned to power in 1974 even more firmly committed to the use of selective industrial policy. The 1975 Industry Act augmented the 1972 law by establishing the National Enterprise Board (NEB) as a holding company for state-owned enterprises and providing for the conclusion of planning agreements as a condition of assistance. The act also enabled the government to require firms to disclose information; however, only one planning agreement was concluded (with Chrysler), and the latter provision was never implemented (Grant, 1982).

The intent of the industrial policies of the 1970s was to promote the development of new industries and facilitate the modernization of older ones. However, practice diverged from intent. Rescue operations predominated. The National Enterprise Board, charged with the promotion and sponsorship of new industries, actively promoted the development of high-technology industries; however, it was also saddled with a number of the lame ducks, such as Rolls-Royce and British Leyland, which the government felt compelled to sustain. The net effect was to expand the government's portfolio of both profitable and declining industries. The Conservative government, led by Margaret Thatcher, has since reversed this trend by selling off more profitable firms, limiting the NEB's ability to borrow funds and, in general, replacing selective measures with market-oriented policies (Grant, 1982).

Thus far, we have said relatively little about trade union support of or participation in industrial or economic policies. Trade union involvement must be considered both in terms of formal modes of access (the ways in which unions are plugged into the political system) and in terms of trade union participation in policy coalitions and the postwar social bargain. The former are well known. Trade unions in Britain are connected to the system through their affiliation with the Labour party, through direct consultation with politicians or bureaucrats, through participation in tripartite structures such as the NEDC and its economic development committees, and, more recently, the sectoral working parties established under the 1975 Industry Act. Close contact, however, does not necessarily mean influence; although British trade unions have been involved in economic and industrial policies, rarely have they been able to shape policies to their taste.

Neither their connections with the Labour party nor their participation in tripartite structures grant the trade unions or the Trades Union Congress (TUC) control over party or government policies. Ties between the unions and the Labour party are frequently strained, and tripartite structures in Britain are weaker than in other countries. Although trade unions control a preponderant proportion of the votes in the Labour party's annual conference, the unions are rarely sufficiently unified to dictate policy to the party. Except on matters directly affecting them, the party leadership acts independently of the trade unions. Close ties permit trade union leaders to influence politicians, but these same links can be used to persuade trade union leaders to endorse government policies. This has been especially true when Labour is in power: confronted with the tasks of ensuring profits in a mixed economy, Labour governments have frequently requested trade unions to accept voluntary wage restraint (Panitch, 1977a). When this has occurred, the unions have usually acceded to the government's request. However, as Panitch points out, this has typically resulted in increased militancy at the base and the eventual collapse of incomes policies. As a result, trade union influence is problematic. When the Labour party is in opposition and party leaders feel that it is desirable to move closer to the unions, union influence can be considerable; this was the case in the early 1970s, following a major disagreement over Labour's attempt to regulate the trade unions in 1969. However, as the experience of the late 1970s illustrates, this can be reversed when Labour is in power.

Labour governments have been equally independent on matters of industrial policy and the management of nationalized industries. In Labour party and Trades Union Congress doctrine, the nationalization of industry has been regarded as the principal tool for asserting public control over the economy. However, the nationalization of industry has rarely been used as a device for asserting greater trade union or worker control over industry (Bornstein and Gourevitch, 1984). Although trade unionists have occasionally held seats on the boards of nationalized firms, the predominant pattern has been to establish public corporations with autonomous managements and no co-determination or worker control. Nor were trade unions granted anything more than a minor role in the operation of the industrial policy instruments established in the 1970s: although trade unionists were represented on both the National Enterprise Board and the sectoral working parties (SWPs) which operated under the aegis of the National Economic Development Council, trade unions had little direct influence over industrial policy.[9] As a result, with the exception of changes in work rules negotiated during collective bargaining, trade unions have had little voice in structural policy or investment decisions.

The absence of trade union influence reflects both Labour party predilections and trade union priorities. In the immediate postwar period, the Trades Union Congress regarded public ownership not as a device for changing the economic system but rather as a means of ensuring full employment and a more equitable distribution of wealth; when Keynesianism proved to be an adequate substitute, interest in nationalization faded (Bornstein and Gourevitch, 1984). Later, in the 1970s, when the crises of the British economy were more apparent, the TUC stressed planning and nationalization as steps toward socialism, and argued for a greater role for unions in economic decision making. However, public control was not seen as means for implementing structural policies, and neither planning, nor nationalization, nor trade union participation was given priority (Bornstein and Gourevitch, 1984). Labour party and TUC priorities are amply demonstrated by the 1975 Social Contract, negotiated by the Wilson government and the TUC. In addition to promising repeal of the Conservatives' Industrial Relations Act and enjoining Labour to forswear statutory incomes policies, the Social Contract was to have given trade unions a voice in economic planning and industrial policy decisions. However, tensions resulting from three years of wage restraint, which the Social Contract forbade, wrecked the agreement well before these provisions could be implemented (Bornstein, 1984; Bornstein and Gourevitch, 1984).

Tripartite relationships are equally problematic. Tripartite arrangements work best where all relevant interests are represented and able to make decisions which bind themselves and the other parties. Britain's experiment in tripartism, the National Economic Development Council, was flawed in several ways. First, NEDC decisions were not binding on unions, business and government, which meant that there was no way of implementing them (Shonfeld, 1965; Hall, 1984). Second, although tripartism was intended as a device to reconcile and harmonize the interests of labour and capital, the NEDC was not fully representative of British capital. In contrast to other countries we have been discussing, there is a major division in Britain between finance and industrial capital (Longstreth, 1979). British finance capital is internationally oriented. In contrast, British industrial interests are domestically oriented. Although banks provide long-term finances, firms raise investment capital on the stock market or, more typically, out of profits (Zysman, 1983). British industrial interests, organized in the Confederation of British Industries (CBI), were represented in the NEDC, along with the TUC. However, finance capital, in many respects the stronger interest, was not present. In the absence of finance capital, it would have been difficult for industrial interests to complete their side of any bargains struck with labour (Hall, 1984).

Our analysis suggests that British trade unions have had little direct influence over industrial policy decisions. Nevertheless, it would be a mistake to think that the trade unions or workers were entirely absent from such decisions. Although the available evidence is limited, workers and their unions have been active in pressing for the rescue of declining firms. A shop stewards' inquiry into the failure of the trade union movement to secure greater control over industrial policy, *State Intervention in Industry: A Workers' Inquiry* (Newcastle Trades Council, 1980), indicates that shop stewards pressed for intervention in a number of instances. These include demands for the nationalization of Tyneside, Merseyside, and Swan Harbour shipyards, the development of alternative proposals for Lucas Aerospace, and the formation of a nationwide shop stewards' coalition, the Power Engineering Industry Trade Union Commission (PEITUC), which lobbied the government for the assignment of contracts for new electricity generating equipment to Parsons and other power engineering firms in a way which would preserve employment. The report also indicates considerable division between shop stewards and trade unions, and is critical of the trade unions for ignoring shop stewards' proposals and not pressing their demands on the Labour party (Newcastle Trades Council, 1980). In a somewhat different vein, Brian Hogwood's study of the takeover of the British shipbuilding industry (1979) indicates the existence of pressures from the unions to avoid redundancies as well as considerable disagreement among the many craft-based unions operating in the industry; these typically involved demarcation disputes, layoffs, and the reorganization of work. Ovenden's study of the nationalization of the steel industry (1978) documents similar rivalries among trade unions operating in that industry and argues that the positions of the two largest unions, the British Iron, Steel, and Kindred Trades Association (BISAKTA) and the National Union of Blast Furnacemen (NUB), on both nationalization and workers' control were largely reactive. Impetus for nationalization came largely from the Labour party, while proposals for workers' control came from the National Craftsmen's Coordinating Committee (NCCC), a coalition of smaller unions operating in the industry (Ovenden, 1978).

These diverse cases suggest trade unions lack any sustained influence in British industrial policy. Although unions are a factor which policy makers are likely to take account of in their decisions, a variety of circumstances limit trade union influence. In addition to relations with the Labour party and the limits of tripartite institutions, the highly decentralized structure of the British trade union movement is a further obstacle. The Trades Union Congress has little control over affiliated unions and the prevalence of craft organizations means that there are invariably a large number of unions operating in any one firm or industry. Rivalries among unions make it difficult to reach agreement on common positions, other than the defence of existing jobs, a position which British unions frequently take. Deeper involvement would put the movement at risk. The TUC's problem is aptly summed up by A.G. Jordan's comments on trade union participation in the planning agreements espoused by the Labour party in the mid-1970s. Two such agreements were signed, one with Chrysler and one with the National Coal Board. Paraphrasing Gerald Kaufman (1980), a minister in the Department of Industry at the time, Jordan notes that:

> The TUC, asked if unions at the national level would like to be signatories, hastened to decline. The unions realized full well that planning agreements might involve redundancies as part of internal restructuring and to become party to those redundancies would be internally damaging to the unions. (Jordan, 1981, pp. 111–12)

Our analysis shows that British trade unions are not equipped to do much more than react to events and proposals. That, of course, does not mean that the TUC lacks a position on industrial policy. On the contrary. In addition to general commitments to nationalization and economic democracy, the TUC endorses selective import controls to protect British markets from foreign competition, reflationary measures, and withdrawal from the European Economic Community. The trade unions also favour aid to industries, both to rescue firms from collapse and to promote technological innovation; and believe that such aid should be linked to planning agreements that specify the nature of the investment and the impact it would have on labour (Grant, 1982; Evans, 1980; Martin and Ross, 1980). How widely shared such sentiments are and whether they are likely to receive priority are other matters. For the moment, British unions are busy trying to defend previous prerogatives.

We have now considered trade union involvement in diverse settings. The cases we have examined suggest that, for most of the postwar period, there was little *direct* trade union involvement in industrial policy. In France, unions were excluded from policy processes and had no direct impact on industrial policy. In Britain, unions had some impact, but no sustained role in economic or industrial policy. Although we have not yet discussed them, the same could be said of Canada and the United States. Even in countries such as the Netherlands and Sweden, where trade unions were incorporated far more closely into economic policy making, trade unions had little influence over industrial policies. Although, in these instances, unions participated in policy coalitions which promoted economic growth and full employment, the predominant policies were general rather than specific, and unions had no control over investments.

More recent patterns contrast with those of earlier years. In the United States and Canada, trade unions have participated in defensive coalitions seeking protection for ailing industries. In Sweden and the Netherlands, trade unions have been involved in the reorganization of sectors in decline. In the next section, we will explore this in greater detail.

Trade Unions and the Politics of Industrial Decline

The last ten to fifteen years provide fertile ground for exploring trade union involvement in industrial policy. In contrast to the earlier postwar period, changing patterns of international competition, together with growing retrenchment and restructuring in older sectors of the economy, have tempered expectations of unlimited growth and altered the context in which the postwar social bargain operated. Trade unions can no longer be certain that capital will provide investments to generate or sustain employment. Instead, firms in a number of sectors have shifted to more capital-intensive investments, or moved production to cheaper locations, or sought protection, subsidies, or other forms of government assistance. The question we must consider is whether trade unions, which were previously excluded from direct involvement in industrial policy, have been able to use either market power or political power to inject themselves into such decisions and, if they are involved, what role they play.

In our discussions of the Netherlands and Sweden, we noted instances in which trade unions were involved in industrial policy. In this section, we will examine these and other cases in greater detail. In doing so, we will attempt to delineate the circumstances in which trade unions are likely to be involved and the extent to which they are likely to be able to exercise influence over industrial policy decisions. Our cases fall into two distinct patterns. In one, trade unions participated in defensive coalitions which lobbied for protection. In the other, trade unions were involved in the reorganization of declining industries.

The Politics of Defensive Coalitions

The United States

The cases presented in Zysman and Tyson, *American Industry in International Competition* (1983), enable us to examine the politics of protection in several industries. Studies of textiles, steel, and the colour television industry demonstrate several common features. First, the predominant response of U.S. industries that have perceived themselves to be threatened by foreign competition has been to seek exemption from the liberal international order which the United States actively promoted in the postwar era. With the exception of the colour television industry, there were few attempts to move production offshore or to upgrade products or processes in order to retain comparative advantage. Second, coalitions seeking protection have been able to take advantage of the multiple points of access which the American political system provides; the Congress, with its strong local and regional representation, shifting coalitions, and its ability to block or modify federal government proposals, has been a favoured point of access. Third, although trade unions frequently have been enlisted as participants in protective coalitions, there is little evidence that trade unions have either initiated the process or been able to define the terms of the discussion. Instead, trade unions join employers in an uneasy coalition in order to preserve jobs.

The efforts by the textile and apparel industries to obtain protection from foreign competition (Aggarwal and Haggard, 1983) are typical. Postwar battles to secure protection date back to the liberalization of trade in the 1930s and particularly to the textile industry's response to cotton support programs which increased the cost of cotton fibres. Confronted with higher costs, the industry's principal response was to seek protection against lower-cost Japanese imports. Although different segments of the industry were not affected in the same way, cotton fibre producers were able to recruit woollen and synthetic textile producers, apparel manufacturers, and labour unions into the coalition; other segments of the textile industry were brought along when restraints on cotton imports (principally from Japan) encouraged foreign producers to shift into other fabrics (pp. 252–53, 265ff.). As noted, the more fragmented apparel manufacturers were also enlisted, although many might have benefited from lower cost imports. Labour unions, constantly confronted with the problem of maintaining their strength in an industry that was shifting from unionized to non-unionized locations, were also brought, somewhat reluctantly, into the coalition for protection. Although, in 1958 Senate hearings, the United Textile Workers of America argued that the problems of the industry were domestic and not international, and proposed the creation of a Textile Development Agency (which was to be charged with promoting research and development and the administration of manpower programs including a shorter working week and retraining and retirement programs), the textile unions supported efforts to exempt the textile industry from the 1962 Trade Act (Aggarwal and Haggard, 1983, pp. 266–68). Subsequently, unions took part in the coalitions promoting the Long Term Agreement, the Multi-Fiber Arrangement, and other devices to restrict imports. A similar coalition emerged in the footwear industry. Although initially unsuccessful, in 1977 joint appeals from the AFL-CIO and the American Footwear Industries Association resulted in an orderly marketing agreement restricting imports (Yoffie, 1983, pp. 338–39).

Defensive coalitions also operated in the American steel and colour television industries. Borrus (1983) examines steel industry responses to foreign competition. Rather than rebuilding or modernizing their plants, U.S. producers responded to Japanese product and process innovations by seeking protection in order to preserve their market share. Labour was an integral part of the coalition. In 1967, the United Steelworkers and the steel producers collaborated in a campaign to secure relief from imports. Both lobbied the Congress in order to force the U.S. government to negotiate a voluntary restraint agreement; this was to give the industry time to adapt (p. 84). In 1974, the same coalition was instrumental in the designation of steel as a sector which could be the subject of special discussions during trade negotiations (p. 85). In 1977, following the negotiation of a costly contract and a wave of layoffs and plant closures, demands for protection intensified. Local union leaders and public officials formed the Steel Communities Coalition, and a bipartisan steel caucus emerged in the U.S. Congress. Pressures there resulted in the appointment of the Task Force on Steel, directed by Undersecretary of the Treasury, Anthony Solomon, and charged with the formulation of a comprehensive program for steel (pp. 90–92). Under considerable pressure from the industry, the Solomon task force proposed incentive schemes for modernization; assistance to ease costs of adjustment; a trigger-price mechanism to prevent dumping on U.S. markets; and a tripartite committee to facilitate cooperation among unions, business, and government (pp. 93–96). The Solomon plan recognized the need for restructuring, but left the task to the industry. The larger firms responded by shifting investments from steel to other sectors (pp. 98–99).

In the colour television industry, the way in which the defensive coalition emerged was somewhat different. When Japanese colour television receivers began to capture a larger share of the American market in the late 1960s and the early 1970s, management and unions pursued separate strategies. Firms filed appeals under fair trade legislation, but at the same time began to shift production of components offshore in order to reduce costs. Anxious to preserve jobs, unions petitioned for relief under the 1962 Trade Expansion Act (Millstein, 1983, p. 123). The unions and firms differed on tax treatment for multinationals and the application of tariffs to components and assemblies produced offshore (p. 124). Separate actions and petitions continued until 1975, when unions and firms came together in COMPACT, a coalition of ten AFL-CIO unions and domestic television receiver and components manufacturers seeking restrictions on imports of finished products (p. 128). Further manoeuvres forced the U.S. government to negotiate an orderly marketing agreement with Japan in 1977. This required the Japanese to shift a portion of their final assembly to the United States, but did nothing to prevent American firms from shifting their production offshore (pp. 132–36ff.).

These cases suggest clear limits to the extent of trade union cooperation and influence in defensive coalitions. Essentially, trade unions and firms set aside adversarial relations long enough to petition a third party, the government, for assistance and relief from foreign competition. As Aggarwal and Haggard and other authors in the Zysman and Tyson volume suggest, protection is the "lowest common denominator" on which the trade unions and manufacturing interests can agree. Typically, the firms or business associations involved control the definition of the issues at stake, and there is no thought of involving government or trade unions in management of firms. Instead, both are kept at arm's length and enlisted only when their assistance is explicitly required. Unions may in some instances initiate the process, or lobby separately, but they are unable to impose alternative definitions or solutions.

Canadian Textiles

Although the permeability of the U.S. Congress provides fertile ground for lobbying, defensive coalitions are not confined to the United States. In their study of the textile and clothing industry in Canada and France, Mahon and Mytelka (1983) examine the operation of a similar defensive coalition in Canada. Beginning in the late 1960s, the Canadian Textile Institute enlisted the textile unions and the provinces of Ontario and Quebec in a campaign against low-cost imports. Lobbying efforts resulted in the development of a new textile policy by the newly formed Department of Industry, Trade and Commerce. Launched in 1971, this policy combined import controls with programs designed to encourage adaptation and modernization. In order to secure import quotas, textile firms had to submit adjustment plans to a Textile and Clothing Industry Board. The ensuing review enabled the board to comment on adjustment plans and encourage firms to modernize production and adapt to changing conditions in international trade. However, this involved only firms petitioning for relief and not the industry as a whole. The policy worked more effectively in textiles, where the larger firms adapted, than in the more fragmented clothing sector (pp. 563–71).

Although the policy which emerged in Canada differed somewhat from that which evolved in the United States, the role of trade unions was similar: unions served principally as co-petitioners in defensive coalitions. However, in Canada the industry brief was addressed to the cabinet and the new policy was formulated by a government department concerned with both domestic industry and foreign trade. As Mahon and Mytelka point out, demands for protection pitted the industry and trade branches against each other, and resulted in a policy which combined temporary protective measures with incentives for adjustment.

Trade Unions and Industrial Restructuring

In the course of our examination of trade union participation in Dutch and Swedish economic policy, we considered several instances in which trade unions had participated in the restructuring of firms or sectors in decline. Trade unions were involved in the restructuring of the Dutch textile industry and in the reorganization of Swedish shipbuilding. Although one can raise doubts about the extent of trade union influence, the Dutch and Swedish experiences indicate that there are circumstances, other than participation in defensive coalitions, in which trade unions are involved in industrial policy decisions. In the Dutch and Swedish cases, factors leading to the involvement of trade unions included previous traditions of cooperation, legal rights of factory councils to be consulted about impending changes, and the support of governments anxious to preserve employment. In the Dutch case, the market power of the trade unions — unions had become more militant in the early 1970s and workers had occupied ENKA's Breda plant — also played a role. In order to delineate these circumstances more fully, we need to explore a wider range of cases.

West Germany and Austria provide further examples of countries with traditions of cooperative labour relations and systems of co-determination which inject unions into industrial policy decision. Austria has an intricate web of corporatist policy-making structures which Germany lacks. Italy has no tradition of cooperative labour relations, but unions there nevertheless have been able to exploit market power in order to gain a voice in industrial policy.

Austrian Textiles and Steel

A recent study by Peter Katzenstein (1984) provides detailed treatment of trade union involvement in industrial policy in Austria. As in the Netherlands and Sweden, trade unions in Austria are incorporated into policy processes. However, the institutions and structures of corporatism are far more pervasive. The economy is closely regulated by an Economic Council and Chambers of Labour and Agriculture, as well as wage and price commissions. Unions and employers share power in a variety of settings, including government structures, informal commissions, and the boards of directors of Austria's nationalized industries. The system gives trade unions considerable influence. Trade union federations are consulted on major policy decisions, and both economic policies and the management of nationalized industries have been geared toward full employment. In addition, Austrian legislation requires that shop stewards be consulted about proposed reorganizations and closures. Throughout the postwar period, Austrian industries have been accorded moderate protection (Austria was slower to remove tariffs than other countries). More recently, the Austrian government has intervened and granted credits in order to ease the impact of change in the steel and textile industries.

Austrian policies reflect the nearly equal balance between Catholic and Socialist parties and the ways in which these two parties have shared power. From 1946 to 1966, both parties participated in a grand coalition, allocating power in proportion to parliamentary strength. Since 1966, single-party governments have been in office. However, early practices of power-sharing and proportional allocation have continued. According to Katzenstein, trade union influence stems not only from the strength and position of the Socialists, who were in power from 1970 until 1983, but also from the size of the nationalized sector and the concomitant weakness of business. Nationalized industries include two-thirds of the fifty largest firms, with virtually half of the national product, and the two largest banks are also in state hands. The influence of private business is also diluted by the presence of a labour wing in the Catholic party, the principal avenue for business representation (Katzenstein, 1984).

Katzenstein's studies of the steel and textile industries demonstrate the position of Austrian trade unions. In the case of steel, the industry, nationalized since the war, had served as an instrument of overall economic policy. For a time, lower steel prices subsidized other industries, and a large workforce was maintained in order to sustain full employment. When the industry ran into difficulties in the 1970s, employment was maintained and investment continued. However, mounting losses made this practice difficult to sustain. In the late 1970s, VEW, the industry's specialty steel subsidiary, felt compelled to reduce capacity. Three distinct plans, proposing layoffs, short time, or wage cuts, were rejected by the factory council. Instead, a plan was negotiated which avoided layoffs but required workers to take ten unpaid vacation days. In 1979, cuts in fringe benefits were proposed, and in 1981 layoffs were again broached. In each instance, the factory council acceded to some changes, but nevertheless succeeded in reducing the scope of redundancies. Cutbacks were coupled with provisions for aid to the communities affected, as well as with compensatory measures for workers on short time or taking early retirement (Katzenstein, 1984).

Trade unions were also involved in the merger and reorganization of textile firms in eastern Austria. As in the case of steel, the unions were involved from the start and were willing to accept reductions in the workforce in order to create a more efficient industry. When large infusions of cash failed to stem losses, the textile union acceded to further layoffs and, eventually, to the failure of the firm. However, workers and subcontractors were cushioned from the impact by generous compensatory measures (Katzenstein, 1984).

West Germany

In their examination of West German responses to crises, Esser and Fach (1983) discuss instances in which West German trade unions were involved in industrial restructuring. These include the reorganization of the coal industry from 1958 onward, the restructuring of the Ruhr and Saar steel industries in the late 1970s and early 1980s, reductions in shipbuilding capacity, layoffs in the automobile industry, and rescues of firms, such as AEG Telefunken, in difficulty. Trade unions participated both through workers' representatives on firms' boards of directors and through ad hoc "crisis cartels" assembled to devise schemes for firms or sectors in difficulty. Other participants typically included the large investment banks, Länder (provincial) governments, and the federal economics ministry (pp. 107–108). Reflecting commitments to structural modernization and adaptation to the market, reorganization schemes typically involved rationalization of production rather than recourse to protection. In many of the cases cited (the reorganization of the Ruhr and Saar steel industries and cutbacks in Volkswagen production are examples), the trade union IG Metall negotiated compensatory social plans. These eased the impact of layoffs by encouraging early retirements and providing special redundancy pay (pp. 111–20).

Trade union involvement in restructuring reflects both the integration of the German trade union movement and the schemes of co-determination in effect in most industries. Relations between unions and employers are both cooperative and adversarial, although the latter element is often neglected in more stereotypical images of *"Modell Deutschland."* Their cooperative stance means that trade unions can be useful allies when restructuring is on the agenda. However, co-determination is also a factor. In the coal and steel industries, where full parity co-determination operates (workers and owners have equal representation on boards of directors), trade union representatives are inextricably involved in decisions. In other industries, the practice is less extensive: the 1952 Works Council Act confined workers' representation on firms' boards of directors to one-third. The 1976 revisions to this act stopped short of full parity, but still provided workers and trade union representatives with information and an additional arena in which they could press their views (Esser and Fach, 1983).

Italian Textiles

Trade unions in the Italian textile industry have been closely involved in industrial policy decisions. In his examination of textile unions and restructuring in the 1970s, Michael Contarino (1984) found that trade unions were influential in three of the five regions studied. However, in contrast to many of the other cases we have considered, the Italian trade unions were not incorporated into national-level tripartite structures. Instead, trade union involvement took place against a background of growing market power of the trade unions, increased cooperation among Italy's three trade union federations, and growing trade union interest in industrial policy. The strikes of the hot autumn of 1969 demonstrated the potential market power of Italian trade unions. In 1972, Italy's three national trade union federations, the Communist-led CGIL, the Christian Democratic CSIL and the Social Democratic UIL, coordinated their efforts by concluding a Pact of Federation. Although this did not unify the three federations, it committed them to an interventionist posture which included gaining control over industrial restructuring (chap. 21). The national position was echoed in the textile federation (FULTA), which coordinated the efforts of each federation's textile union. The FULTA position endorsed restructuring but argued that it should take place in ways which, at a minimum, would increase employment or would assure the competitiveness of firms. FULTA stressed the importance of technology and investment and the need to upgrade production and marketing and called for national and regional planning, credit facilities, support for research and development and marketing, and for the use of credit to prevent the decentralization of production from placing workers beyond union influence or protection (chap. 2). Protection was regarded as at best a temporary measure.

Although FULTA was unable to realize its demands nationally, local and regional organizations were nevertheless involved in industrial policy. Contarino examined trade union influence in the restructuring of the textile, clothing, and footwear sectors in five areas: Busto Arsizio (Lombardy); Turin; two "Red-belt" areas, Prato and Carpi; and the Veneto. Trade union influence varied considerably. In Busto Arsizio, the local FULTA, which assumed an interventionist or "propositional" posture, responded to the threatened closure of a major firm, Cantoni, which would have resulted in more than 2,000 layoffs, by proposing a counter-plan indicating ways in which the firm could be reorganized. This involved some cutbacks, sale of non-productive assets, new capital and new marketing strategies. A one-day general strike, coupled with national and regional backing and a threat of a factory occupation, backed up the FULTA position. Negotiations with the firm and the regional government led to the acceptance of an alternative plan. This committed the firm to re-absorb some of the affected workers and arranged compensation from special government funds for others (Contarino, 1984, chap. 3). In contrast, the textile unions in Turin, operating in a different context with different traditions, assumed an oppositional stance when confronted with the prospect of layoffs of Montedison and other firms. The unions opposed the layoffs but were unable to prevent them (chap. 4).

In Prato and Carpi, Communist domination of local and regional governments was a factor in what Contarino describes as local neo-corporatism. Contarino argues that both the Italian Communist party (PCI) and the FULTA promoted the growth and competitiveness of firms, and supported research and development and market research in order to facilitate adaptation. In effect, both accepted the logic of the market and encouraged technological change, but at the same time sought to cushion workers from the adverse effects by emphasizing manpower programs and improvements in the quality and skill level of work. Confronted with plans for the rationalization of firms and changes in the organization of work, particularly growing decentralization of workplaces, the unions responded both by explaining the necessity of change to workers and by developing schemes which pushed restructuring in directions desired by the unions. The potential market power of the well-organized and well-disciplined unions and the ability of Communist-controlled local governments to mediate between unions and firms assured that union plans would gain a hearing. In addition, as in Busto, unions were able to offer concessions such as a six-day work week, which permitted more intensive use of machinery and made the union-sponsored schemes more acceptable to the firms involved (chap. 5).

The position of the textile unions in Carpi and Prato contrasted sharply with their role in the Veneto, a Christian Democratic region. In this case, divisions among the textile unions inhibited a coordinated approach, and local and regional governments were far less concerned about the impact of restructuring on employment or ensuring that unions were consulted. As a result, unions had far less leverage in the process (chap. 6).

The ability of textile unions to gain a voice in the restructuring of the industry reflects not only the context in which the unions operated but also the ability to deploy market power behind plausible alternatives. As we noted, the textile unions' efforts were part of a broader strategy to gain a voice in industrial policy. Although many of the Italian trade union federations' initiatives fell short of the mark, trade union influence was not confined to textiles. In his examination of crisis response in Italy, Michael Kreile (1983) asserts that trade unions enjoyed a veto over industrial policy (p. 216). Although Kreile does not cite specific sectoral decisions, he argues that trade unions were influential both in the diversion to the south of increasingly large proportions of state holding-company investment, and in insisting that industrial policies be job-oriented. As examples of the latter, Kreile cites the operation of GEPI, a public-financing agency involved in the rescue of firms, and its mandate to ensure the re-employment of workers displaced by cutbacks or closures, and generous compensatory schemes for workers affected (pp. 206–216). Unfortunately, Kreile does not indicate whether these or other measures were passed with the assent of the trade union movement or merely put forward in the interest of placating unions.

Trade Union Involvement Further Considered

We have now examined trade union involvement in industrial policy in a variety of settings. The cases we have considered demonstrate two general patterns: the first, which characterizes unions in Canada and the United States, is participation in defensive coalitions lobbying for protection from imports. The second, characteristic of the Netherlands, Sweden, Austria, West Germany and, to a certain extent, Italy, is trade union participation in the reorganization of declining sectors or firms in difficulty. These cases are strikingly similar: trade unions were drawn, or perhaps propelled, into discussions about the fate of weaker firms or industries, and were able to review and comment on restructuring plans. In some instances, trade unions vetoed restructuring schemes, but, in most cases, their influence was confined to cushioning the impact on workers or regions by delaying or preventing layoffs, spreading cutbacks over several regions, and securing compensatory measures such as preferential hiring, retraining schemes, early retirement, subsidies for shorter hours, or extended unemployment benefits. In exchange, trade unions endorsed restructuring and sanctioned some redundancies. Finally, in these cases, recourse to protection was at best a minor element.

Why are trade unions involved in industrial policy? The role of legitimizing industrial change could be taken as an explanation, but the matter is not quite so simple. Although trade unions were involved in the cases we have considered, they were left out in many others: the French textile industry, where unions were systematically "marginalized," is one example; the entire gamut of British industrial policy is another. If trade unions were drawn in to lubricate the process of change and make it more acceptable in some countries, why were they excluded in others?

Because many of the cases occurred in countries with long traditions of corporatism, it is tempting to suggest that the inclusion of trade unions is simply an extension of national tripartism to sectoral decisions. However, this would not explain trade union involvement in West Germany or Italy, or for that matter in the Netherlands, where relations between unions and employers have been increasingly strained since the 1960s. Similarly, although factory councils and formal systems of co-determination figured in many of our cases, providing unions with either information or a forum in which to make their views heard, it did not figure in all of them; nor could co-determination, in and of itself, provide an explanation.

If we want to understand the circumstances in which trade unions are involved, or involve themselves in industrial policy, we need to explore the problem from the perspective of the participants: capital, labour and government. We need to ask why capital would want to include labour, why labour would want to be involved, what resources it could bring to bear to ensure that it was, and whether governments would have particular reasons to involve labour.[10]

Let us begin with capital. We have already suggested one reason why capital might want to involve labour: to legitimize restructuring. However, this desire is not universal. If we were to survey the full gamut of restructuring decisions, including plant closures, shifts in investment or location, or changes in technology or production processes, we would discover that trade unions were involved in at best a minority of cases.

Why is labour excluded? The most plausible explanations are that, in most circumstances, capital has no need to include labour and that including labour would reduce management prerogatives. Lest this appear circular, let us consider it in further detail. In settings in which property rights and the exercise of management prerogatives are considered sacred, businesses have little need to legitimize investment or disinvestment decisions. If they want to close plants, they do it; consulting unions would make the process more difficult. When unions are included, it is for a reason. This might be because plant closures and disinvestment decisions are regarded as illegitimate, or because firms are legally required to do so, or because a third party, typically government, insists on it as a condition for granting assistance. Alternatively, trade unions might be included because they have sufficient market power to disrupt the firm or society if they are excluded.

This helps to explain the patterns we have observed. In Canada and the United States, firms have little reason to include unions except as co-petitioners in pleas for protection from imports. In the Netherlands, Sweden, Austria and West Germany, official policies have been geared toward full employment. Disinvestment decisions are not as legitimate and, at a minimum, require some explaining. In his examination of industrial policy in Austria and Switzerland, Katzenstein (1984) argues that prevailing norms and traditions of social partnership in both countries encouraged consultation; Lundmark (1983) and Contarino (1984) make similar arguments about the policy cultures of social democratic Sweden and the Communist-controlled regions of Italy. We can extend the argument to the Netherlands and Germany. However, this is only part of the story. As Katzenstein points out, norms are reinforced by practice, and practices can change over time. In the countries we have been studying, practices of consultation are reinforced by both law and political relationships. Although co-determination laws are invariably weaker than many trade unionists would desire, they nevertheless draw unions into debates on restructuring. We have already alluded to workers' representation on the boards of directors of West German firms. In Austria, plant reorganizations require the consent of shop stewards (Katzenstein, 1984). In Sweden, a 1976 law requires firms to negotiate with unions not only on hiring and firing, but on changes in the organization of work or the operation of the firm (Martin, 1984, pp. 262–63). Dutch law requires that firms give notice of proposed mergers and present reorganization plans to factory councils. Finally, the presence of parties of the left in government, alone or in coalition with others, or even in opposition with reasonable prospects of returning to power, may directly or indirectly reinforce proclivities toward consultation.

In addition, the market power of trade unions is important; if trade unions lacked minimal ability to disrupt firms by witholding their labour, it is doubtful that trade unions would be involved in either macro-economic policy or industrial restructuring. In the case of the Italian textile industry, the market power of unions was a major factor propelling unions into industrial policy decisions. Similarly, market power was a factor in the Dutch textile industry. The reorganizations which Langdon studied took place in the 1970s, in a period when restiveness at the base and an increased frequency of wildcat strikes had forced Dutch trade unions to assume a more militant posture. In one case, ENKA-Breda, the occupation of the plant forced reconsideration of the proposed shutdown. In the other two, mass demonstrations and the prospect that the unions might walk out of sectoral discussions helped to reinforce trade union demands (Langdon, 1980). Even so, neither market power alone, nor market power combined with proclivities to consult unions, can fully explain trade union participation in industrial policy: the impact of market power depends in large measure on how firms and government respond to it. If firms or government are willing to tolerate long strikes or social unrest, trade unions' market power will be less effective than if firms or government are anxious to maintain social peace.

Let us consider the matter from the perspective of the trade unions. If participation in industrial restructuring involves little more than legitimizing layoffs or plant closures, why should trade unions want to be involved? There are a number of possible considerations. One is that many trade unions may not want to be included because there are few gains to be made; another is that standing by and letting things happen without attempting to influence the course of events may be equally unpalatable. A third is that unions may believe that there are gains to be made, and that by participating they may prevent or delay redundancies or at least secure concessions which protect the workers involved. If we survey trade unions in the countries we have been studying, we find all of these perspectives represented. Many Canadian, U.S. and British unions have avoided inclusion in industrial or economic policy decisions because the costs, such as loss of support and diminished freedom of action, outweighed prospective gains. French unions, with their maximalist posture, took a similar tack, but are divided on their approach now that a socialist government is in office. Austrian, Swedish, West German and Italian unions have taken the opposite approach and involved themselves in the interest of protecting workers as best they can. Dutch trade unions now take a middle position; in the late 1960s and early 1970s, trade unions participated in a number of sectoral commissions, but have since withdrawn from many of these.

A number of factors condition trade union attitudes toward participation in industrial restructuring. One, to which we have already alluded, is the style and posture of the trade unions and the ways in which these are shaped by both past experience and available opportunities. As Gourevitch et al. (1984) point out, trade unions are products not only of their pasts, but also of the web of relationships in which they currently find themselves. Even if union leaders desire it, changing strategies may be difficult because of member expectations, the demands made by kindred political parties, and the costs of abandoning established channels or practices. Katzenstein (1984) argues that unions and other actors are unable to escape the corporatist networks in which they are involved. One could make a similar argument about the Netherlands: despite the frustrations of sectoral tripartism, which led unions to abandon sectoral commissions, trade unions still talk to employers and government regularly in a number of commissions attached to the Social and Economic Council.

Second, the political climate is important. Many of the instances of social partnership at the sectoral level which we observed took place in countries in which social democratic parties were in power alone or in coalition with others, or in countries with governments anxious, for one reason or another, to promote employment. The bourgeois coalition in office in Sweden from 1976 to 1982 was a notable example of this. In Italy, the weakness of the Italian state may have created openings for trade union initiatives which do not normally exist in other countries, or if they do, go unnoticed by trade unions. Equally, however, governments which do not make employment their primary goal may create a climate in which trade union participation in industrial policy is difficult even if trade unions are favourably predisposed. As we have already noted, there are costs involved in participation; trade unions risk losing the support of their members if they sanction layoffs or offer concessions without getting something in return. More often than not, it is governments who bear the costs of concessions. If governments are unwilling to foot the bill, then unions may find that the risks of participation are too high.

A third factor, which may be of importance, is the way in which trade unions are organized. Mancur Olson (1982) has argued that the broader and more centralized an organization, the more likely it is to take a more general and less particularistic view of questions at hand. Of the trade union movements we have considered, it is indeed the more broadly based and centralized movements which have participated in both national economic policies and sectoral reorganizations. More decentralized organizations, such as the AFL-CIO and the Canadian Labour Congress, and trade union movements in which craft organization predominates, such as the British, are considerably less involved in either national economic policies or sectoral reorganizations. However, this does not mean that these unions are uninvolved in industrial policy. Instead, the kinds of policies which these organizations pursue are different. Some of the more narrowly based U.S. and Canadian unions have been active in seeking protection for various industries, and the AFL-CIO has been calling for a national industrial policy for the United States. Similarly, British trade unions have vigorously defended jobs and more recently have sought import controls to protect British industries.

Although there is a difference in the kinds of policies pursued, it is not at all clear that it is the breadth of trade unions' point of view which affects the nature and extent of participation in industrial policy. Opportunities for participation may vary considerably. In addition, larger and more centralized organizations may simply have more resources and staff available, making them better equipped to formulate alternative policies; in contrast, highly fragmented trade unions, organized according to craft, lack both the personnel and the flexibility to develop and pursue alternative plans. Even so, highly centralized organizations may find the selective aspects of industrial policy to be potentially too divisive to make them worth bothering about; instead, pursuing more general policies, such as the expansionary measures most trade union federations demand, helps to maintain common positions and keep the organization together.

Let us come back to the main argument. We have now considered reasons why capital might want, or perhaps feel compelled, to involve trade unions in industrial policy, and some of the reasons why trade unions might or might not want to be included. At several junctures, we have alluded to the importance of government and suggested that, in some countries, government policies play an important role both in decisions regarding the inclusion of trade unions and in creating conditions under which trade unions are likely to participate. However, we have said little about governments or their reasons for including trade unions in industrial policy decisions or circumstances under which they are likely to do to so. Why do some governments include trade unions in industrial policy decisions while others exclude them?

One possible explanation is that in certain countries, prevailing norms and traditions of social partnership require the inclusion of labour. Another is that some governments, typically of the left, include labour as a matter of course, or because they feel it necessary to do so in order to maintain their bases of support. A third possible explanation is that labour is included for instrumental reasons such as securing union cooperation and facilitating industrial restructuring. As we have already noted, most of the countries in which trade unions were involved in industrial restructuring had long traditions of social partnership, and parties of the left were prominent in many, but not all, of the governments in power during the periods under discussion.

If we want to understand the reasons why some governments actively seek to include unions while others exclude them, we need to consider not only prevailing policy culture and the political colour of governments, but also the content of most industrial policies and the circumstances under which they are implemented. Much of the industrial policy debate focusses on the desirability of positive or offensive industrial strategies. In practice, however, most industrial policy involves the rescue and reorganization of declining firms or industries. Although in some instances this may be accomplished by erecting tariff barriers, or granting subsidies and loans, the process frequently entails reorganizing production in order to reduce costs and increase profits. Involving trade unions in this process can serve a variety of purposes: unions may be asked to consent to layoffs or plant closures, guarantee industrial peace, restrain wages, bend seniority rules, accept the introduction of new technologies and changes in organization of work, and, at the same time, explain the necessity of change to their members. In addition, in certain circumstances, governments may also use union support and union willingness to make concessions as devices for persuading firms to remain in the country, maintain production, and make the investments required to ensure their long-run viability.

Including trade unions thus can be an important device for legitimizing industrial policies, minimizing conflict, and lubricating the process of change. Nevertheless, involving trade unions also entails certain costs. Unions must defend both the long-term and the short-run interests of their members. As such, unions are likely to resist layoffs, closures, and changes in the definition of work unless either governments or employers are willing to guarantee some jobs and finance compensatory measures. The price which stronger or more militant unions exact may be greater than either governments or employers are willing to pay; and governments, particularly if they feel that workers and their unions have few alternatives, may choose instead to risk higher levels of industrial conflict and unrest. Decisions to include or exclude trade unions will reflect not only government goals and the extent to which governments are sympathetic to capital or labour, but also the likelihood that trade union participation will produce the desired result.

If we examine the trade union movements that have been involved in industrial restructuring, a striking pattern emerges: with the exception of Italy, the trade unions that were regularly involved in industrial restructuring have tended to be more centralized organizations known to place long-run concerns, such as the viability of firms or industries, ahead of more immediate demands. In contrast, trade union movements with well-established traditions of militancy, resistance to elimination of redundancies, and opposition to changes in work rules (such as the British and the French) have been excluded from involvement in decisions regarding industrial restructuring, even when parties of the left were in power.

The principal exceptions to these two major patterns are instances in which the risks of bankruptcy or closure are so great that unions can be forced to make concessions in order to save the industry; the Chrysler bailout in the United States is a notable example. This suggests that the inclusion of trade unions reflects not only traditions of social partnership, the ideological proclivities of governments, or obligations that certain parties may owe to trade unions, but also the likelihood that trade unions will assume a cooperative posture.

We have now explored reasons why capital, labour, and government might want to involve trade unions in industrial policy. Our examination suggests two distinct patterns: in one, relatively strong trade unions allow themselves to be incorporated into tripartite structures and become less overtly militant, but nevertheless use their political strength either to ensure that they are regularly consulted on economic and industrial policy decisions or to secure the passage of laws requiring consultation. Trade unions are included in industrial policy decisions because laws and prevailing norms require it, and because unions can be expected to temper their demands, accept changes, and cooperate in the reorganization of firms and sectors, even if this means loss of jobs. Unions are included in order to legitimize and facilitate the process.

In the second pattern of union involvement, the incorporation of trade unions into tripartite structures has either failed or never been attempted, and trade unions, which are typically more militant, remain outside normal policy processes. Trade unions are excluded from most industrial policy decisions because there is no legal or cultural requirement, nor any instrumental reason why they should be included. Unless trade unions are either enlisted as co-petitioners for subsidies or protection, or included in order to wring concessions from them, involving trade unions would result in demands which firms and government would prefer, and are able, to avoid.

The argument suggests that the inclusion or exclusion of trade unions depends largely on past traditions and practices and the kind of policy culture which has emerged. However, this should not be overstated. Past traditions can easily be broken if one or more participants can muster sufficient support to impose alternative practices or policies. At present, the trend in many countries is toward exclusion of trade unions. This reflects both the increasing costs of compensatory measures and the increased ability, in a period of protracted unemployment, to resist trade union demands and reverse previous gains. Excluding unions is part of a broader strategy of reducing costs, allowing greater flexibility, and increasing profits in order to ensure investment. Although this is one way to ensure the long-run viability of firms, one can question whether it is the most desirable.

Including trade unions in industrial policy can also serve a number of purposes. In addition to the rather uncomfortable role of explaining changes to their members, trade unions could be included in order to ensure that the social consequences of change are taken into account, and to monitor the process of change. This latter role could be particularly important. Most industrial policies involve direct or indirect subsidies to capital in order to ensure the survival and long-run viability of industries. However, governments typically lack any direct control over the ways in which firms use subsidies and, in particular, whether they make the required investments. It is possible that trade unions could be enlisted in order to monitor subsidies and ensure that they are used for the purposes prescribed.

Taking this route would require including trade unions in restructuring decisions. Unless unions were completely inclined to accept government and management points of view, this would involve making some concessions to the trade unions. This in turn would entail certain costs (at a minimum, financing compensatory measures for displaced workers) and would risk entrenching unions in the process. However, it would also result in certain gains: one of the reasons why governments subsidize industry is not only to ensure the viability of the firm but also to preserve jobs. The latter is an interest that trade unions and many governments have in common. Whether trade unions should or would want to participate on this basis is another matter. Our survey suggests that this will depend in large measure on the extent to which their interests and the interests of their members are taken into account.

Notes

This paper was completed in October 1984.

1. Only recently are books beginning to appear that deal with this question. Katzenstein (1984) examines the influence of trade unions in Austrian and Swiss industrial policy. Lange, Ross, and Vannicelli (1982) and the recently published companion volume (Gourevitch et al., 1984) deal with union attitudes to industrial policy in their examinations of trade union responses to the current economic crisis.

2. The literature is vast: in addition to studies treating individual national trade unions, there is a growing comparative literature. See, for example, the articles in Hayward (1980); Lange, Ross, and Vannicelli (1982); Gourevitch et al. (1984). Literature on incomes policies is considerable; see, for example, Flanagan, Soskice, and Ulman (1983); Ulman and Flanagan (1971). The literature on neo-corporatism is of direct relevance here; see, for example, Panitch (1977b; 1980); Lehmbruch (1977).

3. The literature on industrial policy is a composite of several literatures. These include literature on the economics of industrial policies, a growing literature on international trade, and earlier literature on economic planning. There is surprisingly little on the politics of industrial policy. The author of a recent British book on the subject is apologetic in suggesting that political scientists might have something to say about the subject. See Grant (1982).

4. See, for example, Magaziner and Reich (1982).

5. See, for example, Pinder, Hosomi, and Diebold (1979); Diebold (1980); Pinder (1982a). For an economist's model of how defensive coalitions operate, see Burton (1983).

6. See, for example, Zysman (1983) or Grant (1982). For articles which do consider the role of trade unions directly or indirectly, see Gunter (1975) and Hager (1982). In addition, Zysman and Tyson (1983) contains a series of case studies which treat the role of trade unions.

7. The concept of a policy coalition is prominent in the literature on the domestic sources of foreign economic policy, which examines the way in which coalitions of diverse interests, e.g., agriculture, labour, and different manufacturing, financial or commercial interests, come together in support of or opposition to protective tariffs or free trade. The literature treats support of or opposition to protective tariffs as a product of the ways in which coalitions are orchestrated and sectors define their interests. Interests reflect not only product cycles and the position of different sectors in the international economy, but also the activities of leaders and parties, who select and emphasize particular issues and programs. Interests may be involved either as direct participants and advocates of a particular point of view, or as passive or indirect participants brought along because of specific benefits or side payments which compensate for adverse effects of the main policy or because followers are enlisted in support of a particular leader. See Gourevitch (1984); Kurth (1979); Katzenstein (1978).

8. The Japanese case is similar to the French. The Ministry of International Trade and Industry used protection and a variety of selective incentives in order to encourage the growth of designated industries. Trade unions played a negligible role. See Pempel and Tsunekawa (1979).

9. The lack of trade union influence is borne out by diverse sources. Wilson et al. (1982) surveyed 150 strategic decisions in 30 British organizations and concluded that trade union influence was minimal. For the most part, union involvement was confined to personnel matters, and white collar unions were far more active than industrial unions. In most instances, unions reacted rather than initiated.

10. This section draws on the notion of political exchange, which Alessandro Pizzorno developed in order to explain variations in strike rates. See Pizzorno (1978).

Bibliography

Aggarwal, Vinod K., with Stephan Haggard. 1983. "The Politics of Protection in the U.S. Textile and Apparel Industries." In *American Industry in International Competition: Government Policies and Corporate Strategies*, edited by John Zysman and Laura Tyson, pp. 249–313. Ithaca, N.Y.: Cornell University Press.

Apple, Nixon. 1980. "The Rise and Fall of Full Employment Capitalism." *Studies in Political Economy* 4 (Autumn): 5–39.

Blank, Stephen. 1977. "Britain: The Politics of Foreign Economic Policy, the Domestic Economy, and the Problem of Pluralistic Stagnation." *International Organization* 31 (4): 674–721.

Bornstein, Stephen. 1984. "States and Unions: From Postwar Settlement to Contemporary Stalemate." In *The State in Capitalist Europe: A Casebook*, edited by Stephen Bornstein, David Held, and Joel Krieger, pp. 54–90. London: Allen and Unwin.

Bornstein, Stephen, and Peter Gourevitch. 1984. "Unions in a Declining Economy: The Case of the British TUC." In *Unions and Economic Crisis: Britain, West Germany, and Sweden*, edited by Peter Gourevitch et al., pp. 13–88. London: Allen and Unwin.

Borrus, Michael. 1983. "The Politics of Competitive Erosion in the U.S. Steel Industry." In *American Industry in International Competition: Government Policies and Corporate Strategies*, edited by John Zysman and Laura Tyson, pp. 60–106. Ithaca, N.Y.: Cornell University Press.

Burton, John. 1983. *Picking Losers . . . ? The Political Economy of Industrial Policy*. Hobart Paper 99. London: Institute of Economic Affairs.

Cohen, Stephen S. 1977. *Modern Capitalist Planning: The French Model*. Berkeley: University of California Press.

Contarino, Michael. 1984. "The Politics of Industrial Change: Textile Unions and Industrial Restructuring in Five Italian Localities." Ph.D. dissertation, Harvard University.

de Hen, P.E. 1980. *Actieve en re-actieve industriepolitiek in Nederland*. Amsterdam: de Arbeiderspers.

de Vries, John. 1978. *The Netherlands Economy in the Twentieth Century*. Assen, The Netherlands: van Gorcum.

Diebold, William, Jr., ed. 1980. *Industrial Policy as an International Issue*. New York: McGraw-Hill.

Esping-Andersen, Gosta. 1981. "From Welfare State to Economic Democracy." *Political Power and Social Theory* 2: 111–40.

Esping-Andersen, Gosta, and Roger Friedland. 1982. "Class Coalitions in the Making of Western European Economies." *Political Power and Social Theory* 3: 1–52.

Esser, Josef, and Wolfgang Fach, with Kenneth Dyson. 1983. " 'Social Market' and Modernization Policy: West Germany." In *Industrial Crisis: A Comparative Study of the State and Industry*, edited by Kenneth Dyson and Stephen Wilks, pp. 102–27. New York: St. Martin's Press.

Estrin, Saul, and Peter Holmes. 1983. "French Planning and Industrial Policy." *Journal of Public Policy* 3 (1): 131–48.

European Trade Union Confederation. 1982. "Industrial Policy in Western Europe." Report adopted by the ETUC Executive Committee on March 25, 1982.

European Trade Union Institute. 1981. "Industrial Policy in Western Europe," edited by John Evans. Report of a conference, November.

Evans, Moss. 1980. "Import Controls Are the Key to Industrial Planning." *Public Administration* 19: 3–4.

Flanagan, Robert J., David W. Soskice, and Lloyd Ulman. 1983. *Unionism, Economic Stabilization, and Incomes Policies: The European Experience*. Washington, D.C.: Brookings Institution.

Gourevitch, Peter Alexis. 1984. "Breaking with Orthodoxy: The Politics of Economic Policy Responses to the Depression of the 1930's." *International Organization* 38 (Winter): 95–129.

Gourevitch, Peter, Andrew Martin, George Ross, Stephen Bornstein, Andrei Markovits, and Christopher Allen. 1984. *Unions and Economic Crisis: Britain, West Germany, and Sweden*. London: Allen and Unwin.

Grant, Wyn. 1982. *The Political Economy of Industrial Policy*. London: Butterworth.

Green, Diana. 1983. "Strategic Management and the State: France." In *Industrial Crisis: A Comparative Study of the State and Industry*, edited by Kenneth Dyson and Stephen Wilks, pp. 161–92. New York: St. Martin's Press.

Gunter, Hans. 1975. "Trade Unions and Industrial Policies in Western Europe." In *Industrial Policies in Western Europe*, edited by Steven J. Warnecke and Ezra N. Suleiman, pp. 93–117. New York: Praeger.

Hager, Wolfgang. 1982. "Industrial Policy, Trade Policy, and European Social Democracy." In *National Industrial Strategies and the World Economy*, edited by John Pinder, pp. 236–64. Totawa, N.J.: Allanheld, Osmun.

Hall, Peter. 1984. "Patterns of Economic Policy: An Organizational Approach." In *The State in Capitalist Europe: A Casebook*, edited by Stephen Bornstein, David Held, and Joel Krieger, pp. 21–53. London: Allen and Unwin.

Hayward, Jack, ed. 1980. *Trade Unions in Politics in Western Europe*. London: Frank Cass.

Hogwood, Brian. 1979. *Government and Shipbuilding: The Politics of Industrial Change*. Westmead, England: Saxon House.

Jordan, A.G. 1981. "Iron Triangles, Woolly Corporatism and Elastic Nets." *Journal of Public Policy* 1 (1): 95–123.

Katzenstein, Peter. 1978. *Between Power and Plenty*. Madison: University of Wisconsin Press.

———. 1984. *Corporatism and Change: Austria, Switzerland, and the Politics of Industry*. Ithaca, N.Y.: Cornell University Press.

Kaufman, Gerald. 1980. *To Be a Minister*. London: Sidgwick and Jackson.

Kreile, Michael. 1977. "West Germany: The Dynamics of Expansion." *International Organization* 31 (4): 774–808.

———. 1983. "Public Enterprise and the Pursuit of Strategic Management: Italy." In *Industrial Crisis: A Comparative Study of the State and Industry*, edited by Kenneth Dyson and Stephen Wilks, pp. 193–219. New York: St. Martin's Press.

Kurth, James. 1979. "The Political Consequences of the Product Cycles: Industrial History and Political Outcomes." *International Organization* 33 (1): 1–34.

Langdon, Stephen. 1980. "Industrial Restructuring and the Third World: The Case of Dutch Textile Manufacturing, 1965–79." Unpublished.

———. 1981. "North/South, West and East: Industrial Restructuring in the World Economy." *International Journal* 36: 766–92.

Lange, Peter, George Ross, and Mario Vannicelli. 1982. *Unions, Change, and Crisis: French and Italian Union Strategy and the Political Economy*. London: Allen and Unwin.

Lehmbruch, Gerhard. 1977. "Liberal Corporatism and Party Government." *Comparative Political Studies* 10: 91–126.

Lereuz, Jacques. 1975. *Economic Planning and Politics in Britain*. London: Martin Robertson.

Longstreth, Frank. 1979. "The City, Industry and the State." In *State and Economy in Contemporary Capitalism*, edited by Colin Crouch, pp. 157–91. London: Croom Helm.

Lundmark, Kjell. 1983. "Welfare State and Employment Policy: Sweden." In *Industrial Crisis: A Comparative Study of the State and Industry*," edited by Kenneth Dyson and Stephen Wilks, pp. 220–44. New York: St. Martin's Press.

Magaziner, Ira, and Robert Reich. 1982. *Minding America's Business: The Decline and Rise of the American Economy*. New York: Harcourt Brace Jovanovich.

Mahon, Rianne, and Lynn Krieger Mytelka. 1983. "Industry, the State, and the New Protectionism: Textiles in Canada and France." *International Organization* 37 (4): 551–81.

Maier, Charles S. 1977. "The Politics of Productivity: Foundations of American International Economic Policy After World War II." *International Organization* 31 (4): 607–33.

Markovits, Andrei S., and Christopher S. Allen. 1980. "Power and Dissent: The Trade Unions in the Federal Republic of Germany Re-examined." In *Trade Unions in Politics in Western Europe*, edited by Jack Hayward, pp. 69–86. London: Frank Cass.

_____. 1984. "Trade Unions and Economic Crisis: The West German Case." In *Unions and Economic Crisis: Britain, West Germany, and Sweden*, edited by Peter Gourevitch et al., pp. 89–189. London: Allen and Unwin.

Martin, Andrew. 1979. "The Dynamics of Change in a Keynesian Political Economy: The Swedish Case and Its Implications." In *State and Economy in Contemporary Capitalism*, edited by Colin Crouch, pp. 88–121. London: Croom Helm.

_____. 1981. "Economic Stagnation and Social Stagnation in Sweden." In *Monetary Policy, Selective Credit Policy and Industrial Policy in France, Britain, West Germany, and Sweden*. Report of the U.S. Congress Joint Economic Committee. Washington, D.C.: U.S. Government Printing Office.

_____. 1984. "Trade Unions in Sweden: Strategic Responses to Change and Crisis." In *Unions and Economic Crisis: Britain, West Germany, and Sweden*, edited by Peter Gourevitch et al., pp. 190–359. London: Allen and Unwin.

Martin, Andrew, and George Ross. 1980. "European Trade Unions and the Economic Crisis: Perceptions and Strategies." In *Trade Unions in Politics in Western Europe*, edited by Jack Hayward, pp. 33–67. London: Frank Cass.

Millstein, James. 1983. "Decline in an Expanding Industry: Japanese Competition in Color Television." In *American Industry in International Competition: Government Policies and Corporate Strategies*, edited by John Zysman and Laura Tyson, pp. 106–41. Ithaca, N.Y.: Cornell University Press.

Netherlands. 1981. Advisory Commission on Industrial Policy. *A New Spirit for Industry*. The Hague: Ministry of Economic Affairs.

_____. 1982. Advisory Commission on the Progress of Industrial Policy. *Review of Activities*. The Hague: Ministry of Economic Affairs.

Netherlands Scientific Council for Government Policy. 1980. *Industry in the Netherlands: Its Place and Future* (English translation published in 1982). Report to the Netherlands Government, no. 18. The Hague: Staatsuitgeverij.

Newcastle Trades Council. 1980. *State Intervention in Industry: A Worker's Inquiry*. Newcastle-upon-Tyne.

Olson, Mancur. 1982. *The Rise and Decline of Nations*. New Haven: Yale University Press.

Ovenden, Keith. 1978. *The Politics of Steel*. London: Macmillan.

Panitch, Leo. 1977a. "Profits and Politics: Labour and the Crisis of British Capitalism." *Politics and Society* 7 (4): 477–507.

_____. 1977b. "The Development of Corporatism in Liberal Democracies." *Comparative Political Studies* 10: 61–90.

_____. 1980. "Recent Theorizations of Corporatism: Reflections on a Growth Industry." *British Journal of Sociology* (June): 159–87.

Pempel, T.J., and Keiichi Tsunekawa. 1979. "Corporatism without Labor: The Japanese Anomaly." In *Trends toward Corporatist Interest Intermediation*, edited by Philippe C. Schmitter and Gerhard Lehmbruch, pp. 231–71. Contemporary Political Sociology, Vol. 1. Beverly Hills, Cal.: Sage.

Pinder, John, ed. 1982a. "Causes and Kinds of Industrial Policy." In *National Industrial*

Strategies and the World Economy, edited by John Pinder, pp. 41–52. Totawa, N.J.: Allanheld, Osmun.

———. 1982b. *National Industrial Strategies and the World Economy*. Totawa, N.J.: Allanheld, Osmun.

Pinder, John, Takashi Hosomi, and William Diebold. 1979. *Industrial Policy and the International Economy*. Triangle Papers 19. New York: The Trilateral Commission.

Pizzorno, Alessandro. 1978. "Political Exchange and Collective Identity in Industrial Conflict." In *The Resurgence of Class Conflict in Western Europe since 1968*, edited by Colin Crouch and Alessandro Pizzorno, Vol. 2, pp. 277–98. New York: Holmes and Meier.

Pontusson, Jonas. 1983. "Comparative Political Economy of Advanced Capitalist States: Sweden and France." *Kapitalistate* (no. 10/11): 43–73.

———. 1984. "Labor and Industrial Policy in Sweden." Paper presented at the 1984 meeting of the American Political Science Association in Washington, D.C.

Salvati, Michele, and Giorgio Brosio. 1979. "The Rise of Market Politics: Industrial Relations in the Seventies." *Daedalus* 108 (Spring): 43–71.

Shonfeld, Andrew. 1965. *Modern Capitalism: The Changing Balance of Public and Private Power*. London: Oxford University Press.

Ulman, Lloyd, and Robert J. Flanagan. 1971. *Wage Restraint: A Study of Incomes Policies in Western Europe*. Berkeley: University of California Press.

van Doorn, Kees, Gerrit Dubbeld, Pieter Rosielle, and Frans van Waarden. 1976. *De beheerste vakbeweging: Het NVV tussen loonpolitiek en loonstrijd, 1959–1973*. Amsterdam: van Gennep.

Wassenberg, Arthur F.P. 1982. "Neo-corporatism and the Quest for Control: The Cuckoo Game." In *Patterns of Corporatist Policy-Making*, edited by Gerhard Lehmbruch and Philippe C. Schmitter. Beverly Hills, Cal.: Sage.

Wilson, David C., Richard J. Butler, David Cray, David J. Hickson, and Geoffrey R. Mallory. 1982. "The Limits of Trade Union Power in Organizational Decision-Making." *British Journal of Industrial Relations* 20 (3): 322–41.

Windmuller, John P. 1969. *Labor Relations in the Netherlands*. Ithaca, N.Y.: Cornell University Press.

Wolinetz, Steven B. 1983a. "Neo-corporatism and Industrial Policy in the Netherlands." Paper presented at the annual meeting of the Canadian Political Science Association in Vancouver, B.C., June 6–8.

———. 1983b. "Wage Regulation in the Netherlands: The Rise and Fall of the Postwar Social Contract." Paper presented at the Council for European Studies, Fourth Annual Conference of Europeanists in Washington, D.C., October 13–15.

Yoffie, David B. 1983. "Adjustment in the Footwear Industry: The Consequences of Orderly Marketing Agreements." In *American Industry in International Competition: Government Policies and Corporate Strategies*, edited by John Zysman and Laura Tyson, pp. 313–49. Ithaca, N.Y.: Cornell University Press.

Zysman, John. 1983. *Governments, Markets, and Growth: Financial Systems and the Politics of Industrial Change*. Ithaca, N.Y.: Cornell University Press.

Zysman, John, and Laura Tyson, eds. 1983. *American Industry in International Competition: Government Policies and Corporate Strategies*. Ithaca, N.Y.: Cornell University Press.

10

Federalism and the Politics of Industrial Policy

ALLAN TUPPER

In modern democracies, the content of national industrial strategies provokes intense controversy, mainly over the balance between government intervention and market forces and the appropriate blend of policy instruments. In Canada, federalism adds several vexing questions to such debates. For instance, what is, and what should be, the contribution of each level of government to an industrial strategy? More generally, how can effective public policies be generated in the face of divided jurisdiction and political decentralization?

This essay explores the political issues posed by Canadian federalism for industrial policy making, dividing the discussion into three sections. The first delineates the role and contribution of each level of government to the formulation of industrial policies. Here I argue that a concern with measuring which level of government is dominant is not useful, because such a focus overlooks federalism's combination of active governments in Ottawa and the provinces. Moreover, generalizations about the "interventionist" character of different national industrial policies should be treated cautiously. While Canadian governments are interventionist as compared with governments in the United States and Australia, they intervene less actively and differently than, for example, the governments of France or Sweden.

The second section probes the interactions between governments and pays particular concern to areas of cooperation and conflict. My theme is that, while governments seldom pursue industrial policies that are clearly contradictory, there remains a lack of policy coordination between the federal and provincial governments and between provincial governments themselves. In most major areas of industrial policy, each government pursues its ends with scant reference to the goals of the other actors.

In the third section, the contemporary Canadian experience is compared with that of two other modern federations, the United States and Australia. The findings suggest that, because of the different character and development of federalism in these countries, their experience holds no blueprint for Canadian reformers. In both countries, but especially in the United States, the regional governments possess fewer economic powers than the Canadian provinces. One interesting finding that emerges, however, is that Canadian observers may have exaggerated the integrity of the internal "common markets" in both Australia and the United States. For in both countries governments, in defiance of constitutional guarantees, have erected various internal barriers to trade. In this area, comparison suggests that differences between federal states are those of degree, not of kind. More speculatively, I maintain that intergovernmental conflict in matters of industrial policy making may be on the wane as governments come to realize that cooperation might be mutually beneficial.

The Role of Governments in Industrial Policy in Canada

In this section, which sketches the influence of the federal and provincial governments on industrial policy, the analysis is suggestive rather than exhaustive. I try to note trends, but do not claim to catalogue the full range of federal and provincial policies. In particular, I focus on procurement policy, grants and incentives to industry, and the role of Crown corporations. Such topics as commercial policy, macroeconomic policies, and taxation, while important as instruments of industrial policy, are not examined explicitly.

The Federal Role

While it is commonplace to remark upon, if not lament, the passing of Ottawa's dominance in Canadian federalism, the federal government remains an active force in industrial policy making. While challenged and constrained in some measure by the provinces, the federal government wields powerful industrial policy levers comparable to those of a unitary state. Ottawa controls fiscal, monetary, and commercial policy, manages a large stable of state corporations, offers a range of loans, grants, and subsidies to private enterprise, exercises extensive regulatory powers, and employs an activist purchasing policy. The following examples provide some insight into the federal role.

• On average, the federal government spends three times as much on trade and industry as the provinces *combined* ($865 million in 1979–80 compared to a provincial total of $333 million).[1]

- In 1980, governmental investments in and loans outstanding to the private sector were estimated at $19.1 billion, with a further $29.4 billion in loan guarantees and insurance. The federal share was 74 and 95 percent respectively.[2]
- In 1980, the Federal Business Development Bank had loans outstanding slightly in excess of $2 billion. The largest provincial financial intermediary was the Ontario Development Corporation, with loans outstanding of less than $200 million.[3]

Such data remind us that Ottawa is a potent force in Canadian industrial policy. Its expenditures often outstrip those of all the provinces combined. Its policy alternatives are more complex than those of the provinces and embrace instruments, like tariffs, where no formal provincial role exists. Thus, observers must carefully distinguish rhetoric from reality when discussing Ottawa's demise.

Like other modern states, the Canadian government offers programs of financial assistance to industry. In the main, the former Department of Industry, Trade and Commerce (IT&C) and now the Department of Regional Industrial Expansion have administered Ottawa's tangle of industrial loans and grants, which despite their range and importance have been curiously immune from scholarly evaluation. As for political controversy, the New Democratic Party decried many industrial policies as a form of "welfare" for large corporations during the 1972 federal election campaign, but such objections have been the exception rather than the rule.

The range and diversity of federal programs of assistance to industry make it difficult to generalize about policy intentions. However, the most thorough and contemporary study advances the following points:[4]

- Direct federal aid to industry grew rapidly in the 1965–71 period when a dozen new programs were inaugurated. Since then expenditures have not increased significantly.
- Most federal assistance seeks to generate investment. The promotion of research and development and the development of export markets are lesser priorities.
- No master plan or "industrial strategy" underpins Ottawa's largesse. Both prosperous and declining industries have received roughly comparable shares of assistance. Only three broad categories of firms can be said to have received disproportionate assistance — those where tariff protection is very low, those engaged in research, and those which are dominant employers in regions.

As well as undertaking policies designed to enhance the competitiveness of industry, the federal government has, since the early 1960s, assumed a direct role in influencing the location of industry and the promotion of economic activity in Canada's slow-growth regions, notably Quebec and

Atlantic Canada. The most important manifestation of Ottawa's new role was the creation in 1969 of the Department of Regional Economic Expansion (DREE) which was given wide-ranging powers to promote economic development.[5] In contrast to IT&C, DREE stressed the need for intergovernmental collaboration if regional disparities were to be overcome. In 1973, the department launched the General Development Agreements that provided vehicles for joint federal-provincial planning and funding of economic projects deemed central to provincial priorities.[6]

One of DREE's policies — the Regional Development Incentives Act (RDIA) — has been particularly controversial. The act seeks to lure firms to slow-growth areas and to encourage the expansion of existing firms in the same areas. The main inducement is one-time federal grants to a maximum of $6 million to corporations locating in designated areas. Although expenditures under the RDIA were modest (around $491 million between 1969 and 1978) when compared to IT&C expenditures, the act evoked debates about federal economic policy and government-business relations. One objection was that the RDIA provided windfalls to corporations by financing investments that would occur anyway, without a subsidy. More importantly, the RDIA and other DREE activities symbolized for many, including the province of Ontario, a threatening interference with market forces which they felt should be the prime determinant of industrial location. In the critics' view, the Canadian economy was not strong enough to tolerate a politically inspired, and ultimately irrational, dispersion of economic activity. In other words, promoting robust industry and balancing regional distribution of economic activity struck many observers as incompatible objectives. In contrast, other critics maintained that DREE was too passive, too dependent upon the response of corporations, and too weak to impose its views on other federal agencies and institutions. DREE's activities also focussed attention on such questions as the reasons for the persistence of regional disparities, the best mix of policies to alleviate them, and the proper role for governments in influencing industrial location.

Much to the chagrin of textbook economists and free-traders, government purchasing is employed as a policy instrument in advanced economies. The state's control over large purchases of goods and services enables it to employ its purchasing power in pursuit of various objectives. In Canada, through a complex web of regulations, the federal government favours Canadian suppliers. However, considerable confusion surrounds the political and economic objectives of federal purchasing policy. This confusion is heightened by the fact that the politicians and administrators appear to have considerable discretion in this area, and because the essence of public policy is nowhere spelled out in detail. It appears that current practice seeks to satisfy several objectives, including the protection of domestic industry from import competition, the sustenance of technology-based industry, and baser partisan objectives.

A revered distinction between the political economies of Canada and the United States is the greater reliance of Canadian governments on public ownership as a policy instrument. In this country, federal Crown corporations have played a vital role in the transportation and communications industries. The Canadian National Railways, Air Canada, and the Canadian Broadcasting Corporation were established to maintain and extend infrastructure in the face of an inhospitable environment, a timid private sector, and the U.S. presence. After World War II, the federal government expanded its role and launched the entities that were to become the Federal Business Development Bank, the Export Development Corporation, and the Canada Mortgage and Housing Corporation. Such financial intermediaries were designed to fill "gaps" in capital markets, to assist disadvantaged groups, and to supplement private financial institutions.

Since the 1960s Canadian public enterprise has proliferated, assumed new roles, and generated controversies.[7] The rapid growth of Petro-Canada has made that firm a significant actor in the oil and gas industry, an area traditionally the preserve of the private sector. And through the acquisition of Canadair and deHavilland Aircraft, Ottawa has assumed a role in the civil and military aviation industries. The establishment of the Cape Breton Development Corporation in 1967 marked the first time that a federal state firm had been created explicitly for the purpose of maintaining employment. At the same time, Crown corporations like Atomic Energy of Canada Ltd., the CNR, and Air Canada have diversified their operations, placed more emphasis on profitability, and competed directly against private firms. Such developments have expanded political controversies about government's role in the marketplace.

In an impressive survey published in 1983, John W. Langford and Kenneth J. Huffman analyzed the scope and economic significance of federal Crown corporations.[8] Their sample of 61 Crown corporations that performed explicitly commercial functions reveals that these firms employ 183,106 persons, control assets in excess of $53 billion, and owe $18.5 billion to other lenders. Whether the growth of Crown corporations has added much coherence to federal industrial policy is another question. The Liberals and Progressive Conservatives appear divided, at least rhetorically, about the value of such corporations as policy instruments. Moreover, as noted by Harvey Feigenbaum,[9] the tendency of large state corporations to place their own goals above those of governments has evoked considerable concern about their effectiveness as interventions.

Another development is the federal government's tendency to intervene in the economy through mixed enterprises and equity investments. In this vein, the Langford-Huffman survey notes that 80 per cent of federal mixed enterprises have been created since 1970. The Canada Development Corporation, originally a mixed enterprise itself, acquired whole or partial ownership of many firms and thereby blurred the boundaries between public and private sectors. The Canada Development Investment Corporation, which was established in 1982, may serve as a state holding company responsible for directing and coordinating other Crown corporations and government investments in the private sector. A related development is Ottawa's growing disposition to extend loan guarantees to large firms and to refinance, or "bail out," distressed corporations. Such interventions, and the resulting political controversies reflect Ottawa's greater willingness to intervene at the level of the firm and to become involved in the restructuring of industry.

This brief review of federal industrial policy reveals the government as an active player in shaping the economy. Moreover, Canadian federalism's division of power between the federal and provincial governments has raised no major barriers to Ottawa's exercise of a range of instruments. What is open to question, however, is the effectiveness, not the scope, of federal industrial policy. Diverse critics are united in the view that Ottawa's industrial policies are piecemeal, uncoordinated, and guided by no master plan. In postwar Canada, Ottawa has been unable to develop, generate support for, or implement a coherent set of national economic objectives. There is no "national policy."

Explanations for this state of affairs are legion. One view holds that successive Liberal governments have been divided over such questions as the role of government in the economy and economic nationalism. As a result, policy has meandered under the varying influences of different factions and ideologies. As a recent U.S. study argues, because of domestic divisions, Canadian industrial policy is more interventionist than that of the United States, but less interventionist than that of Japan and several western European states.[10] Another explanation sees the absence of federal leadership as a function of changes in Canadian federalism, as growing provincial economic prowess and the related regional specialization of the economy have prevented decisive federal action in the face of economic decline. More recently, Stephen Clarkson has maintained that a resurgence of American nationalism under the Reagan Administration has limited Ottawa's options.[11] For example, federal plans to advance an interventionist industrial strategy were shelved in the aftermath of Washington's opposition to the National Energy Program.

Since the federal election of 1980, the federal government has employed its powers to reverse centrifugal tendencies in Canadian federalism and to reassert Ottawa's dominance. Among the major policies enacted were the National Energy Program, constitutional provisions which stressed an entrenched Charter of Rights, and alterations to federal-provincial fiscal relations. Such initiatives, collectively labelled the "Third National Policy" by Donald Smiley,[12] were designed to enhance the power, prestige, and visibility of Ottawa at the expense of the provincial governments. Further evidence of Ottawa's growing desire to act independently of the provinces was the reorganization of federal economic development departments in January 1982. Salient features of this reorganization included:

- the disbanding of DREE and IT&C and their replacement by the Department of Regional Industrial Expansion (DRIE);
- a clarification and expansion of the roles of the former Ministry of State for Economic Development which became the Ministry of State for Economic and Regional Development (MSERD); and
- the establishment in each province of regional offices of MSERD headed by a Federal Economic Development Coordinator.

The effect of such changes are not yet fully understood, and they remain the subject of political and scholarly controversy.[13] However, the reorganization does reflect a federal desire to abandon such efforts at federal-provincial cooperation as the General Development Agreements and to generate regional policies independent of the provincial governments.

The Provincial Role

The continuing vitality of the provincial governments remains, in the words of a leading student, the "great mystery" of Canadian federalism.[14] Instead of collapsing under the supposedly nationalizing imperatives of national transportation and communications systems and citizen mobility, the provinces have in the 1970s approached economic management with renewed vigour.

With the passage of time, scholarly views on the provincial role have become more favourable. Once portrayed as incompetents in economic matters, the provinces are now sometimes seen as progressive and able economic actors. Illustrative of this change in attitude is the argument advanced by Michael Jenkin in his study of federal and provincial industrial policies. According to Jenkin, the provinces, unable to use such major levers as monetary policy and trade policy, have relied on more direct instruments of intervention. Moreover, their concern with the local effects of corporate decision making has led them into more intimate relationships with firms than Ottawa has generally experienced. The "micro" approach to industrial policy is analagous to the industrial policies pursued by the interventionist democracies of western Europe and Japan. Such arguments led Jenkin to conclude: "many of the creative and innovative aspects of industrial policy today in Canada are to be found not at the national level, but within provincial jurisdictions."[15]

The diversity of the provinces makes difficult and unwise the advancement of general truths about their industrial polices. However, at least two generalizations can be safely made. First, no province is willing to allow either federal economic policy or market forces to be the exclusive determinant of its economic structure. Particularly since the 1960s, the provinces have undertaken policies that modify the impact of both factors. Second, although all provinces aspire to greater control over their economies, they differ in their capacity and willingness to intervene. Alberta is often said to exhibit the fiscal resources and political will to mount an industrial strategy while the less prosperous governments in Atlantic Canada, ever dependent on federal largesse, are less inclined to pursue independent policies.

Hinterland and Metropolitan Strategies

The eight hinterland provinces have often lamented their subordinate status in comparison with the metropolitan core of Ontario and Quebec. Relatively sparsely populated, far from major markets, and subject to the usual vicissitudes of resource-based economies, the western and Maritime provinces have sought to diversify. As noted earlier, the government of Alberta in the 1970s is generally thought to have developed the most comprehensive industrial blueprint. At the heart of Alberta's strategy are efforts to steer the provincial economy away from its dependence on oil and natural gas, to limit the impact of external forces on the local economy, and to employ ownership of natural resources to shift economic and political power westward.[16] In so doing, Alberta has rejected the notion of "force-fed" industrialization based on subsidized secondary manufacturing. Instead, it seeks to further upgrade natural resources within the province and to develop technology-based industry in Edmonton and Calgary. The development of an indigenous petrochemical industry, with its technology base, dependence on feedstock availability, and high salaries is the centrepiece of Alberta's policy.

Other provinces, notably Saskatchewan, British Columbia, and Newfoundland, appear committed to industrial policies comparable in intent to Alberta's. That is, they see their salvation in increased provincial control over natural resources and in the further upgrading of resources within provincial boundaries. None of these provinces, as essentially hinterland areas, now sees much sustenance in the development of secondary manufacturing. However, as each province boasts a different resource base, important differences remain in the policies that are being and can be pursued. For example, in its efforts to extend provincial control over potash, oil, natural gas, and uranium, Saskatchewan has relied on Crown corporations. On the other hand, Alberta has generally rejected public ownership and has opted instead for "mixed" ownership corporations, notably the Alberta Energy Company, which is jointly owned by the provincial government and many individual investors.

As the most populated province and the home of more than 50 percent of Canadian manufacturing capacity, Ontario remains this country's industrial heartland. Indeed, its diversified economy has long been the envy of other provinces. Ontario's prosperity is attributable to much more than favourable federal policies and natural advantages. As H.V. Nelles has demonstrated, the government of Ontario was pursuing policies of public ownership, resource processing within provincial boundaries, and assistance to industry early in this century.[17] Rather ironically, Ontario is the architect of many policies that are now employed by hinterland provinces in the pursuit of "province building." Until the mid-1970s, however, Ontario was able to stand back from the competitive struggle for industry that preoccupied other provinces.

Deteriorating economic performance has recently led the government of Ontario to assume a more active economic role. Ontario shares several problems with other mature manufacturing areas, notably competition from countries that have significantly lower production costs, lesser tariff protection, and technological backwardness. And like all metropolitan areas that are deficient in oil and gas, Ontario has had to adjust to changes in the price and availability of fuels. These problems are compounded by the "branch plant" nature of Ontario's economy. Indeed, as political and economic power in the United States shifts from the northeast to the southwest, Ontario's attractiveness as a branch plant location has declined. Such compelling trends have led the provincial government to establish new Crown corporations, to provide grants and loans to major firms, and to rationalize and expand its industrial assistance policies. The consequences of Ontario's newfound interest in industrial policy are not yet known. Michael Jenkin has suggested, however, that Ontario's need for industrial restructuring, particularly if extensive federal assistance is required, could well cause further conflict between centre and periphery, and between Ontario and Quebec over the regional distribution of federal assistance.[18]

Quebec's industrial policy is perhaps the most interesting and complex of the ten provincial governments. It is often said to be the most interventionist and nationalistic, although a recent study by Phillipe Faucher, André Blais, and Robert Young deflates both assertions by comparing levels of expenditure and the objectives of industrial policy in Ontario and Quebec.[19] The objectives of Quebec's industrial strategy are to transform the province's industrial structure so as to reduce its dependence on labour-intensive industries like footwear, textiles, and food processing, to encourage technological innovation, and to enhance the role of "modern" industries. In this vein, Quebec policy makers have often pointed to Ontario's more modern and diversified economy. Over the last two decades, they have often asked why there is an economic division of labour between the two metropolitan provinces.

One theme in the rhetoric of Quebec industrial policy is the need to nourish small businesses which in the main are owned and controlled by francophones. Such firms often have serious problems, including low productivity, technological backwardness, and an inability to penetrate export markets. In response, Quebec governments have extended to them financial, marketing, and technical assistance. As well as assisting small francophone firms, the government has employed industrial incentives as levers to increase the number of French Canadian managers and to enhance the use of French in industry.

Since its election in 1976 the Parti québécois, as a social democratic government, might have been expected to chart a new course for Quebec's industrial strategy. Such has not been the case. The PQ has not deviated much from the directions set by its nominally more conservative predecessors. It has argued that "discriminatory" federal economic policy accounts for Quebec's industrial underdevelopment as compared with Ontario, but the province's policies are in fact in the mainstream. The PQ continues to stress the role of francophone businesses, to emphasize Quebec's hydro potential as a source of economic development, to call for the modernization of secondary industry, and to welcome foreign investment.

Instruments of Provincial Intervention

In all provinces, departments usually known as Industry or Industry and Trade develop and administer industrial policies. Such departments provide technical and managerial assistance to business, distribute research on export markets and conduct trade missions. They are supplemented by provincial Crown corporations whose role is to extend financial assistance to firms seeking to establish or expand their operations within the province. Examples include Nova Scotia's Industrial Estates Ltd., the Société de développement industriel du Québec and the Ontario Development Corporation and its affiliates. Although their mandates vary, such institutions seek to generate and maintain employment in secondary industry. In so doing, they supply financial assistance in a variety of forms and are capable of tailoring assistance to the needs of firms. Such Crown corporations were conceived as "lenders of last resort," which were to supplement private financial institutions, but this passive role has been abandoned in favour of a more aggressive posture.

Most provinces have programs that provide outright grants to industry. Different reporting conventions make it difficult to estimate the amounts involved, but Jenkin's study advanced the figure of $80 million for 1979–80. His estimate includes outright grants only and excludes more subtle forms of subsidy. Provincial ownership of hydro utilities in most provinces provides ample scope for subsidization, as does the common practice of extending loans at below market rates.

One controversial element of provincial industrial policy is the use of government purchasing policies that favour local bidders. Such practices are certainly not new, but their employment has recently become more visible and controversial. Governments, for obvious reasons, are unwilling to provide complete information on their purchasing practices and the extent of preference offered. It now appears, however, that all provinces extend some form of preference to local suppliers, although only Newfoundland, Nova Scotia, and British Columbia admit to the existence of outright preferences for local suppliers under all circumstances.[20] Quebec's policy as outlined in 1977 is perhaps the most comprehensive. It includes a general price preference for Quebec suppliers and measures to limit bids to Quebec suppliers under certain circumstances. Even Ontario, which has publicly waged a campaign against "buy provincial" policies and now advocates a 10 percent price preference for *Canadian* suppliers, admits to favouring provincial suppliers in some cases. For example, Ontario's municipalities are required to buy rapid transit equipment only from Ontario sources. Such policies, which are based on political rather than economic reasoning, have been criticized as challenges to the integrity of the Canadian market. But governments have been unable to agree either upon limits to preferential purchasing policies or upon a coordinated intergovernmental approach.

An inescapable feature of the provinces' economic role is their expanded use of public enterprise. Indeed, in no other federation are the regional governments so involved in public ownership of industry. The scope of the provincial public enterprise sector has been thoroughly studied recently. In their comprehensive survey, Aidan Vining and Robert Botterell conclude that there are 233 provincial Crown corporations which account for assets in excess of $62 billion.[21] The "hydros" remain the major provincial Crown corporations, but 48 percent of all provincial Crown corporations have been established since 1970.

Until recently, provincial entrepreneurship was limited to the provision of economic infrastructure, notably the generation and transmission of electricity in all the large provinces except Alberta, telephone service in the Prairie provinces, and railroads in British Columbia and Ontario. One obvious exception is the group of Crown corporations established by the CCF government in Saskatchewan in 1944. These firms, which competed directly with private enterprise and which ventured into the manufacturing and resource sectors, used to be the objects of unrelenting attack by business interests. However, four decades later, Saskatchewan's once heretical example has been emulated by most other provinces. Provincial Crown corporations play a large part in the oil and natural gas industries, industrial financing and reorganization, steel, automobile insurance in four provinces, and a range of manufacturing concerns. The election of NDP governments in Manitoba, Saskatchewan, and British Columbia in the 1970s helps account for some of the recent growth in provincial entrepreneurship, but Progressive Conservative governments in Ontario and Alberta have also been active.[22] And through such devices as "mixed enterprises," joint ventures, and the acquisition of equity in private firms, the provincial governments have extended further into the private sector and established new relationships with business interests.

Nowhere are these tendencies more visible than in Quebec. Since the nationalization of hydro-electricity by the Lesage Liberals in 1962, Quebec's stable of Crown corporations has proliferated to include Sidbec (steel) SOQUEM (mineral exploration), SOQUIP (oil and gas) and the Société de développement industriel (industrial financing and reorganization). Boasting assets in excess of $20 billion, Quebec's Crown corporations and their subsidiaries now number several hundred. Such state corporations undertake political and social functions, as well as purely economic ones. In Quebec, Crown corporations are committed to the promotion of French as a working language in industry, the employment and advancement of francophone managers, and the development of Quebec-based and -controlled firms in the private sector.

The Alberta Heritage Savings Trust Fund (AHSTF) and the Caisse de dépôt et placement du Québec (Caisse) are provincial institutions whose size and economic significance puts them in a class by themselves. As established in 1976, the AHSTF was charged with investing a portion of Alberta's royalties from oil and natural gas. But considerable confusion surrounds the goals of the Trust Fund, which now exceeds $13 billion. The Alberta government maintains that some of its money must be employed to diversify and strengthen the Albertan economy. Other objectives include improving the quality of life and providing a revenue source which can be tapped when resource revenues begin to decline. The Caisse was established in 1965 by Premier Jean Lesage's Liberal government. It was empowered to invest the assets of the Quebec Pension Plan and now receives deposits from other sources as well. At time of writing (1984), the Caisse's assets exceed $16 billion, $3.5 billion of which are investments in the common stocks of such Canadian corporations as Alcan, Canadian Pacific, Bell Canada, and Domtar.

In outlining the rationale for the Caisse, Premier Lasage emphasized that it was destined to be more than a passive investor. Indeed, it would seek investments that were both profitable and in the long-term interests of Quebec's economic development. This fusion of developmental and fiduciary goals has been frequently acknowledged by government spokesmen since 1965. However, the Parti québécois' deployment of the Caisse has evoked bitter controversies about its role in Canada's federalism. The Caisse's desire to appoint directors to the boards of companies in which it had major shareholdings was seen as particularly insidious. When the Caisse sought representation on Canadian Pacific's board, the federal government intervened with Bill S-31 which sought to prohibit certain provincial government investments in interprovincial transportation companies. The debate over this bill focussed attention on the issue of government investment in private firms and the propriety of provincial government investment in significant national firms.[23] To date, no intergovernmental agreement has been struck on this important issue.

Conclusion

This survey of the roles of government in industrial policy reveals the existence of active governments in both Ottawa and the provinces. The federal government pursues a plethora of policies aimed at stimulating investment, ensuring the competitiveness of industry, and influencing the location of firms. It operates a large public enterprise sector. At the same time, the Constitution has posed no obvious roadblocks to a significant economic role for the provincial governments. Without permission from other members of the federation, provinces may subsidize industries, prefer local suppliers in government contracts, and own firms engaged in interprovincial commerce. In recent years, most provincial governments have articulated comprehensive industrial policies. Alan C. Cairns has aptly characterized the status quo in industrial policy with the following words: "Both levels of government are strong. Neither can dominate the other. Both pursue increasingly comprehensive and integrated goals with a consequent decline in their willingness to defer to the interests of external governments."[24]

Before probing the interplay of governments, it is important to remind ourselves that Canadian industrial policies, when compared with those of several other states, are not particularly interventionist. For example, Canadian governments do not, either individually or collectively, engage in anything akin to French indicative planning, nor do they exhibit any powerful desire to embrace such a system. Moreover, Canada's public enterprise sector, while large, is not employed systematically and coherently in pursuit of broader policy objectives. No clear and consistent objectives guide the use of government procurement. The planned restructuring of troubled and/or promising industries is seldom undertaken.

As John Zysman effectively argues, a country like Canada, where the state lacks direct control over the allocation of finance, is ultimately unable to implement a *dirigiste*, planned approach to industrial restructuring.[25] And as well as lacking the capacity to allocate credit selectively, Canadian governments, like those of the other Anglo-American democracies, are limited in their interventions by the continuing power of laissez-faire ideas. Advocates of interventionist, nationalistic industrial policies remain a minority in Canada, particularly among businessmen who seem heavily influenced by the anti-government rhetoric of their U.S. counterparts.

Intergovernmental Relations in Canada

This section examines the interaction of Canadian governments in the sphere of industrial assistance policy. It does so by first examining federal-provincial cooperation and conflict. It then studies the dynamics of interprovincial relations. The recent debate about the integrity of the Canadian common market is also reviewed. This issue is important as a substantive problem in itself and as a microcosm of the political conflicts of interest described in the previous sections.

Federal-Provincial Relations

Federal-Provincial Cooperation

In a recent essay, André Blais, Phillipe Faucher, and Robert Young maintain that contemporary scholarship on federalism exaggerates the amount and intensity of intergovernmental conflict, downplays instances of cooperation, and employs hyperbole when describing inter-governmental relations.[26] There is some truth to this argument. In the field of industrial policy, governments have often been able to collabo-rate effectively; policy making is not always a "zero-sum" game. On the other hand, there are important limits to cooperation, limits that have implications for the content of industrial policy.

As noted earlier, the General Development Agreements, negotiated between DREE and each province, represent successful instances of intergovernmental collaboration. Established in 1973, the GDAs provide a framework under which more specific subsidiary development agree-ments are negotiated and funded. They recognize the need for cooper-ative identification of economic opportunities and priorities and coordi-nated intergovernmental action if regional disparities are to be reduced. In recognition of the different fiscal circumstances of the provinces, Ottawa financed up to 90 percent of projects in Newfoundland, 80 percent of those in Nova Scotia and New Brunswick, 60 percent of those in Quebec, and only 50 per cent of those in Alberta, British Columbia, and Ontario. The agreements embraced a range of schemes including the rehabilitation of Quebec's steel and pulp and paper industries and infra-structure upgrading throughout the Maritimes.

Other instances of cooperation merit attention. In the early 1970s the federal government, Alberta, and Saskatchewan were able to achieve a planned expansion of the steel industry in Western Canada, even though both provinces harboured ambitions about the development of steel-making capacity in their own jurisdictions. Similarly, the federal govern-ment has recently been able to implement a major expansion of Canada's helicopter industry in Quebec without alienating Ontario, which also has a major interest in the industry. And Jenkin notes how the federal government intervened when it appeared that Ontario and Quebec were about to start a bidding war for investment in their pulp and paper industries.[27] The result was a successful federal-provincial agreement that prevented interprovincial competition, but also tailored assistance to the needs of each province. Finally, Stephen Clarkson describes as a "positive experience" the federal-provincial collaboration in preparing Canada's position for the Tokyo round of negotiations on the General Agreement on Tariffs and Trade.[28]

The GDA experience and the cases cited above suggest that intergovernmental agreement is possible, especially when either the number of issues or the number of governments involved are limited. As the agenda broadens and the number of participants increases, the prospect for intergovernmental consensus on industrial policy matters is reduced. The outcome of the 1978 First Ministers' Conference on the Economy supports this contention. There the eleven governments and their advisers were unable to agree on signficant policy questions. As analyzed by Julia Eastman and Douglas Brown, the conference was a spectacle of political posturing, partisan disagreements, and, to a degree, ideological discord.[29] All this overlay intergovernmental disagreements about the content of an industrial strategy, the best policy instruments, and the location of industry. Such "limits to consultation" suggest that Canadian federalism presently precludes the development of an aggressive, interventionist industrial strategy. However, as Stephen Clarkson maintains, "federal-provincial collaboration and consensus on separate sectoral issues is entirely within the realm of the possible."[30]

As noted above, there are several preconditions to effective intergovernmental collaboration. A further problem is that, in a competitive federation, each level of government must believe that it is receiving its share of political credit and visibility. Thus, independent of broader conflicts of interest, governments and their bureaucracies have their own internally generated drives for status, power, and expansion. In a federal state, such drives often become entangled with substantive policy issues. Indeed, one of the reasons for Ottawa's abandonment of the GDA approach was that the provincial governments were reaping considerable political credit for the results of the agreements, even though much federal money was involved. Moreover, the GDA approach reduced Ottawa's status insofar as the federal government, through its own emphasis on bilateral agreements, became "just another government" with no special roles or prerogatives in industrial policy.

Federal-Provincial Conflict

Over the last two decades, Canadian federalism has endured debates about the regional effects of federal industrial policy and the interests it serves. At the heart of such debates is the assertion, advanced by the western provincial governments in particular, that federal initiatives are attuned to the needs of industry in central Canada, insensitive to the needs of hinterland provinces, and based upon the need to preserve a division of labour between a manufacturing core and resource-producing hinterlands. Such flaws in federal policy are seen as inevitable, given

Ottawa's need to respond to the political demands of the heavily populated, industrialized centre.

At the Western Economic Opportunities Conference in Calgary in 1973, the federal government and the western provincial governments convened to examine ways to promote regional development. The conference was the scene of unrelenting attacks on Ottawa's "discriminatory" policies. The policies of the Department of Industry, Trade and Commerce and federal purchasing regulations were criticized as detrimental to Prairie manufacturing and of disproportionate benefit to central Canadian firms. Moreover, DREE's initiatives, while welcomed, were said to be offset by larger IT&C expenditures which strengthened central Canada's hegemony. Although provincial spokesmen called for greater federal expenditures on western industrial development, their real objectives were more regionally sensitive federal policies, a greater federal recognition of the region's resource-based prowess, and federal actions that facilitated regional upgrading or resources. Above all, Ottawa was told to abandon its image of the Canadian economy as predicated upon a regional division of economic activity.

Governments in the Atlantic provinces have sometimes echoed similar sentiments, although their weaker economies and generally better political relations with Ottawa have discouraged them from acting as aggressively as their western counterparts. The provincial governments in the region do occasionally lament Ottawa's inability to formulate policies that generate self-sustaining growth. They resent, moreover, their status as dependents on federal largesse and their lack of autonomy in industrial policy. But ultimately, the Atlantic governments acknowledge the need for a federal government strong enough to redistribute wealth in the Canadian federation and are willing to work cooperatively with Ottawa. They have long supported a major role for DREE, even though they have complained that its policies are offset by federal transportation, industrial, and fiscal policies that centralize economic activity in Ontario and Quebec.

Under Premier Peckford, Newfoundland's anti-federal rhetoric distinguishes it from its more contented neighbours in Atlantic Canada. Newfoundland has repeatedly challenged federal policies in the fisheries and offshore and has done so with a venom uncommon for governments in the region. However, the Maritime provinces have not emulated Newfoundland's aggressive posture. They prefer to maintain good working relationships with the federal government on whose large expenditures they rely.

Hinterland protests about the "bias" of federal policy are as old as Canada itself. A newer development is Quebec's view that federal industrial policies serve Ontario's needs alone. At the heart of the Parti québécois' analysis is the notion that the province's economic backwardness and poor economic performance are as much the product of federal economic policy as the workings of the marketplace. Several important postwar policies — notably the auto pact, which allegedly works against Quebec; the St. Lawrence Seaway, which is said to have undercut Montreal's status as a port; and the National Oil Policy of 1961, which hurt Quebec's ambitions in petrochemicals — are seen to enhance or tolerate the concentration of dynamic industries in Ontario. While Quebec admits to receiving a large share of DREE expenditures, it criticizes such funds as band-aids which have exerted a perverse economic impact. As Quebec struggled to transform its industrial structure, DREE has encouraged new investment in backward industries like textiles.

The provincial governments' arguments about the inadequacies of federal policy have not been unanimously endorsed. Quebec's complaints about federal "discrimination" have been rejected as poorly documented and politically inspired. Moreover, Kenneth Norrie maintains that the Prairie governments have overestimated the impact of federal policy on the west's industrial structure. Market forces, not public policy, account for the concentration of secondary industry in central Canada. As Norrie argues: "The geographically peripheral areas of the country are just not feasible sites to naturally attract most types of secondary industry. . . . Hinterland regions do not become industrial centres in a market economy, and the distribution of manufacturing industries across Canada is a simple reflection of this fact."[31] Such arguments have not exerted much influence on intergovernmental disagreement about industrial policy.

It is tempting to dismiss provincial grievances about the content of federal industrial policy as empty rhetoric which has no impact on Canadian industrial policy. Such a view is, however, mistaken. For provincial government critiques exert major, albeit sometimes subtle, influences on public policy. In a very direct way, incessant provincial criticisms of federal industrial policy have converted debates about industrial policy into intergovernmental wrangles about the location of economic activity. Federalism gives questions about industrial location a prominence unthinkable in a unitary state. Ottawa in particular has difficulty articulating and implementing industrial policies that do not take into account the spatial distribution of industry. Perhaps more importantly, federalism, with its bias toward regional issues, distorts the industrial policy agenda and downplays the signficance of such problems as the overall impact of government and the relationships between government, industry, and labour.

Under contemporary Canadian federalism, the provincial governments may offset federal policies that appear to "centralize" economic activity or to "discriminate" against regions. A particularly dramatic deployment of provincial powers occurred in 1974 when Alberta attempted to cut off feedstock to the Petrosar petrochemical plant in Sarnia. Petrosar, as a symbol of Ontario's hegemony, was seen as a challenge to Alberta's efforts to establish a petrochemical industry. In the ensuing struggle, Ottawa was denounced for tolerating, if not encouraging, the expansion of petrochemicals in Ontario.

Such overt regional conflicts of interest are rare, and few provinces have recently matched Alberta's truculence in federal-provincial relations. However, the provinces have the potential to employ their powers in defiance of federal initiatives, and Ottawa must take this into account. As a result, the federal government can seldom move decisively to implement industrial policies. In a regionally specialized economy, industrial policy often assumes the guise of a zero-sum game where one region's loss is another's gain. Moreover, there is assumed to be inherent antagonism both between the heartland and the peripheries and between the goals of the federal and provincial governments. A major consequence of such antagonism is a diminished federal capacity to articulate national policies.

So far, the focus of this section has been on the capacity of the provinces to constrain Ottawa. The federal government, however, has frequently and aggressively employed its policy-making powers so as to shape provincial priorities. Indeed, Anthony Careless' study of regional development policy demonstrates how Ottawa has taken the initiative in defining problems and proposing solutions[32] while the provinces, seldom consulted, have simply reacted to federal interventions. The federal government, which has ample financial resources as well as a desire to enhance its political visibility, has often pursued policies that reduced provincial autonomy. In the same vein, research by Blais, Faucher, and Young reveals how Ontario and Quebec's interest in regional policy has followed, rather than led, major federal policies.[33] They suggest that the pattern of federal initiative–provincial reaction is the norm in most spheres of industrial policy, although compelling evidence to this effect is lacking. Such findings remind us that Ottawa is a potent force in federalism, more than capable of forcing the provincial hand.

Earlier I argued that Canadian federalism shows a bias toward regional issues and an obsession with industrial location, and I discussed some of the troublesome results. There is, however, a brighter side to this picture. While Canada, as a series of regionally specialized economies, can probably not develop a single, all-embracing industrial policy, an effective industrial strategy might well be based on a series of regional policies. If such an approach were taken, federalism might under certain circumstances be a positive force in the articulation and achievement of policy since our brand of federalism focusses attention on regional economic specialization and the regional effects of national policies. Moreover, the provincial governments, close to the action and endowed with resource ownership, may complement the federal government's pan-Canadian and international focus.

Such harmony can be neither assumed nor guaranteed. Harvey

Lithwick and John Devlin argue that the 1981 federal white paper on economic development simply asserted that regional goals and overall national prosperity could be readily meshed.[34] No clear proposal emerged, however, as to how regional strengths could be used as building blocks or how economic diversification, an important goal of the hinterlands, could be achieved. Moreover, a regionally based industrial policy must have proper political foundations. A federal state, like contemporary Canada, in which the various governments try to enhance their status, may not be fertile ground for the seeds of regional cooperation.

Interprovincial Relations

Interprovincial rivalries and conflicts further complicate Canadian industrial policy. As provinces have expanded their economic roles, they have engaged in fairly frequent and intense competition for industry. Provincial governments are now attempting to offer concessions to industry that are comparable to those of their neighbours. At least three governments seek to nurture petrochemical industries while another six harbour ambitions in steel. In its most extreme form, interprovincial competition for industry has degenerated into bidding wars for new industry. A revealing example of such activity occurred in 1978 when Ontario, Quebec, and several U.S. states openly bid for new automobile plants.

Such competition has few positive consequences, as interprovincial rivalries merely add another element of conflict to intergovernmental relations. Provinces see their neighbours as rivals and resent the suggestion that federal intervention is required to curb their internecine strife. Moreover, corporations may be the major beneficiaries of interprovincial rivalries, as they skillfully play competing governments off against each other. The bargaining power of governments and their capacity to direct the course of provincial development are reduced when they assume that capital is a scarce commodity which in the absence of appropriate inducements will locate elsewhere. It is certainly difficult for a government to gauge the amount and nature of subsidy required to lure a corporation. In fact, governments may subsidize business investments that might have been made without financial inducements. Intergovernmental competition, then, increases the price paid for new investment.

No province benefits from this competition, but some may lose more than others. The governments of Atlantic Canada, already overcommitted in some areas, must keep stretching their resources to compete for industry with provinces that are better situated. Wealthy provinces like Ontario, which already enjoy natural advantages, may "outbid" other provinces. In an ironic way, therefore, competitive industrial strategies may exacerbate regional economic disparities, although this outcome is clearly the reverse of that sought by the provinces that are less well situated. A contrary position maintains that, given lower wages in their jurisdictions, the poorer provinces need not offer incentives comparable to those of the more prosperous ones. Some U.S. data support this argument, but compelling Canadian evidence has not yet been forthcoming. Further research is required into the economic consequences of interprovincial rivalries.

Interprovincial competition may also exert an impact on labour relations policy although this is difficult to document. The reason is that in the poorer provinces a docile, unorganized labour force may be a major attraction for investors. Governments in these provinces may abandon certain progressive forms of labour legislation or adopt hard-line stances toward labour so as to stay competitive as a site for investment. Such thinking may have led the government of Nova Scotia to amend its Trade Union Act so as to make it difficult to unionize interrelated plants of the same firm. The government has not convincingly denied that such legislation was drafted to satisfy Michelin Tires which, as a notoriously anti-union employer, demanded government action to block union organization in its Nova Scotia plants. In return, Michelin allegedly agreed to build a third plant. Similar logic can be applied to the content of environmental legislation, although here too evidence is lacking.

Most provinces have admitted the existence of interprovincial competition for investment and many have condemned the practice although efforts to curb such behaviour have failed. For example, in performing its new role as guardian of the Canadian common market, the government of Ontario has failed to convince other provinces to eschew "buy provincial" purchasing policies. As well, Ontario's recent efforts to improve its relations with Alberta and to enter into agreements which stressed the linkages and common interests between a resource-producing province and a manufacturing one were ignored in Edmonton. Nor have any agreements been struck on the use of industrial grants and incentives. The reasons for the reluctance of the provinces to curb competition are rooted in their preoccupation with provincial, rather than regional or national, impacts of industrial policy. Provincial governments see no reason to welcome industrial developments which, while perhaps economically sound, seem to confer disproportionate benefits on other provinces. To the extent that provincial governments wield any economic powers, an element of competition appears inevitable under federalism.

Some diminution of interprovincial competition may result from the western provinces' growing commitment to resource-led industrial strategies. The Prairie economies now rest on different resource bases, and both Alberta and Saskatchewan have abandoned efforts to force feed secondary industry. As a result, these provinces are unlikely to compete frequently for industry. Similarly, governments in the Maritimes now claim to have abandoned the quest for footloose firms that characterized their economic strategies in the 1960s and 1970s. They claim to seek smaller, indigenous firms which are linked with established industries. However, competition for industry may intensify between Ontario and Quebec. As noted earlier, the government of Ontario is now more willing to use its policy powers in defence of provincial interests, and both provinces face serious problems in their manufacturing industries. Recent disputes about the location of new automobile plants reveal that both governments are sometimes willing to extend large subsidies to corporations.

The Common Market Problem

The tendency of the provinces to engage in competitive industrial policy making is symptomatic of a broader concern about the integrity of the Canadian common market. At the heart of the debate is a concern that growing appetites for intervention have led to a proliferation of policies that impede the flow of factors of production and thereby reduce economic efficiency. Weak industries are fostered and Canada's modest domestic market is further fractured. The issue is interesting both as a substantive policy question and as a reflection of conflicts of interest within Canadian federalism.

The common market controversy evokes questions both about the nature of federalism and about the role of governments in the economy. Some proponents of strengthened guarantees of the common market are concerned about the growing economic prowess of the provinces and their capacity to erect internal barriers. Other advocates of a purer common market fear the expanded role of governments in the economy and seek to reduce that influence for ideological reasons. As John R. Hayes has argued in his comparative study of economic mobility in federations: "Finally — but this is more controversial — additional protection for free movement could make a useful contribution to setting salutory limits on the role of governments in the ownership and control of business enterprises."[35]

How significant is the economic impact of barriers to trade? No consensus emerges on this question. For example, Donald Smiley has argued: "Canadians pay a heavy material price for their failure to sustain a domestic common market."[36] But recent work by John Whalley challenges Smiley's assertion. Whalley concludes that the economic impact of internal barriers to trade has been exaggerated and that perhaps too much attention has been paid to the problem. On the issue of preferential provincial procurement policies, Whalley's rough guess is that two per cent of interprovincial trade is involved.[37] Another view is provided by Thomas J. Courchene who argues that most measures of the economic consequences of protectionism ignore "dynamic efficiency losses."[38] Courchene worries that protectionism stifles the entrepreneurship that is required in a competitive world economy. In his view such losses, although hard to quantify, are significant. Similarly, Jenkin maintains that "buy provincial" procurement policies have weakened segments of the Canadian electrical equipment industry.[39] This is so because manufacturers, in order to obtain major provincial contracts, must often establish a local production facility. As a result, the industry is weak, fragmented, and unable to exploit export opportunities. Such effects are rarely made explicit in economic analyses.

One area of consensus is that many federal policies also distort the Canadian common market. DREE grants, freight rates, and various aspects of Ottawa's energy policies are examples of federal initiatives that inhibit the flow of factors of production. The recognition that internal barriers to trade are often federally imposed, and indeed often exist in unitary states, led Courchene to warn against seeing federalism as "a degenerate form of economic union."[40]

The explicitly economic consequences of internal barriers to trade are secondary to the political significances of such policies. The very existence of beggar-my-neighbour policies contributes to distrust in intergovernmental relations, because they symbolize the intentions of individual governments to pursue their own courses and to insulate their economies from external forces. The unwillingness of Canadian governments to debate their respective contributions to economic distortions reflects enduring conflicts of interest within the federation. And, in a basic way, their failure to grapple with the issue of economic union reveals their inability to address the cumulative impact of government policy on the economy.

These tendencies are illustrated by the results of the First Ministers' Conference on the Constitution held at Ottawa in 1980. One agenda item dealt with federal proposals to strengthen the common market by constitutionally entrenching the mobility rights of citizens, clarifying section 121 of the BNA Act, and extending federal powers over trade and commerce. Underlying Ottawa's position was the view that provincial protectionism was too widespread and that serious political and economic problems were resulting. The federal position was supported only by Ontario, the province with the largest stake in the status quo.

The other provinces assailed the federal position. Not surprisingly to those with even a passing acquaintance with Canadian federalism, the alliance between Ontario and Ottawa evoked the suspicions of the hinterland provinces. Moreover, the provinces attacked the federal proposals as a "power grab" which curtailed provincial powers but did not reduce Ottawa's capacity to intervene. Under this deluge of provincial criticism, the economic union issue was shelved. It has not been resurrected in important intergovernmental forums.

Conclusions

Canadian federalism is characterized by active, but poorly coordinated, governments in Ottawa and the provinces. Although the policies of individual governments are not often contradictory, policy making does tend to be unilateral as governments tend more and more to pursue their own self-interest instead of looking for benefits in interdependence. Ottawa's abandonment of the GDA approach and its efforts to bypass provincial governments in industrial policy making attest to the tendency toward unilateral action.

Canadian governments have shown no real willingness to employ their large public sectors in a coordinated, let alone creative, manner. No intergovernmental agreement has been reached on the role of public procurement or industrial incentives as policy tools. The bitter conflict over Bill S-31, the corporate shareholding limitation act, reveals disagreement about the role of Crown corporations and government investment in firms as part of an industrial strategy. Ontario's efforts to stress the economic linkages between the manufacturing core and resource-producing provinces were resisted by Prairie provincial governments as a self-interested attempt to bolster the status quo.

Perhaps by its very nature, industrial policy generates conflicts of interest. As governments expand their economic roles, their ability to give evidence of proficient economic management becomes a determinant of their success. Accordingly, they tend to object to the policies of other governments that reduce their autonomy or seem to usurp their powers. Conflict also flows from the contrasting perspectives of the federal and provincial governments. The provinces, as custodians of smaller economies, often see particular industrial developments and projects as central to their future prosperity. The federal government, given its responsibility for the entire economy, may appear indifferent to local developments which may seem insignificant on a national scale. Finally, such conflicts are magnified under Canadian federalism with its history of regional animosities. Modern industrial policies have rekindled the old centre-periphery tensions and pointed up Canada's heterogeneity.

The spirit of this essay, like most recent scholarship on Canadian federalism, is pessimistic. A more benign federalism, however, may now be emerging, and the conflict-ridden 1970s may be replaced by a somewhat more harmonious era. Politicians cannot engage in ever escalating struggles with other governments without damaging their own interest. Still the conceptions of the political elite about the limits of conflict and cooperation are decidedly complex. Richard Simeon's classic study *Federal-Provincial Diplomacy* is replete with insight into such conceptions, but his study is now somewhat dated.[41] We need to know much more about such ideas before we can speak authoritatively.

Even casual observers of recent Canadian politics realize that Canadian governments see some benefit in the pursuit of strategies that are at least rhetorically confrontationist. Governments in the three most westerly provinces and Newfoundland, for example, have portrayed Ottawa as an alien force. Federal indifference to their plight is used to justify autarchic development strategies and often to deflect the electorate's attention from local problems. The electoral prowess of the Lougheed and Peckford governments, two of the most strident, attests to the success of such political designs. But there are limits to such strategies. Governments, particularly during periods of relative affluence, may impress their electorates with confrontationist tactics and schemes of economic provincialism. But the overzealous pursuit of such policies and strategies might ultimately be the seeds of a government's destruction. For a government (and Premier Peckford's administration may be a good example) that is overly aggressive and constantly rejects olive branches may unintentionally raise to prominence a separatist option. Such a focus may heighten the concern of hinterland citizens about the vulnerability of their small, open economies and strengthen their commitment to the larger political community which, while sometimes unjust, offers some hope for economic stability. Accordingly, a government, if relentlessly dedicated to a truculent, quasi-independent course, limits its political options dramatically. It may either pursue its logic to its conclusion and risk defeat and replacement by a more conciliatory regime or moderate its own potentially self-defeating drives. Federalism, and its attendant complex of divided citizen loyalties, may constrain the divisive tendencies of its governments.

Intergovernmental conflict may also be reduced in times of economic decline. Put differently, continuing and intense discord in Canadian federalism may in itself be a product of the relatively affluent 1970s. Governments in a federation may be more inclined to expand their powers and wealth when they realize they are struggling for a larger piece of an expanding pie. But in an era of decline, intergovernmental conflict may become a luxury in the eyes of citizens and politicians alike. Conflict, particularly that flowing from the status concerns of governments, may be frowned upon and avoided where possible. Governments themselves may sense that citizens are not particularly concerned at the best of times with the jurisdictional squabbles that preoccupy elites. In a period of economic trauma, a government caught playing out ancient rivalries may be seen as a destructive not a creative force. The ability to cooperate, on the other hand, may simultaneously become a virtue. My sense is that Canadian governments, with the possible exception of Newfoundland, have recently been disciplined by such logic.

The Experience of Other Federations

This section looks at the literature on the politics of industrial policy in the modern U.S. and Australian federations with a view to answering two questions. First, do they exhibit more or less intergovernmental conflict than is seen in Canada? Second, does comparison yield insight into institutional or policy reforms that could improve Canadian federalism and be readily adapted to Canadian conditions?

The United States

The contemporary U.S. federation provides a contrast to the Canadian in two ways. First, the U.S. federal system is more centralized than its Canadian counterpart: Washington is the decisive force. Second, there remains in the United States a hostility to an active economic role for government. While U.S. governments, both federal and state, do intervene in the economy, their interventions are often reluctant, public ownership is seldom employed, and industrial policies are not explicitly coordinated. Neither level of government exhibits a commitment to economic intervention equivalent to either its Canadian or Australian confreres. For these reasons, the U.S. case is not readily comparable with the recent Canadian pattern. In a centralized federation where governments are unwilling to pursue certain industrial policies there is by definition limited intergovernmental conflict about the content of industrial strategy.

Like other modern governments, Washington undertakes industrial assistance policies designed to promote research and development, to enhance productivity, and to encourage the exploitation of foreign markets. The scope and complexity of federal assistance to industry makes efforts and quantification difficult, but several surveys reveal a plethora of programs and substantial expenditures. For example, a study by Ira Magaziner and Robert Reich estimated that in 1980 federal assistance to enterprise (including infrastructure expenditures, research and development, and loans and guarantees outstanding) amounted to $303 billion.[42] Of this total, $40 billion was accounted for by loans, insurance, and guarantees in support of exports while another $17.9 billion was consumed by programs of assistance for small business. In 1980, the federal government spent more than $94 billion on goods and services. Such purchasing power, which makes Washington the nation's largest single consumer of goods and services, is governed by a web of protectionist regulations. The "Buy America" Act and related provisions guarantee domestic suppliers a distinct advantage in the quest for government contracts.

Direct government assistance to individual firms is alien to established patterns of industrial policy in the United States. The bailout of Chrysler, Penn Central, and Lockheed are major departures from the hands-off posture of federal industrial policy makers. The public enterprise sector in the United States is the smallest of any of the OECD countries.

Washington spends some money on the rehabilitation of depressed regions. For example, the Economic Development Administration of the

Department of Commerce spent $483 million for such purposes in 1980. However, the U.S. federal government pursues no explicit policy of balanced regional economic growth. Indeed, in the United States, market forces are viewed as the proper determinants of industrial location. Over the past two decades, U.S. administrations have been loath to interfere with the shift of population and industry from the once dominant industrial northeast to the now dynamic southwestern sun belt. Daniel P. Moynihan, a Democratic Senator from New York, neatly captured the American orthodoxy about regional policy when he remarked: "Sometimes it is necesssary to think like an economist."[43]

The content of U.S. industrial policy is now a major political issue. In the face of deteriorating economic performance, the alleged deindustrialization of the northeast, and import competition, critics have condemned Washington's policies as inadequate. They maintain that the commitment to the virtues of unhindered markets blinds Americans to the need for aggressive intervention if the United States is to achieve an industrial renaissance.[44] In other words, the U.S. economy has suffered from too little intervention, not too much. But in contrast to the situation in Canada, the literature and public debate about U.S. industrial policy is devoid of explicit references to federalism. For those seeking more intervention, Washington is the saviour.

The state governments use some industrial policy levers, but their policies are less interventionist and sophisticated than those of the larger Canadian provinces. The role of state governments is perhaps best described as promotional. That is, their principal economic role is to promote their jurisdiction as a site for the location and expansion of industry. Unlike the Canadian provinces, the state governments are not really concerned with industrial diversification or the quality and nature of industry. Rather, their preoccupation is with generating investment and jobs and creating a suitable business climate. Policies aimed at restructuring extant firms and industries, promoting research and development, and enhancing productivity are uncommon at the state level, although Rhode Island has recently unveiled an industrial policy.

To attract industry, the state tax system is often ingeniously deployed so as to encourage plant expansion and new investments. Tax incentives are supplemented by a range of grants, low-interest loans, and loan guarantees whose complexity and cost to the public purse have yet to be catalogued. Anti-union labour legislation may also be used especially, but not exclusively, in the southern states.

The so-called "Commerce" clause in the U.S. Constitution provides consitutional protection for the common market. Such protection however is not so absolute as to prevent the state governments from engaging in practices that restrict the flow of factors of production. For example, state procurement policies are frequently protectionist; some 34 states favour, in differing ways, state or domestic producers. In several states, also, steel has been accorded special protection. The governments of Ohio and Pennsylvania, where steel-making is very significant, have implemented measures designed to limit the use of imported steel in state-funded projects. Such protectionism has survived political and constitutional attacks on its legitimacy. As in Canada, efforts to strike intergovernmental accords on purchasing policy have failed. For example, only seven states have accepted the principles embodied in the American Bar Association's model purchasing code.[45] Such findings suggest that state governments impose barriers to the flow of goods and services, notwithstanding constitutional protection of the common market.

Australia

The contemporary Australian experience is closer to the Canadian than the American, although firm conclusions are difficult given the paucity of literature on Australian industrial policy. Like Canada, Australia is a vast, sparsely populated federation whose economy is anchored on the export of natural resources. The Australian states are less heterogeneous than their Canadian counterparts, but marked differences exist in their economic structure and prosperity. New South Wales and Victoria are heavily populated and industrialized while Queensland and Western Australia are sparsely populated, resource-rich hinterlands. South Australia and the island state of Tasmania boast neither resource-based nor industrial prosperity. The outlying states resent the economic, political, and cultural hegemony of Victoria and New South Wales. The Commonwealth government, like Ottawa, is frequently portrayed as the instrument of the more populated states.

As the national government, Canberra wields decisive powers in the industrial sphere, including those instruments conventionally employed by modern governments under advanced capitalism, although public enterprise is not very important in Australia. Interestingly, the Commonwealth government, unlike its Canadian counterpart, has no agency dedicated to regional industrial development. The state governments, through a combination of Crown ownership of resources and state jurisdiction over them, are also important economic actors. However, the Australian states, while clearly more significant than the U.S. ones, lack the fiscal clout of the Canadian provinces and are accordingly restrained in their industrial strategies. Contemporary state industrial policies are not particularly coherent or complex, but they do rest on the manipulation of several policy instruments. John Warhurst, an Australian political scientist, has described the efforts of the states to pursue industrial growth as follows:

This has been done through a whole range of schemes either to assist in the expansion of firms already located within State boundaries or to attract new firms or new investment. The schemes include assistance with transport costs, concessions on electric power, preference given to local firms in government purchasing, assistance with management and technical advice, decentralization incentives, provision of factories on a lease-back basis, taxation concessions and others.[46]

As in the other established federations, such instruments are employed competitively. And, as the list of policy instruments reveals, the Australian states employ policy levers that challenge the common market.

During the 1970s, intergovernmental relations in Australia, like those in Canada, were adversely influenced by changes in the supply and value of nonrenewable resources. The resource-rich states, especially Queensland and Western Australia, resisted Canberra's efforts to expand its influence in resource policy and to redistribute the benefits of resource development from producing to consuming regions. As in Canada, such efforts to extend federal jurisdiction evoked intergovernmental conflict. At the most elementary level, the resistance of the states to Canberra's enhanced role reflects the reflex reaction of governments under federalism to preserve their power and status against the expansionary tendencies of the upper level. As well, intergovernmental conflict, especially that between the Commonwealth and Queensland and Western Australia, reflects enduring conflicts of interest between the industrialized core and the hinterlands, who see Canberra as the instrument of metropolitan interests. Such deep-rooted conflicts may be exacerbated in the Australian case by partisan differences between state and Commonwealth governments, but, as in Canada, explicitly partisan conflict is of secondary importance. However, as Garth Stevenson argues, federal policy makers in Australia hold unflattering views about their political and bureaucratic counterparts in the states.[47] Canberra views the state governments as conservative actors who routinely pursue short-sighted policies. In Stevenson's view, such sentiments fan intergovernmental conflict.

The Australian case provides Canadian reformers with no obvious blueprint. As in Canada, intergovernmental conflict over industrial and resource policy is routine. Policy making is frequently competitive, especially between the state governments, and, as noted earlier, resource policy has exacerbated Commonwealth-state relations in the 1970s. But in the face of discord, Australian federalism has generated no noteworthy mechanisms for the better intergovernmental coordination of industrial policy.

Conclusion

Our brief foray into comparative federalism yields no powerful lessons for Canadians. The U.S. experience is very different from the Canadian: in the United States, the federal government is the fountainhead of important economic policy. As a result, Canada's preoccupation with intergovernmental conflict and policy coordination has no parallels in U.S. politics. In contrast, Australia reveals characteristics of policy making roughly comparable to those in Canada, such as centre-periphery conflict, state-led challenges to the economic union, and frequent intergovernmental friction. However, the Australian case, while comparable to the Canadian, advances no clear agenda of reform for Canadians. No innovative institutional arrangement or policies are evident in Australian industrial policy making. "Made in Canada" reforms are thus necessary.

Conclusions

Our survey reveals that both federal and provincial governments are active in industrial policy making in Canada, and generally more active than their counterparts in Australia and the United States. Intervention in the economy has evoked continuing intergovernmental controversy about the proper direction and content of Canadian industrial policy. In particular, the provinces, with the exception of Ontario, have denounced federal policies as insensitive to local interests and serving the needs of the more-industrialized areas. Such reasoning has prompted the provinces to launch, with varying degrees of vigour, industrial strategies designed to offset the effects of federal policies and market forces. As well, both levels of government have given priority to the articulation of industrial policy and economic management in general. Under these circumstances, governments become jealous guardians of their jurisdictional prerogatives and powers. In turn, policy making becomes influenced, not only by objective economic concerns, but also by strategies aimed at enhancing the visibility and status of governments themselves. Ottawa's retreat from the General Development Agreement approach and interprovincial competition for industry are evidence of these tendencies. In such important areas as purchasing codes, public investment strategies, and the use of grants and incentives, Canadian governments remain at odds.

One solution to the problems of the status quo is to prescribe a reduction in the role of government in the economy. Put simply, to the extent that governments reduce their appetites for intervention, intergovernmental conflict will be correspondingly reduced. But no evidence suggests that Canadian governments are much interested in reducing their economic roles. A broader question is whether an open economy like Canada's can prosper without the sustenance of government intervention.

If neither level of government is willing to limit its intervention and if neither seems prepared to cede significant powers to the other, only one obvious option presents itself. Governments must acknowledge the scope of their intervention, their interdependence, and their capacity to exert a perverse effect on the economy in the absence of coordination. Put somewhat differently, if Canadian governments are individually committed to intervention, serious efforts must be made to ensure that the benefits of such intervention are not lost through intergovernmental conflict. The growing tendency to "go it alone" is not a feasible option in the era of interdependent governments.

For reasons specified in this study, Canadian federalism creates impressive, but not insurmountable, obstacles to intergovernmental cooperation. But before greater harmony is achieved, a change in attitude must occur. Government, scholars, and interested parties in the private sector must learn to exploit federalism as a useful force in the development of industrial policies. This would entail abandoning various assumptions about the inherently problematic nature of economic policy making under Canadian federalism. It would also require recognition of the fact that federalism may allow for the generation of regionally sensitive and effective industrial policies. For provincial governments, with their knowledge of their own relatively small economies, may be useful partners of a national government which has a broader, more complex, and more heterogeneous constituency. In the absence of other options, governments should entertain the possibility that Ottawa and the provinces can act as partners in industrial development.

Notes

This paper was completed in July 1984.

1. Michael Jenkin, *The Challenge of Diversity: Industrial Policy in the Canadian Federation*, study prepared for the Science Council of Canada (Ottawa: Minister of Supply and Services Canada, 1983), p. 153.

2. Allan M. Maslove, "Loans and Guarantees: Business as Usual versus the Politics of Risk," in *How Ottawa Spends: The Liberals, the Opposition, and Federal Priorities*, edited by G. Bruce Doern (Toronto: James Lorimer, 1983), p. 125.

3. Economic Council of Canada, *Intervention and Efficiency* (Ottawa: Minister of Supply and Services Canada, 1983), p. 18.

4. André Blais, Phillipe Faucher, and Robert Young, "L'aide financière directe du gouvernement fédéral à l'industrie canadienne, 1960–1980," Notes de recherche no. 12 (Montreal: Université de Montréal, Département de science politique, 1983).

5. For an overview of DREE's rationale see Anthony Careless, *Initiative and Response: The Adaptation of Canadian Federalism to Regional Economic Development* (Montreal: McGill-Queen's University Press, 1977), chap. 10.

6. For details see Donald J. Savoie, *Federal-Provincial Collaboration: The Canada–New Brunswick General Development Agreement* (Montreal: McGill-Queen's University Press, 1981).

7. For an overview see Marsha Gordon, *Government in Business* (Montreal: C.D. Howe Institute, 1981).

8. John W. Langford and Kenneth J. Huffman, "The Uncharted Universe of Federal Public Corporations," in *Crown Corporations in Canada: The Calculus of Instrument Choice*, edited by J. Robert S. Prichard (Toronto: Butterworth, 1983), pp. 219–301.

9. Harvey Feigenbaum, "The Politics of Public Enterprise," a study prepared for the Royal Commission on the Economic Union and Development Prospects for Canada (Ottawa: 1984).

10. Peter Morici et al., *Canadian Industrial Policy* (Washington, D.C.: National Planning Association, 1982).

11. Stephen Clarkson, *Canada and the Reagan Challenge* (Toronto: James Lorimer for the Canadian Institute for Economic Policy, 1982).

12. Donald Smiley, "A Dangerous Deed: The Constitution Act 1982," in *And No One Cheered*, edited by Keith Banting and Richard Simeon (Toronto: Methuen, 1983).

13. For a useful overview of the debate see Peter Aucoin and Herman Bakvis, "Organizational Differentiation and Integration: The Case of Regional Economic Development Policy in Canada," paper presented to the Annual Meeting of the Canadian Political Science Association, Vancouver, B.C., June 1983.

14. Alan C. Cairns, "The Governments and Societies of Canadian Federalism," *Canadian Journal of Political Science* 10 (December 1977), p. 699.

15. Jenkin, *The Challenge of Diversity*, p. 45.

16. For details see John Richards and Larry Pratt, *Prairie Capitalism: Power and Influence in the New West* (Toronto: McClelland and Stewart, 1979), especially chap. 9.

17. H.V. Nelles, *The Politics of Development: Forests, Mines, and Hydro-Electric Power in Ontario, 1849–1941* (Toronto: Macmillan, 1974).

18. Jenkin, *The Challenge of Diversity*, chap. 4.

19. André Blais, Phillipe Faucher, and Robert Young, "L'aide directe au secteur manufacturier, Québec-Ontario," *Journal of Canadian Studies* 18 (Spring 1983): 54–78.

20. For details see Jenkin, *The Challenge of Diversity*, pp. 92–93.

21. Aidan R. Vining and Robert Botterell, "An Overview of the Origins, Growth, Size and Functions of Provincial Crown Corporations," in *Crown Corporations in Canada: The Calculus of Instrument Choice*, edited by J. Robert S. Prichard (Toronto: Butterworth.

22. For an excellent overview of the use of public enterprise by different political parties see Marsha Chandler, "State Enterprise and Partisanship in Provincial Politics," *Canadian Journal of Political Science* 15 (December 1982): 711–40.

23. For details see Allan Tupper, "Bill S-31 and the Federalism of State Capitalism," Discussion Paper 18 (Kingston: Queen's University, Institute of Intergovernmental Relations, 1983).

24. Cairns, "The Governments and Societies of Canadian Federalism," p. 721.

25. John Zysman, *Governments, Markets, and Growth* (Ithaca, N.Y.: Cornell University Press, 1983).

26. André Blais, Phillipe Faucher, and Robert Young, "The Concept of Province-Building: A Critique," paper presented to the Annual Meeting of the Canadian Political Science Association, Vancouver, B.C., June 1983.

27. Jenkin, *The Challenge of Diversity*, pp. 129–34.

28. Clarkson, *Canada and the Reagan Challenge*, p. 301.

29. Douglas Brown and Julia Eastman, *The Limits of Consultation: A Debate among Ottawa, the Provinces and the Private Sector on an Industrial Strategy* (Ottawa: Minister of Supply and Services Canada, 1981).

30. Clarkson, *Canada and the Reagan Challenge*, p. 310.

31. Kenneth H. Norrie, "Some Comments on Prairie Economic Alienation," *Canadian Public Policy* 2 (Spring 1976), p. 213.

32. Careless, *Initiative and Response*.

33. Blais, Faucher, and Young, "L'aide directe au secteur manufacturier, Québec–Ontario," and "The Concept of Province-Building: A Critique."

34. N. Harvey Lithwick and John Devlin, "Economic Development Policy: A Case Study in Underdeveloped Policy Making," in *How Ottawa Spends, 1984*, edited by Allan M. Maslove (Toronto: Methuen, 1984), pp. 122–66.

35. John A. Hayes, *Economic Mobility in Canada: A Comparative Study* (Ottawa: Minister of Supply and Services Canada, 1982), p. 6.

36. Donald Smiley, *Canada in Question: Federalism in the Eighties*, 3d ed. (Toronto: McGraw-Hill Ryerson, 1980), p. 163.

37. John Whalley, "Induced Distortions of Interprovincial Activity: An Overview of the Issues," in *Federalism and the Canadian Economic Union*, edited by M.J. Trebilcock et al. (Toronto: University of Toronto Press for the Ontario Economic Council, 1983), p. 178.

38. Thomas J. Courchene, "Analytical Perspectives on the Canadian Economic Union," in *Federalism and the Canadian Economic Union*, edited by M.J. Trebilcock et al. (Toronto: University of Toronto Press for the Ontario Economic Council, 1983), pp. 95–97.

39. Jenkin, *The Challenge of Diversity*, p. 93.

40. Courchene, "Analytical Perspectives," p. 107.

41. Richard Simeon, *Federal-Provincial Diplomacy* (Toronto: University of Toronto Press, 1972).

42. Ira C. Magaziner and Robert B. Reich, *Minding America's Business: The Decline and Rise of the American Economy* (New York: Vintage Books, 1983), p. 241.

43. Daniel P. Moynihan, "The Politics and Economics of Regional Growth," *The Public Interest* 51 (Spring 1978), p. 8.

44. As an example see Robert B. Reich, *The Next American Frontier* (New York: Times Books, 1983).

45. W. C. Graham, "Government Procurement Policies: GATT, the EEC, and the United States," in *Federalism and the Canadian Economic Union*, edited by M.J. Trebilcock et al. (Toronto: University of Toronto Press for the Ontario Economic Council, 1983), p. 383.

46. John Warhurst, *State Governments and Australian Tariff Policy* (Canberra: The Australian National University, Centre for Research on Federal Financial Relations, 1980), p. 15.

47. Garth Stevenson, *Mineral Resources and Australian Federalism* (Canberra: The Australian National University, Centre for Research on Federal Financial Relations, 1977), p. 30.

ABOUT THE CONTRIBUTORS

Michael M. Atkinson is Associate Professor in the Department of Political Science, McMaster University, Hamilton.

André Blais is Associate Professor in the Department of Political Science, University of Montreal, and is also the Research Coordinator for the Industrial Policy section, which is part of the Politics and Political Institutions Research Area, Royal Commission on the Economic Union and Development Prospects for Canada.

Marsha A. Chandler is Professor in the Department of Political Science, University of Toronto.

Andrew B. Gollner is Associate Professor in the Department of Political Science, Concordia University, Montreal.

David Marsh is Professor in the Department of Government, University of Essex, Colchester, England.

Lynn Krieger Mytelka is Professor in the Department of Political Science, Carleton University, Ottawa.

Allan Tupper is Associate Professor in the Department of Political Science, University of Alberta, Edmonton.

Conrad Winn is Associate Professor in the Department of Political Science, Carleton University, Ottawa.

Steven B. Wolinetz is Associate Professor in the Department of Political Science, Memorial University of Newfoundland, St. John's.

THE COLLECTED RESEARCH STUDIES

Royal Commission on the Economic Union and Development Prospects for Canada

ECONOMICS

Income Distribution and Economic Security in Canada (Vol.1), *François Vaillancourt, Research Coordinator*

Vol. 1   Income Distribution and Economic Security in Canada, *F. Vaillancourt* (C)*

Industrial Structure (Vols. 2-8), *Donald G. McFetridge, Research Coordinator*

Vol. 2   Canadian Industry in Transition, *D.G. McFetridge* (C)
Vol. 3   Technological Change in Canadian Industry, *D.G. McFetridge* (C)
Vol. 4   Canadian Industrial Policy in Action, *D.G. McFetridge* (C)
Vol. 5   Economics of Industrial Policy and Strategy, *D.G. McFetridge* (C)
Vol. 6   The Role of Scale in Canada–US Productivity Differences, *J.R. Baldwin and P.K. Gorecki* (M)
Vol. 7   Competition Policy and Vertical Exchange, *F. Mathewson and R. Winter* (M)
Vol. 8   The Political Economy of Economic Adjustment, *M. Trebilcock* (M)

International Trade (Vols. 9-14), *John Whalley, Research Coordinator*

Vol. 9   Canadian Trade Policies and the World Economy, *J. Whalley with C. Hamilton and R. Hill* (M)
Vol. 10 Canada and the Multilateral Trading System, *J. Whalley* (M)
Vol. 11 Canada–United States Free Trade, *J. Whalley* (C)
Vol. 12 Domestic Policies and the International Economic Environment, *J. Whalley* (C)
Vol. 13 Trade, Industrial Policy and International Competition, *R. Harris* (M)
Vol. 14 Canada's Resource Industries and Water Export Policy, *J. Whalley* (C)

Labour Markets and Labour Relations (Vols. 15-18), *Craig Riddell, Research Coordinator*

Vol. 15 Labour-Management Cooperation in Canada, *C. Riddell* (C)
Vol. 16 Canadian Labour Relations, *C. Riddell* (C)
Vol. 17 Work and Pay: The Canadian Labour Market, *C. Riddell* (C)
Vol. 18 Adapting to Change: Labour Market Adjustment in Canada, *C. Riddell* (C)

Macroeconomics (Vols. 19-25), *John Sargent, Research Coordinator*

Vol. 19 Macroeconomic Performance and Policy Issues: Overviews, *J. Sargent* (M)
Vol. 20 Post-War Macroeconomic Developments, *J. Sargent* (C)
Vol. 21 Fiscal and Monetary Policy, *J. Sargent* (C)
Vol. 22 Economic Growth: Prospects and Determinants, *J. Sargent* (C)
Vol. 23 Long-Term Economic Prospects for Canada: A Symposium, *J. Sargent* (C)
Vol. 24 Foreign Macroeconomic Experience: A Symposium, *J. Sargent* (C)
Vol. 25 Dealing with Inflation and Unemployment in Canada, *C. Riddell* (M)

Economic Ideas and Social Issues (Vols. 26 and 27), *David Laidler, Research Coordinator*

Vol. 26 Approaches to Economic Well-Being, *D. Laidler* (C)
Vol. 27 Responses to Economic Change, *D. Laidler* (C)

---

* (C) denotes a Collection of studies by various authors coordinated by the person named.
  (M) denotes a Monograph.

POLITICS AND INSTITUTIONS OF GOVERNMENT

Canada and the International Political Economy (Vols. 28-30), *Denis Stairs and Gilbert R. Winham, Research Coordinators*

Vol. 28 Canada and the International Political/Economic Environment, *D. Stairs and G.R. Winham* (C)

Vol. 29 The Politics of Canada's Economic Relationship with the United States, *D. Stairs and G.R. Winham* (C)

Vol. 30 Selected Problems in Formulating Foreign Economic Policy, *D. Stairs and G.R. Winham* (C)

State and Society in the Modern Era (Vols. 31 and 32), *Keith Banting, Research Coordinator*

Vol. 31 State and Society: Canada in Comparative Perspective, *K. Banting* (C)

Vol. 32 The State and Economic Interests, *K. Banting* (C)

Constitutionalism, Citizenship and Society (Vols. 33-35), *Alan Cairns and Cynthia Williams, Research Coordinators*

Vol. 33 Constitutionalism, Citizenship and Society in Canada, *A. Cairns and C. Williams* (C)

Vol. 34 The Politics of Gender, Ethnicity and Language in Canada, *A. Cairns and C. Williams* (C)

Vol. 35 Public Opinion and Public Policy in Canada, *R. Johnston* (M)

Representative Institutions (Vols. 36-39), *Peter Aucoin, Research Coordinator*

Vol. 36 Party Government and Regional Representation in Canada, *P. Aucoin* (C)

Vol. 37 Regional Responsiveness and the National Administrative State, *P. Aucoin* (C)

Vol. 38 Institutional Reforms for Representative Government, *P. Aucoin* (C)

Vol. 39 Intrastate Federalism in Canada, *D.V. Smiley and R.L. Watts* (M)

The Politics of Economic Policy (Vols. 40-43), *G. Bruce Doern, Research Coordinator*

Vol. 40 The Politics of Economic Policy, *G.B. Doern* (C)

Vol. 41 Federal and Provincial Budgeting, *A.M. Maslove, M.J. Prince and G.B. Doern* (M)

Vol. 42 Economic Regulation and the Federal System, *R. Schultz and A. Alexandroff* (M)

Vol. 43 Bureaucracy in Canada: Control and Reform, *S.L. Sutherland and G.B. Doern* (M)

Industrial Policy (Vols. 44 and 45), *André Blais, Research Coordinator*

Vol. 44 Industrial Policy, *A. Blais* (C)

Vol. 45 The Political Sociology of Industrial Policy, *A. Blais* (M)

LAW AND CONSTITUTIONAL ISSUES

Law, Society and the Economy (Vols. 46-51), *Ivan Bernier and Andrée Lajoie, Research Coordinators*

Vol. 46 Law, Society and the Economy, *I. Bernier and A. Lajoie* (C)

Vol. 47 The Supreme Court of Canada as an Instrument of Political Change, *I. Bernier and A. Lajoie* (C)

Vol. 48 Regulations, Crown Corporations and Administrative Tribunals, *I. Bernier and A. Lajoie* (C)

Vol. 49 Family Law and Social Welfare Legislation in Canada, *I. Bernier and A. Lajoie* (C)

Vol. 50 Consumer Protection, Environmental Law and Corporate Power, *I. Bernier and A. Lajoie* (C)

Vol. 51 Labour Law and Urban Law in Canada, *I. Bernier and A. Lajoie* (C)

The **International Legal Environment** (Vols. 52-54), *John Quinn, Research Coordinator*

Vol. 52 The International Legal Environment, *J. Quinn* (C)
Vol. 53 Canadian Economic Development and the International Trading System, *M.M. Hart* (M)
Vol. 54 Canada and the New International Law of the Sea, *D.M. Johnston* (M)

Harmonization of Laws in Canada (Vols. 55 and 56), *Ronald C.C. Cuming, Research Coordinator*

Vol. 55 Perspectives on the Harmonization of Law in Canada, *R. Cuming* (C)
Vol. 56 Harmonization of Business Law in Canada, *R. Cuming* (C)

Institutional and Constitutional Arrangements (Vols. 57 and 58), *Clare F. Beckton and A. Wayne MacKay, Research Coordinators*

Vol. 57 Recurring Issues in Canadian Federalism, *C.F. Beckton and A.W. MacKay* (C)
Vol. 58 The Courts and The Charter, *C.F. Beckton and A.W. MacKay* (C)

FEDERALISM AND THE ECONOMIC UNION

Federalism and The Economic Union (Vols. 58-72), *Mark Krasnick, Kenneth Norrie and Richard Simeon, Research Coordinators*

Vol. 59 Federalism and Economic Union in Canada, *K. Norrie, R. Simeon and M. Krasnick* (M)
Vol. 60 Perspectives on the Canadian Economic Union, *M. Krasnick* (C)
Vol. 61 Division of Powers and Public Policy, *R. Simeon* (C)
Vol. 62 Case Studies in the Division of Powers, *M. Krasnick* (C)
Vol. 63 Intergovernmental Relations, *R. Simeon* (C)
Vol. 64 Disparities and Interregional Adjustment, *K. Norrie* (C)
Vol. 65 Fiscal Federalism, *M. Krasnick* (C)
Vol. 66 Mobility of Capital in the Canadian Economic Union, *N. Roy* (M)
Vol. 67 Economic Management and the Division of Powers, *T.J. Courchene* (M)
Vol. 68 Regional Aspects of Confederation, *J. Whalley* (M)
Vol. 69 Interest Groups in the Canadian Federal System, *H.G. Thorburn* (M)
Vol. 70 Canada and Quebec, Past and Future: An Essay, *D. Latouche* (M)
Vol. 71 The Political Economy of Canadian Federalism: 1940-1984, *R. Simeon and I. Robinson* (M)

THE NORTH

Vol. 72 The North, *Michael S. Whittington, Coordinator* (C)

COMMISSION ORGANIZATION

Chairman
Donald S. Macdonald

Commissioners

Clarence L. Barber	William M. Hamilton	Daryl K. Seaman
Albert Breton	John R. Messer	Thomas K. Shoyama
M. Angela Cantwell Peters	Laurent Picard	Jean Casselman-Wadds
E. Gérard Docquier	Michel Robert	Catherine T. Wallace

Senior Officers

Executive Director
J. Gerald Godsoe

Director of Policy	*Senior Advisors*	*Directors of Research*
Alan Nymark	David Ablett	Ivan Bernier
Secretary	Victor Clarke	Alan Cairns
Michel Rochon	Carl Goldenberg	David C. Smith
	Harry Stewart	
Director of Administration	*Director of Publishing*	*Co-Directors of Research*
Sheila-Marie Cook	Ed Matheson	Kenneth Norrie
		John Sargent

Research Program Organization

Economics	Politics and the Institutions of Government	Law and Constitutional Issues
Research Director	*Research Director*	*Research Director*
David C. Smith	Alan Cairns	Ivan Bernier
Executive Assistant & Assistant Director (Research Services)	*Executive Assistant*	*Executive Assistant & Research Program Administrator*
I. Lilla Connidis	Karen Jackson	Jacques J.M. Shore
Coordinators	*Coordinators*	*Coordinators*
David Laidler	Peter Aucoin	Clare F. Beckton
Donald G. McFetridge	Keith Banting	Ronald C.C. Cuming
Kenneth Norrie*	André Blais	Mark Krasnick
Craig Riddell	Bruce Doern	Andrée Lajoie
John Sargent*	Richard Simeon	A. Wayne MacKay
François Vaillancourt	Denis Stairs	John J. Quinn
John Whalley	Cynthia Williams	
	Gilbert R. Winham	
Research Analysts	*Research Analysts*	*Administrative and Research Assistant*
Caroline Digby	Claude Desranleau	Nicolas Roy
Mireille Ethier	Ian Robinson	
Judith Gold		
Douglas S. Green	*Office Administration*	*Research Analyst*
Colleen Hamilton	Donna Stebbing	Nola Silzer
Roderick Hill		
Joyce Martin		

*Kenneth Norrie and John Sargent co-directed the final phase of Economics Research with David Smith

9649